Treatment of Depression in Adolescents and Adults

Clinician's Guide to Evidence-Based Practice Series

Treatment of Traumatized Adults and Children
Allen Rubin and David W. Springer, Editors

Substance Abuse Treatment for Youth and Adults
David W. Springer and Allen Rubin, Editors

Psychosocial Treatment of Schizophrena
Allen Rubin, David W. Springer, and Kathi Trawver, Editors

Treatment of Depression in Adolescents and Adults
David W. Springer, Allen Rubin, and Christopher G. Beevers, Editors

Published by John Wiley & Sons, Inc., Hoboken, New Jersey.

Published simultaneously in Canada.

For general information on our other products and services, please contact our Customer Care Department within the United States at (800) 762-2974, outside the United States at (317) 572-3993 or fax (317) 572-4002.

Wiley also publishes its books in a variety of electronic formats. Some content that appears in print may not be available in electronic books. For more information about Wiley products, visit our website at www.wiley.com.

Library of Congress Cataloging-in-Publication Data:

Springer, David W.
    Treatment of depression in adolescents and adults / David W. Springer, Allen Rubin, Christopher G. Beevers.
        p. cm.–(Clinician's guide to evidence-based practice series ; 4)
    Includes bibliographical references and index.
    ISBN 978-0-470-58759-1 (pbk.); 978-1-118-01538-4 (ePDF); 978-1-118-01539-1 (eMobi); 978-1-118-01540-7 (ePub)
    1. Depression in adolescence–Treatment. 2. Evidence-based medicine. I. Rubin, Allen. II. Beevers, Christopher G. III. Title.
    RJ506.D4S67 2011
    616.85'2700835–dc22   2010047240

Printed in the United States of America

10 9 8 7 6 5 4 3 2 1

Clinician's Guide to
Evidence-Based Practice Series

Treatment of Depression in Adolescents and Adults

Edited by
DAVID W. SPRINGER, ALLEN RUBIN,
and CHRISTOPHER G. BEEVERS, EDITORS

WILEY

John Wiley & Sons, Inc.

Contents

Series Introduction

One of the most daunting challenges to the evidence-based practice (EBP) movement is the fact that busy clinicians who learn of evidence-based interventions are often unable to implement them because they lack expertise in the intervention and lack the time and resources to obtain the needed expertise. Even if they want to read about the intervention as a way of gaining that expertise, they are likely to encounter materials that are either much too lengthy in light of their time constraints or much too focused on the research support for the intervention, with inadequate guidance to enable them to implement it with at least a minimally acceptable level of proficiency.

This is the fourth in a series of edited volumes that attempt to alleviate that problem and thus make learning how to provide evidence-based interventions more feasible for such clinicians. Each volume is a how-to guide for practitioners—not a research-focused review. Each contains in-depth chapters detailing how to provide clinical interventions whose effectiveness is being supported by the best scientific evidence.

The chapters differ from chapters in other reference volumes on empirically supported interventions in both length and focus. Rather than covering in depth the research support for each intervention and providing brief overviews of the practice aspects of the interventions, our chapters are lengthier and more detailed practitioner-focused how-to guides for implementing the interventions. Instead of emphasizing the research support in the chapters, that support is summarized in Appendix A. Each chapter focuses on helping practitioners learn how to begin providing an evidence-based intervention that they are being urged by managed care companies (and others) to provide, but with which they may be inexperienced. Each chapter is extensive and detailed enough to enable clinicians to begin providing the evidence-based intervention without being so lengthy and detailed that reading it is too time consuming and overwhelming. The chapters also identify resources for gaining more advanced expertise in the interventions.

We believe that this series is unique in its focus on the needs of practitioners and in making empirically supported interventions more feasible for them to learn about and provide. We hope that you will agree and that you will find this volume and this series to be of value in guiding your practice and in maximizing your effectiveness as an evidence-based practitioner.

Allen Rubin, Ph.D.
David W. Springer, Ph.D.

Acknowledgments

Special thanks go to four Wiley staff members who helped make this series possible. In alphabetical order they are: Peggy Alexander, vice president and publisher; the late Lisa Gebo, senior editor; Sweta Gupta, editorial program coordinator; and Rachel Livsey, senior editor.

About the Editors

David W. Springer, PhD, LCSW, is the associate dean for academic affairs and a university distinguished teaching professor in the School of Social Work at the University of Texas at Austin, where he is also investigator of the Inter-American Institute for Youth Justice and holds a joint appointment with the Department of Psychology. Dr. Springer received his PhD in Social Work from Florida State University, where he also received a Master of Social Work degree and a Bachelor of Arts in Psychology. Dr. Springer's social work practice experience has included work as a clinical social worker with adolescents and their families in inpatient and outpatient settings and as a school social worker in an alternative learning center with youth recommended for expulsion for serious offenses. His interest in developing and implementing effective clinical interventions continues to drive his work. His areas of interest include: evidence-based substance abuse and mental health treatment with youth; forensic social work with juvenile delinquents; intervention research with adolescents; and applied psychometric theory and scale development. He currently serves on the editorial board of several professional journals and on the National Scientific and Policy Advisory Council of the Hogg Foundation for Mental Health. Dr. Springer has co-authored or co-edited several other books, including: *Substance Abuse Treatment for Criminal Offenders: An Evidence-Based Guide for Practitioners*; *Developing and Validating Rapid Assessment Instruments*; *Social Work in Juvenile and Criminal Justice Settings* (3rd ed.); and *Handbook of Forensic Mental Health with Victims and Offenders: Assessment, Treatment, and Research*. Dr. Springer recently served as chair of a Blue Ribbon Task Force consisting of national and regional leaders, which was charged with making recommendations for reforming the juvenile justice system in Texas. In recognition of his work with the Blue Ribbon Task Force, the National Association of Social Workers (NASW), Texas Chapter/Austin Branch, selected Dr. Springer as the 2008 Social Worker of the Year.

Allen Rubin, PhD, is the Bert Kruger Smith Centennial Professor in the School of Social Work at the University of Texas at Austin, where he has been a faculty member since 1979. While there, he worked as a therapist in a child guidance center and developed and taught a course on the assessment and treatment of traumatized populations. Earlier in his career he worked in a community mental health program providing services to adolescents and their families. He is internationally known for his many publications pertaining to research and evidence-based practice. In 1997 he was a co-recipient of the Society for Social Work and Research Award for Outstanding Examples of Published Research for a study on the treatment of male batterers and their spouses. His most recent studies have been on the effectiveness of EMDR and on practitioners' views of evidence-based practice. Among his 12 books, his most recent is *Practitioner's Guide to Using Research for Evidence-Based Practice*. He has served as a consulting editor for seven professional journals. He was a founding member of the Society for Social Work and Research and served as its president from 1998 to 2000. In 1993 he received the University of Pittsburgh, School of Social Work's Distinguished Alumnus Award. In 2007 he received the Council on Social Work Education's Significant Lifetime Achievement in Social Work Education Award.

Christopher G. Beevers, PhD, is an associate professor and director of the Mood Disorders Laboratory (http://www.psy.utexas.edu/MDL) in the Department of Psychology at the University of Texas at Austin. He is also a licensed psychologist in the state of Texas. Dr. Beevers received his PhD in Clinical Psychology from the University of Miami and completed his post-doctoral training in mood disorders research in the Department of Psychiatry and Human Behavior at Brown University. Dr. Beevers' research examines the etiology, maintenance, and treatment of depression. His most recent work examines the effectiveness of a cognitive bias modification program as an adjunctive treatment for depression. He is also currently investigating genetic, neural, and behavioral associations with cognitive vulnerability to depression. Dr. Beevers has received research funding from the National Institute of Mental Health (NIMH) and the Department of Defense. He currently serves on the editorial board of several leading journals in his area of research, including the *Journal of Consulting and Clinical Psychology, Behavior Therapy, and Cognitive Therapy and Research*. He has been a grant reviewer for national and international organizations, including the National Institutes of Health, Swiss National Science Foundation, Netherlands Organization for Scientific Research, and the National Institute for Health Research (United Kingdom). In 2006 he received the President's New Researcher Award from the Association of Behavioral and Cognitive Therapies. In 2009 he was a Beck Scholar at the Beck Institute for Cognitive Therapy and Research.

About the Contributors

David Baruch, MA, is a PhD student in clinical psychology at the University of Wisconsin–Milwaukee. His clinical interests include the treatment of depression and the integration of spirituality to enhance treatment efficacy of ESTs. David's primary research interests include the development of protocols to maximize homework completion in therapy, to integrate spirituality into ESTs for depression, and to design novel means of training therapists in ESTs.

William Bowe is a PhD student in clinical psychology at the University of Wisconsin–Milwaukee. His clinical interests include the treatment of depression, borderline personality disorder, and impulse control disorders using empirically supported interventions. In line with his clinical work, William's primary research interests are the development and dissemination of empirically supported treatments for depression that are culturally adapted for underserved ethnic minority populations.

Andrew Busch is a postdoctoral fellow at the Centers for Behavioral and Preventive Medicine at the Alpert Medical School of Brown University. His research interests include behavioral treatments for depression and the adaptation of Behavioral Activation for novel populations.

Esteban V. Cardemil is an associate professor at Clark University in Worcester Massachusetts. He received his PhD in clinical psychology from the University of Pennsylvania. His research focuses on the effects of race, ethnicity, and social class on psychopathology, and he has developed a particular focus on the development of prevention interventions for depression. Dr. Cardemil has written extensively about the process of adapting evidence-based practice for different cultural groups, and he is currently the principal investigator of a National Institute of Mental Health–funded grant to examine the help-seeking process for depression among Latino men.

Jonathan W. Kanter, PhD, is associate professor, director of the Depression Treatment Specialty Clinic, and Psychology Department Clinic Coordinator at the

Department of Psychology at the University of Wisconsin–Milwaukee. He is also a core scientist with the Center for Addictions and Behavioral Health Research at the University of Wisconsin-Milwaukee. Dr. Kanter has published more than 50 articles and chapters on behavioral activation, behavioral theory of depression, and using the therapeutic relationship in behavior therapy and has presented numerous workshops and talks on these topics. Currently, Dr. Kanter is funded by the National Institute of Mental Health to develop Behavioral Activation for Latinos with depression and is the recipient of an NIMH award to his clinical training program as a Program of Excellence in Empirically Validated Behavioral Treatments.

James P. McCullough Jr., PhD, is distinguished professor of psychology and psychiatry at Virginia Commonwealth University where he has worked since 1972. He developed the Cognitive Behavioral Analysis System of Psychotherapy (CBASP) during the early 1970s, the only psychotherapy model constructed specifically for the treatment of the chronically depressed patient. He has conducted psychotherapy research with the chronic patient for almost four decades. Dr. McCullough has served as a principal investigator in three national randomized clinical trials involving more than 2,200 chronically depressed outpatients. In addition, he has participated in the American Psychiatric Association's revisions of the *DSM-IV* and *DSM-V* unipolar mood disorder nomenclature.

Oswaldo Moreno is a clinical psychology doctoral student at Clark University in Worcester, Massachusetts. He serves as a graduate research assistant on an NIMH-funded mixed-methods investigation of help-seeking for depression among Latino men. His research interests are in the area of mental health disparities and mental health care in Latinos, as well as religiosity/spirituality among Latinos.

Cory F. Newman, PhD, ABPP, is director of the Center for Cognitive Therapy, and associate professor of psychology in psychiatry at the University of Pennsylvania School of Medicine. Dr. Newman is a diplomate of the American Board of Professional Psychology, with a specialty in behavioral psychology, and a founding fellow of the Academy of Cognitive Therapy. Dr. Newman has served as both a protocol therapist and protocol supervisor in a number of large-scale psychotherapy outcome studies, including the Penn-Vanderbilt-Rush Treatment of Depression Projects. Dr. Newman is also an international lecturer, having presented scores of cognitive therapy workshops and seminars across the United States and Canada, as well as 13 countries in Europe, South America, and Asia. Dr. Newman is the author of dozens of articles and chapters on cognitive therapy for a wide range of disorders and has co-authored four books, including *Bipolar Disorder: A Cognitive Therapy Approach* (APA, 2001).

J. Kim Penberthy, PhD, is director of training for the Center for Addiction Research and Education and associate professor in the Department of Psychiatry & Neurobehavioral Sciences at the University of Virginia School of Medicine. She is the North

American representative for the CBASP Network International and co-investigator on over ten large NIH-funded psychopharmacotherapy trials for depression and/or addiction. Dr. Penberthy's research focus is on development and implementation of evidence-based treatments for chronic depression as well as for addictions and co-occurring disorders, with a focus on acquisition learning. She conducts and supervises clinical research and practice. In addition, Dr. Penberthy publishes and lectures internationally on these and related topics.

Paul Rohde, PhD, is a senior research scientist at Oregon Research Institute (ORI) and has 22 years of experience as a research scientist with a substantive focus on the etiology, treatment, and prevention of adolescent depression and comorbid psychopathologies. Dr. Rohde received his PhD from the University of Oregon in 1988 and has been a licensed psychologist since 1990. He has directed or co-directed 21 federally funded research projects, including five randomized controlled trials (RCTs) evaluating adolescent depression treatment interventions and two RCTs evaluating adolescent depression prevention interventions. His most recent adolescent depression treatment research includes participation in TADS (Treatment for Adolescents with Depression Study), which evaluated the effectiveness of Cognitive Behavioral Therapy (CBT) and fluoxetine for the treatment of adolescent major depression, and his direction of a NIDA-funded study evaluating service delivery methods for integrating CBT and family-based treatment for adolescents with comorbid depressive and substance use disorders.

Monica Sanchez is a clinical psychology doctoral student at Clark University in Worcester, Massachusetts. She completed her undergraduate work at the University of California, Berkeley. Using a community participatory approach, her research focuses on understanding the particular mental health needs of minority and disadvantaged communities. She is currently studying the role that cultural definitions of mental illness, in addition to cognitive factors, play in mental health help-seeking for Latinos.

CHAPTER 1

Introduction: Evidence-Based Practice for Major Depressive Disorder

Christopher G. Beevers

Major depressive disorder (MDD) is a common, recurrent, and impairing condition that predicts future suicide attempts, interpersonal problems, unemployment, substance abuse, and delinquency (Kessler & Walters, 1998). According to the World Health Organization, 121 million people are currently suffering from MDD and it is a leading cause of disability worldwide among people 5 years old and older. The annual economic cost of MDD in the United States alone is staggering—$70 billion in medical expenditures, lost productivity, and other costs (Greenberg, Stiglin, Finkelstein, & Berndt, 1993; Philip, Gregory, & Ronald, 2003). Further, MDD accounts for more than two-thirds of the 30,000 reported suicides each year (Beautrais et al., 1996). Given this enormous impact at societal and individual levels, there is a clear need to develop and disseminate efficacious treatments for this disorder.

Fortunately, a number of empirically supported interventions are available for depressed adolescents and adults. In-depth descriptions of some of the most established treatments are included in this book—Cognitive Behavioral Therapy (CBT), Behavioral Activation (BA), and Cognitive Behavioral Analysis and System of Psychotherapy (CBASP). We include chapters on the application of CBT with adolescents and adults. Further, we include a chapter on how to apply these interventions to diverse populations, such as people with diverse racial and ethnic backgrounds. Each chapter provides a detailed, clinician-focused guide on how to implement these interventions. A review of the research base for each intervention is included in Appendix A.

Prior to reviewing the contents of each chapter in this introduction, we first provide an overview of how depression is defined, a brief description of its epidemiology, and then how depression is typically assessed. We then review other treatments (both pharmacological and nonpharmacological) that have empirical support for the treatment of depression but are not included in this volume. We finish with a brief overview of this volume's chapters.

Major Depressive Disorder: Definition, Epidemiology, and Course

The *Diagnostic and Statistical Manual of Mental Disorders* (4th edition—*DSM-IV*) defines Major Depressive Disorder (MDD) as the presence of five (or more) of the following nine symptoms during the same 2-week period:

1. Depressed mood most of the day, nearly every day.
2. Markedly diminished interest or pleasure in almost all activities (anhedonia).
3. Significant weight loss/gain or decrease/increase in appetite.
4. Insomnia or hypersomnia.
5. Psychomotor retardation or agitation.
6. Fatigue or loss of energy.
7. Feelings of worthlessness (or excessive or inappropriate guilt).
8. Diminished ability to concentrate or make decisions.
9. Recurrent thoughts of death.

Symptoms must be present most of the day, nearly every day, and should represent a significant change from previous functioning. Importantly, one of the nine symptoms has to be either depressed mood or anhedonia. In adolescents or children, irritable mood can be substituted for depressed mood. Less than 5% of depressed adolescents typically endorse anhedonia (Rohde, Beevers, Stice, & O'Neil, 2009), so depressed or irritable mood tends to be the hallmark symptom of adolecent depression. Significant weight loss or gain is typically defined as 5% or more change in body weight in a month when not dieting. These symptoms must cause significant distress or impairment in social, occupational, or other important areas of functioning. Finally, these symptoms should not be attributable to substances (e.g., drug abuse, medication changes), medical conditions (e.g., hypothyroidism), or the death of a loved one.

Recent epidemiological research indicates that the 12-month prevalence rates for MDD was 6.6% (95% CI, 5.9%–7.3%) among adults residing in the United States. Lifetime prevalence for MDD was 16.2% (95% CI, 15.1%–17.3%). Put differently, approximately 13.5 million adults experienced MDD in the past year, and 34 million adults have experienced MDD at some point in their lives. Approximately 51% who experienced MDD in the past year received health-care treatment for MDD, although treatment was considered adequate in only 21% of the cases (Kessler, Berglund et al., 2003). Thus, MDD is a prevalent and pervasive mental health disorder that is unfortunately not treated optimally in the United States.

Obtaining adequate treatment is important, as the course of MDD tends to be relatively prolonged. One of the largest studies of MDD recovery among individuals seeking treatment found that 50% of the sample recovered from MDD by 6 months, 70% within 12 months, and 81% within 24 months. Approximately 17% did not recover within the 5-year follow-up period (Keller et al., 1992). The first 6 months represents a particularly important time period for MDD recovery, as the rate of MDD recovery significantly slows after 6 months. Similarly, Kessler (2009) writes that time to recovery of MDD in nontreatment-seeking populations "appears to be highly variable, although epidemiological evidence is slim" (p. 29). One study found that 40% had recovered from MDD by 5 weeks and 90% had recovered within 12 months (McLeod, Kessler, & Landis, 1992). Another study reported that mean time to recovery was 4 months and that approximately 90% had recovered by 12 months (Kendler, Walters, & Kessler, 1997). Taken together, these data suggest that most participants from a community sample recover from MDD within 12 months.

Risk for MDD is especially pronounced during adolescence (Blazer, Kessler, McGonagle, & Swartz, 1994; Lewinsohn, Hops, Roberts, & Seeley, 1993). Prevalence rates range from 10% to 18.5% (Kessler & Walters, 1998). This is especially true for adolescent girls, who are approximately twice as likely to experience depression as adolescent boys (Hankin et al., 1998). Longitudinal studies show that increases in MDD prevalence for women occur at approximately 15 years of age and persist into adulthood (Hankin et al., 1998; Kessler, Berglund et al., 2003; Lewinsohn, Hops et al., 1993; Nolen Hoeksema & Girgus, 1994; Prinstein, Borelli, Cheah, Simon, & Aikins, 2005).

Treatment for adolescents with subthreshold symptoms of MDD may be particularly important, as adolescents with elevated symptoms (but who do not meet criteria for MDD) are at high risk for future onset of MDD. Lewinsohn, Roberts, and colleagues et al. (1994) found that elevated depressive symptoms was one of the most potent risk factors for future MDD onset over the subsequent year out of dozens of risk factors. Seeley, Stice, and Rohde (2009) recently examined a broad array of putative risk factors (e.g., parental support, negative life events, depressive and bulimic symptoms, substance use, attributional style, body dissatisfaction, physical activity, social adjustment, delinquency) for MDD onset in a longitudinal study of 496 adolescent girls 15 to 18 years old. Among 18 variables tested, the strongest predictor of future MDD onset was subthreshold depressive symptoms. Girls with elevated symptoms were at approximately five times greater risk for future MDD onset than girls with low symptoms (28% versus 6%).

Unfortunately, treatment utilization among depressed adolescents is also lacking. Approximately 60% of adolescent with MDD receive treatment (Lewinsohn, Rohde, & Seeley, 1998). Individual outpatient psychotherapy administered by a mental health provider is the most common form of treatment. Adolescents with more severe depression, a comorbid condition, a past history of MDD, a history of suicidal attempts, and academic problems, and females were more likely to receive treatment.

However, those who had received treatment were not less likely to relapse into another episode of depression during young adulthood (Lewinsohn et al., 1998). This suggests that the typical treatment received by depressed adolescents may not have been effective at changing the underlying cause of depression onset.

Assessment of Depression

A number of questionnaires and diagnostic interviews are available to assess depression symptoms and MDD in adolescents and adults. We review these assessments for adults and adolescents separately.

Adults

The Structured Clinical Interview for *DSM-IV* Axis I Disorders (SCID) diagnoses is the most common method for determining whether an adult meets criteria for MDD (and many other *DSM-IV* diagnoses). This is a semistructured interview that inquires about current and past symptoms. Length of an SCID interview can be quite variable—individuals with no past or current symptoms can complete the interview in about 15 minutes. Individuals with more complex symptom presentations can take several hours to complete a SCID interview. A typical SCID interview takes about 90 minutes. With adequate interviewer training, the SCID interview has excellent reliability and has been used extensively in depression research. Determining the validity of the SCID is more complex, as it is typically used as the gold standard to determine a diagnosis. Nevertheless, there is ample evidence that an SCID diagnosis converges with diagnoses derived from other diagnostic interviews (First, Spitzer, Williams, & Gibbon, 1995). For more detail on the SCID, see http://www.scid4.org/.

The World Health Organization (WHO) Composite International Diagnostic Interview (CIDI) is a psychiatric diagnostic interview designed to be administered by nonclinicians. The CIDI assesses for most Axis I disorders (including MDD) as defined by the *DSM-IV* and the ICD-10. It also assesses service use, use of medications, and barriers to treatment. There is substantial evidence for the reliability and validity of the CIDI. It has been translated into numerous languages and is typically used in large-scale epidemiological studies (Kessler, Berglund et al., 2003). For more information, see http://www.hcp.med.harvard.edu/wmhcidi/index.php.

The Mini-International Neuropsychiatric Interview (MINI) is another diagnostic interview that was developed jointly by psychiatrists and clinicians in the United States and Europe (Sheehan et al., 1998). It is much briefer than the SCID and CIDI, with an administration time of approximately 20 minutes. It assesses 15 of the most common *DSM-IV* Axis I disorders, including current and past history of MDD. Due to its brevity, it is often used as a screening interview that is subsequently confirmed with a subsequent in-depth diagnostic interview. It also has excellent reliability and validity (Sheehan et al., 1997). For more information, see https://www.medical-outcomes.com/index.php.

A number of self-report and interviewer-based assessments of depression severity are also available. The most commonly used interview-based depression severity assessments with adults include the Hamilton Rating Scale for Depression (HAM-D) and the Inventory of Depressive Symptomatology (IDS). The 17-item HAM-D was originally developed in 1960 and subsequently revised a number of times (Hamilton, 1960). It has been used primarily in antidepressant medication trials. The HAM-D has been criticized on the basis that it has poor content validity (may overemphasize somatic symptoms, which are especially responsive to antidepressant medication treatment), having a nonoptimal response format for many items, several items do not appear to discriminate people at high and low ends of the depression continuum, and other psychometric flaws (Bagby, Ryder, Schuller, & Marshall, 2004).

As a result, a newer interview-based assessment of depression severity, the IDS, is gaining popularity (Rush, Thomas, & Paul-Egbert, 2000). The 30-item IDS (and the 16-item Quick IDS) assess the severity of depression symptoms in the past seven days. The items measure all *DSM-IV* symptoms of MDD, although a total score is typically used to assess depression severity. There is much evidence to suggest that the IDS has good psychometric properties, including good internal reliability, test-retest reliability and adequate content, criterion, and construct validity (e.g., Rush et al., 2003). The IDS has been translated into more than 20 different languages and is used widely in medical research. Items can be added to the IDS to facilitate computation of the HAM-D total score within the IDS interview. Further, there is also a self-report version of the IDS to be completed by patients. The IDS (and its corresponding short and self-report versions) are available for download at http://www.ids-qids.org/index.html.

There are also a number of other excellent self-report assessments of depression severity. The Beck Depression Inventory-II (BDI-II) is a 21-item self-report questionnaire that is among the most commonly used instrument to assess depression severity (Beck, Steer, & Brown, 1996). It is often used in research involving psychological treatments. The BDI-II has demonstrated adequate internal consistency, test-retest reliability, and construct validity (Dozois, Dobson, & Ahnberg, 1998). A score of 12 or less is considered nondepressed, whereas a score of 20 or greater typically indicates moderate or greater depression severity (Dozois et al., 1998). To obtain the BDI-II, see http://www.pearsonassessments.com/HAIWEB/Cultures/en-us/Productdetail.htm?Pid=015–8018–370&Mode=summary.

Alternatively, the Center for Epidemiologic Studies—Depression (CESD) is another common assessment of depression severity (Radloff, 1977). The CESD was developed to be a brief self-report scale designed to measure depression severity in the general (nonpsychiatric) population. It has 16 items that measure the severity of depression symptoms in the past week. It has very good internal consistency and test-retest reliability. Validity was established by correlating the CESD with other depression inventories and clinical ratings of depression (Radloff, 1977). A 10-item version has also been developed (Irwin, Artin, & Oxman, 1999). It is a widely used depression scale, particularly when the majority of the sample is expected to be currently depressed.

Adolescents

The Kiddie-Sads-Present and Lifetime version (K-SADS-PL) is a semistructured diagnostic interview designed to assess severity ratings of symptomatology as well as current and past episodes of psychopathology in adolescents according to *DSM-IV* criteria (Kaufman et al., 1997). The full interview assesses more than 35 mental health diagnoses, including MDD. The K-SADS-PL is administered to parents and the adolescent. Other sources of information may also be incorporated (e.g., school reports) into a summary rating. It is typically recommended to start the interview with the adolescent first, followed by the parents. Clinical judgment is required when there are discrepancies in the content of the reports from adolescents and parents. The K-SADS has been found to have acceptable test-retest reliability (k's = .60 – 1.00), inter-rater reliability (k's = .60 –1.00), and internal consistency (alpha's = .68 – .84) for MDD ratings, and to discriminate between disordered and nondisordered adolescents (Ambrosini, 2000; Kaufman et al., 1997; Lewinsohn et al., 1993). For more information, see http://www.wpic.pitt.edu/ksads/default.htm.

The Children's Depression Inventory is a 27-item, self-report assessment of depression severity that was developed for children and adolescents between the ages of 7 and 17 years (Kovacs, 1992). Each item describes a symptom, and the adolescent rates the severity of each symptom over the past two weeks on a 3-point scale. A 10-item version is also available. The normative sample was ethnically and geographically diverse. Internal consistency and test-retest reliability are excellent. There are five subscales (negative mood, interpersonal difficulties, negative self-esteem, ineffectiveness, and anhedonia), although using the CDI total score is the most common approach to assessing symptom severity. For more information on the CDI, see http://www.pearsonassessments.com/pai/.

Evidence–Based Treatment for Depression: Interventions Not Included in This Volume

There are a number of treatments for depression that have empirical support indicating that the treatment is effective for the treatment of depression. Of course, we preferred to include an in-depth review of each and every one of these treatments in this book. However, this was not practical or feasible. Instead we selected a variety of treatments that have a solid research base, and each chapter provides an in-depth description of a treatment. Rather than inadvertently convey that these are the only effective treatments for depression, we now provide a brief overview of other treatments that have a solid research base that are not included, for one reason or another, in this text.

Pharmacological Treatments

Several classes of medications are used to treat depression. Three basic types of antidepressant medications include tricyclic antidepressants, monoamine oxidase inhibitors (MAOIs), and serotonin-specific reuptake inhibitors (SSRIs). There are some newer antidepressant medications that do not fit neatly into these categories because they have different mechanisms of action (e.g., venlafaxine and nefazedone). The efficacy rates for these newer antidepressant treatments are comparable to the efficacy rates of SSRIs (Stahl, Entsuah, & Rudolph, 2002).

Tricyclic Medications Prior to the introduction of SSRIs, tricyclic medications were the most commonly prescribed antidepressant medications. Although the exact mechanism of action is not completely understood, tricyclic medications reduce the transmission of norepinephrine by blocking its reuptake and allowing for norepinephrine to pool in the synapse. This leads to decreased production of norepinephrine (i.e., downregulation). These medications can take two to eight weeks before a therapeutic effect occurs, which may be due to neurogenesis (nerve growth) in the hippocampus (Santarelli et al., 2003). Tricyclic mediations can produce a number of side effects including blurred vision, dry mouth, constipation, drowsiness, and weight gain. As a result, 40% of patients stop taking these medications, even though with careful management these side effects can disappear. Tricyclic medications improve depression symptoms in approximately 50% of patients; if we exclude patients who stopped taking the medication, improvement rates climb to 70% (Depression Guideline Panel, 1993). Taking excessive doses of these medications can be lethal, so individuals with suicidal tendencies should be monitored closely.

MAOIs These antidepressant medications block the enzyme MAO, which degrades neurotransmitters such as serotonin and norepinephrine. As a result, more of these neurotransmitters are available in the synapse, leading to downregulation. MAOIs appear to be as effective as tricyclic medications and have fewer overall side effects (Depression Guideline Panel, 1993). However, people prescribed MAOIs have significant food restrictions. They cannot consume food or drinks that contain tyramine, such as cheese, red wine, or beer. Doing so can lead to significant increases in blood pressure that in some cases can be fatal. MAOIs can also interact with other commonly used drugs, such as cold medicine. As a result, MAOIs are not often prescribed.

SSRIs SSRIs are the most commonly prescribed class of antidepressant medication and are generally considered the first choice for antidepressant treatment. These medications block the reuptake of presynaptic serotonin, leaving more available at the receptor site. This facilitates increased serotonin production over time. Although this class of drugs is relatively new, the efficacy of SSRIs is comparable to MAOI and tricyclic medications. Approximately 50% experience symptom improvement, but depression fully remits in only about 25% to 30% of patients (Trivedi et al., 2006). SSRIs have fewer side effects than the other antidepressant medications, thus accounting for their popularity despite similar efficacy compared to older treatments. Most common side effects include physical agitation, sexual dysfunction, low sexual desire, and sleep difficulties.

Placebo Response

Although antidepressant medication treatment is a common and accepted form of treatment for depression, there is some controversy about whether it is more effective than pill placebo (Moncrieff & Kirsch, 2005). That is, do antidepressant medications improve symptoms beyond the effect of believing that medication treatment will be effective? A recent study addressed this question using meta-analysis of six studies that compared antidepressant medication to pill placebo (Fournier et al., 2010). In short, this study found that antidepressant treatment was only mildly more effective than placebo for people with relatively low symptoms of depression, whereas a clinically significant benefit of antidepressant medication compared to placebo was observed for patients with more severe forms of depression. Thus, medication treatment may be particularly beneficial for individuals with more severe forms of the disorder. However, this study was based on only six studies (718 patients) involving two antidepressant medications (paroxetine and imipramine), so much more work needs to be done in this area.

Antidepressant Treatment With Adolescents

Far less is known about the treatment efficacy of antidepressant medication in adolescents. A recent meta-analysis indicated that antidepressant treatment appears to be effective for adolescents (Bridge et al., 2007). Across 13 clinical trials and 2910 participants 7 to 17 years old, overall response to treatment was 61%, compared to 50% for placebo. Adolescents had a better response to antidepressant treatment relative to placebo than children, but this was due to a stronger placebo response in children. Overall response rate to antidepressant treatment (not accounting for differences in placebo response) for adolescents and children was very similar (62% versus 65%). The efficacy of antidepressant treatment was inversely related to the duration of depressive disorder. This suggests that providing adolescents treatment earlier in the course of the depressive episode may be beneficial. Fluoxetine (Prozac) is currently the only medication approved by the U.S. Food and Drug Administration (FDA) for the treatment of depression in children and adolescents (ages 8 and older).

Recently, there has been some concern that antidepressant medications may increase risk for suicidal ideation and behavior among a subset of adolescents. The FDA reviewed placebo-controlled clinical trials of SSRIs involving 2,200 youth and found that risk for suicidal thinking or behavior was double among those receiving SSRIs versus placebo, although base rates for suicidal behavior were relatively low

(4% versus 2%). In response, the FDA adopted a serious "black box" label warning, indicating SSRIs could increase the risk of suicidality in youth. The FDA also recommended especially close monitoring in the first four weeks of SSRI treatment, a time period when suicidal ideation and behavior were most likely to occur. Interestingly, epidemiological research indicates that increased SSRI prescriptions are associated with lower rates of completed suicide in adolescents and children (Gibbons, Hur, Bhaumik, & Mann, 2006). Further, after instituting a "black box" warning, prescriptions for SSRIs decreased and rates of completed suicide subsequently increased among children and adolescents (Gibbons et al., 2007). Thus, this is a highly contentious issue, with conflicting evidence about whether SSRIs contribute to or prevent suicidal behavior.

Psychological Treatments

In this section, we review interpersonal psychotherapy, marital therapy, family treatment, and psychological treatment with adolescents.

Interpersonal Psychotherapy (IPT) There is substantial evidence that IPT is an effective treatment for depression. It is generally recommended as an acute treatment for adult depression by numerous guidelines and panels (e.g., Depression Guideline Panel, 1993). IPT has been shown to be equally effective as acute antidepressant treatment with amitriptyline for the reduction of depression symptoms, and combined treatment (IPT + amitriptyline) was more effective than either treatment alone (Weissman et al., 1979). Further, a large multisite study has demonstrated that IPT is equally effective as antidepressant treatment with imipramine and CBT for the treatment of mild depression and that IPT demonstrated a slight advantage over CBT for the treatment of more severe forms of depression (Elkin et al., 1989).

The IPT treatment manual has been translated into numerous languages and implemented around the world. Later we provide a brief overview of the concepts and techniques of IPT. For more detail, treatment manuals are available for IPT with depressed adults (Weissman, Markowitz, & Klerman, 2000), depressed adolescents (Mufson, Moreau, Weissman, & Klerman, 1993), and for delivery in group formats (Wilfley, MacKenzie, Welch, Ayres, & Weissman, 2000).

IPT is based on the notion that life events influence the onset and expression of depression. The main goal of IPT is to help the patient better understand and cope with depression by making connections between current life events and the onset of symptoms. This is achieved in part by helping patients to overcome interpersonal problems in an effort to improve life circumstances and relieve depression. Its focus is on current events and relationships, rather than on past relationships or problems. IPT techniques include (a) an *opening question:* patients provide information regarding their current mood state and events that contributed to the current mood; (b) *communication analysis:* patients review an important affectively charged life event; (c) *exploration of patient's wishes and options:* patients review desired outcomes for the situations described in session; (d) *decision analysis:* patients decide which options to use in future life situations, and (e) *role playing:* patients practice implementing new strategies and solutions to interpersonal problems.

Treatment with IPT typically lasts 12 to 16 weeks when implemented in clinical trials, although longer versions of IPT have been developed (Klerman, DiMascio, Weissman, Prusoff, & Paykel, 1974). The early phase of treatment involves a diagnostic evaluation, presentation of the IPT framework, and a review of the patient's psychiatric history. Reviewing key interpersonal relationships is a major focus of this phase. The therapist also identifies life difficulties that contribute to the patient's depressive symptoms in one of four key areas: (1) grief, (2) role disputes, (3) role transitions, and (4) interpersonal deficits. The middle phase of treatment focuses on remediating these problem areas. For instance, if the main issue is the patient's difficulty with social skills, much of the treatment will be focused on improving those skills (e.g., via role plays with the therapist). The final phase of treatment helps the patient to consolidate the gains, identify potential weaknesses, and develop a plan to cope with increases in depression should they occur again.

Marital Therapy Although there is good evidence that marital therapy can be used to successfully treat marital discord (Beach, Jones, & Franklin, 2009), there is emerging evidence that martial therapy can effectively treat depression. Three studies found that behavioral marital therapy was equally effective for treating depression as cognitive therapy, and both were superior to a waitlist control (Beach & O'Leary, 1992; Emanuels-Zuurveen & Emmelkamp, 1996; Jacobson, Dobson, Fruzzetti, Schmaling, & Salusky, 1991). Behavioral martial therapy had the additional benefit of reducing marital discord to a greater extent than cognitive therapy. Other forms of marital treatment have been shown to be effective, such as spouse-aided cognitive therapy (Emanuels-Zuurveen & Emmelkamp, 1997), cognitive marital therapy (Teichman, Bar-El, Shor, & Sirota, 1995), and IPT modified for couples (Markowitz, Weissman, & Gabbard, 2009), although the evidence base is somewhat smaller for these forms of treatment.

Given the success of Behavioral Marital Therapy (BMT) for the treatment of depression, we provide a brief review of this intervention (for a more thorough review, see Beach et al., 2009). BMT is a relatively brief time-limited (approximately 10 weeks) treatment that is indicated for couples when one partner is depressed and marital discord is present. Initially, therapists identify relationship stressors and develop a plan to eliminate them, while simultaneously increasing the number of positive interactions between the couple. Ideally, this phase of treatment will improve depressed mood and prepare the couple for the second phase of treatment aimed at restructuring the marital relationship. The main focus of this second phase of treatment is to improve communication between partners, engage in more productive and healthy problem solving, and improve day-to-day interactions between the couple. Most of the work in BMT occurs during this phase. The final phase of treatment involves preparation for termination from treatment and setting a plan to cope with future stressors that may increase vulnerability to depression and marital discord.

Family Treatment Family-based treatment is another type of intervention that appears to be effective for depression. For instance, severely depressed patients who received family treatment were more likely to improve and report less suicidal ideation than patients who did not receive family treatment (Miller et al., 2005). Although there are a number of family-based treatments, the McMaster approach appears to be effective for treating adult depression (Miller, Ryan, Keitner, Bishop, & Epstein, 2000).

This treatment takes a systems approach to understanding dysfunction within the family. It assumes that: (a) all parts of the family are interrelated; (b) one member of the family cannot be fully understood in isolation from the rest of the family; and (c) family structure, organization, and interactions influence family members' behavior. At the beginning stages of treatment, family functioning is evaluated in six domains: problem-solving, communication, roles, affective responsiveness, affective involvement, and behavior control. The family and the therapist then develop a contract, which identifies the expectations, goals, and commitments regarding treatment. Treatment is then initiated to mitigate identified problems. Treatment focuses on behavioral changes via task setting that occurs between sessions. Subsequent sessions then focus on evaluating the success of those assignments and then planning future tasks that build on prior successes. A number of techniques are also explored during the session to help improve the family's ability to communicate and change the problems without the help of the therapist. The final stages of treatment focus on summarizing treatment, setting long-term goals, and determining whether future follow-up treatment is necessary. For more detail, see Epstein, Bishop, Miller, and Keitner (1988).

Psychological Treatment With Adolescents Although CBT treatment has the most empirical support for the psychological treatment of adolescent depression (see Appendix A), evidence is accumulating for other forms of treatment. For instance, two studies have documented the efficacy of adolescent IPT (IPT-A) for depressed adolescents versus brief supportive therapy (Mufson, Weissman, Moreau, & Garfinkel, 1999) and waitlist (Rosselló & Bernal, 1999). Further, in a study involving training community clinicians to deliver the intervention, IPT-A outperformed treatment as usual (Mufson et al., 2004), with 50% recovering from depression in IPT-A versus 34% in treatment as usual. Adolescents receiving IPT-A also reported significantly better improvement in overall functioning and social functioning at the end of treatment than those who received treatment as usual. Thus, IPT-A is considered an efficacious treatment for adolescent depression (David-Ferdon & Kaslow, 2008).

Family-oriented treatment also appears to be an efficacious treatment for adolescent depression. One of the first studies compared systemic behavior family therapy (SBFT) to CBT and supportive therapy for the treatment of depression. SBFT identifies the presenting problems within the family and then focuses on changing dysfunctional interaction patterns and improving communication within the family. At the end of acute treatment (12 to 16 sessions), 17% of CBT participants, 32% of SBFT participants, and 42% of the supportive treatment participants still met criteria for MDD. However, by the 2-year follow-up, more than 80% had recovered from MDD and treatment did not predict who was more likely to recover. Thus, although this literature is sparse and much more work is needed, family treatment may work less efficiently than CBT for treating adolescent depression, but longer-term outcomes appear to be comparable.

Combined Pharmacological and Psychological Treatment

Given that pharmacological and psychological treatments can be effective in isolation, a related question is whether combining these treatments can improve depression treatment outcomes further. A number of studies have examined this question, including several meta-analyses. One meta-analysis found that adding psychotherapy to antidepressant treatment almost doubled the response rate compared to antidepressant treatment alone (Pampallona, Bollini, Tibaldi, Kupelnick, & Munizza, 2004). Participants in the combined treatment were also less likely to drop out of treatment compared to those who only received medication.

However, the picture is less clear when examining the impact of adding pharmacotherapy to psychotherapy. One review found that combined treatment was not more effective than psychotherapy for less severe forms of depression, but a significant advantage was observed for combined treatment for more severe recurrent depressions (Thase et al., 1997). Yet another review indicates that combined treatment compared to single treatment leads to small improvements in depression (Friedman et al., 2004). Overall, combined treatment in adults may be beneficial; however, the effects tend to be modest and are probably best indicated for more severe forms of depression.

Relatively fewer studies have examined the efficacy of combined treatment in adolescents. The Treatment for Adolescents with Depression Study (TADS) is a large multisite clinical research study examining the effectiveness of antidepressant medication, CBT psychotherapy, and their combination among adolescents 12 to 17 years old (Treatment for Adolescents with Depression Study Team, 2003). This study was conducted at 13 clinics across the United States (at a cost of $17 million) and involved 439 adolescents. After 12 weeks of treatment, 71% receiving combined treatment, 61% receiving fluoxetine (Prozac), 44% receiving CBT, and 35% receiving pill placebo were much or very much improved (Treatment for Adolescents with Depression Study Team, 2004). After 18 weeks of treatment, results were similar, as combination treatment was still most effective. By 36 weeks, the response rate was highest for combination treatment (86%), but response rates for fluoxetine and CBT had caught up (81% each)(Treatment for Adolescents with Depression Study Team, 2007). Interestingly, rates of suicidal thinking or behavior were highest in fluoxetine only (15%), compared to combined treatment (8%) and CBT alone (6%). Given adolescents' rapid responses to combined treatment, these data suggest combining CBT with fluoxetine may be the quickest, most effective, and safest treatment for adolescent depression.

Evidence–Based Treatment for Depression: Interventions Included in This Volume

This book includes six chapters. In this chapter we provide background information about how depression is defined and measured. We also review effective treatments for adolescent and adult depression that are not included in this volume. In the remainder of this chapter, we provide a preview of interventions that are included in the subsequent chapters.

In Chapter 2, Paul Rohde reviews Cognitive Behavioral Treatment (CBT) for use with adolescents. He describes a group-based treatment for adolescent depression based on the Adolescent Coping With Depression (CWD-A) course. This course has outstanding empirical evidence for its efficacy, which is reviewed in Appendix A. Dr. Rohde also describes individual CBT treatment for depressed adolescents. The approach is consistent with treatment provided in the Treatment for Adolescent Depression Study (TADS). Incidentally, Dr. Rohde is a member of the Treatment for Adolescent Depression Study team, and he helped implement the CBT intervention in TADS. This chapter reviews the general structure of CBT sessions and provides an in-depth review of core CBT skills, such as goal setting, behavioral activation, and countering cognitive distortions. He then reviews optional CBT skills, such as problem solving, social skills, and relaxation. These can be implemented based on the adolescents' needs and duration of treatment. Throughout the chapter, Dr. Rohde uses case examples to illustrate his points.

In Chapter 3, Cory Newman reviews the application of CBT to adult depression. Before reviewing the CBT mechanics, he provides an excellent review of commonly held myths about CBT and succinctly describes why each is, indeed, a myth. For instance, he debunks the notion that CBT has to be short-term, that the therapeutic relationship does not matter in CBT, and that CBT is simply replacing negative thoughts with the power of positive thinking. Next, he reviews how to conceptualize depression from a CBT perspective and provides two illuminating case examples. He then reviews the core techniques used in CBT when treating depressed adults. Note that there is some overlap with techniques discussed in Chapter 2; however, you will see a number of unique approaches as well. For instance, in addition to reviewing activity scheduling and responding to negative thoughts, he also reviews how to incorporate role-play, homework, and behavioral experiments. He also reviews how to apply CBT to suicidal clients—suicidal ideation and behavior is a common symptom of depression and Dr. Newman provides excellent advice on how to treat suicidal clients from a CBT perspective. Finally, he concludes with a review of additional issues that arise during CBT for depression, such as how to identify the client's strengths, what to do when a depressed person takes on a "depressive identity," or how to work with hopelessness. Together, Chapters 2 and 3 provide an in-depth review of CBT for depression and also discuss clinical issues that often arise during treatment but are often not addressed in treatment manuals or the research literature.

Although the research support for CBT for depression is impressive, the question was raised whether behavioral activation (BA) alone would be sufficient for the treatment of depression. A pioneering dismantling study compared the efficacy of BA versus CBT, with very encouraging results for BA (Jacobson et al., 1996). As a result of that study, BA treatment was developed and it is now an empirically supported treatment. In Chapter 4, Jonathan Kanter, William Bowe, David Baruch, and Andrew Busch review a variant of BA that includes the core features of the BA treatments that have been developed. They provide a rich overview of the theory behind BA and its general principles. They discuss how to convey the BA rationale to clients and how to deal with clients' reactions to the conceptualization. Activity scheduling is a hallmark technique of BA. Thus, much of Chapter 4 is devoted to reviewing this technique in detail. They also incorporate a review of clients' values—this approach is used to help make behavioral activation more meaningful. Ideally, clients are working toward goals that are personally meaningful and are consistent with their own values. The inclusion of values is a recent and cutting-edge addition to BA. They also review common barriers to treatment success, such as avoidance and failure to complete homework assignments. This chapter includes a number of detailed case descriptions, which help to illustrate this intervention. Although BA may sound straightforward, after reading this chapter, you will quickly see that this intervention is much more complex than the name implies.

Although depression is typically thought of as episodic, with periods of well-being interspersed with periods of depression, for some people depression takes a much more chronic course. Remission from MDD may be incomplete, or the MDD episode may persist for much longer than commonly expected. About 3% of the population suffers from this type of chronic depression (Kessler et al., 1994). Importantly, chronic forms of MDD are associated with impaired work performance, poorer social functioning (Wells, Burnam, Rogers, Hays, & Camp, 1992), increased health care utilization (Weissman, Leaf, Bruce, & Florio, 1988), and higher rates of attempted suicide (Klein et al., 1998) than are more acute forms of depression. Despite the large societal impact of chronic depression, until recently, few psychological treatments had been developed and shown to be effective for treating chronic depression.

In Chapter 5, James McCullough and Jennifer Penberthy describe the leading psychological treatment for chronic depression, Cognitive Behavioral Analysis System of Psychotherapy (CBASP). CBASP is one of the only treatments specifically developed for the treatment of chronic depression. In Chapter 5, the authors use a case study to illustrate the application of CBASP. They present a client who has been chronically depressed for approximately 2 years and then walk the reader through a course of CBASP treatment. They start with obtaining a psychiatric history, followed by collecting an interpersonal history. Next, a situational analysis is presented. This is a key CBASP intervention that involves reviewing past situations and identifying coping strategies employed in those situations. Over time, situational analysis helps clients to identify more effective ways of coping with stressors and increases their self-efficacy in those situations. Thus, CBASP shares many features of CBT, but also places much greater emphasis on interpersonal aspects of a client's life.

In Chapter 6, Esteban Cardemil, Oswaldo Moreno, and Monica Sanchez tackle the tremendously important yet difficult issue of how to apply evidence-based practice to diverse populations. They correctly point out that much work on empirically supported treatments for depression has been conducted with people from European-American middle-class backgrounds. Thus, this raises the question of whether we need to adapt these interventions for other populations, and if so, how? Cardemil and colleagues propose that we should tailor interventions according to the needs of different populations. They provide several suggestions for how to adapt evidence-based treatments for diverse populations. This advice is based on empirical research with diverse populations, which is consistent with the philosophy of evidence-based practice. We believe this issue is critically important, as clients from diverse backgrounds who are seeking treatment are likely to become the norm rather than the exception.

We hope that after reading the various chapters in this volume you will have a better appreciation and understanding of evidence-based treatments for adolescents and adults with depression. Moreover, we hope that these descriptions inspire you to incorporate these techniques into your own practice or perhaps motivate you to receive additional training on one or more of the approaches reviewed in this volume. Ultimately, we hope you find this book to be of value for treating depressed clients. If you have feedback about any aspect of the book that you would like to share with us, do not hesitate to contact us at beevers@psy.utexas.edu or dwspringer@austin.utexas.edu.

References

Ambrosini, P. J. (2000). Historical development and present status of the Schedule for Affective Disorders and Schizophrenia for School-Age Children (K-SADS). *Journal of the American Academy of Child and Adolescent Psychiatry, 39,* 49.

Bagby, R. M., Ryder, A. G., Schuller, D. R., & Marshall, M. B. (2004). The Hamilton depression rating scale: Has the gold standard become a lead weight? *American Journal of Psychiatry, 161,* 2163–2177.

Beach, S. R. H., Jones, D. J., & Franklin, K. J. (2009). Marital, family, and interpersonal therapies for depression in adults. In I. H. Gotlib & C. L. Hammen (Eds.), *Handbook of depression* (2nd ed., pp. 624–641). New York, NY: Guilford Press.

Beach, S. R. H., & O'Leary, K. D. (1992). Treating depression in the context of marital discord: Outcome and predictors of response of marital therapy versus cognitive therapy. *Behavior Therapy, 23,* 507–528.

Beautrais, A. L., Joyce, P. R., Mulder, R. T., Fergusson, D. M., Deavoll, B. J., & Nightingale, S. K. (1996). Prevalence and comorbidity of mental disorders in persons making serious suicide attempts: A case-control study. *American Journal of Psychiatry, 153,* 1009–1014.

Beck, A. T., Steer, R., & Brown, G. K. (1996). *Beck Depression Inventory (BDI-II).* San Antonio, TX: Psychological Corp.

Blazer, D. G., Kessler, R. C., McGonagle, K. A., & Swartz, M. S. (1994). The prevalence and distribution of major depression in a national community sample: The National comorbidity survey. *American Journal of Psychiatry, 151,* 979–986.

Bridge, J. A., Iyengar, S., Salary, C. B., Barbe, R. P., Birmaher, B., Pincus, H. A., . . . Ren, L. (2007). Clinical response and risk for reported suicidal ideation and suicide attempts in pediatric antidepressant treatment: A meta-analysis of randomized controlled trials. *JAMA, 297,* 1683–1696.

David-Ferdon, C., & Kaslow, N. J. (2008). Evidence-based psychosocial treatments for child and adolescent depression. *Journal of Clinical Child and Adolescent Psychology, 37,* 62–104.

Depression Guideline Panel. (1993). *Clinical practice guideline: Depression in primary care.* Rockville, MD: Department of Health and Human Services, Agency for Health Care Policy and Research.

Dozois, D. J. A., Dobson, K. S., & Ahnberg, J. L. (1998). A psychometric evaluation of the Beck Depression Inventory-II. *Psychological Assessment, 10,* 83–89.

Elkin, I., Shea, M. T., Watkins, J. T., Imber, S. D., Sotsky, S. M., Collins, J. F., ... Glass, D.R. (1989). National Institute of Mental Health treatment of depression collaborative research program: General effectiveness of treatments. *Archives of General Psychiatry, 46,* 971–982.

Emanuels-Zuurveen, L., & Emmelkamp, P. M. G. (1996). Individual behavioural-cognitive therapy v. marital therapy for depression in maritally distressed couples. *British Journal of Psychiatry, 169,* 181–188.

Emanuels-Zuurveen, L., & Emmelkamp, P. M. G. (1997). Spouse-aided therapy with depressed patients. *Behavior Modification, 21,* 62–77.

Epstein, N. B., Bishop, D. S., Miller, I. W., & Keitner, G. I. (1988). *Treatment manual—Problem centered systems therapy of the family.* Providence, RI: Brown University Family Research Program.

First, M., Spitzer, R., Williams, J., & Gibbon, M. (1995). *Structured clinical interview for DSM-IV—Patient version.* New York, NY: Biometrics Research Department, New York State Psychiatric Institute.

Fournier, J. C., DeRubeis, R. J., Hollon, S. D., Dimidjian, S., Amsterdam, J. D., Shelton, R. C., et al. (2010). Antidepressant drug effects and depression severity: A patient-level meta-analysis. *JAMA, 303,* 47–53.

Friedman, M. A., Detweiler-Bedell, J. B., Leventhal, H. E., Home, R., Keitner, G. I., & Miller, I. W. (2004). Combined psychotherapy and pharmacotherapy for the treatment of major depressive disorder. *Clinical Psychology: Science and Practice, 11,* 47–68.

Gibbons, R. D., Brown, C. H., Hur, K., Marcus, S. M., Bhaumik, D. K., Erkens, J. A., et al. (2007). Early evidence on the effects of regulators' suicidality warnings on SSRI prescriptions and suicide in children and adolescents. *American Journal of Psychiatry, 164,* 1356–1363.

Gibbons, R. D., Hur, K., Bhaumik, D. K., & Mann, J. J. (2006). The relationship between antidepressant prescription rates and rate of early adolescent suicide. *American Journal of Psychiatry, 163,* 1898–1904.

Greenberg, P. E., Stiglin, L. E., Finkelstein, S. N., & Berndt, E. R. (1993). The economic burden of depression in 1990. *Journal of Clinical Psychiatry, 54*, 405–418.

Hamilton, M. (1960). Development of a rating scale for depression. *Journal of Neurology, Neurosurgery, and Psychiatry, 23*, 56–62.

Hankin, B. L., Abramson, L. Y., Moffitt, T. E., Silva, P. A., McGee, R., & Angell, K. E. (1998). Development of depression from preadolescence to young adulthood: Emerging gender differences in a 10-year longitudinal study. *Journal of Abnormal Psychology, 107*, 128–140.

Irwin, M., Artin, K. H., & Oxman, M. N. (1999). Screening for depression in the older adult: Criterion validity of the 10-item center for epidemiological studies depression scale (CES-D). *Archives of Internal Medicine, 159*, 1701–1704.

Jacobson, N. S., Dobson, K., Fruzzetti, A. E., Schmaling, K. B., & Salusky, S. (1991). Marital therapy as a treatment for depression. *Journal of Consulting and Clinical Psychology, 59*, 547–557.

Jacobson, N. S., Dobson, K. S., Truax, P. A., Addis, M. E., Koerner, K., Gollan, J. K., . . . Gortner, E. (1996). A component analysis of cognitive-behavioral treatment for depression. *Journal of Consulting and Clinical Psychology, 64*, 295–304.

Kaufman, J., Birmaher, B., Brent, D., Rao, U., Flynn, C., Moreci, P., . . . Williamson, D. (1997). Schedule for affective disorders and schizophrenia for school-age children-present and lifetime version (K-SADS-PL): Initial reliability and validity data. *Journal of the American Academy of Child and Adolescent Psychiatry, 36*, 980–988.

Keller, M. B., Lavori, P. W., Mueller, T. I., Endicott, J., Coryell, W., Hirschfeld, R. M., . . . Shea, T. (1992). Time to recovery, chronicity, and levels of psychopathology in major depression. A 5-year prospective follow-up of 431 subjects. *Archives of General Psychiatry, 49*, 809–816.

Kendler, K. S., Walters, E. E., & Kessler, R. C. (1997). The prediction of length of major depressive episodes: Results from an epidemiological sample of female twins. *Psychological Medicine, 27*, 107–117.

Kessler, R. C., & Wang, P. S. (2009). Epidemiology of depression. In I. H. Gotlib & C. L. Hammen (Eds.), *Handbook of depression* (2nd ed., pp. 5–22). New York, NY: Guilford.

Kessler, R. C., Berglund, P., Demler, O., Jin, R., Koretz, D., Merikangas, K. R., et al. (2003). The epidemiology of major depressive disorder. Results from the National Comorbidity Survey Replication (NCS-R). *JAMA, 289*, 3095–3105.

Kessler, R. C., McGonagle, K. A., Zhao, S., Nelson, C. B., Hughes, M., Eshleman, S., . . . Wittchen, H. U. (1994). Lifetime and 12-month prevalence of DSM-III-R psychiatric disorders in the United States. Results from the National Comorbidity Survey.

Kessler, R. C., & Walters, E. E. (1998). Epidemiology of DSM-III-R major depression and minor depression among adolescents and young adults in the National Comorbidity Survey. *Depress Anxiety, 7*, 3–14.

Klein, D. N., Norden, K. A., Ferro, T., Leader, J. B., Kasch, K. L., Klein, L. M., ... Schwartz, J. E. (1998). Thirty-month naturalistic follow-up study of early-onset dysthymic disorder: Course, diagnostic stability, and prediction of outcome. *Journal of Abnormal Psychology, 107*, 338–348.

Klerman, G. L., DiMascio, A., Weissman, M. M., Prusoff, B. A., & Paykel, E. S. (1974). Treatment of depression by drugs and psychotherapy. *American Journal of Psychiatry, 131*, 186–191.

Kovacs, M. (1992). *Children's depression inventory manual.* Toronto, Canada: Multihealth Systems.

Lewinsohn, P. M., Hops, H., Roberts, R. E., & Seeley, J. R. (1993). Adolescent psychopathology: I. Prevalence and incidence of depression and other DSM-III-R disorders in high school students. *Journal of Abnormal Psychology, 102*, 133.

Lewinsohn, P. M., Roberts, R. E., Seeley, J. R., Rohde, P., Gotlib, I. H., & Hops, H. (1994). Adolescent psychopathology: II. Psychosocial risk factors for depression. *Journal of Abnormal Psychology, 103*, 302–315.

Lewinsohn, P. M., Rohde, P., & Seeley, J. R. (1998). Treatment of adolescent depression: Frequency of services and impact on functioning in young adulthood. *Depression and Anxiety, 7*, 47–52.

Markowitz, J. C., Weissman, M. M., & Gabbard, G. O. (2009). Applications of individual interpersonal psychotherapy to specific disorders: Efficacy and indications. In *Textbook of psychotherapeutic treatments* (pp. 339–364). Arlington, VA: American Psychiatric Association.

McLeod, J. D., Kessler, R. C., & Landis, K. R. (1992). Speed of recovery from major depressive episodes in a community sample of married men and women. *Journal of Abnormal Psycholology, 101*, 277.

Miller, I. W., Keitner, G. I., Ryan, C. E., Solomon, D. A., Cardemil, E. V., & Beevers, C. G. (2005). Treatment matching in the posthospital care of depressed patients. *American Journal of Psychiatry, 162*, 2131–2138.

Miller, I. W., Ryan, C. E., Keitner, G. I., Bishop, D. S., & Epstein, N. B. (2000). The McMaster approach to families: Theory, assessment, treatment and research. *Journal of Family Therapy, 22*, 168–189.

Moncrieff, J., & Kirsch, I. (2005). Efficacy of antidepressants in adults. *BMJ, 331*, 155–157.

Mufson, L., Dorta, K. P., Wickramaratne, P., Nomura, Y., Olfson, M., & Myrna, M. W. (2004). A randomized effectiveness trial of interpersonal psychotherapy for depressed adolescents. *Archives of General Psychiatry, 61*, 577.

Mufson, L., Moreau, D., Weissman, M. M., & Klerman, G. L. (1993). *Interpersonal psychotherapy for depressed adolescents.* New York, NY: Guilford.

Mufson, L., Weissman, M. M., Moreau, D., & Garfinkel, R. (1999). Efficacy of interpersonal psycho-therapy for depressed adolescents. *Archives of General Psychiatry, 56*, 573–579.

Nolen Hoeksema, S., & Girgus, J. S. (1994). The emergence of gender differences in depression during adolescence. *Psychological Bulletin, 115*, 424–443.

Pampallona, S., Bollini, P., Tibaldi, G., Kupelnick, B., & Munizza, C. (2004). Combined pharmacotherapy and psychological treatment for depression: A systematic review. *Archives of General Psychiatry, 61*, 714–719.

Philip, S. W., Gregory, S., & Ronald, C. K. (2003). The economic burden of depression and the cost-effectiveness of treatment. *International Journal of Methods in Psychiatric Research, 12*, 22–33.

Prinstein, M. J., Borelli, J. L., Cheah, C. S. L., Simon, V. A., & Aikins, J. W. (2005). Adolescent girls' interpersonal vulnerability to depressive symptoms: A longitudinal examination of reassurance-seeking and peer relationships. *Journal of Abnormal Psychology, 114*, 676.

Radloff, L. S. (1977). The CES-D scale: A self-report depression scale for research in the general population. *Applied Psychological Measurement, 1*, 385–401.

Rohde, P., Beevers, C. G., Stice, E., & O'Neil, K. (2009). Major and minor depression in female adolescents: Onset, course, symptom presentation, and demographic associations. *Journal of Clinical Psychology, 65*, 1339–1349.

Rosselló, J., & Bernal, G. (1999). The efficacy of cognitive-behavioral and interpersonal treatments for depression in Puerto Rican adolescents. *Journal of Consulting and Clinical Psychology, 67*, 734–745.

Rush, A. J., Thomas, C., & Paul-Egbert, R. (2000). The inventory of depressive symptomatology (IDS): Clinician (IDS-C) and self-report (IDS-SR) ratings of depressive symptoms. *International Journal of Methods in Psychiatric Research, 9*, 45–59.

Rush, A. J., Trivedi, M. H., Ibrahim, H. M., Carmody, T. J., Arnow, B., Klein, D. N., . . . Markowitz, J. C. (2003). The 16-item quick inventory of depressive symptomatology (QIDS), clinician rating (QIDS-C), and self-report (QIDS-SR): A psychometric evaluation in patients with chronic major depression. *Biological Psychiatry, 54*, 573–583.

Santarelli, L., Saxe, M., Gross, C., Surget, A., Battaglia, F., Dulawa, S., . . . Weistaub, N. (2003). Requirement of hippocampal neurogenesis for the behavioral effects of antidepressants. *Science, 301*, 805–809.

Seeley, J. R., Stice, E., & Rohde, P. (2009). Screening for depression prevention: Identifying adolescent girls at high risk for future depression. *Journal of Abnormal Psychology*, *118*, 161–170.

Sheehan, D. V., Lecrubier, Y., Sheehan, K. H., Amorim, P., Janavs, J., Weiller, E., . . . Hergueta, T. (1998). The mini-international neuropsychiatric interview (M.I.N.I): The development and validation of a structured diagnostic psychiatric interview for DSM-IV and ICD-10. *Journal of Clinical Psychiatry*, *59*, 22.

Sheehan, D. V., Lecrubier, Y., Sheehan, K. H., Janavs, J., Weiller, E., Keskiner, A., . . . Schnika, J. (1997). The validity of the mini international neuropsychiatric interview (MINI) according to the SCID-P and its reliability. *European Psychiatry*, *12*, 232.

Stahl, S. M., Entsuah, R., & Rudolph, R. L. (2002). Comparative efficacy between venlafaxine and SSRIs: a pooled analysis of patients with depression. *Biological Psychiatry*, *52*, 1166–1174.

Teichman, Y., Bar-El, Z., Shor, H., & Sirota, P. (1995). A comparison of two modalities of cognitive therapy (individual and marital) in treating depression. *Psychiatry: Interpersonal and Biological Processes*, *58*, 136–148.

Thase, M. E., Greenhouse, J. B., Frank, E., Reynolds, C. F., III, Pilkonis, P. A., Hurley, K., . . . Grochocinski, V. (1997). Treatment of major depression with psychotherapy or psychotherapy-pharmacotherapy combinations. *Archives of General Psychiatry*, *54*, 1009–1015.

Treatment for Adolescents with Depression Study Team. (2003). Treatment for adolescents with depression study (TADS): Rationale, design, and methods. *Journal of the American Academy of Child and Adolescent Psychiatry*, *42*, 531–542.

Treatment for Adolescents with Depression Study Team. (2004). Fluoxetine, cognitive-behavioral therapy, and their combination for adolescents with depression: Treatment for adolescents with depression study (TADS) randomized controlled trial. *JAMA*, *292*, 807–820.

Treatment for Adolescents with Depression Study Team. (2007). The treatment for adolescents with depression study (TADS): Long-term effectiveness and safety outcomes. *Archives of General Psychiatry*, *64*, 1132–1143.

Trivedi, M. H., Rush, A. J., Wisniewski, S. R., Nierenberg, A. A., Warden, D., Ritz, L., . . . Norquist, G. (2006). Evaluation of outcomes with citalopram for depression using measurement-based care in STAR*D: Implications for clinical practice. *American Journal of Psychiatry*, *163*, 28–40.

Weissman, M. M., Leaf, P. J., Bruce, M. L., & Florio, L. (1988). The epidemiology of dysthymia in five communities: Rates, risks, comorbidity, and treatment. *American Journal of Psychiatry*, *145*, 815–819.

Weissman, M. M., Markowitz, J. C., & Klerman, G. L. (2000). *Comprehensive guide to interpersonal psychotherapy*. New York, NY: Basic Books.

Weissman, M. M., Prusoff, B. A., DiMascio, A., Neu, C., Goklaney, M., & Klerman, G. L. (1979). The efficacy of drugs and psychotherapy in the treatment of acute depressive episodes. *American Journal of Psychiatry*, *136*, 555–558.

Wells, K. B., Burnam, M. A., Rogers, W., Hays, R., & Camp, P. (1992). The course of depression in adult outpatients: Results from the medical outcomes study. *Archives of General Psychiatry*, *49*, 788–794.

Wilfley, D. E., MacKenzie, R. K., Welch, R. R., Ayres, V. E., & Weissman, M. M. (2000). *Interpersonal psychotherapy for groups*. New York, NY: Basic Books.

2
Cognitive Behavior Therapy Treatment for Adolescents

Paul Rohde

Given the high prevalence and significant public health burden of adolescent depression, a number of interventions designed to treat this condition have been developed and evaluated in randomized controlled trials. Current treatments for depressed adolescents include various psychosocial interventions, pharmacotherapy, and combination treatments (medication plus psychotherapy). Several randomized controlled studies have examined the efficacy of both individual- and group-based psychosocial interventions for depressed adolescents (Curry, 2001; Kaslow & Thompson, 1998; Reinecke, Ryan, & DuBois, 1998). Cognitive-behavioral therapy (CBT) has been evaluated most frequently and has been found to be superior to wait-list control and often is more efficacious than a number of alternative treatments (e.g., Brent et al., 1997; Kahn, Kehle, Jenson, & Clark, 1990; Stark, Reynolds, & Kaslow, 1987; Vostanis, Feehan, Grattan, & Bickerton, 1996; Wood, Harrington, & Moore, 1996) and comparable to interpersonal psychotherapy for adolescents (Rosselló & Bernal, 1999).

The primary goal of cognitive therapy is to help the depressed person become aware of pessimistic and negative thoughts, depressotypic beliefs, and causal attributions in which the person blames him- or herself for failures but does not take credit for successes. Once these depressotypic thinking patterns are recognized, the client is taught to develop and substitute more realistic cognitions for these counterproductive ones. The primary goal of behavior therapy is to increase engagement in activities that either elicit positive reinforcement or avoid negative reinforcement from the environment. CBT interventions combine cognitive and behavioral strategies to address the problems that commonly characterize depressed individuals (e.g., pessimism; internal, global, and stable attributions for failure; low self-esteem; low engagement in pleasant activities; social withdrawal; anxiety and tension; low social support and increased conflict). CBT interventions generally focus on specific and current actions and cognitions as targets for change, have a fair degree of structure and consistency in the session organization, incorporate the use of homework assignments, and are relatively brief (generally fewer than 20 sessions).

Two Cognitive Behavior Therapy Interventions

This chapter focuses on two forms of CBT for adolescent depression: group and individual therapy. The group-based CBT is the Adolescent Coping with Depression (CWD-A) course (Clarke, Lewinsohn, & Hops, 1990) and the individual-based CBT focuses on the psychosocial intervention developed for evaluation in the Treatment of Adolescents with Depression Study (TADS; Curry et al., 2003; TADS Team, 2004).

Group Therapy: The CWD-A Course

The CWD-A course consists of 16 two-hour sessions conducted over eight weeks for mixed-gender groups of up to 10 adolescents. The course is structured to provide training in mood monitoring, social skills, pleasant activities, relaxation, constructive thinking, communication, problem solving, and relapse prevention. Participants receive a workbook that provides structured learning tasks, short quizzes, and homework forms. To encourage generalization of skills to everyday situations, adolescents are given homework assignments that are reviewed at the beginning of the subsequent session. The therapist manual and client workbook for the CWD-A course are available at no cost at http://www.kpchr.org/public/acwd/acwd.html.

The CWD-A has been evaluated in several randomized controlled trials and has been found to be superior to wait-list control and a life-skills tutoring comparison group, but not significantly better than usual HMO care. Research support for the CWD-A is summarized in Appendix A.

Individual Therapy: TADS CBT

TADS evaluated the immediate and long-term effectiveness of different treatments and combinations of treatments for depression. Specifically, the project compared individual CBT, fluoxetine, combination CBT/fluoxetine, and a pill placebo with clinical management in 439 adolescents with major depression. TADS consisted of a 12-week acute treatment phase (after which, adolescents receiving pills only were unblinded), 6 weeks of graduated maintenance treatment, 18 weeks of maintenance treatment, and a one-year open follow-up. The CWD-A course was one of the two source CBT interventions on which the TADS CBT program was based. Information regarding TADS and the TADS CBT manuals are available at no cost at https://trialweb.dcri.duke.edu/tads/index.html.

A summary of TADS research appears in Appendix A. Overall, TADS found that treatment with either fluoxetine monotherapy or in combination with CBT accelerated the response for depression in adolescents, and the addition of CBT enhanced the safety of pharmacotherapy.

The General Structure of Cognitive Behavior Therapy Sessions

CBT sessions are moderately structured, with the goal of balancing skill training and supportive, empathic listening. Although the focus of each session varies depending on the specific skills being addressed and the needs of the individual client, CBT sessions have a fairly consistent format, which is described to the adolescent in the first session.

Most sessions begin by creating a session agenda, checking in with the adolescent regarding depression symptoms since the last session, and reviewing homework assignments from the previous session. Creating an agenda collaboratively helps the adolescent know what topics will be covered in the session—there are no secrets. Knowing what to expect helps diminish the client's anxiety and helps him or her stay on track. Mood monitoring—one of the core CBT skills discussed later in this chapter—provides an efficient method of quickly monitoring whether any particularly difficult experiences occurred since the last session. Helping clients establish the habit of doing their homework between sessions is based on the assumption that applying CBT skills to the adolescent's day-to-day life is where real change occurs. If the homework has not been done, the therapist brainstorms solutions with the client to increase the likelihood of future success and attempts to complete as much of the homework in the session as possible. When homework has been completed, the adolescent should be strongly reinforced and encouraged to make an internal attribution for that accomplishment.

The middle portion of most CBT sessions is devoted to learning a new skill or refining work on a skill that was introduced in an earlier session. CBT skills are most relevant to a client when they are linked to the adolescent's personal concerns and life experiences. Skills can be taught using a variety of techniques, including brief lectures, modeling, role-playing, and Socratic questioning. Adolescents are encouraged to learn a variety of skills, with the expectation that not all skills may be useful to them but that we do not know *a priori* which skills will have the most powerful influence in improving their mood.

The final portion of each session is devoted to addressing any additional issues raised by the adolescent and planning a homework assignment for the upcoming week. Often, non-CBT therapists (and many beginning CBT therapists) do not devote enough time to planning the homework assignment. To maximize the effectiveness of homework assignments, the therapist needs to make sure of several things: that the adolescent understands and accepts the rationale for homework, knows how to complete the assigned homework, has a plan for how he or she will remember to do the assignment outside of session, anticipates problems to completing the assignment, and brainstorms solutions to address these potential problems. The therapist should be clear and specific when developing the homework assignment and questions should be encouraged to anticipate potential problems. Prior to ending each session, the therapist can tell the client the general focus of the next session. Letting clients know in advance what to expect keeps things out in the open, making them "informed consumers." This is a respectful way to keep the adolescent engaged in therapy and hopefully increases the probability of continued attendance.

As is true of any psychotherapeutic intervention, CBT with depressed adolescents needs to be conducted in the context of a strong working alliance and therapeutic relationship among the adolescent, parents, and the therapist. Essential therapist characteristics include the capacity for accurate empathy, warmth, genuineness, and an ability to establish rapport with a diverse range of adolescents and parents. At times the therapist who works with the adolescent must maintain an alliance both with the teenager and the parents in the face of conflict between the two.

Parent Participation

Parents and other guardians are an integral part of the adolescent's social system. They are typically the ones who have sought treatment for their teen, and they are often instrumental in ensuring treatment attendance. In addition, several factors involving the parents (e.g., marital discord, high parental expectations, poor problem-solving skills, low rates of pleasant activities involving the family) often contribute to maintaining the adolescent's depression. For these reasons, parents are viewed as important members of the treatment team that is joined together against a common enemy—the adolescent's depression. In TADS CBT, parents participate in treatment both by attending individual psychoeducation sessions and conjoint teen-parent sessions. In these psychoeducation sessions, the therapist reviews the skill-based modules with the parents, apprises them of the treatment and progress toward goals, and helps them understand ways in which they can reinforce their child using these skills at home. In conjoint teen-parent sessions, family members work together to identify and improve problem areas. In addition, during individual sessions with the adolescents, the TADS CBT therapist may "check in" with the parents for up to 10 to 15 minutes at the start of the session. The purpose and components of the parent sessions are described in more detail in Wells and Albano (2005).

For group CBT, a parallel group intervention for the parents of depressed adolescents was developed as a companion to the CWD-A course (Lewinsohn, Rohde, Hops, & Clarke, 1991). The parent course has two primary goals: inform parents of the CWD-A material in order to encourage support and reinforcement of the adolescent's use of skills; and teach parents the communication and problem-solving skills that are being taught to their son or daughter. Parents meet with a separate therapist weekly for 2-hour sessions that are conducted at the same time as the teen group. Two joint sessions are held in the seventh week during which the adolescents and the parents come together to practice these skills on issues that are salient to each family. Workbooks have been developed for the parents to guide them through the sessions (also available at the general CWD-A website http://www.kpchr.org/public/acwd/acwd.html). We evaluated the impact of the parent course in the first two research trials evaluating the CWD-A course but, contrary to expectation, did not find significantly higher depression recovery rates with parental participation in either study. It may be that more intensive or integrated methods of intervening with parents in the treatment of depressed adolescents are necessary.

Stages of Cognitive Behavior Therapy

Like other depression interventions, CBT occurs in three stages: acute, continuation, and maintenance treatment. Acute treatment, which aims to achieve a full recovery from the depressive episode, consists of a relatively brief number of weekly sessions, typically 12 to 18, and is focused on forming a therapeutic alliance, developing goals, and learning skills to combat depression. In the early sessions of acute treatment, basic behavioral and cognitive skills (e.g., mood monitoring, pleasant activities) are introduced, followed by more complex and individually tailored skills in latter sessions (e.g., social skills, negotiation, and compromise). Continuation treatment occurs after the adolescent has achieved a strong response to care. These sessions begin to occur less frequently (biweekly or monthly) and are aimed at consolidating gains and preventing relapse, with no introduction of new skills. The last session or sessions in the continuation stage is devoted to developing a thorough relapse-prevention plan. Maintenance treatment, which aims to maintain gains and prevent recurrence, can last a few months to a few years, depending on the previous depression history, and generally consists of less frequent sessions (e.g., every 6 to 8 weeks). Homework is regularly assigned across all three stages of treatment.

Core Depression Cognitive Behavior Therapy Skills

By definition, cognitive-behavioral therapy requires the use of concepts and techniques to change both cognitions and behavior (actions). In the treatment of depression, the behavioral component focuses on increasing the frequency of pleasant ("fun") activities, and the cognitive component focuses on identifying and challenging frequent negative thoughts. In treatments that adopt a predominantly cognitive approach, core schema can be identified and changed but these types of treatments require a fairly long duration and have not been evaluated extensively in clinical trials with depressed adolescents. Prior to the behavioral and cognitive work that forms the basis of CBT, a model of change is taught, along with mood monitoring to track progress. These four skills (i.e., Treatment Rationale, Mood Monitoring, Behavioral Activation, Cognitive Restructuring) are components of all CBT approaches with depressed adolescents. Later we review each of these skills by describing the rationale for their inclusion in the treatment of depression, the format that is generally used to teach the skill, and common challenges that can arise for each skill area. Transcriptions from CWD-A course sessions are provided to illustrate the delivery of core CBT skills. After describing the core CBT skills for depression, additional optional skills are described that can be incorporated into treatment, depending on the specific needs of the depressed adolescent.

Treatment Rationale and Goal Setting

In this section, we review the relevancy and importance of treatment rationale and goal setting in CBT.

Why It's Relevant

The first CBT session is generally conducted with both the adolescent and his or her parent(s). Based on the CBT premise that treatment should start with a model of change that is shared with the client, the therapist educates the family about the cognitive-behavioral model of depression and the treatment that is derived from this model. It's important to have a model or rationale for treatment and to share that rationale with the client. The treatment model provides a "map" for treatment, and just like a road map, is only a representation of the real terrain; the model may not contain all the factors that led to the adolescent's depression. The treatment model does, however, serve as a guide to get the person from where they are to where they want to be. Most people who enter the course feel that they have little or no control over their moods and giving them a model gives them a sense of control and hope.

Additional aims for the first CBT session are to elicit a list of the initial treatment goals from the adolescent and parents, link those goals to the CBT model, and begin establishing a collaborative therapeutic alliance with both the adolescent and parents.

How It's Implemented

After a brief introduction, the CBT therapist obtains a description from the adolescent and parents of the presenting problems. This information is helpful in personalizing the subsequent presentation of the CBT model of depression and treatment. Knowing the pressing concerns of the family and linking those concerns to the treatment model are important in fostering hopefulness that treatment will be of benefit to the specific problems the client is experiencing.

The CBT model of depression is based on the following assumptions. First, depression is more than "feeling bad." It is a disorder that changes a person's mood, thinking, behavior, and biology. Second, depression has many possible origins; there is no single cause that applies to everyone. Third, effective treatments for depression are available, and CBT has received some of the strongest research support.

The CBT model for depression has the following components: (a) Personality can be thought of as a three-part system consisting of actions, thoughts, and emotions. In the CWD-A course, this three-part system is called the Personality Triangle. (b) Each part of our personality affects the other two parts. If a person changes one component, the other two parts of the triangle will be impacted. (c) A series of negative feelings, thoughts, or actions can cascade into a "downward spiral." Conversely, positive actions, thoughts, and feelings can build on each other to improve a person's outlook, creating an "upward spiral." These spirals are just the parts of the Personality Triangle going from one point to another. Examples of both Downward and Upward spirals reported by depressed adolescents are shown in Figures 2.1 and 2.2. (d) It is difficult to change emotions directly. Instead, it is much easier to change negative thoughts or actions, which will change emotions. (e) The skills taught in CBT aim to help the young person change her or his actions and thoughts, with the ultimate goal of improving one's mood. Clients need to become aware of their actions, thoughts, and feelings; to evaluate how positive and helpful these actions, thoughts, and feelings are; and, if they are not helpful, they need to learn new skills for behaving and thinking in ways that are more positive and constructive. (f) Change takes time and effort. It is important to learn a variety of skills and then evaluate which specific tools will be most beneficial to the individual. (g) Once these skills are learned and used outside of the session, adolescents can become their own therapist.

Once the therapist has reviewed the CBT conceptualization, the family is asked to identify its goals for treatment ("How would you know that treatment had been

Figure 2.1   Example of a Downward Emotional Spiral Completed by a Depressed Male Adolescent

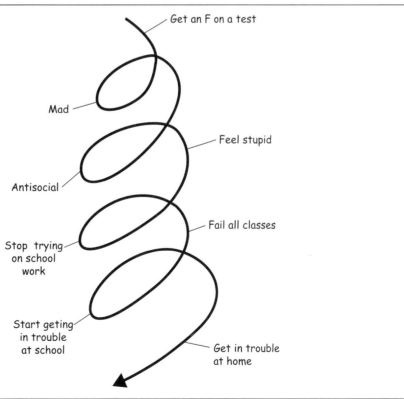

Figure 2.2   Example of an Upward Emotional Spiral Completed by a Depressed Female Adolescent

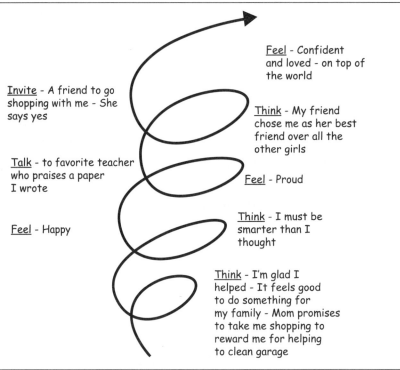

helpful?''). Goals act as guides to treatment. In addition, the ability to articulate and achieve one's goals is a valuable skill in its own right. The therapist first obtains a description of the adolescent's goals and then asks whether the parents can support their child's goals before asking parents for their own treatment goals for the adolescent. It will probably be necessary to break the initially presented goals into smaller, specific steps for change. Almost all goals will involve changes in actions or cognitions, and the therapist should quickly and clearly link the family's specific treatment goals to the general CBT model and the corresponding CBT skills that will be learned and practiced. Knowledge of the individual targets for change will help the therapist develop the initial case conceptualization for this specific client and the potential need for supplementary CBT skill modules.

Common Challenges and Possible Responses

The treatment rationale and goals for change are discussed in the first session, which is obviously extremely important in terms of setting the stage for the rest of treatment. Several difficulties can emerge that disrupt the positive process. First, by working with both the adolescent and his or her parents, the therapist may not create an adequate therapeutic alliance with the adolescent. This is most common if the parents require and receive the bulk of the therapist's attention or if the adolescent-parent relationship is particularly strained. If this problem becomes evident in session, the therapist should attempt to conduct a second, individual session with the adolescent as quickly as possible (ideally in a few days). If you know before the first session that there is a high degree of conflict between the adolescent and parent(s), it may be preferable to conduct two sessions, one with only the adolescent and the second with just the parents. These can occur back-to-back on the same day.

It is fairly common that the adolescent and/or parents do not accept the CBT model of depression. This can occur because the person sees depression as a problem in "brain chemistry," which requires medication or genetics or as the result of severe negative events occurring in early childhood. If questions arise, perhaps the best response is to acknowledge that the adolescent or parent may be correct—we cannot know the initial cause of depression for a specific individual and it is not yet well-established who responds best to medication and who responds best to CBT. Reassure the family that CBT has been shown to be a highly effective treatment for many depressed adolescents. If the adolescent reports significant past trauma, the therapist should empathize with the adolescent and acknowledge that his or her life may have been extremely difficult. These factors are things that we may not be able to change in CBT for depression. We will, however, be able to focus on parts of the adolescent's current life that are most under her or his direct control.

Describing the rationale for treatment can take a fair amount of time and be quite didactic. Therapists can overwhelm, or fail to connect with, the family if they attempt to cover the material too quickly. Personalizing the material regarding the model of depression and CBT wherever possible will greatly increase the family's ability to remain attentive and involved in the session. The therapist should repeatedly check in with the family to ensure that the descriptions make sense to them and are relevant.

In the area of goal setting, one common challenge is that the adolescent's goals appear unreasonable. In this case, the therapist can take a stance of an inquisitive listener and accept the teen's goals as a reasonable starting point, but then help to break the goals down into manageable chunks. You may want to let the teen know that he or she may not be able to achieve the long-term goal during the course of therapy but that there can be meaningful progress toward it.

Another common problem is that the goals are overly vague ("I want to do good in school"). To be useful, goals must be broken down into manageable units and defined in concrete, measurable terms such as, "I want to get a B in math." Ideally, steps toward a clearly defined goal are articulated and roles are clearly defined. For example, "I will ask my teacher for additional assistance in math after school and my parents will check my homework and meet with the school personnel to discuss additional resources in the school."

Lastly, the therapist needs to carefully respond to any discrepancies between goals articulated by the adolescent and the parents. It is essential to acknowledge and discuss these discrepancies. Unrealistic parental goals can in some cases be gently challenged without disrupting the therapeutic alliance. If parents and adolescent state goals that appear clearly incompatible, it might be most helpful to defer those topics for discussion in a subsequent session, concentrating your efforts on mutually agreed upon goals, especially those that are most applicable to the CBT model of change.

Mood Monitoring

In this section, we review the relevancy and importance of mood monitoring in CBT. Additionally, we provide a clinical example of mood monitoring in group CBT.

Why It's Relevant

Mood monitoring is a basic skill that is taught to depressed adolescents as a way of tracking how they feel. It is generally taught in the first session and is one of few skills discussed in each session throughout treatment. Mood monitoring serves several functions. First, it provides important baseline information regarding how the adolescent is feeling at the beginning of treatment. Second, mood monitoring gives the therapist and the adolescent a common language when discussing emotions. For example, in the CWD-A course (which uses a 1- to 7-point mood monitoring scale), when the adolescent reports that her mood was a "1" (i.e., the saddest she ever felt), that means something very different from when her mood was a "3" (below average but much closer to neutral). Third, it helps to challenge the cognitive distortion that "I'm always depressed" by showing clients that, while their moods may not fluctuate from terrible to fantastic, they almost always vary from bad to at least "less bad" or even "average." Fourth, mood monitoring helps the adolescent learn which specific situations or times of the day or week are associated with feeling more or less sadness or irritability. Then, instead of having a vague sense of what contributes to feeling better or worse, teens will understand their depression better and feel more empowered to do something about it. Once situations have been identified that are associated with feeling better, the goal will be to increase such activities. Thus, mood monitoring leads naturally into the Pleasant Activities module. Fifth, mood monitoring can help the client identify which skills in the course have the most powerful effect on improving his or her mood.

How It's Implemented

Mood monitoring requires that upper and lower mood anchors be defined and that a mood monitoring form be used daily. In TADS CBT, mood anchors are created using the 11-point Emotions Thermometer. The session begins by teaching teenagers that emotions vary in strength, and that by using an Emotions Thermometer, they can understand not only what they are feeling, but also how strong that emotion is. Adolescents are taught to rate emotions, ranging from 0 (very bad) to 10 (very good). To provide concrete anchor points for the thermometer, the therapist asks the teen to recall two or three experiences in which he or she felt bad, and two or three in which he or she felt good, and to rate these experiences, generating experiences that vary in intensity so that the whole thermometer range can be used. This exercise provides an opportunity to highlight to the adolescent that feelings range from good to better, and bad to worse, and concomitantly, that even though it might seem like they feel bad all the time, by using the Emotions Thermometer they can see how their emotions change over time.

Next, the mood monitoring form is introduced as a way to track each day the situations, events, and thoughts connected with feeling good or bad. Using several examples, teens are taught to rate their moods using the Emotions Thermometer. It is helpful to use examples that the teenager has brought up in the session to illustrate how to use the mood monitor. For homework, the client is instructed to notice and record situations that happen in the morning, afternoon, and evening each day of the week that are associated with feeling good or feeling bad.

A similar approach is used in the CWD-A course, except that the mood monitoring form uses a 7-point scale rating best and worst mood for the adolescent. Once mood anchors are created, group members are asked to rate their average moods once each day at approximately the same time, usually in the evening after dinner or right before going to bed. An example of mood monitoring with a week of mood ratings is shown in Figure 2.3. All of the forms mentioned in this chapter are available at no cost at the two websites listed earlier.

Clinical Example: Mood Monitoring Review in Group CBT

Therapist (T): And what's our goal in being here? What's the main thing we really want to do in this group?

Adolescent 1 (A1): Change how you feel.

T: And we keep track of how we feel by doing what?

A1: Writing on this. [He points to something on table.]

T: Right! Did you fill it out this week? Every day, preferably at the same time, you want to fill this out. And what is really important about this especially when you're trying to make positive changes is that you look at this every day because it is going to help you see that how you feel is related to what you do. And if you want to change what you do or how you feel, you have to look at both pieces. Did anyone have any trouble with this, have trouble assigning a number?

Adolescent 2 (A2): I did.

T: How come?

A2: Just cause I don't really know the happiest time in my life.

A1: Yeah, I kind of had that problem, like every day I don't really know if I had a good day or what it feels like, do you know what I mean?

Figure 2.3 A Mood Monitoring Form With Mood Anchors and Seven Days of Mood Ratings

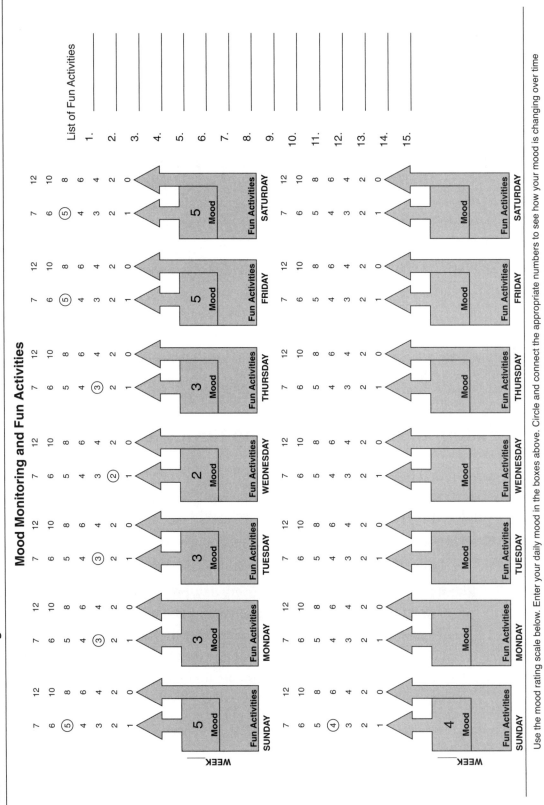

T: So by the end of the day, it felt like so much stuff had happened it was hard to tell if it was a good day or not?

A2: Yeah, I've just been so used to having bad days that I really don't know if it's been a good day or not.

T: Those are two different questions. I heard you say that you aren't sure what the best—we talked about 1 and 7 in terms of those as our anchors—1 is freezing cold and 7 is boiling hot and everything in between is a different grade of temperature—so 1 is our worst day and 7 is our best. One thing you could be asking yourself is if you think you had a great day, ask "Could I have had a better day?" and if you say yes, then that wasn't your best day. But it is going to be hard if you don't have an anchor. So when we started this last week, what did you identify as the anchor for your best mood?

A2: I couldn't do it.

T: When you try and think about that, what comes up?

A2: Nothing.

T: What kinds of numbers do you have? Are you feeling kind of in the middle?

A2: Yep.

T: Do you have days that you feel or can you think of a memory that was above a 6?

A2: Yes, but I always think my day could be better.

T: In your memory, have you ever had a completely, totally great day? [Talking to the first adolescent] Marcus, what did you use for a 7? Last week, what was your anchor for your best day?

A1: I went down to my grandpa's and me and him, well we . . . basically I changed the brakes on my car and had a good day with him. I saw my uncle, and I hadn't seen him in about a year and while I was doing that stuff, they were telling me positive things like, "Wow, you did that in 15 minutes," and then on top of that when my mom got off work, she was basically like complimenting me for doing that and for staying out of trouble and doing something that basically could help me for my future.

T: That's wonderful. It's a great example that a 7 day doesn't have to be something totally unusual but can be just a really, really good day. Thanks for sharing that. [Talking to another group member] How did you do with this, Allison? In the lobby before group, you said you had had a mostly good week. [Looking at her mood monitoring form] It looks like you've had several good days and then you have a few hard days. What was going on during your harder days?

Adolescent 3 (A3): What do you mean by harder days?

T: Well, this looks like a super good day, but this one was lower.

A3: I went to court.

T: So that is certainly something that could bring one down. But then it went back up here; do you remember what was going on, say, on Saturday?

A3: I had a good time with a nice friend.

T: So, spending time with good people. Great job keeping track! So what about you now? [Talking to another group member] You had a range of mood scores. Did you notice anything that was going on when your mood went up to 5 and then when it went down to 3?

A4: My days off.

T: Days off from school or work?

A4: Both—sometimes yeah.

T: You guys are awesome for remembering to do your homework. Would you like a Starburst and a Hershey's Kiss or two of each.

A4: No, I'm good.

T: How did you guys figure out the average of the day? Like if you had a crummy morning but then you were feeling better at the end of the day, how did you work that out?

A4: I did the day at my highest point.

T: So you went with what was most extreme?

A4: Yeah, if I have something really good happen . . . It's not like I make it up . . . I got Alzheimer's and so like when I was feeling really good or really crappy, I just remember that.

T: Well, you might consider doing an average of the day, *if* you can remember. How about you guys, how did you figure out how to do it?

A3: I separated all the good things from the bad things and then how many of each happened.

T: You guys are really thoughtful. I'm really impressed. How about you, Marcus?

A1: I just took the things I did differently each day out of my usual routine each week, so like anything I did during my free time I took how that was. If I didn't do anything really interesting, I figured the routine was pretty lame.

T: So, for you it is the pieces that are out of the routine.

Common Challenges and Possible Solutions

Mood monitoring can present several challenges to the CBT therapist. As in the example, some clients have trouble creating an upper anchor ("I've never had a 7 day. My life has always been bad"). Emphasize that each person's life has been different and that each person's highs and lows therefore are different. Encourage the adolescents to carefully review their entire lives and look for a time (even if it was fairly brief) when they were their very happiest. It could have been a trip or a time when something really nice happened to them, a special party or celebration, a time when they had a good friend or pet that they loved very much. That becomes their 7. If you still receive resistance, ask them to choose a time when they were the least depressed.

Many depressed adolescents experience a range of emotions throughout the day. Encourage them to try to average their moods for the day. If this is difficult, ask them to describe a recent day that had a wide variety of changes and help them come up with an average (or, if applicable, ask the group to suggest how they would rate the day). It's important to not let one negative event overshadow how they felt for the majority of that day.

Other common obstacles with mood monitoring are that the client forgets to complete the form or finds it overwhelming. In either of these cases, attempt to reconstruct the information and fill out the tracking form as completely as possible in the session and help the adolescent decide on one time in the evening to look back over their day and record their mood, as well as a particular place where the form will be kept (e.g., on a bedside table, in her or his backpack with other "homework"). They may need to put a reminder somewhere in the house or ask their parent to remind them.

Lastly, mood anchors are generally created in the first session and the therapist needs to be prepared for the adolescent to reveal childhood traumas or other severe negative events when creating the lower mood anchor. Acknowledge the intensity of emotions while remaining calm. If you are conducting group CBT, you might offer to talk more with the adolescent in private after group. Be sure to check in with the adolescent before the session is completed to assess his or her current emotional state. Additional treatment, specifically focused on the trauma, may be necessary. Consult with a supervisor or colleagues regarding ethical/reporting obligations.

Increasing Fun Activities: Behavioral Activation

In this section, we review the relevancy and importance of behavioral activation in CBT.

Why It's Relevant

Sessions designed to increase pleasant activities are based on the assumption that relatively low rates of positive reinforcement are critical antecedents of depressive episodes (Lewinsohn, Biglan, & Zeiss, 1976). Research has shown that the association between our moods and our positive activities level is surprisingly strong. This is a simple but powerful tool in feeling better. Like depressed adults, depressed adolescents often stop engaging in activities that once were enjoyable. Their repertoire of fun activities frequently is reduced to a small number of solitary, relatively passive activities (e.g., computer videogames, watching television, listening to potentially depressing music).

To increase their fun activity level, depressed adolescents are taught basic self-change skills, including (a) identifying activities that are enjoyable for them, (b) keeping track, or "baselining," their current pleasant activity level, (c) looking at the connections between their activity level and mood, (d) setting a realistic goal for increased pleasant activities, (e) developing a contract to do more fun activities, and (f) reinforcing themselves for achieving the goals of their contract.

How It's Implemented

The therapist begins by explaining the rationale for this skill, which is to increase the level of pleasant activities. Three categories of fun activities—social, success, and physical—appear to have the most powerful influence on our moods. For most individuals, doing things with other people has a more positive impact on their moods than doing things alone. "Success" activities refer to doing things that we are particularly competent at or completing a difficult task. Last, a growing body of research is documenting the powerful effect exercise has on an individual's mood. Our goal is to have adolescents do at least a few activities in each of these three categories.

Once the rationale is established, generate a personalized list of pleasant activities, having the adolescent think of as many fun activities as possible. Be specific and include easy-to-accomplish activities, such as making a phone call or doing little things around the house. Given that you will usually have had a few sessions with the adolescent, you can provide a reminder of previously mentioned enjoyable activities if he or she is unable to remember them. Continue until the adolescent has generated a list of at least 10 activities.

Next, review the list to select specific activities to track and increase. Potential mood-enhancing activities should meet the following criteria: (a) personally enjoyable to the adolescent, (b) active rather than passive, (c) inexpensive, (d) not harmful to oneself or others, (e) can be done at least weekly, and (f) do not require the cooperation of many other people. If the adolescent is experiencing significant psychomotor retardation or is unable to identify pleasant activities, the therapist may need to begin with activity scheduling (Brent & Poling, 1997). If activity scheduling is indicated, a weekly schedule is created in which the adolescent identifies activities to do at specific times each day, including simple, routine activities, such as eating breakfast, taking a shower, and so on. The teen does the activities and then rates each activity on two dimensions: mastery (sense of accomplishment) and pleasure (enjoyment level), using the 0- to 10-point scale similar to the Emotions Thermometer. Once pleasurable activities are identified in subsequent sessions, they can become the focus for behavioral activation.

Once the list of approximately 10 to 20 activities has been generated, the therapist needs to determine a baseline rate of activity. This can be done either by assessing the rate of activity engagement for the previous three or four days or having the client track her or his activity level (and mood) for 1 or 2 weeks, without specifically aiming to increase that activity level.

After baseline data have been collected, the therapist and the adolescent review the associations between mood and fun activity levels. This is generally done by graphing the adolescent's mood relative to his or her activity level; a sample form is shown in Figure 2.4. The mood and fun activities form provides a pictorial representation of the association between number of fun activities and the adolescent's daily mood ratings. The form also contains the list of fun activities that she was tracking. After mood and fun activity rates for several days are graphed, the therapist reviews the graphs to determine whether the client's mood is related to activity level. For most but not all depressed adolescents, there is a fairly clear association between their moods and activity levels, for at least some of the days that were tracked. The therapist should focus on the associations that establish the principle that what we do affects how we feel. Common reasons for a nonassociation are discussed below.

Once the association between activity and mood has been established, the adolescent is asked to make a specific effort to change what she or he is doing. The therapist assists adolescents in reviewing their baseline information and selecting a slightly higher level of fun activities. This goal should be specific and realistic. Depressed adolescents often have unrealistically high expectations of what they can accomplish and set themselves up for failure. When selecting the minimum number of fun activities she or he will aim for, it is advisable to aim for a number that is only one or two higher than their lowest activity levels during the baseline period. Although not essential, it is always helpful to create a written contract to do a certain number of fun activities each day for the next few weeks. Along with the contract, adolescents identify meaningful rewards for meeting their daily and weekly goals. Again, rewards are optional but increase the likelihood of success.

Clinical Example: Generating Fun Activities in Group CBT

Therapist (T): So there are three kinds of activities that we are looking at tracking—we are going to track them in our diaries. Can you take a wild guess at what those three activities are? [Names of the three categories are listed on the board]

Adolescent 1 (A1): Social, success, and physical activities.

T: Bing, bing, bing!! You got it! I want to make a list of each kind of fun activity. Can one of you take notes on the board while we are doing this?

Adolescent 2 (A2): Do we have to? Why do we have to take notes?

Adolescent 3 (A3): My wrist is broken. [Note: not true]

T: So, Maria gets to be the lucky one.

Adolescent 4 (A4): Why do we have to? Your notes are right there.

T: It's much easier for some people to see it when it is on the board. At various times I'm going to ask each of you to do something like this, so you might as well get it over with.

Figure 2.4 A Mood Monitoring Sample Graph

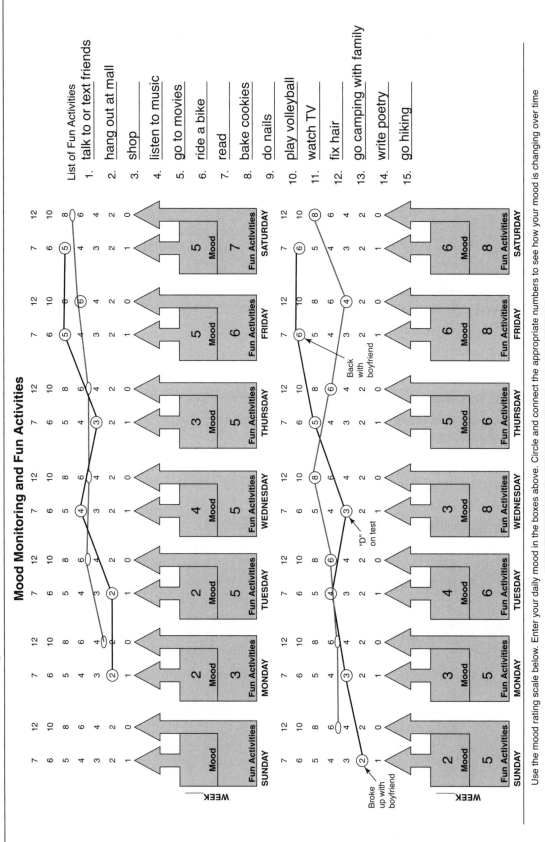

A2: So, like, what if I'm mentally retarded or something?

T: Let's talk about what kinds of fun activities there are. What are social activities? These are just times spent with other people. So what is an example of a social activity?

A1: Have a girlfriend.

A4: Band practice.

T: Write down on your worksheet the ones that are good for you, the ones you can relate to. What are some other social activities—not that you necessarily do but that can be done?

A1: Smoke a bong with all of your friends while riding a bike.

A3: You don't do that.

T: Riding a bike could be a physical activity. What else? What are some other social activities?

Adolescent 5 (A5): Me and my friend, what we do is—I don't know what you call it, but I'll be behind him while he's driving and like if someone cuts him off—we like to box the driver in.

T: Let me be clear—these fun things are supposed to be safe and legal.

A1: Shopping.

T: Good. What kind of shopping? What do guys shop for?

A1: Clothes, CDs, movies.

T: [Pause] Okay, so success activities are experiences that make you feel like you have done something really well—like when you have achieved something or you do something that you have been trying to do for a while. What's a success activity for you?

A5: Writing songs.

T: Great one.

A3: Doing graffiti.

T: So tell me how graffiti is a success activity.

A3: Creating art.

T: Can you do art in other ways? What are some other activities that make you feel like you have accomplished something? Do any of you work?

A1: Actually going to school is a big one. As boring as it is, I really feel good when I actually go to class.

T: That is a really good point.

A4: Actually doing my homework, and turning it in.

T: Does that actually make you feel good? Sometimes people say that and don't really mean it.

A4: No, it really does.

Adolescent 6 (A6): If I actually graduated with good grades, I would be so proud of myself.

T: Graduating is a great one. What about other success activities? Are there things that your friends tell you that you're good at—even if it is telling jokes.

A2: My friends tell me I'm good at a lot of things.

T: Do you drive? Are you a good driver?

A2: A lot better than lots of other people.

T: Okay, so that could be another success activity. This is actually the area where people have the most difficulty coming up with things for themselves.

A6: My friends think I'm funny.

T: Do you feel good when people laugh when you are trying to be funny?

A6: Yeah.

T: Being funny is both a social and a success activity.

A2: There are other things I'm good at.

T: Let's hear it.

A2: Videogames, and I'm good at making people smile and pretty good at sports and . . . I don't know . . . I'm good at "Facebooking."

T: How about physical activities? Someone already said bike riding. What are some other physical activities?

A1: I like swimming.

A5: Bowling.

A1: Working out, but that costs money.

T: Okay, think of different sports. Even if you don't play them, think of the different sports that might be fun to do.

A3: Soccer, hockey, foosball . . . .

T: Are any of you skateboarders?

A3: I tried, but I didn't like it.

A1: Going to the gym, and making my family happy.

T: What do you do to make them happy?

A1: I don't know, help out, clean up, and watch my little brother and stuff.

T: That's very sweet. No one has said that before. [Pause] Okay, we're getting a lot of good activities. How about a few more? What did you use to do when you were younger?

A5: I don't remember.

A6: Wherever my dad took me.

A2: Yeah, like going on vacations.

T: That works, but what I want are activities you can do—like if I sent you home today and said, "Do 10 fun activities," you can't go on a vacation. So what are things you can do this week? I know you've all been little kids, so as little kids you played all the time. What kinds of things did you like to do?

A1: Play with my dog.

A5: Have a girlfriend.

T: Girls are already on the board. [Pause] Do you guys all get a sense of some of the activities that might fit better for you on your sheet there?

Common Challenges and Possible Responses

A number of factors can interfere with behavioral activation. First, depressed adolescents sometimes select activities that they believe should be enjoyable but in reality are not pleasant for them. If this appears to have happened, gently question whether other activities might be more enjoyable.

Second, some depressed adolescents are overwhelmed with the assignment of tracking all of the activities on their list. If recording all of the activities on their list appears to be too demanding, focus on one or two activities that appear to be particularly reinforcing for the adolescent and work on engaging them in that specific activity as the homework. Other adolescents may state that they don't "feel like" doing the activities. Gently remind them of the personality triangle (increasing their activity level has to occur prior to the improvement in mood) and encourage them to try this as an experiment.

A third common challenge is that many of the listed activities are impractical (e.g., too expensive or contingent on factors out of the adolescent's control). If this occurs, augment the list with additional activities that are more likely to occur. There are many fun activities that cost nothing. Brainstorm with the adolescent, asking group members if available, to help generate possibilities. Write no/low-cost fun activities on the board for all group members to consider.

Fourth, some adolescents are focused on activities with negative long-term consequences ("The only things I like to do are doing drugs and having sex with my boyfriend"). Rather than arguing with the adolescent to reduce potentially dangerous activities, the therapist can aim to increase the repertoire of activities. Ask the adolescent what she or he did before using drugs, partying, or having romantic relationships. Encourage them to generate a list containing a variety of activities with a variety of individuals. You may need to encourage more solitary activities (e.g., reading, listening to music, art, pets). The therapist may also need to assess potential for danger to self.

Fifth, some adolescents have busy schedules with a high level of required activities, either related to school, work, or home chores. This is a fairly common issue. If the adolescent's time is truly quite limited, that means that she or he will need to be particularly creative in engaging in the fun activities that have the most "bang for their buck" (as opposed to selecting fun activities that are only minimally helpful, like watching TV). The therapist may need to talk with the parent/guardian to see if the adolescent can be relieved of some chores or responsibilities. This may not be possible. Regarding schoolwork, check to see how efficient the teen is being with her or his study time. Often, if school pressures are high, the adolescent is spending quite a bit of "study time" managing anxiety levels or complaining with friends about workload demands. It may be necessary to work with the parents to free up the adolescent's schedule to accommodate more fun activities.

Some depressed adolescents are already engaging in many activities that theoretically could be enjoyable, but they are sabotaging these activities with negative self-talk. If this appears to be the case, gather information on the adolescent's negative cognitions during homework review, making notes for subsequent work on cognitive distortions. Other adolescents may be engaging in potentially enjoyable social activities but failing to enjoy the events because of social skill deficits. If this appears to be the case, an emphasis on social skills would be warranted.

Occasionally, adolescents increase their activity levels but report no corresponding improvement in mood. There are several possible explanations: (a) The teen did not keep accurate records. Respectfully ask whether this might be a possibility and help the teen complete the diary correctly. (b) They have not chosen activities that have the strongest effect on their mood. (c) There may be a time lag between doing more fun activities and a mood improvement. It may take more time for the behavioral activation to have a noticeable effect. (d) Some unusually stressful situation occurred during this time that is clouding the association between fun activities and mood. (e) They are doing the fun activities but negative self-talk is sapping any potential enjoyment out of the activity. If this is the case, other CBT skills, especially cognitive restructuring, may be more effective in elevating their mood and will eventually help the adolescent genuinely benefit from behavioral activation.

Cognitive Distortions and Realistic Counter-Thoughts: Cognitive Restructuring

In this section, we review the relevancy and importance of cognitive restructuring in CBT; additionally, a clinical example is provided to explain the use of the CAB method in group CBT.

Why It's Relevant

Patterns of maladaptive thinking (e.g., automatic negative thoughts) negatively influence emotions and behaviors (Beck, 1995). In CBT, a fundamental intervention is teaching teens to identify and challenge errors in thinking or cognitive distortions. Certain cognitive styles or maladaptive patterns of thinking (e.g., overlooking the positive aspects of a situation) can halt treatment progress or lead to depression relapse. Therefore, it is necessary to teach the depressed client how to identify and then to counteract negative irrational thinking patterns.

Once the adolescent understands the concept of cognitive distortions and has begun to identify common automatic negative thoughts, the therapist moves on to the next skill, which is to "talk back" to automatic negative thoughts and cognitive distortions by formulating and using realistic counter-thoughts.

How It's Implemented

This skill builds on the adolescent's understanding of mood monitoring and launches into the next step of examining the role of thoughts in negative moods. Usually, the adolescent will have completed several weeks of mood monitoring, linking feeling states to specific situations, and may have already begun to identify thoughts associated with certain trigger situations. The therapist now works to more directly examine the associations between thoughts and feelings and how to begin developing more realistic and helpful thoughts.

Work on changing negative thinking can begin by providing the adolescent with a simplified list of commonly described cognitive distortions (e.g., Beck et al., 1979; Burns, 1980). After reviewing this list, the teen is asked to begin identifying the negative thinking of others; it is generally easier to see the cognitive distortions of others rather than our own. In TADS CBT, the client reads a series of hypothetical scenarios entitled "Dear Problem Solver" letters, which are designed to illustrate cognitive distortions (e.g., catastrophizing, black-and-white thinking, missing the positive, jumping to conclusions). In the CWD-A course, cartoon strips with popular characters that appeal to adolescents (e.g., Garfield the cat) are used to illustrate depressotypic thoughts and alternate positive thoughts that may be used to counter them. Once the adolescent can accurately identify these distortions in others, the therapist has an opportunity to help the adolescent apply the list of distortions directly to his or her own experiences.

There are three general approaches used to change thinking in depressed adolescents. The first method is to increase positive thinking and decrease negative thinking. This approach is similar to the concept of "positive affirmations" and may be most appropriate for younger adolescents. Adolescents need to begin tracking the thoughts that they have on a regular basis and to distinguish thoughts from feelings. The basic goal is to increase the ratio of positive to negative thoughts, using positive statements generated by the client, the therapist, or other group members.

The second method is to challenge irrational or unrealistic thinking. This technique probably is the most developmentally advanced concept in CBT with depressed adolescents and may be difficult for some adolescents. The approach incorporates elements for identifying and challenging negative and irrational thoughts in depressed adults, but these techniques have been modified and simplified for use with adolescents. A three-column mood-monitoring form can be introduced on which the adolescent records upsetting events, negative thoughts associated with the situation, and resulting emotions. In the CWD-A course, the three components are called the *activating event* (A), the *belief* (B), and the *consequence* (C). The skill of examining one's ABCs is called CAB Method because we apply it to our life when we find ourselves having a negative emotion or consequence. Once the negative, untrue, or unhelpful thought is identified, the adolescent is taught to develop a positive counter-thought, which is a new thought that is on the same topic as the original negative belief but is more true and positive. Using examples of automatic negative thoughts from the client's recent experiences, the therapist teaches the adolescent a variety of methods to question negative thinking. Techniques can include (a) looking for contradictory evidence (e.g., "Is this thought even true? Is there any evidence that this thought is not completely correct?"), (b) Socratic questioning (e.g., "Is there any other way to look at the situation?" "How would I talk with a friend who had the same trigger?"), and (c) aspects of acceptance (e.g., "So what if this thought is true? Can I accept it and try to move on with my life?"). Role-playing and role reversal are often helpful, with the therapist and adolescent switching roles and the therapist modeling "stuck" negative automatic thinking and having the adolescent suggest alternative thoughts, acting as the therapist. An example of a CAB form completed by a depressed adolescent is shown in Figure 2.5. The five-column form from cognitive therapy with depressed adults (i.e., describing the event, automatic negative thoughts, initial emotions, realistic

Figure 2.5   Example of a Completed CAB Form

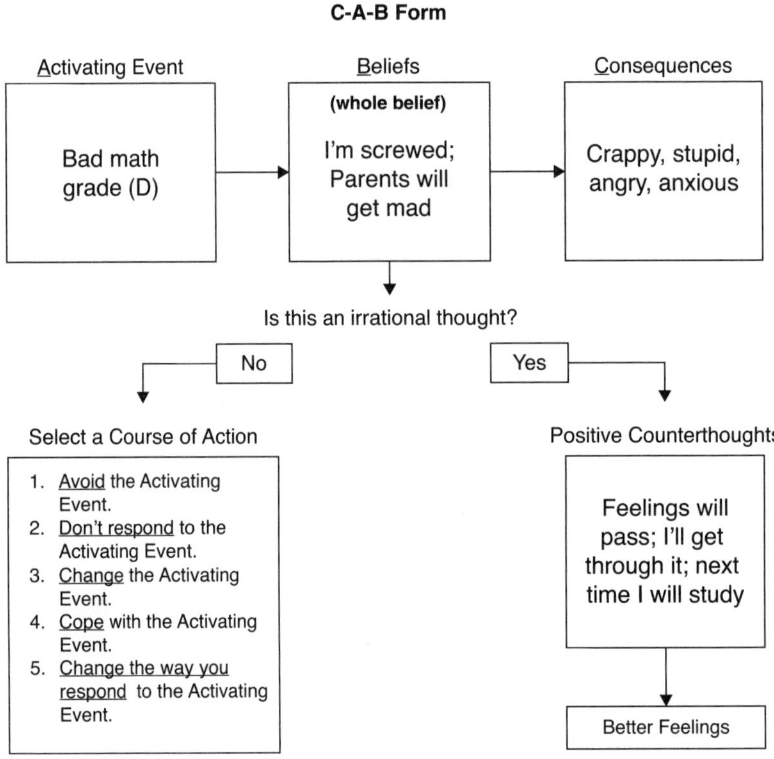

counter-thoughts, and subsequent emotions) provides a clear and powerful structure for tracking this process.

The third method of cognitive work consists of several additional techniques the adolescent can use to break the cycle of negative thinking. These techniques, some of which are commonly used with depressed adults, include journaling, writing a letter to the person that is never sent, "worry time" (set aside a specific and limited time, usually 5 to 15 minutes once a day, during which the person only dwells on all the worries and concerns in their life), "thought-stopping" (saying to yourself "stop!" whenever you catch yourself having a common negative thought), and the "rubber-band technique" (in which the client wears a rubber band and lightly snaps themselves when they catch themselves back in a common negative thought). A description of these methods of responding to negative thinking is included in the CWD-A therapist manual.

Clinical Example: Explaining the CAB Method in Group CBT

Therapist (T): [After reviewing cartoon examples] So, it's pretty easy to figure out when you're looking at cartoons like this what the negative belief is, right? Because you can see it all laid out there and figure it out, but it is a lot harder to do that when it's real life, when it's your own life.

Adolescent 1 (A1): It depends on the situation. I was in class with my friends and they were all joking around and making fun of the teacher, and I thought I can't believe I am even with you people—we are going to get kicked out of class!

T: Hold on to that because we are going to do your own situations in a minute. A lot of times when you are in a situation that is making you feel negatively, whether it is making you feel angry or unhappy or uncomfortable, whatever it is, the first thing that you notice is your feeling, right? So far the first thing we've always been looking at is a thought—what is the thought that the people in the cartoon are having? But usually, when you are in your own life and in your own head, your thought isn't the first thing you recognize; it's how you feel. You recognize that you are feeling sad or annoyed or angry or whatever. We have a method that we call the CAB Method. And so the equation in the CAB Method looks like this: A + B = C. It's the same equation that we have been using on these cartoons. So C is what we are going to call the consequence of the situation—it's the feeling. That is how you feel—just like in this Garfield cartoon—the consequence was that Garfield felt ashamed and embarrassed.

So consequence or C is the feeling you have. And A is the activating event—the trigger or the situation that led to you feeling that way. So in that cartoon, the trigger was that dad is wearing dumb clothes and making you go out in public with him. And then B is the belief that you have; it's the negative thought that you have about the trigger that makes you feel that way. So that is why it is A + B = C. So the thought that you have (B) about the trigger plus what is happening (A) leads you to feel the way that you feel (C). When we are analyzing our situations, we always start here with the C; it's usually the easiest thing for us to notice. And then once we know what we are feeling, we fill that in the box on this form. So you figure out how you are feeling and then you say, hey, what's going on that is making me feel this way? That's the second piece of the equation—the activating event or trigger. Okay, so now you know what is going on and then you ask, what is my belief about this situation that is making me feel this way? And that is usually the hardest thing to figure out, so that's why we do it last. That is why we call it the CAB Method because you start with C—you start with your negative feelings—the consequence. Then you figure out the activating event and then you figure out the belief. So, it's CAB. That's the order that you analyze it in.

Clinical Example: Practice Developing Counter-Thoughts in Group CBT

T: I want to spend some time practicing how to develop positive counter-thoughts. Here is a sheet of negative thoughts that people in this group have had. I want to go through these together and think of a more positive counter-thought for each negative thought. The first one is, "I need the love and approval of every important person in my life—especially my parents."

Adolescent 1 (A1): If they don't love me for who I am, I don't need their love.

T: Okay, that's one possibility. There is no one single right answer for any of these. There are in fact a million possibilities that will work. Another possibility might be, "I'm not going to compromise myself for anyone," or "I'm fine just the way I am." Another way to go about that one is, "There are certain people whose opinions are more important to me than others." And "If everybody doesn't like me, that's fine." Now what about the second statement, "I have to be popular or smart all the time in everything I do in order to feel like I'm worth something."

Adolescent 2 (A2): Someone actually said that?

T: Yes, these are actual thoughts people in this group have had. Jean, what do you think about that one—if you are thinking I have to be the smartest all the time or I am worthless. What is a positive counter-thought to that one you could have?

Adolescent 3 (A3): It's kind of hard 'cause I'm like never smart.

T: So this is kind of a thought that you've had. What is a positive counter-thought? What is a more positive and more realistic way of looking at that situation?

A3: I'm not smart.

T: No, that is still a negative thought.

A3: I'm not very smart but I'm better at other things than some people are.

T: There you go. "There are things that I am better at than other people." Can you think of a different positive counter-thought, Jesse?

Adolescent 4 (A4): I don't have to appeal to other people's standards to feel like I'm worth something.

A2: I tell myself that all the time because people give me a hard time because I can't read well and whatnot and like whatever—I can probably outride you on my bike anytime.

T: Everybody is smart in different ways. There are probably some things you guys can do a lot better than me. That's just the way the world works.

A1: I can probably play drums better than both of you.

T: Okay, let's move on to number three, "People who do just one thing that I disapprove of should be punished."

A2: Yeah, they should be killed.

T: What is a positive counter-thought you can say for that? That's a thought that a lot of people have when they are really angry.

A4: There are always two sides to every story.

T: So maybe there is a different side that I don't understand.

A1: Life is a two-way street.

T: Good. Sometimes people respond to that one with "Live and let live" or "Who am I to judge?" How about number four, "My unhappiness is someone else's fault, and I can't help feeling the way I do."

A3: It's all my fault, no one else's, except for my own.

T: How about, "I'm in control. I have control over my feelings." That is what you are saying essentially, right?

A3: Looking at the bad side of things.

T: So you are making a choice, right? I have the choice. The flip side of that thought is that "I have the power to make myself feel better."

Clinical Example: Working With Personal Examples in Group CBT, Part 1

Therapist: It's really easy to blame external circumstances for the way that you feel, right? To say that person made me angry or that person made me sad.

Adolescent 1 (A1): Like the other day, I was hanging out with this girl and I kind of like her and even though we kind of like joke around and whatnot, I started talking to my friend and asked him about her, because he knew her longer than I did and he was like, yeah she doesn't really want to have anything to do with you, and I said like, oh really, and she is sitting right next to me while he's saying this and so like I look at her and ask her, do you like really not want to have anything to do with me? And she doesn't say anything. So, I ask her, you don't have to tell me—you can plead the fifth; it's okay. But obviously if you plead the fifth, you're guilty, it's obvious, and she says, yeah, I plead the fifth. I was like, oh great. So all day long after that I wanted to go beat somebody up.

T: Yeah, lots of negative thoughts, I would imagine. So that's a great example of a negative situation.

A1: I still drove her home from the party.

T: That was very gentlemanly of you.

A1: And I like hung out with her for three hours after that and I felt really bad and the whole time I was trying to make it good, so she couldn't tell that I felt kind of bad about it and whatever, and we were all hanging out for like three hours and . . . .

T: So, Jordan, tell me what was a negative thought that you were having in that situation.

A1: I don't know. I was trying to figure out what the hell is wrong with me, am I really that annoying?

T: Okay, so there is one negative thought.

A1: And then later that night she pointed out that she really doesn't know me and that I jump into relationships kind of like head first.

T: This is a really great example because this is a common situation that happens to lots of people. So let's go with that. If the negative thought is, "I must be really annoying because she doesn't want anything to do with me," what is a positive counter-thought that you can make for that negative thought?

A1: She just doesn't know me that well.

T: Did that make you feel better when you thought that?

A1: Yeah, after she told me that I felt better and I was like, oh okay, at least she isn't like the rest of these people here who don't want to have anything to do with me because there are a lot of people that don't want anything to do with me. I mean I understand because I can be a very loveable person and whatnot, but if you piss me off I will beat you up. There is no hesitation whatsoever, I will turn on a dime.

T: So, what we are doing here is talking about exactly what you are talking about. It is really easy to turn on a dime. A lot of us have tempers like that that just kind of kick in and snap really easily, and this kind of positive counter-thought stuff even though it may seem kind of silly, sometimes is a really good way to be able to combat that. Because a lot of time when you have negative thoughts, they are just so automatic and they are really irrational and you're not really thinking about them, right? What we are trying to do is to actually argue with your own thoughts, and people don't do this enough. A lot of times people just think that their thoughts are automatically true. I mean, I thought it, so of course it must be true, right? We know that that is not always the case. So when you catch yourself thinking negatively, what you want to do is to challenge that thought. This doesn't come easily to a lot of adults, so that is why we want to practice it. Think back to that example with the girl—if you are thinking about the girl who said "if this guy doesn't go out with me, I'm a total loser forever." What is a way that you can challenge that thought if that was a thought that you had—what would you say to yourself?

A1: I would probably be like . . . I don't know, that has never really happened to me.

T: If it did, try to imagine. How would you argue with yourself, how would you challenge it?

A1: I don't know, probably be like, she's just some dumb person who doesn't know me very well.

T: Clearly she doesn't know enough about me to know what would be good about going out with me. So, one question you can ask is, is this thought really true? That is essentially how you argue with any thought you have. You have to ask yourself, is this really true, is that actually the case that I am a total failure forever if I don't get a date? Probably not—the thought is irrational.

Clinical Example: Working With Personal Examples, Part 2

Adolescent 1 (A1): I hate it when my female goes out and hangs out with the guys without me. Cause like it's just not right—I trust her but some of the guys . . .

Therapist (T): That is a perfect situation. One of your assignments for next week is going to be to use this method to analyze some situations in your life. So, I want to think about that situation, your girlfriend is hanging out with some other guys. If we are using the CAB Method, where do we start?

A1: C.

T: What is C?

A1: Feelings.

T: Yes, exactly! The first thing you usually recognize is how you are feeling. So how are you feeling in that situation?

A1: I'm sad, I guess.

T: It can be a bunch of different things. Sad is one thing it sounds like. Jealous? Angry? Suspicious?

A1: Suspicious.

T: So once we have our C—once we have our feeling; what do we want to know next in our CAB Method?

A1: Our trigger.

T: Yes, our activating event.

A1: It's because she is hanging out with other guys. I even get jealous when my girlfriend is hanging out with her other girlfriends.

T: So what is the Belief that you have about her hanging out with other people that is making you feel this way?

A1: The guys could be trying to do something with her.

T: So, she is being unfaithful to me.

A1: No, I'm not saying she is; I'm saying the guys are.

T: Isn't she involved in that situation?

A1: Well, she could be. It isn't necessarily with or without her permission. Just in general. It's just that I've had that happen a few times.

T: So, somebody is going to do something to her or with her. If she is not with me, something could happen and I can't be there to stop it. That is your belief. If she is not with me, something bad is going to happen. Good. So once we know your belief, we ask is that a rational or an irrational belief?

A1: Rational, I don't know.

T: Okay, is it true?

A1: It could be in the middle.

T: It could or could not be.

A1: It depends on who she is with. If she is with my friends, I can trust them.

T: Chances are . . . my guess would be is that every time that she is not with you, chances are she is not going to get hurt. I mean everyone can get hurt sometimes, right? But chances are she probably is not going to.

A1: So, it is probably irrational.

T: I would think it is an irrational belief. So following this, it is an irrational belief, then what is a more realistic way that you could think about that same situation that might make you feel better?

A1: Nothing is going to happen; she is going to be fine.

T: She is usually with good people; she is going to be okay, I trust my friends. That is a perfect situation, Taylor. Thanks for sharing that with me.

A1: It happens all the time.

T: You did really a good job with this. It seems like you can really do this. So that is the kind of thing I want you to do for next time. I'm going to copy this because this is a really good example.

A1: Sure, you can have it, go for it.

Common Challenges and Possible Responses

Some depressed adolescents have difficulty identifying their negative automatic thoughts and accepting the possibility that thoughts can be changed. If this occurs, the therapist can start with identifying thoughts in more familiar neutral arenas, such as thoughts related to preferences in music or friends, and identify the ways that the thoughts have changed over time. Alternatively, the therapist can give clients hypothetical events (e.g., Your mother tells you you're lazy, You graduate from high school) and ask them to record at least two different emotions they might have in reaction to the event and to rate these emotions on a mood-monitoring scale. The therapist helps the client understand that different ways of thinking about the same event or trigger led to different emotions.

These skills are demanding and some adolescents will be unable to successfully learn the underlying concepts of this skill in a way that can be used in their daily life. When the client is young or immature, it may be more effective to focus on using positive statements or affirmations instead of attempting to have the adolescent develop realistic counter-thoughts on their own. If attempts to teach the concept of realistic counter-thoughts are unsuccessful, the therapist should clearly convey the message that the client is not at fault, otherwise they may generate additional negative attributions ("I'm so stupid that I can't even understand therapy").

Some adolescents feel powerless over their thinking ("I can't control what I think. Thoughts just pop into my head"). The therapist should assure the adolescent that this is like learning any other skill—if they practice, they will become better. Also, remind them that they have changed their thinking about other important topics, such as their friends, in the past. Occasionally adolescents get preoccupied with finding the one "right" counter-thought. The therapist needs to clearly emphasize that there is no single correct response to a negative automatic thought. The value of a counter-thought depends on whether it is believable and whether it helps the client feel more positive and accepting of the event.

A common dilemma is that, although exaggerated, a depressed person's negative thoughts sometimes are fairly accurate. As cognitive therapists, are we attempting to encourage our clients to look at the world through rose-colored glasses? No. If you try and push an overly optimistic thought, it will not be believable to the adolescent and will be rejected. A more helpful approach is to aim toward thoughts that are just slightly more positive than the client's view of reality. The therapist needs to validate accurate negative thoughts and acknowledge that it is perfectly realistic to think negatively when negative things happen. If the person remains stuck in that negative thinking, however, it may no longer be as helpful.

When working on this skill, sometimes therapists can become argumentative with their clients. The therapist cannot force this skill on their client. A helpful stance to take is that we teach our clients these skills with the clear understanding that it is up to them to decide if and when they will use these skills.

Optional CBT Skills

In addition to the core skills of mood monitoring, behavioral activation, and cognitive restructuring that are included in all forms of CBT for depressed adolescents, several additional skills can be incorporated into treatment, based on the potential duration of care and the specific needs of the adolescents. These optional modules are reviewed next. As acute treatment ends, either transitioning into less frequent maintenance care or treatment termination, the CBT therapist consolidates gains in a final "Skill Integration/Relapse Prevention" session, which is also described.

Problem Solving

In this section, we review the relevancy and importance of problem solving in CBT.

Why It's Relevant

Many depressed adolescents have impaired problem-solving skills or experience psychosocial stressors that contribute to the maintenance of their depression. Often, because of concentration difficulties, pessimism, passivity, or slowed thinking, depressed adolescents find it difficult to generate new options to problems in their life, systematically evaluate these options, and make a plan for change. Teaching a structured method to solve problems can combat such obstacles and help clients adaptively cope with problems that would otherwise lead to continued feelings of hopelessness or powerlessness.

How It's Implemented

The CBT therapist's first task is to lay the groundwork for problem solving as a skill by explaining to the adolescent that everyone faces problems in their lives and that it is important to have a way to solve problems so that they do not lead to pessimism or depression. Next, the therapist can introduce a general method for problem solving with practice situations. Different versions of CBT use different forms of problem solving, but all include a clear and specific definition of the problem, a period of brainstorming without criticizing potential solutions, an evaluation of the generated solutions, and the selection of a small number of changes to implement. In TADS CBT, for example, the problem-solving method was named RIBEYE to facilitate recall of the various problem solving components. This acronym stands for: Relax, Identify the problem, Brainstorm, Evaluate the solutions, say Yes to one, and Encourage yourself.

The specific components can first be taught with the adolescent discussing solutions to the problems of other teenagers. In TADS CBT, "Dear Problem Solver" letters are provided that contain elements of common problems for teenagers (e.g., curfew, grades, conflicts with parents). After reading these letters, clients are asked to define the problem and to generate as many possible solutions as they can without worrying whether the solutions are good or bad. After brainstorming solutions, the therapist helps the client look at the potential negative and positive consequences of each option, and then to make a hypothetical choice.

Once the adolescent has practiced the basic steps of problem solving with a few examples, the therapist reviews the components of problem solving more formally and begins applying the skills to real-life situations for the individual client. Problem solving is practiced in the session through a series of role plays, and then selected solutions are assigned as homework for the upcoming week. If the therapist has no contact with the parents, the adolescent may be required to explain the process of problem solving to his or her parents prior to using it at home, which can be a demanding requirement for many depressed adolescents. Based on the client's age, developmental status, and situation at home, the therapist will need to determine the extent and complexity of home practice assignments involving problem solving.

Common Challenges and Possible Responses

Problem solving can be an extremely useful tool for the majority of depressed teens. However, several difficulties may occur when teaching this skill. First, adolescents may try to use the skill to tackle their most complex and difficult problems without adequate practice. This is understandable because those are the problems that seem to be the most important in their lives. They may, however, become frustrated and feel hopeless when the process does not work right away. Therapists should encourage their clients to stick with smaller, less entrenched difficulties until they become more proficient at the process and may need to suggest specific issues or topics to work on that are likely to be met with success. After the concepts and skills are learned, they can then be applied to the more severe and potentially explosive difficulties.

A second common challenge is that adolescents (and parents) find it difficult to brainstorm solutions or hear the brainstormed solutions of others without evaluating them at the same time. Particularly for adolescents with strong negative thinking styles, repeated brainstorming practice with gentle reminders ("Let's brainstorm first; we'll evaluate later") will be essential to allow them to entertain a variety of solutions instead of quickly dismissing the problem as hopeless.

A third common challenge is that some adolescents think this kind of a problem-solving process is unrealistically demanding, saying things like, "You want me to use this every time I have a problem? This could take all day!" To address this criticism, encourage the adolescent to use parts of the problem-solving process. For example, almost all teens can benefit from describing the problem in clear, specific, and behavioral terms. In addition, many clients report that brainstorming solutions allows them to slow down and calm down to think more clearly about their options. In general, the probability of arriving at a successful solution increases as the adolescent uses more of the problem-solving components.

Social Skills

In this section, we review the relevancy and importance of social skill building in CBT.

Why It's Relevant

Several studies have demonstrated that depressed adolescents and adults often have a number of social skill deficits or difficulties that may contribute to the onset and maintenance of their depression. To address these deficits, various methods of improving social skills are often incorporated into CBT. Social-skill training can give adolescents numerous opportunities to learn and practice a variety of techniques, including basic "friendly skills" (e.g., look at people, smile), how to start a conversation, how to meet new people, how to join and leave a social group, and how to give and receive feedback. These skills are first taught in-session using role plays and then through home practice assignments to work on specific aspects of the adolescent's interpersonal behavior.

As part of their social skill deficits, many depressed adolescents have difficulties with appropriate assertiveness. Many depressed adolescents are overly passive, sometimes failing to express their frustrations until they blow up at someone (often a parent) in an aggressive manner. Some depressed adolescents experience pressure from deviant peers or coercion from a boyfriend or girlfriend and are unable to resist these pressures. The therapist needs to convey to the adolescent that assertiveness is not a personality trait but rather it is a skill that with practice can be learned. Clients who learn how to be assertive in difficult interpersonal situations feel better and have a greater likelihood of getting what they want or need out of a situation.

In group CBT, social skills often occur early in treatment to facilitate group cohesion and success with other skills that are common components of CBT, such as increasing fun activities, active listening, and effective problem solving.

This CBT skill is for depressed adolescents who are having difficulty making and keeping friends. These skills are not intended to change underlying personality characteristics such as shyness or introversion, but can provide adolescents with tools to improve their interactions with other adolescents and with adults and interrupt any negative downward spirals.

How It's Implemented

The CWD-A course contains a great deal of material on social skills that can be implemented in both individual and group CBT. These skills include basic components of social interactions, such as meeting, greeting, and talking with people. Specifically, through role-playing and discussion, adolescents learn a variety of skills to help meet other people (e.g., making eye contact, smiling) and helpful ways to start a conversation (e.g., developing appropriate greetings, asking open-ended questions). Additional practical skills covered include listening skills, skills for ending a conversation, and skills for joining and leaving group conversations. The therapist discusses important differences in social interactions involving adults versus adolescents, and men versus women.

When role plays are used, the therapist can start by modeling poor conversation skills and having the teen comment on observable conversation errors, such as slouching, looking at the floor, changing topics abruptly, and so on. The therapist can then model more effective social skills with the adolescent playing the role of a peer. To help solidify learning the new skill, the adolescent then reverses roles with the therapist and practices employing effective conversation skills.

If assertiveness training is indicated, the terms *passive, aggressive,* and *assertive,* are clearly defined, with examples of each type of response in common interpersonal situations. Once these concepts are understood, the therapist moves into personal situations in which the client has responded either passively or aggressively. In addition to understanding the adolescent's behavior, it is important to identify the negative thoughts that were associated with either the passive or the aggressive response. Three general steps are helpful when generating an assertive response. First, clients need to recognize how they feel about the situation. Second, they express that emotion, using an "I statement." Third, they ask for a different course of action. Assertiveness training is especially productive if it includes as much behavioral rehearsal as possible, including role playing the potential responses of the other person. Homework for this skill can include writing the steps for being assertive on index cards and practicing the assertive response to a real-life interpersonal situation.

Common Challenges and Possible Responses

Some depressed adolescents may not have a realistic view of their social skillfulness ("I already know this stuff. I don't need to do this, I have plenty of friends"). When a teen does not recognize the need for learning social skills, therapists are encouraged to normalize learning these skills. For example, sharing how everyone can benefit from reviewing and practicing these skills helps to relieve the pressure that a teen might feel, perhaps thinking that he or she is being singled out as needing the skill. Point out that these skills can be useful when interviewing for a job or trying to get an apartment.

Talking about social skills is not sufficient; in-session practice is essential in learning and fine-tuning these techniques. Shy adolescents may initially feel awkward about the role plays, particularly if they are uncomfortable talking about and placing themselves in unfamiliar social situations. Therefore, it may be necessary for the therapist to reassure the client that feeling somewhat uncomfortable in a new group is a universal phenomenon. To many teens, role plays feel quite artificial at first. This problem can be minimized by prefacing the practice with the acknowledgment that the role plays *are*, to a degree, artificial, but that they can be useful to learn and practice a new skill, which eventually will need to be practiced in the client's real life. When the adolescent first plans to try these new ways of interacting, the therapist should encourage the teen to carefully choose people who are safe and supportive for the initial practice. It is important for the adolescent to know that social skills can be learned just like any other skill. Although these techniques may feel difficult or awkward initially, with practice, the results can be rewarding.

Negative thoughts associated with social skill deficits are likely to occur when working on these techniques. The therapist should be alert to such negative automatic thoughts (e.g., "People don't like me," "I'll never be able to make friends"), as it is important to help the teen identify and challenge those thoughts.

Perhaps the most common challenge to learning the skills of assertion is that it requires a troublesome interpersonal situation to occur in close proximity to the session. Often, the adolescent is unable to practice this skill after the session because the most relevant situation requiring an assertive response does not happen or is not under the adolescent's control (e.g., the challenging person does not interact with your client that week). In this situation, the therapist can help the client develop (and practice) a response plan to be used in the future, when the opportunity presents itself. A second challenge to teaching assertiveness is that the adolescent inadvertently goes from passivity to aggression, bypassing the assertive response. If this happens when the adolescent is interacting with her or his parents, it may be necessary to carefully review this skill with the parents to forewarn them of what to expect and what to reinforce.

Relaxation

In this section, we review the relevancy and importance of relaxation techniques in CBT.

Why It's Relevant

Many depressed adolescents experience tension and anxiety, especially during social situations or when taking tests at school. This tension and anxiety often interferes with effective interpersonal functioning and reduces the pleasure they derive from potentially enjoyable activities. Teaching depressed adolescents to relax in situations that are typically stressful enables them to better implement the social skills they learn in the CWD-A course and to enjoy pleasant activities, many of which are socially oriented.

How It's Implemented

If relaxation is going to be taught, the therapist introduces the relaxation module by indicating that the adolescent has mentioned times when she or he feels "stressed out." The therapist explains that feeling stressed makes it difficult to cope with issues that arise and that feeling tense breeds additional problems to implementing the first step of the RIBEYE method of problem solving, if it is being included in treatment. The therapist describes the technique to be practiced, demonstrates it, invites the client to practice the skill, and gives appropriate feedback and guidance regarding how the skill is used.

Two relaxation methods are often taught in CBT with depressed adolescents. The first technique presented, called the Jacobson method (Jacobson, 1929), consists of participants systematically tensing and relaxing the major muscle groups throughout the body until they are fully relaxed. The client progresses through all the major muscle groups with corresponding movements, such as making a tight fist for 5 seconds and then relaxing the hand for 10 seconds. This relaxation technique can be introduced early in treatment because it is easy to learn and thus provides the adolescent with an initial success experience. Many adolescents use the Jacobson method to help them fall asleep at night. If progressive muscle relaxation is practiced, it is important to elicit feedback from the adolescents as to how they feel after the relaxation exercises by having them rate their feelings on the Emotions Thermometer or by using a small finger thermometer or temperature measure called a *Bio-Dot* that provides numerical data on whether their skin temperature is increasing, which is a sign of relaxation.

The second, more inconspicuous technique, the Benson method (1975), is introduced midway through the CWD-A course. This technique involves sitting comfortably in a quiet place and repeating a calming word or phrase as one exhales. Adolescents also learn a variation called the *quick Benson*, which is more portable. Modifications of this method can include deep breathing with a self-statement such as "I'm relaxing" and "I'm keeping my cool," deep breathing with self-statements and counting backward, or deep breathing with pleasant imagery such as asking the teenager to think of an appealing outdoor scene. Tension-reducing options, such as leaving the negative situation for a period of time and going out for a walk, are also introduced.

For both relaxation techniques, the practice may be recorded so the teen can take the recording home and listen to the techniques for review. Additionally, the therapist may write brief guidelines or reminders about how to practice the methods on index cards for the teen to follow at home. With regard to the homework assignments, the teen may rate his or her level of tension before and after the relaxation technique along with the associated automatic thoughts.

Common Challenges and Possible Responses

The most common challenge in learning any relaxation method is that many adolescents will not experience a strong relaxation response in their initial practice. This is common and may even be predicted. Encourage them to try these methods at least a few times before making a decision regarding the method's usefulness.

In addition, many adolescents initially report that they are unable to stop intrusive thoughts. Again, this can be anticipated and predicted. Encourage clients to try to focus on their breathing when other thoughts come into their minds. Assure them that this will get easier with practice. Using this skill yourself will allow you to describe your own methods of dealing with this experience, which can further help your clients.

If a finger thermometer or Bio-Dot is used, the device may not register any skin temperature change. Assure the teen that every body functions a little differently and they may need to practice this technique a few times before a change can be detected. Also, the finger thermometer or Bio-Dots are not always accurate. Ask if they experienced the subjective sensation of being more relaxed. If they did, that's the main point.

The therapist needs to tailor the relaxation techniques to the needs of the adolescent. For example, progressive muscle relaxation may be helpful to teens with generalized anxiety disorder or insomnia, but it is contraindicated for adolescents with panic attacks, and it is not likely to be helpful for adolescents with social phobia. In general, briefer relaxation methods are more likely to be used by teens than the more time-consuming technique of progressive muscle relaxation.

Last, parents may be instrumental in encouraging the effective use of relaxation techniques, such as allowing the teen to leave a room for a brief "cooling-off period" without being reprimanded for avoiding parent/teen interactions.

Communication

In this section, we review the relevancy and importance of learning effective communication patterns in CBT.

Why It's Relevant

In addition to difficulties creating and maintaining positive social interactions, depressed adolescents may have communication skill deficits with their parents, siblings, peers, teachers, and co-workers that contribute to their depression. Changing ineffective communication patterns is one way to change behavior that can lead to positive changes in relationships and emotions.

Communication work in CBT for depressed adolescents generally focuses on the basic skills of active listening and expressing feelings, both positive and negative ones.

How It's Implemented

This module is comprised of two separate but interrelated skills: listening and expressing feelings. Listening is taught first and is related to incidents that the adolescent may have brought up previously where communication breakdowns were connected to feeling depressed. For the therapist to effectively teach listening, two important concepts need to be conveyed to the adolescent: (a) one can listen even when one disagrees, and (b) one can learn or improve listening and other communication skills with effort and practice. Active listening (i.e., restating the sender's message in your own words) can be contrasted with partial listening (i.e., discussing the same topic but shifting the focus from the sender to the listener) and irrelevant listening (i.e., changing the topic, which is surprisingly common).

In order to provide practice in listening skills, role-playing is useful. One way to do this is for the adolescent and therapist to role-play debates on current controversial topics. First, the therapist should find out the teen's stance on a particular topic. Then, while the therapist argues the opposite position, the teen is instructed to listen closely and summarize what was said. After correctly summarizing the therapist's stance, the teen presents his or her position on the topic, which the therapist listens closely to and summarizes. This practice provides an opportunity to highlight the difference between listening and agreeing, and to target any negative thoughts or cognitive distortions that may be contributing to ineffective communication.

Listening as a skill lays an essential foundation for teaching the second aspect of communication: expressing positive and negative feelings. Communicating both types of information takes the same form, using I-statements (e.g., When you ___, I feel ___."). Role playing is essential and the therapist can use feedback, modeling, and humor to teach and practice these basic communication skills.

Common Challenges and Possible Responses

One of the difficulties in teaching depressed adolescents listening and expressing skills is that other members of their families have similar communication styles or deficits. Families of depressed adolescents may develop maladaptive or hostile communication patterns that contribute to the teens' continuing depression or to their risk for recurrence. When you observe high rates of negative communication behaviors or hostility during conjoint parent-teen sessions, it is extremely important to build on what the teen has been taught by also teaching parents these listening and communication skills. Occasionally, an adolescent's home environment is not safe or conducive to practicing communication. If this appears to be the case, the adolescent can be encouraged to seek safer partners to practice the skills with (e.g., a grandparent, friend, boy/girl friend, teacher).

Another common challenge is that the teen finds it difficult to stay calm enough to either listen or express feelings effectively. For these adolescents, additional work on relaxation or affect regulation (described later) may be necessary before they are able to successfully employ their newly learned communication skills. These situations can be practiced in-session repeatedly prior to the adolescents broaching these issues in their homes.

Last, active listening will feel stilted and artificial to almost all adolescents ("This is dumb, nobody talks like this"). Although you do not want to argue with the adolescents, tell them that there *are* many adults who do use this communication style but that it needs to be done in a natural, rather than robotic, manner. Remind them that the way they are communicating now may not be working well for them (fights with parents, problems in school, etc.) and that you are just asking them to try something different and see what happens. Most new skills feel awkward at first. This is also a good place to use humor to capture their attention.

Affect Regulation

In this section, we review the relevancy and importance of affect regulation in CBT.

Why It's Relevant

Affect regulation can be introduced if the therapist has noticed that the adolescent has difficulty coping with emotionally arousing situations. This skill is used to enhance a teen's ability to control sudden changes in mood and to develop a detailed plan for coping with situations that trigger intense emotions (Rotheram, 1987). Adolescents who become too emotionally aroused, in either anger or anxiety, will be unable to effectively employ the other coping strategies they have learned through CBT.

How It's Implemented

The therapist introduces this skill area to the client as a way of "keeping feelings under control." In an empathetic manner, the therapist explains to the teen that it is difficult to remember how to use skills he or she has worked on in treatment because the teen becomes very anxious or upset. The therapist then asks the teen to look at a blank Emotions Thermometer and name the way he or she feels when about to lose control. The emotions will likely vary between feeling "stressed," "frustrated," or "angry." The teen is asked to label the higher end of the Emotions Thermometer with a term that connotes feeling out of control (e.g., *about to explode*) and to label the opposite end *feeling in control* or *relaxed*. At the intermediate points on the Emotions Thermometer, the client is asked to identify physiological, psychological, and behavioral cues indicating escalation toward the out-of-control end of the spectrum (e.g., tension in specific body areas, increased speech volume, agitation, slamming doors).

Once behavioral anchors have been developed for various points on the Emotions Thermometer, the adolescent is asked to indicate the point on the thermometer at which the situation becomes "too hot to handle." That point is labeled the *Boil Over Point*. The adolescent is then asked to choose a point and accompanying cues to serve as signals that he or she needs to "do something" to calm down before arriving at the Boil Over Point. This point is labeled the *Action Point*, or the point where the adolescent is still able to use his or her skills to avoid an explosive outburst.

The therapist then works with the teens to identify specific steps that they can take at the Action Point (e.g., taking a walk, leaving the house with a family member, choosing an activity from the Pleasant Activity list).

Collaborating with parents during a portion of this intervention is helpful so that they can add their observations regarding these occurrences. Parents should also be involved so that they can cooperate with the plan. Parents may need to be encouraged to avoid engaging in behaviors that are likely to escalate the situation (e.g., continuing to pursue an argument with the teen who is about to explode). Both parents and teen should develop a plan for a "cooling off" period with each party going to a different location should the need arise.

To reinforce the newly learned skill, an index card listing each step the adolescent may take when her or his emotions approach the Action Point can be made along with helpful counter-thoughts and specific action steps. A similar index card can be given to the parent, listing what the teen may do and how the parent may assist.

Common Challenges and Possible Responses

The most common challenge in this area is that the adolescent successfully learns affect regulation strategies in the session but "forgets" to employ these coping skills when experiencing intense emotional reactions in real life. It is important to rehearse a scenario similar to the one that might trigger an intense emotion and walk the client through each step of the plan. To encourage generalization and effective use of this skill, the therapist can work with the client to select one or two such scenarios that may occur in the near future and discusses a specific action plan. The adolescent is encouraged to imagine and "walk through" each example and practice the new method of responding. In subsequent sessions, use of the Action Plan can be reviewed and revisited, if necessary.

Skill Integration/Relapse Prevention

In this section, we review the relevancy and importance of skill integration and relapse prevention in CBT.

Why It's Relevant

The final session in acute CBT treatment is aimed at reviewing progress in treatment, determining which skills have been most helpful, and developing a plan to avoid depressive episodes in the future. This session is an opportunity for the therapist to highlight gains that the client has made and to reinforce the connection between CBT skills and the achievement of those gains. Some adolescents will be completing their treatment, whereas others may be transitioning to less frequent maintenance therapy. In addition, the therapist works with the client to anticipate future stressors that might trigger a downward spiral and create a response plan to prevent future depressive episodes. Stressors include both common daily hassles (especially when chronic) and major life events. To the extent that the adolescent can anticipate these experiences and develop a response plan for each stressor, she or he will be more prepared to handle them effectively. Of course, many major life events are unpredictable, but some are known and should be planned for (e.g., graduation, leaving home, starting a career, possible marriage). For all adolescents, but in particular those who are hopeless or perfectionistic, therapists should clearly convey that continued practice with the cognitive and behavioral skills that were taught in treatment will make additional progress possible.

How It's Implemented

This integration/prevention session must be individually tailored to the particular adolescent. If at all possible, parents are involved in this session, especially if additional treatment is warranted. The format of this session is slightly different from previous sessions because the emphasis is on reviewing skills, as opposed to learning new ones. After reviewing homework from the previous session, the therapist reviews progress that has been made toward goals that were set at the beginning of care and, if applicable, any steps that still need to be taken toward these goals. Next, the therapist and the adolescent review the skills that were learned in treatment and discuss which particular skills were most helpful. It is important to emphasize to the client that positive changes were achieved during the course of treatment as a result of using these skills. Next, the therapist discusses the concept of major and minor stressors and how each may lead to a downward negative spiral potentially leading back into depression. The therapist works with the client to identify as many stressors as possible, developing a response plan for each stressor, should it occur. The response plan for each stressor should include at least one CBT skill from treatment as a tool to successfully cope with this occurrence. For clients who have not benefited significantly from treatment, this is an opportunity to discuss other treatment options and to provide referrals, if required.

Common Challenges and Possible Responses

For the majority of depressed adolescent clients, the Skill Integration/Relapse Prevention session is an opportunity to celebrate treatment progress. For adolescents who have experienced a positive response to CBT, the therapist works to ensure that adolescents recognize that much of this response is a consequence of their efforts and involvement in treatment. One challenge is that some adolescent clients experience a drop in their mood as termination approaches. Adolescents who are suddenly quite negative to treatment after having been active and positive clients may be undergoing difficulties related to transitioning to life without treatment. Make sure to remind them about the progress they have made. Praise their efforts . . . large or small. Remind them of how they were feeling before treatment. Be very specific about what skills were noticeably helpful for them. Also, encourage them to increase their "fun activities" levels for the next week or so to help with the transition. Again, work with them to be specific about what they will do.

That said, some adolescents will have made relatively little progress, and the challenge in these situations is to help the clients remain optimistic about the possibility of help. Encourage clients to notice the small steps that they have taken toward their goals, and highlight that some progress is substantially better than none. Encourage the teen to continue using the skills that appeared to have improved his or her mood the most. Also, talk about that fact that the next stage of treatment, if this will be occurring, will provide additional opportunities for progress toward goals and skills practice. If other treatments will replace or augment CBT in the future, the main goal of this session will be to educate the teen and parents that several different treatment options exist and that lack of success in CBT does not mean that other treatments will not help.

Indications and Contraindications for Cognitive Behavior Therapy With Depressed Adolescents

Research studies are now available that support the use of both psychosocial and pharmacological treatments, alone or in combination, for adolescents with depressive illness (see Appendix A). This developing field, however, has not been without controversy. Even the best-supported psychotherapy interventions, including CBT, have not consistently fared well in comparison to other active interventions. Similarly, antidepressant medication studies have not been universally positive; in some studies, SSRIs (selective serotonin reuptake inhibitors) have been associated with elevated rates of serious adverse events. Significant controversy has arisen regarding the safety of antidepressants with depressed adolescents, and close monitoring of young patients treated with antidepressant medications has been strongly suggested by both regulatory agencies and professional organizations. From a risk/benefit perspective, findings from TADS and other well-powered trials currently suggest that the "best practice treatment" for adolescent depression consists of a combination of SSRIs and CBT. However, many adolescents and parents have concerns about antidepressant usage, and some adolescents are unwilling or unable to tolerate the side effects of medications. Future research needs to address whether the positive effects of combination treatment are specific to CBT or could be obtained with other, more broadly available forms of psychotherapy.

We know that comorbidity interferes with the treatment of depression, in both adolescents and adults. We previously examined several hypotheses concerning the potentially negative impact of lifetime psychiatric comorbidity on participation in, and benefit from, the CWD-A course (Rohde, Clarke, Lewinsohn, Seeley, & Kaufman, 2001). Although the total number of comorbid disorders was unrelated to depression recovery, having a lifetime diagnosis of substance abuse/dependence was associated with a slower time to depression recovery, and adolescents who had a lifetime history of attention-deficit and disruptive behavior disorders at intake were more likely to experience depression recurrence during follow-up. That research does not indicate that CBT is inappropriate or ineffective for youth with multiple disorders, but that the speed of response and maintenance of gains may be impacted by certain comorbidities.

We examined in TADS the predictors and moderators of response to acute treatments (Curry et al., 2006). Adolescents who were younger, less chronically depressed, higher functioning, less hopeless, with less suicidal ideation, fewer melancholic features or comorbid diagnoses, and greater expectancies for improvement were more likely to benefit more acutely than their counterparts from all forms of treatment—CBT, fluoxetine, or combination treatment. These variables were general predictors of a positive response. Most clinicians and families, however, are interested in treatment moderators, or the variables that predict which specific treatment may be indicated. We found two patterns of treatment moderation. For adolescents with more severe depression, as measured by symptom severity or high levels of cognitive distortions, combination treatment was not superior to fluoxetine alone, whereas adding CBT to medications did improve outcomes for adolescents with mild to moderate depression. Although we had expected combination treatment to have its strongest effect with the most severely depressed adolescents, it appears that in the acute stage of treatment there is no immediate symptomatic benefit of adding CBT to medications for these teens. Such adolescents may simply be unable to obtain symptom relief from psychotherapy until their depression has improved to some extent. Thus, CBT monotherapy would not be considered the optimal treatment for adolescents who are severely depressed.

The second moderator in TADS involved family income and was a situation where CBT as a monotherapy fared very well. For adolescents from families with low- or middle-income levels, fluoxetine alone was equivalent to combination treatment (and both were superior to the pill placebo). However, for the quarter of the TADS sample that were in families with high income, adolescents were as likely to benefit from CBT alone as from combined treatment, and fluoxetine alone was not superior to pill placebo. It was not clear from the variables we had collected what factors related to socioeconomic status (SES) mediated the relatively superior response to CBT in adolescents from high-income families. In conclusion, depression severity, cognitive distortions, and family income level may help clinicians to choose between various interventions, including CBT, provided either as a monotherapy or in combination with an evidence-based medication.

Additional Readings and Continued Training

This chapter has been designed to provide only an introduction to CBT with depressed adolescents. For additional readings on this topic, the clinician is first referred to both therapist manuals for the CWD-A course and TADS CBT. Both manuals provide a fairly comprehensive review of relevant information. In 2005, the journal *Cognitive and Behavioral Practice* devoted its second issue of Volume 12 to the treatment of adolescent depression, with articles written by TADS collaborators, and those articles address a number of pertinent issues. Additional training prior to providing CBT with depressed adolescents is highly recommended for the novice therapist. If group CBT will be provided, two training approaches seem to work the best. The first approach is to pair the trainee therapist with an experienced leader. As treatment progresses, the trainee assumes an increasingly active role. Advantages of this approach include working with actual depressed adolescents, more direct supervision, and more personalized practice. The major limitation of this approach, however, is that an experienced CWD-A course facilitator needs to be available. In addition, only one therapist can be trained at a time. The second approach consists of conducting a "mock" CWD-A course. Each session is conducted in a start-stop manner to allow time to review the rationale for section and discuss problems. Advantages of this approach include having the opportunity to learn the goals and structure of all sessions before being in a room of depressed adolescents and the ability to train a large number of therapists. Disadvantages of this approach are that it requires other therapists who are interested in learning this intervention and that less experienced therapists will not have direct experience using the materials with actual adolescents. Given that many therapists are unable to receive CBT training for adolescent depression, my colleagues and I have developed a computer-based training that therapists can do at their home or office. Information on this product, called "Mastering the Coping Course: Interactive Training for the Adolescent Coping With Depression Course," can be found at Applied Behavior Science press: http://www.appliedbehaviorscience.com/absp.htm. Whatever training approach is taken, ongoing supervision is recommended for therapists who are new to this approach or client population.

In conclusion, cognitive-behavioral therapy aims to serve as a comprehensive, yet practical, treatment approach for working with depressed adolescents. CBT has been shown to be an effective, nonstigmatizing, and cost-efficient treatment for depression. The goal of this chapter was to introduce the intervention to clinicians and to offer practical advice related to providing these specific skills to their depressed adolescent clients, in either a group or on an individual basis. CBT is highly flexible, and with relatively minor modifications, this form of therapy can be successfully implemented into a broad range of clinical practice.

References

Beck, A. T., Rush, A. J., Shaw, B. F., & Emery, G. (1979). *Cognitive therapy of depression*. New York, NY: Guilford Press.

Beck, J. S. (1995). *Cognitive therapy: Basics and beyond*. New York, NY: Guilford Press.

Benson, H. (1975). *The relaxation response.* New York, NY: William Morrow.

Brent, D., & Poling, K. (1997). *Cognitive therapy treatment manual for depressed and suicidal youth.* Pittsburgh, PA: University of Pittsburgh.

Brent, D. A., Holder, D., Kolko, D., Birmaher, B., Baugher, M., Roth, C., . . . Johnson, B. A. (1997). A clinical psychotherapy trial for adolescent depression comparing cognitive, family, and supportive therapy. *Archives of General Psychiatry, 54,* 877–885.

Burns, D. (1980). *Feeling good.* New York, NY: Signet.

Clarke, G., Lewinsohn, P. M., & Hops, H. (1990). *The adolescent coping with depression course.* The therapist manual and the adolescent workbook may be downloaded for free at http://www.kpchr.org/public/acwd/acwd.html

Curry, J. (2001). Specific psychotherapies for childhood and adolescent depression. *Biological Psychiatry, 49,* 1091–1100.

Curry, J., Rohde, P., Simons, A., Silva, S., Vitiello, B., Kratochvil, C., . . . Reinecke, M. (2006). Predictors and moderators of acute outcome in the treatment for adolescents with depression study (TADS). *Journal of the American Academy of Child and Adolescent Psychiatry, 45,* 1427–1439.

Curry, J. F., Wells, K. C., Brent, D. A., Clarke, G. N., Rohde, P., Albano, A. M., . . . March, J. S. (2003). Treatment of adolescents with depression study (TADS) cognitive behavior therapy manual: Introduction, rationale, and adolescent sessions. Available for free download at https://trialweb.dcri.duke.edu/tads/index.html

Jacobson, E. (1929). *Progressive relaxation.* Chicago, IL: University of Chicago Press.

Kahn, J., Kehle, T., Jenson, W., & Clark, E. (1990). Comparison of cognitive-behavioral, relaxation, and self-modeling interventions for depression among middle-school students. *School Psychology Review, 19,* 196–211.

Kaslow, N. J., & Thompson, M. P. (1998). Applying the criteria for empirically supported treatments to studies of psychosocial interventions for child and adolescent depression. *Journal of Clinical Child Psychology, 27,* 146–155.

Lewinsohn, P. M., Biglan, A., & Zeiss, A. (1976). Behavioral treatment of depression. In P. Davidson (Ed.), *Behavioral management of anxiety, depression, and pain* (pp. 91–146). New York, NY: Brunner/Mazel.

Lewinsohn, P. M., Rohde, P., Hops, H., & Clarke, G. (1991). *Leaders' manual for parent groups: Adolescent coping with depression course.* Available at http://www.kpchr.org/public/acwd/acwd.html

Reinecke, M. A., Ryan, N. E., & DuBois, D. L. (1998). Cognitive-behavioral therapy of depression and depressive symptoms during adolescence: A review and meta-analysis. *Journal of the American Academy of Child and Adolescent Psychiatry, 37,* 26–34.

Rohde, P., Clarke, G. N., Lewinsohn, P. M., Seeley, J. R., & Kaufman, N. K. (2001). Impact of comorbidity on a cognitive-behavioral group treatment for adolescent depression. *Journal of the American Academy of Child and Adolescent Psychiatry. 40,* 795–802.

Rosselló, J., & Bernal, G. (1999). The efficacy of cognitive-behavioral and interpersonal treatments for depression in Puerto Rican adolescents. *Journal of Consulting and Clinical Psychology, 67,* 734–745.

Rotheram, M. (1987). Evaluation of imminent danger for suicide among youth. *American Journal of Orthopsychiatry, 57,* 102–110.

Stark, K., Reynolds, W., & Kaslow, N. (1987). A comparison of the relative efficacy of self-control therapy and a behavioral problem-solving therapy for depression in children. *Journal of Abnormal Child Psychology, 15,* 91–113.

Treatment for Adolescents with Depression Study Team (2004). The treatment for adolescents with depression study (TADS): Short-term effectiveness and safety outcomes. *Journal of the American Medical Association, 292,* 807–820.

Vostanis, P., Feehan, C., Grattan, E., & Bickerton, W. (1996). A randomized controlled out-patient trial of cognitive-behavioral treatment for children and adolescents with depression: Nine-month follow-up. *Journal of Affective Disorders, 40*, 105–116.

Wells, K., & Albano, A. M. (2005). Parent involvement in CBT treatment of adolescent depression: Experiences in the treatment for adolescents with depression study (TADS). *Cognitive & Behavioral Practice, 12*, 209–220.

Wood, A., Harrington, R., & Moore, A. (1996). Controlled trial of brief cognitive-behavioural intervention in adolescent patients with depressive disorders. *Journal of Child Psychology and Psychiatry, 37*, 737–746.

3
Cognitive Behavior Therapy for Depressed Adults

Cory F. Newman

Introduction

Cognitive-behavioral therapy (CBT) is well established as an empirically supported treatment for unipolar depression in adults. This statement sounds straightforward enough, until we realize that depression is actually a highly heterogeneous disorder, often coinciding with comorbid clinical problems that complicate the clinical picture, and manifesting itself in differing levels of severity and/or chronicity that impact the course of the illness and the scope of the treatment that is required (Whisman, 2008). Thus, although there are core features of cognitive therapy for depression that can be succinctly identified and described, the delivery of these procedures requires individualized knowledge of a given client's problems; careful attention to the vicissitudes of the therapeutic relationship; flexibility in conducting the treatment so that it seems most relevant, compelling, and promising to the client; and attention to complications that would otherwise interfere with treatment. Therefore, this chapter presents cognitive therapy of depression as a well-defined, sensible, empirically supported set of operations with clear objectives, while also devoting considerable time to the description and illustration of special issues and complications that often arise in everyday practice.

The Cognitive–Behavioral Model of Depression

One of the central features of cognitive-behavioral therapy for depression is its emphasis on the psychological significance of clients' negatively biased beliefs about themselves, the world around them, and their future (Beck, Rush, Shaw, & Emery, 1979). Clinically depressed clients tend to believe that they lack the ability to cope with difficult circumstances (helplessness), that others are happier and more competent (inadequacy), and that the future is bleak (hopelessness). The clients' depressotypic thinking is perpetuated by cognitive processes that maintain it. For example, depressed clients may selectively attend to instances in their lives when they had setbacks but fail to pay similar attention to evidence of their accomplishments and successes. Similarly, depressed clients who have suffered personal disappointments or rejections may conclude that they are all alone and nobody cares, when in fact there may be a number of important people in their lives who try to offer friendship and support. "Such biases in information processing often lead depressed individuals to neglect their interpersonal relationships and to give up prematurely in trying to achieve important goals. The result is a deepening of their pessimism, a worsening of their mood, and a vicious cycle of further withdrawal" (Newman & Beck, 2009, p. 2857).

CBT for depression also focuses on the clients' actions, in that depressed clients often demonstrate problems with fatigue, low motivation, and withdrawal from activities that otherwise could give them a sense of mastery and pleasure. The inactivity of the depressed clients leads to low positive reinforcement, few opportunities for experiencing joy, and stagnation or regression in feeling a sense of personal growth and empowerment. This interacts negatively with the clients' negative cognitive biases to produce even more self-reproach, helplessness, and hopelessness. In the most severe cases, depressed clients believe that life is so unremittingly painful and unrewarding that suicide may be the only "answer."

A major aim of CBT is to teach depressed clients the skills of systematically identifying, evaluating, and modifying their thinking styles toward the goal of gaining a more objective and manageable view of their problems, along with constructive ways of addressing them. Session work often emphasizes modification of "hot cognitions"—automatic thoughts and images that are associated with a change or increase in emotion. Another overarching goal of CBT is to increase the clients' involvement in activities that are enjoyable, prosocial, and lead to a sense of accomplishment. This system of therapy is comprised of a core set of cognitive and behavioral techniques used strategically in the context of a comprehensive case conceptualization (Kuyken, Padesky, & Dudley, 2009), facilitated by an understanding, accepting, empathic therapeutic relationship (Gilbert & Leahy, 2007). CBT is time-effective and well-structured, with special emphasis given to "empowering and educating [clients] in psychological skills such as rational responding, objective self-monitoring, formulating and testing personal hypotheses, behavioral self-management, problem-solving, and [other skills]" (Newman & Beck, 2009, p. 2858). CBT therapists collaborate with their clients to devise homework assignments that will reinforce these skills, leading the clients to experience better maintenance of therapeutic gains over the long term (Burns & Spangler, 2000; Rees, McEvoy, & Nathan, 2005), a hallmark of CBT (DeRubeis et al., 2005; Hollon et al., 2005).

To those who have not been formally trained in cognitive-behavioral therapy, it is easy to fall prey to some of the common myths about this psychotherapeutic approach. The following is a brief, nonexhaustive list of such inaccuracies, along with rejoinders that more aptly describe CBT as it is actually delivered in practice and taught to practitioners-in-training.

Myth #1: CBT Is Necessarily Short-Term

CBT is more accurately described as "time effective." Depending on the scope of the client's problems, different cases will require different frequencies of sessions and lengths of treatment. At times, CBT may go on for years (see Giesen-Bloo et al., 2006; Newman, Leahy, Beck, Reilly-Harrington, & Gyulai, 2001). Although practical concerns (e.g., limitations of insurance, grant protocol stipulations) may keep therapy contained within certain limits, cognitive-behavioral therapists recognize that some clients require a longer period of treatment than others. In any case, time is treated like the precious resource that it is—cognitive-behavioral therapists do their best to structure sessions, focus on high-priority topic areas, and assign homework so that clients acquire self-monitoring and self-management skills that facilitate prompt improvement and long-term maintenance. Therapy may not always be short-term, but time is used well.

Myth #2: CBT Pays Little Attention to the Expression of Emotions

The term *cognitive-behavioral therapy* denotes the important role that clients' thought processes and behavioral patterns play in their difficulties and in their learning to function more effectively. However, this is not to say that emotions are not important. Cognitive-behavioral therapists endeavor to help their clients achieve a higher quality of life, including a wider range of emotionality, a greater capacity for hopefulness and joy, improved efficacy in recognizing negative emotions (e.g., anger, grief, fear) so that they may be processed in a healthy way, and (arguably) the ability to find humor in themselves and the occasional absurdities of life (see Newman, 1991). Nevertheless, cognitions and behaviors (by definition) play a central role in cognitive-behavioral therapy, as they provide particularly fruitful points of assessment and intervention.

Myth #3: The Therapeutic Relationship Is an Afterthought in CBT

From its early days, CBT concerned itself with the therapeutic relationship (Beck et al., 1979). Effective CBT is not a mechanistic imparting of techniques, nor is it a process of arid, intellectual debate. Good rapport and a sense of positive, trusting collaboration between therapist and client is essential if the treatment is to have its intended impact (Gilbert & Leahy, 2007). In cases where clients have marked difficulties in getting along with others, the therapeutic relationship in CBT serves as a valuable model for mutual understanding, respect, and good will.

Myth #4: CBT Is Synonymous With "the Power of Positive Thinking"

More accurately, CBT values *constructive, objective* thinking. This means that clients are encouraged and taught to evaluate themselves and their lives so that problems may be identified—not denied—in a way that promotes change without undue self-reproach. As depressive thinking is typified by negatively biased assumptions that promote helplessness and hopelessness (Abramson, Alloy, & Metalsky, 1995; Beck, Wenzel, Riskind, Brown, & Steer, 2006), it is important for CBT to present a relatively optimistic approach. However, cognitive-behavioral therapists do not teach their clients to indulge in idle positive thinking that trivializes their struggles.

Myth #5: CBT Encourages Clients to Avoid Pharmacotherapy

Cognitive-behavioral therapists strive to take an empirical approach to treatment. As such, they *respect the data* in the field of mental healthcare. There is ample evidence that medications can and do play an important role in the treatment of depression and particularly in such disorders as bipolar spectrum illnesses and schizophrenia. The use of medication *per se* is not incompatible with the concurrent delivery of CBT (Wright, 2004). However, cognitive-behavioral therapists address their clients' dysfunctional *beliefs* about medications, such as when the clients maintain that their pills will substitute for the learning of psychological skills, or attribute all their gains to the medicine, thereby deriving little or no boost in self-efficacy, or erroneously hold that potentially helpful medications will rob them of their "true selves."

Case Conceptualization

Although it is customary for clinicians to begin the process of conceptualizing a client's case at the outset of treatment—perhaps in the form of an official "intake" session—the task of understanding the internal and external factors that have led to and maintain the client's present problems is one that is ongoing throughout therapy. As therapists, we may be able to glean a great deal of information about the client by conducting a formal diagnostic evaluation (e.g., the Structured Clinical Interview for the *Diagnostic and Statistical Manual-IV*; First, Spitzer, Gibbon, & Williams, 1996), at which point we may ascertain that the client suffers from a major depressive disorder (see APA, 2000). We will also want to garner a good deal of information about the client's personal history, including his or her important experiences in school, work, family relationships, and important extra-familial relationships. Further, the client's responses at intake may provide us with a reasonable glimpse into his or her cognitive style—how he or she perceives: (a) himself or herself, (b) other people (and the world at large), and (c) the future—the "cognitive triad" (Beck et al., 1979). We may also provide clients with self-report inventories (e.g., the Personality Beliefs Questionnaire: PBQ; Beck et al., 2001) that shed light on maladaptive beliefs that clients may hold. These data are valuable for hypothesizing the ways in which the clients' thought patterns play a role in their psychological difficulties. Collectively, this information puts the therapist in a good position to collaborate with clients in establishing some preliminary goals for therapy that the clients will find relevant and on target.

As therapy progresses, the therapist will come to learn more about the client simply by observing the client's cognitive, behavioral, and emotional reactions to current events in his or her life, as well as to the goings-on in the therapy sessions, including the therapeutic relationship. This information will be incorporated into the case conceptualization, which is a somewhat fluid entity. For example, the therapist may learn that a given depressed client is prone to mistrust what the therapist is saying, becoming wary and taking offense at otherwise benign therapist comments. This would be in contrast to another depressed client who is eager to learn what the therapist has to teach him or her and expresses enthusiasm about the usefulness of the therapeutic dialogue. Some clients seem to have great difficulty in arriving on time for sessions or in doing their therapy homework, whereas others are quite punctual and/or reliably give a good-faith effort to complete their between-sessions assignments. Similarly, there are important differences between depressed clients who are reticent in session, often saying "I don't know" in response to the therapist's questions about their thoughts, versus those clients who readily and willingly engage in spirited, collaborative dialogue with the therapist, offering hypotheses whenever they are asked to contribute their ideas. These sorts of differences between clients become quite germane to their respective case conceptualizations. As such, astute cognitive therapists will use this differential information in the service of under-standing the clients better, communicating more *accurate* empathy, making adjust-ments in their interpersonal style so as to maximize collaboration, and devising goals that are most relevant for the individual clients in question. Therapists who formu-late a good, data-driven case conceptualization will be in the best position to answer the following sorts of questions they may ask themselves during the course of therapy:

➤ What are the client's personal strengths, and how can we use them in the service of maximizing the benefits of therapy?

➤ What are the signs that the client is struggling to understand what I am saying or to understand the purpose of the homework? How can I describe things more clearly or give better rationales so that my client and I can be on the same page?

➤ What are the risks and benefits of my introducing a given issue that I believe is important but that the client has not yet volunteered? How can I express my thoughts about this issue so that it is most acceptable to this particular client?

➤ What are the client's most likely responses to a given intervention? If the client's responses confound my hypotheses, what could be accounting for this? Are there missing data? How can we explore this further and yet maintain a sense of safety and collaboration in the therapeutic relationship?

➤ Which changes would be most therapeutic for this client to make? What procedures would make these changes most durable? How can I determine if the client is actually learning something useful in therapy or is merely being superficially agreeable?

These are but a handful of questions that therapists can entertain, pertinent to the case conceptualization and related treatment plan. The upshot is that a cognitive case conceptualization involves gathering and organizing data about the client's beliefs systems, behavioral patterns, emotional experiences, and interpersonal functioning across situations and longitudinally over time. These data help therapists to construct individualized treatment plans and to make (and test) predictions about how the client will respond. As noted earlier, it is important to identify and utilize the client's personal *strengths* in the service of therapy, as this strategy demonstrates respect for the client and boosts the client's morale and sense of self-efficacy (see Kuyken et al., 2009).

The following are some brief, circumscribed examples of using the case conceptualization to craft the appropriate therapeutic intervention, using the fictitious depressed clients "Hal" and "Fay." Hal (divorced, age 60) presents as a reserved, introspective man who is very pragmatic in his approach to life. He lives alone with his dog and has few friends. He makes quick judgments about people and situations, but rarely vocalizes them. His parents apparently were depressed as well, but never sought treatment, and expressed the attitude that "Life is tough, and doesn't owe you anything." Fay (single, age 32) is more vocal and gregarious and has a number of good friends, though she is quick to compare herself unfavorably to them. She wants to get more out of life, but finds that she inhibits herself from taking personal and vocational risks owing to her lack of confidence and her belief that she cannot deal with disappointment. Fay is aware that life has a lot to offer, but she is worried that she is letting life pass her by. In light of the above information, here are four ways in which the same cognitive therapist may choose to use different interventions with Hal and Fay.

1. Although Hal and Fay are both clinically depressed, the therapist would not assume that they have the same goals for therapy, especially in light of their differing personal styles and contrasting demographics. The therapist would explicitly explore each client's goals individually. However, the therapist would be aware that Hal may downplay the notion of "goals," as he may be apt to construe goal setting as synonymous with "expecting something from life," which goes against what he was taught growing up. Thus, the therapist may phrase the question of goals differently with Hal, asking (perhaps), "What would you like to ask of *yourself*, so that you can make improvements in your mood?" The same therapist may not have to be as careful in his or her choice of words in asking Fay to discuss her goals for therapy.

2. The therapist learns that both Hal and Fay make self-condemning comments, based on a sense that they are "not doing enough." Knowing that Hal is a very practical fellow who has few friends, the therapist may be more inclined to ask Hal the question, "What constructive course of action would you like to take in response to this problem?" rather than ask the question, "What would you tell a close friend who was going through the same thing as you, and who had the same self-reproachful thoughts?" With Fay, a conversationally adept person who is interpersonally active in her life, the therapist may choose to do the opposite, asking her what she would tell a friend in the same situation.

3. Hal and Fay both have problems asserting themselves. However, Hal's difficulties stem from a pessimistic attitude that, "I'm not going to get what I want anyway, so there is no point in saying anything," whereas Fay's hesitation is based on fearing that she will damage her relationship with the other person. Hal rarely tries to speak his mind to others, and has a limited repertoire. Fay ruminates about the myriad comments she would like to make, but can't bring herself to say. In response to these assertion problems, the therapist may choose to work with Hal to test his theory that "you won't get what you want anyway," and therefore to do some behavioral experiments in speaking up. They may choose a couple of relatively benign scenarios (e.g., asking for extra packets of mustard at the deli counter), and determine if this provides evidence that sometimes it is useful to speak up. Then they would try to generalize these findings to more important areas of life (e.g., asking his brother to help out more with their elderly mother). With Fay, the therapist may opt for role-playing exercises in session, so as to take advantage of Fay's strengths in being verbally expressive, all within a safe environment where she would not damage any relationship. This intervention would give Fay some useful exposures to vocalizing her opinions, and to generating some effective but diplomatic responses to the other person's non-cooperative stance (as play-acted by the therapist). After practicing, Fay could try some assertive comments in everyday life that she has been "dying to say," to see how effective she could be in terms of stating her case while preserving the relationship.

4. It is unlikely that Hal is going to dramatically change his interpersonal style, and it probably isn't one of his goals to do so. However, he may benefit significantly from getting back into some activities he used to enjoy that he has neglected for some time, such as doing carpentry work, playing chess (which he can now do on line if he wishes), and fishing. The therapist may also ask Hal if he has any "unfinished business" in his life that is "a thorn in his side." Together they may explore things that still need resolution, and they can turn their attention to these issues as goals for therapy. Examples might include taking a trip he had planned, then postponed, and never rescheduled, or completing an old household project that was "half done for 15 years," or going back to a volunteer job he once liked

but left when he didn't respect the new director of the organization. Getting Hal behaviorally active would be a key to his treatment. For Fay, significant progress will probably hinge on learning to pursue new goals that she had been avoiding for fear of failure and rejection. Already an active and social person, it is likely that she can have more interpersonal success if she learns to reduce her catastrophizing about interpersonal disagreement. In order not to let "life pass her by" (as she feared), it would be necessary to have clear goals to pursue without delay, rather than continue to postpone acting on them out of a sense of low self-efficacy. The therapist would undoubtedly make use of rational responding and role-playing as key techniques (see below).

These are but a few ways in which a conceptual understanding of the clients can lead the therapist to pursue interventions that are maximally relevant for and suited to the individual in question. The following section addresses some of the core interventions in CBT.

Techniques

It is somewhat artificial to separate "techniques" from case conceptualization and the therapeutic relationship, as these three main elements of treatment are best construed as being intertwined and synergistic. CBT techniques that are presented as rote procedures, out of the context of the client's life, and minus a sense of good-natured collaboration with the therapist, are rather "clunky" at best, and may even seem irrelevant and forgettable. As a metaphor, we may view CBT techniques as "products" (e.g., skills, words of wisdom) that we wish to impart to our clients. The case conceptualization is the *map* that will help us transport these products to the right place, in a reasonable time. The therapeutic relationship is the *route* itself, such as a road, a waterway, or a flight path. We want this route to be as smooth as possible, without undue bumps in the road, rapids in the water, or turbulence in flight. Taken together, this metaphor illustrates how the efficacy of therapeutic techniques is buttressed by an accurate case conceptualization and a safe, reasonably smooth therapeutic relationship. In light of this, the following subsections on techniques should be considered in this context. Thus, the order of presentation of the following techniques is not meant to imply priority or primacy, as that depends on the individual case at hand. Further, although the following techniques are presented one at a time, there is no reason that the skilled CBT therapist cannot use combinations of these (and other related) techniques, provided that there is a good rationale for doing so and assuming that the results support their use in this manner. With that in mind, let us proceed with a description of some of the core techniques in the CBT repertoire.

Behavioral Experiments

Although the term *behavioral experiment* seems to imply that this technique is purely in the behavioral realm, it is more completely viewed as an *experiential experiment*, as changing one's behavior in a strategic way has the potential power to alter the client's emotions and thought processes as well. What is a behavioral experiment? Simply put, it is an opportunity to act in a way that is hypothesized to bring about something healthy and positive, even if the client at first doubts that he or she can do it, or cannot fathom that the experiment will result in anything worthwhile. Behavioral experiments are most often enacted as part of a cognitive therapy homework assignment (see Bennett-Levy et al., 2004), but they may also be used in-vivo in the therapy session itself.

As an example of the latter, a depressed man revealed that he had been avoiding checking his work-related e-mail, as he was certain that there would be messages from colleagues questioning his progress on some projects he had been avoiding. Realizing that this sort of avoidance represented poor problem-solving skills and could result in a worsening of consequences for his client, the therapist asked the client what was stopping him from reading such e-mail. The client replied (reflecting his negative assumptions) that he "wouldn't be able to cope with the criticisms" and that reading the e-mail "wouldn't help the situation anyway." At first, the therapist thought he might assign the client the task of opening up all of his work-related e-mail as a behavioral experiment between sessions, but then hypothesized that this client may simply avoid the assignment. Therefore, the therapist suggested an *in-vivo behavioral experiment*, in which the client was invited to use the therapist's computer to read his e-mail on the spot, in session. The following dialogue illustrates how the therapist presented this idea to the client:

> Therapist (T): It sounds as though your negative expectations are preventing you from facing some important things that need your attention. I'm concerned for you. I think this is one of those times when, "What you don't know *can* hurt you." Maybe you and I can start the process of problem solving right now.
>
> Client (C): How?
>
> T: [Pointing to his own desk and computer] Here, take my seat. I'll stand. Log in to your e-mail account right now and let's do the behavioral experiment of looking at your e-mail right now.
>
> C: I really don't want to waste my therapy time by looking at my e-mail.
>
> T: Oh, this wouldn't be a waste of therapy time at all. In fact, it would be two very effective interventions called *exposure to a feared situation* and a *behavioral experiment*. You can see for yourself how well you can deal with the messages that you think are waiting for you, rather than just assuming that you can't deal with them at all, which I think underestimates your coping skills.
>
> C: I don't know. [Pauses] I don't think I can handle it right now.
>
> T: I am here to give you all the moral support you need. I can also help you to begin the process of problem solving if you find that the news is not so good.

This could be a great behavioral experiment in exceeding your expectations about your coping capabilities.

C: It's going to be ugly.

T: That's your prediction. That's what we call a *hot cognition*. Let's not prejudge. Let's see for ourselves. I think we can make great progress today by doing this behavioral experiment right here, right now, no delay.

C: If I fall apart, it's all your fault. [Laughs nervously]

T: That's another hot cognition. By contrast, I have faith in your ability to withstand this little test. Let's go for it, and we'll start solving whatever problems await you.

Not only did this client succeed in doing this behavioral experiment, he exceeded the expectations of the therapist, as the client actually went beyond the intended intervention to send reply e-mail to his colleagues to begin the process of solving the problem that he had heretofore avoided and dreaded. One of the significant benefits of behavioral experimentation is that it sometimes leads to a chain reaction of constructive actions that creates a positive feedback loop.

Activity Monitoring and Scheduling

When depressed clients suffer from anergia and anhedonia, they often scale back the degree to which they engage in potentially productive or rewarding activities, a condition that unfortunately reinforces the client's helplessness and low mood. In response to this problem, CBT therapists often will encourage clients to self-monitor their activities (e.g., via the use of the Daily Activity Schedule, or DAS; see J. S. Beck, 1995), to rate each of their activities in terms of mastery and pleasure (e.g., scales of 0–10 for "Ms" and "Ps"), to study ways in which it might be advantageous to schedule new activities, and to implement gradually increased schedules of activities. This may be done as a freestanding method or in combination with techniques that target the clients' thought processes (see below). Expectedly, when depressed clients feel sluggish and low in motivation, their therapists will need to be understanding and encouraging in making such behavioral prescriptions. The client's collaboration with the behavioral plan is of paramount importance, as is the therapist's ability to inspire their clients to extend themselves toward greater levels of activity, as well as to be patient when clients report at first that they "cannot" enact the planned exercises. Caring perseverance is the key.

The DAS (or other behavioral self-monitoring form) can be particularly valuable as an assessment of how the clients are using and/or structuring their time. A completed DAS (perhaps as an early homework assignment) will provide the therapist with potential hypotheses about the factors that may be maintaining the client's depression. For example, one client's DAS showed that her life was overbooked as she ran from one obligation to another in her efforts to work and go to school while raising a young child alone. She had no time for friends, a relationship, or recreational events, and she reported feeling constantly worn out. The therapist had the sense that this client was courageously coping with the demands of single-parenthood, but was struck by the client's penchant for self-criticism. The therapist came to realize that this client was turning down offers of help from family and friends, fearing that if she accepted their assistance she would be a "burden" to them. By contrast, another depressed client's DAS showed that he was always awake well after midnight and was never out of bed until early afternoon. Many of the items on his DAS were poorly described (e.g., "hanging" and "chilling"), leading the therapist to hypothesize that this client may be using alcohol and drugs on a regular basis, while doing little for a sense of accomplishment or healthy pleasure. The client denied that he was abusing substances, but eventually revealed that he was spending hours each day looking at Internet pornography and feeling helpless in looking for a job. Yet another client's DAS indicated that his days were quite filled with work-related, social, and recreational activities, yet he had described his life as having "an emptiness about it." This incongruity (and in-session discussion thereof) ultimately led to the client's revealing that he was in an on-again, off-again extramarital relationship that left him questioning his morals and life direction. Once again, the potential value of data from the DAS went well beyond a simple accounting of the client's activities to identify significant problems that were not so obvious at the initial self-reporting.

In terms of *scheduling* activities, the following behavioral assignment can be presented to the client in the form of the following instruction—"create more, consume less." Although this behavioral prescription is modest in its concept, many clients find that it is difficult to enact, as it asks them to reduce the "consumptive" activities on which they have come to rely for mood regulation, such as overeating, drinking too much alcohol, using illicit drugs, spending too much money on material goods or gambling, having sex in excessive ways (e.g., multiple, casual partners), and other behaviors that ostensibly "feed their monster" of low impulse control and poor self-image. At the same time, the "create more, consume less" credo asks the clients to increase the degree to which they *create* something good in their lives. It may be useful to assign the clients the homework of generating a list of such creative activities in which to devote more of their time and energy in the service of improving their self-esteem and mood. An abbreviated example of such a list follows:

1. If you used to play a musical instrument, start playing it again. If you already play one, play it more (e.g., take lessons again). The same thing goes for singing.
2. Work in your garden (or outdoors in general) to create something good from the earth for your enjoyment.

3. Compose thoughtful, humorous messages for the important people in your life. This may be in the form of text messages, e-mail, greeting cards, poems, a caring voicemail message, and so on.

4. Write something (e.g., a journal entry, an editorial, an Automatic Thought Record (ATR) (e.g., J. S. Beck, 1995; see below) for your next therapy session—a short story, a paper for a class, a joke, an observation you made today—that you do not wish to forget, and so on.

5. Design a new environment for yourself at home or at work by rearranging things and cleaning so that you are happier with the things that surround your personal space.

6. Create a new physical activity regimen, which may involve formal exercise (e.g., a class at a gym), informal activity (e.g., walk more, use the stairs more), sports, or other forms of active recreation.

7. Engage in a craft such as knitting, crochet, carpentry, sculpting, and so on.

Following the "consume less, create more" theme can be naturally antidepressive, but therapists must be empathic and understanding about the difficulties their clients may encounter in trying to pursue their goals. Enacting this credo requires the client to delay gratification, tolerate discomfort, summon up energy, and think in a constructive manner—all difficult tasks for the depressed individual. Nonetheless, it offers a simple, understandable blueprint for counteracting helplessness and gaining some distance from habitual behaviors that otherwise worsen one's mood and self-esteem.

Role-Playing

Acquiring an effective behavioral repertoire usually requires a process of trial and error. To the degree that someone can take the "error" part of the equation in stride, much learning can be accomplished over the years. Unfortunately, some of our clients are quite averse to making mistakes, owing to personal histories of being unduly punished by important others for not doing things "right," and/or their own self-punitive or catastrophic mindsets regarding what will happen if they dare to try but "fail." When this occurs, clients miss many opportunities to learn new, adaptive behaviors, particularly in the realms of appropriate emotional self-expression, assertiveness, public speaking, and general conversational skills. The resultant deficits in these skill sets aggravates a depressed client's sense of low self-efficacy, leading them to engage in further avoidance of trial-and-error opportunities in life. Especially for such depressed clients (many of whom also evince comorbid anxiety disorders), role-playing represents a promising technique in CBT.

The best way to encourage clients to take part in role-play exercises is for the therapists themselves to show enthusiasm for this intervention. Far too many therapists sidestep this technique because they find it potentially awkward or embarrassing, just like their clients! However, it is possible to look at role-playing as a "no-lose" situation that makes the threat of feeling silly seem like part of the intervention rather than an impediment to its implementation. For the client, it is a win if the role-play succeeds in providing the client with an opportunity to practice a new behavior, and it is a win if it simply stirs up some hot cognitions that can be subject to modification via rational responding (see below). Similarly, for the therapist taking part in a therapeutic role-play, it is a win if he or she is able to model behaviors that are helpful for the clients to emulate; and it is a win if the therapist stumbles, stammers, and/or draws a blank, as this offers the therapist the chance to demonstrate some accurate empathy for the client's difficulties. For example, in the case of a client who struggles to assert herself with her overbearing, hypercritical father, the therapist may elect to play the role of the client, while the client plays the role of the father. If, in the course of the role-play, the therapist is at a loss as to how to respond to the "father's" harsh comments (as portrayed by the client), the therapist can say, "Wow, does he really say things like that to you? That's outrageous! I had no idea what you were up against. Now I see why it's so difficult for you to face him. I guess we really have our work cut out for us." This sort of interaction bolsters the therapeutic relationship, while demonstrating that even a "failed" role-play contributes useful information.

As we can see, role-playing has multiple uses. It offers the opportunity for the client to practice new interpersonal repertoire, in the safety of the therapist's office, with multiple chances to repeat the exercise, thus gaining practice without any of the objective trial-and-error drawbacks that may occur in everyday life outside the office. Role-playing stimulates hot cognitions, in that the clients will likely be emotionally activated in the process, thus helping to identify new, relevant cognitions. It can also be used in the service of reenacting important past situations that clients wish to process, as well as rehearsing upcoming interactions (e.g., a job interview) for which the clients want to prepare. Role-playing can be used in a hypothetical manner, such as when a painfully shy client is asked to read a script (written by the therapist) depicting a highly confident person so as to provide the client with an almost visceral experience in functioning at a higher level. Role playing can depict metaphorical arguments between different parts of the client's experiences, such as when the therapist plays the role of the client's "cynical, pessimistic" self, while the client has to play the role of his or her "aspiring, optimistic" self, providing hopeful rebuttals against the therapist's comments, in the form of a friendly debate. Novel or otherwise useful responses that the client generates in the process of doing such role-plays should be written down as examples of more functional ways of thinking.

Of course, therapists wish to be collaborative with their clients and therefore should not be too forceful in insisting that clients do the role-plays if they flat out refuse. Nonetheless, therapists can assess the clients' catastrophic expectations that inhibit them from taking part in this technique and can nicely ask if they may revisit the option of doing role-plays in future sessions. There is no safer place to practice new behaviors and new ways of thinking than in the privacy of the therapist's office. If clients do not role-play there, it is highly unlikely that they will enact the target behaviors in their lives during the week, where risks may be real and where the clients may only get one chance to speak their minds. In sum, role-playing is a valuable, multipurpose intervention that is probably underutilized, given its therapeutic attributes.

Rational Responding (and Automatic Thought Records)

Rational responding is perhaps the quintessential CBT technique. Therapists teach clients to view their negative emotions (sadness, guilt, anger, shame, etc.) as *cues* to ask themselves the question, "What is going through my mind right now that could be contributing to my feeling this way?" The goal is to teach the clients the skill of spotting their *automatic thoughts* in given situations, to evaluate these thoughts, to test their validity, and to modify them to a more constructive form. Patterns in automatic thoughts may lead therapists and clients to ascertain certain *beliefs* or deeper *schemas* that clients may maintain that adversely affect their emotional lives (see Beck, Davis, & Freeman, 2004; Young, Klosko, & Weishaar, 2003). With training and practice, clients can learn to spot and counteract the thoughts that otherwise would maintain and/or exacerbate their depressive symptoms. Clients use a series of questions (adapted from the ATR; see J. S. Beck, 1995) to help themselves reconsider the validity and/or utility of their thoughts. Such questions include (see Newman & Beck, 2009):

➤ What are some other plausible ways I can look at this situation?

➤ What concrete, factual evidence supports or refutes my automatic thoughts?

➤ What constructive action can I take to deal with this situation?

➤ What sincere, helpful, realistic advice would I give to a good friend in the same situation?

➤ What is the worst-case scenario in this situation? What is the best-case scenario? Now that I have considered both extremes, neither of which is statistically likely to occur, what is the most *likely* outcome?

➤ What are the pros and cons of continuing to believe my automatic thoughts? What are the pros and cons of trying to change my automatic thoughts to make them more constructive and hopeful?

Although all of the earlier questions can be used in the service of testing and modifying depressive thinking, it is not necessary to use all of these questions for all maladaptive thoughts and/or in all cases. This is where it is useful for the therapist to have a good conceptualization of the case, including a firm grasp of the important events of the client's life. For example, if a depressed client has made many unwise decisions in her life and therefore has suffered many losses (e.g., her addiction problems have led her to leave school, lose jobs, and get divorced), there is a basis in fact for her thought, "I've made so many mistakes, and now that my life is damaged and hard to manage, I have nobody to blame but myself." Therefore, the therapist would *not* be so be quick to utilize a question such as, "What concrete, factual evidence supports or refutes my automatic thoughts?" Clearly, there is plenty of hard evidence that supports the client's depressive thinking! However, it may be quite constructive to ask some of the other questions from the earlier list. Let us consider how the therapist and the client, working collaboratively in session, might answer the following three questions:

1. What are some other plausible ways I can look at this situation?

   I have definitely made mistakes, but it doesn't help me if I blame myself. I somehow have to learn from my mistakes and make wiser choices as I try to move forward and regain my life.

2. What constructive action can I take to deal with this situation?

   I will go to 12-step meetings on a regular basis and remain in contact with my sponsor. I will go to community college and finish my associate degree. I will not quit my current job, even though I am dissatisfied with it, because I am not in a position to be picky right now. I need to earn a paycheck and to establish a good work record so I can get a letter of recommendation later on when I try for a better job. I will try to make amends to my brother and sister by paying them back the money I owe them, little by little. This may not guarantee that they will want me in their lives again, but at least I will be doing the right thing and I will feel better about myself.

3. What sincere, helpful, realistic advice would I give to a good friend in the same situation?

   I would tell her that I am proud of her for owning up to her mistakes, but that she doesn't have to kick herself while she is down. I would tell her that I will give her all my moral support for her efforts to improve her life, and I look forward to the day when she can smile and laugh again.

On the other hand, some depressive clients demonstrate a habit of viewing things as being worse than they really are, even when there is little or no evidence to support their pessimism, and even when (to the outside observer) it looks as though they have a lot for which to be grateful in their lives. For example, in the case of a largely successful, competent person who feels like an "imposter," it would be fitting and proper to ask the question: "What concrete, factual evidence supports or refutes my automatic thoughts?" Actually, I have done a lot of good things in my life, and the people closest to me seem to respect and care for me. I don't know why I think I'm an "imposter" who really deserves to be blamed for things, but I guess it's a habit I've gotten into over the years, and now I just assume it's true, even when I haven't done anything horribly wrong.

By using the particular question(s) to fit a given client, the effective cognitive therapist will get the most mileage out of the intervention of rational responding. Of course, the ultimate goal is to teach the clients to use these questions for themselves, perhaps by assigning their use as a routine part of the clients' homework (e.g., doing ATRs).

As noted earlier, clients can take full advantage of this technique by learning to notice when their negative emotionality is exacerbated and asking themselves, "What is going through my mind right now?" Therapists teach their clients to generate hypotheses about what they may be thinking at such moments, explaining that it is not necessary to spell out one's thoughts in a word-for-word, grammatical fashion. Once clients have come up with some ideas about what they might be thinking (and perhaps writing them down in their cognitive therapy journal), they can then systematically apply the list of questions earlier, thus producing more constructive alternatives or rational responses to their initial automatic thoughts. Those clients who take the time to memorize the questions are most apt to be able to use them at critical moments, especially in situations when writing their thoughts is impractical (e.g., in the car).

Figure 3.1 illustrates a completed ATR, including all of the important columns following the date and time, including: (a) situation, (b) automatic thoughts, (c) emotions, (d) alternative responses, and (e) outcome. This ATR illustrates the case of a young woman who became distraught when friends canceled their social plans for the evening, leaving her feeling alone. Note that the client *rates* her degree of belief in her automatic thoughts, as well as her level of emotionality on 0 to 100 scales, both before she generates and writes alternative responses and afterward, so as to gauge the impact of her attempt at using this self-help intervention. The outcome column indicates that this client successfully moderated her extreme automatic thoughts as well as the accompanying feelings of anger, despair, and loneliness. Clients do not always show such improvements when they try to do these ATRs. When this occurs, it serves to cue the therapist to offer helpful feedback to the client, to probe for more information that may be pertinent to a given ATR, and to help the client to try the ATR again. Well-constructed alternative responses on the ATR should either boost the client's morale or teach them something useful, or both. If it does neither, then the ATR needs some revision, and perhaps more involvement from the therapist.

As therapy progresses, greater attention is focused on the client's underlying beliefs and related schemas, such as, "I am incompetent to cope with life as others do," and "I am defective and unlovable" (see Beck et al., 2004; Young et al., 2003). These schemas tend to be associated with more chronic, severe dysphoria and dysfunction, and will prove more difficult to change in treatment. Many repetitions of a full array of behavioral and cognitive techniques (including ATRs) offered by a caring (and inspiring) therapist will be necessary in order to produce positive change, and much practice will be required of the clients (typically via homework assignments) in order to maintain such progress. One particularly evocative technique is

Figure 3.1 Automatic Thought Record

Directions: When you notice your mood getting worse, ask yourself, "**What's going through my mind right now?**" and as soon as possible jot down the thought or mental image in the Automatic Thoughts column.

Date/Time	Situation	Automatic Thought(s)	Emotion(s)	Alternative Response	Outcome
	1. What event, daydream, or recollection led to the unpleasant emotion? 2. What (if any) distressing physical sensations did you have?	1. What thought(s) and/or image(s) went through your mind? 2. How much did you believe each one at the time?	1. What emotion(s) (sad, anxious, angry, etc.) did you feel at the time? 2. How intense (0–100%) was the emotion?	1. (optional) What cognitive distortion did you make? (e.g., all-or-nothing thinking, mind-reading, catastrophizing) 2. Use questions at bottom to compose a response to the automatic thought(s). 3. How much do you believe each response?	1. How much do you now believe each automatic thought? 2. What emotion(s) do you feel now? How intense (0–100%) is the emotion? 3. What will or did you do?
Sat. night around 10pm	At home alone. Plans with "M and H" fell through this evening. Nothing to do but feel alone and sorry for myself.	1. I hate my life. I don't want to go on. Nobody understands. 2. I can't deal with any of this. I'm useless and hopeless and nothing matters anymore.	Anger (80%) Despair (95%) Loneliness (100%)	I am deeply disappointed that I am alone tonight, but that doesn't mean that my whole life is horrible and useless. I am lonely and dissatisfied and that makes me extremely vulnerable when I experience a disappointment like tonight. It doesn't mean I should give up and die. I have to find a way to help myself, such as by writing these Thought Records. My friends do understand, but they can't always be responsible for me. I will help myself.	1. Thoughts 1st thought: 20% 2nd thought: 10% 2. Emotions Anger (0%) Despair (40%) Loneliness (80%) 3. Actions I went for a jog, took a long, hot bath, and curled up with a good book.

Questions to help compose an alternative response: (1) What is the evidence that the automatic thought is true? Not true? (2) Is there an alternative explanation? (3) What's the worst that could happen? Could I live through it? What's the best that could happen? What's the most realistic outcome? (4) What's the effect of my believing the automatic thought? What could be the effect of changing my thinking? (5) What should I do about it? (6) If _____ (friend's name) was in the situation and had this thought, what would I tell him/her?

Source: © J. Beck (1995). Adapted from *Cognitive Therapy: Basics and Beyond*, and used with permission.

imagery reconstruction, the rationale of which is to revisit historical events in the client's life where he or she encountered powerful negative experiences that are hypothesized to have a causal role in the development of the schemas. This technique, which usually requires an entire session, combines aspects of relaxation, guided imagery of the past experience, assessment of the client's feelings and thoughts in that old experience, deliberate manipulation of the memory to include empowering aspects (e.g., the client asserting himself with an abuser, using the communication skills he possesses today), and rational reevaluation of the old thoughts that are pertinent to the schemas. For more in-depth detail on these specialized procedures, the Young et al. (2003) volume is an excellent resource.

There are a number of additional techniques that could be mentioned here (e.g., problem solving), but instead they are described and alluded to in the upcoming sections on homework and working with suicidal clients. Overall, only a central sample of the possible CBT techniques is mentioned in this chapter. For more comprehensive listings and descriptions of a wider range of CBT techniques, see such volumes as Leahy and Holland (2000), and O'Donohue and Fischer (2009).

The Role of Homework in Cognitive Behavior Therapy for Depression

When depressed persons come to a therapist's office, they are often hoping to find a safe place where they can express their feelings without being criticized or rejected. They may hold out some hope that their therapists will offer some words of compassion and wisdom that will make them feel better. Good cognitive-behavioral therapists will provide these conditions, and more. They will provide their depressed clients with an *education* in how to help themselves. They do this by teaching clients the cognitive model, helping them to learn to identify and modify their problematic thoughts and beliefs, guiding them to become more active and productive, and by giving them *homework* that will teach them the skills they need to help themselves. When clients practice their therapy skills via engaging in regular therapy homework assignments, they learn to maintain their therapeutic gains long after the completion of formal sessions (Burns & Spangler, 2000; Rees et al., 2005).

What qualifies as "homework"? There are many possibilities, some of which are listed in Table 3.1. What they have in common is the following: *Therapy homework offers clients the opportunity to educate themselves in improving their ability to understand themselves better, to make deliberate changes in their thoughts and behaviors that will help boost their morale, and to use these skills over time and across situations.* The list of possible homework assignments is very long, limited only by the collective imaginations of the therapist and client. It is often the case that the techniques that are taught in session can double as homework assignments between sessions (e.g., brainstorming solutions to problems or rationally responding to negative, automatic thoughts). Other assignments usually require that the clients take what they learn in the "lab"

Table 3.1 Sample List of Homework Assignments for Clients

1.	Read a handout/chapter in a book/other literature about cognitive therapy.
2.	Listen to your audio-recording of your therapy session.
3.	Keep a daily log of your moods, with ratings.
4.	Keep a daily log of your behavioral activities (Daily Activity Schedule).
5.	Rate your behavioral activities in terms of *mastery* and *pleasure*.
6.	Prospectively plan new activities designed to improve health and mood.
7.	Prospectively plan new activities designed to deal constructively with problems.
8.	Brainstorm ways to solve a difficult problem, and weigh the pros and cons.
9.	Weigh the pros and cons of a difficult decision.
10.	Keep a journal of daily experiences (situations, moods, outcomes, etc.).
11.	Monitor and record thoughts when mood is low.
12.	Use Automatic Thought Records to rationally respond to negative thoughts.
13.	Engage in behavioral experiments to test hypotheses and effect change.
14.	Practice delaying acting on impulse (e.g., eating, smoking).
15.	Communicate with someone you have been avoiding or neglecting.
16.	Assert yourself in an appropriate situation after practicing.
17.	Practice breathing control and relaxation techniques to reduce agitation.
18.	Alter sleep-wake cycle gradually in a functional direction.
19.	If you cannot fall asleep, get up and write down your thoughts.
20.	Catch yourself when you say defeatist comments (e.g., "I can't . . .), and change it to a more hopeful alternative (e.g., "It is difficult, but I'll try to do it."), and document.

(the therapist's office) and apply it in the "field" (the client's everyday life), such as behavioral experiments (see Bennett-Levy et al., 2004).

Ideally, therapy homework assignments should be clearly related to the work that is being done in session, so that the client is most likely to see the relevance of the task. For good measure, it helps if the therapist provides a rationale for the assignment, along with some instructions in how to do the homework. Sometimes, if the therapist introduces the assignment with sufficient time still remaining in the session, it is possible to *start the homework assignment in the therapist's office* as a way to jump-start the client's participation in the task. For example, if the client is being introduced to the ATR, a depressive comment he or she articulated in session can be used as material for the ATR. The therapist and the client can begin working on the ATR together, with the client being asked to complete the remainder of the ATR for homework. The following dialogue illustrates this process:

Therapist (T): This sheet is called an Automatic Thought Record. It's a structured method for recording some of the spontaneous, depressive thoughts you often have. By following the instructions on this sheet and writing down your thoughts, you can put yourself in a position to question those thoughts in a constructive way, so that perhaps you can look at things in a more favorable light and with a sense of positive direction. We did some work on that today in session, and now I would like to encourage you to try to do some of this work on your own during the week.

Client (C): I was afraid of this. My friend said that cognitive therapy involves homework, and I have to tell you that homework and I don't mix well at all.

T: Hmmm. You've got some misgivings about this. Okay. I'm open to hearing your views about this. Tell me about your past experience with homework that makes you have doubts about doing it for therapy.

C: As you know, I have some major learning problems. Attention-deficit, whatever. Just really bad. All I can think of is the frustration and humiliation I went through in school trying to do my homework, and having nobody to help me because my parents were fairly useless, and I was ashamed to tell anybody at school because they just assumed I was being lazy because somehow they thought I was smart. But I know that *I'm totally incompetent when it comes to organizing my thoughts.*

T: First of all, I want to thank you for entrusting that information to me. I didn't realize the extent of your past academic hardship, and I don't think I realized how alone you felt in your frustration, with nobody to help you. I'm really sorry about that.

C: It's not *your* fault.

T: Well, I don't want to add insult to injury now, but I have an idea about how we take something negative and turn it into a positive. Are you interested?

C: What do you mean?

T: Well, did you hear what you just said a minute ago that really put yourself down?

C: I don't know, what did I say?

T: You said something along the lines that you were *totally incompetent in organizing your thoughts.*

C: Yeah, well that's how I feel.

T: We have about 10 minutes left in the session. I could work with you right now to help you get started with the Automatic Thought Record, and we could use that comment as the subject matter under the column that says "automatic thoughts"—that you believe you are "totally incompetent" in organizing your thoughts. That's a terribly self-punishing way to view yourself, and I'll bet we can find some plausible alternative ways to view yourself that are not so condemning of yourself, and therefore not so depressive. Those are the responses that you would write under the column that says "alternative responses."

C: And the column to the left of that is "Situation." Would I write, "In my therapy session?"

T: Yes, and you could even add, "Talking about therapy homework and having doubts." Here, take my copy of the Automatic Thought Record and write that down. I'll get another copy for myself and write the same thing and we can begin this assignment in tandem.

Note that not only is the therapist encouraging the client to do the homework while still expressing empathy for his doubts, but the therapist is also *helping* the client with the work, something the client just lamented that *nobody* ever did for him. Regardless of whether or not the client was overstating his case, the therapist is already providing some evidence that this therapy experience will be more positive than the client expects, especially in sensitive areas such as his sense of competency. The completed version of this hypothetical ATR is presented in Figure 3.2.

When clients have difficulty with homework, it is not so much a problem as an opportunity for the therapist to collaborate with clients to solve the problem, as well as a potential font of data that helps further develop the conceptualization of the case. For example, consider the following hypotheses that address the question, "Why does the client repeatedly neglect to do the therapy homework?" Perhaps the client . . .

➢ Anticipates doing a poor job, feeling humiliated, and being criticized by the therapist.

➢ Expects the homework to fail, which might reinforce his or her sense of hopelessness.

➢ Equates the homework with being given a command, which he or she resents.

➢ Doesn't understand the assignments, but is ashamed to ask.

➢ Doesn't believe that it is an important aspect of therapy, and therefore dismisses it.

➢ Expects that the homework will make him or her feel uncomfortable (or worse).

➢ Maintains the belief that therapy should not involve anything strenuous, like homework.

➢ Does not see the relevance of the homework, and thus does not make it a priority.

In other words, rather than viewing the client's nonadherence to homework only as being problematic, cognitive therapists can use this situation in the service of gaining a better understanding of the client's beliefs. Sometimes the clients will take the initiative and explain their misgivings, such as by saying, "I don't understand how this is going to help me," a comment that can serve as a cue for the therapist to discuss the rationale for therapy homework. However, many clients do not readily spell out their reasons for avoiding the homework, or give reasons that do not adequately explain a *pattern* of neglect (e.g., "I just didn't have time." "I keep forgetting." "I don't know why I never seem to do it."). At such times, cognitive therapists can ask the client some direct questions, phrased nicely and carefully, delivered with a friendly tone. Keeping in mind the hypotheses listed previously, therapists can ask:

Are you concerned that doing the homework will only make things worse?

What are some of your misgivings about the homework? I respect your opinion on this.

Figure 3.2 Automatic Thought Record

Directions: When you notice your mood getting worse, ask yourself, **"What's going through my mind right now?"** and as soon as possible jot down the thought or mental image in the Automatic Thoughts column.

Date/Time	Situation	Automatic Thought(s)	Emotion(s)	Alternative Response	Outcome
	1. What event, daydream, or recollection led to the unpleasant emotion? 2. What (if any) distressing physical sensations did you have?	1. What thought(s) and/or image(s) went through your mind? 2. How much did you believe each one at the time?	1. What emotion(s) (sad, anxious, angry, etc.) did you feel at the time? 2. How intense (0–100%) was the emotion?	1. (optional) What cognitive distortion did you make? (e.g., all-or-nothing thinking, mind-reading, catastrophizing) 2. Use questions at bottom to compose a response to the automatic thought(s). 3. How much do you believe each response?	1. How much do you now believe each automatic thought? 2. What emotion(s) do you feel now? How intense (0–100%) is the emotion? 3. What will or did you do?
Today. Almost at the end of my therapy session.	In my therapy session. Talking about homework and having doubts.	"I'm totally incompetent when it comes to organizing my thoughts." (90%) "I can't do the homework." (95%) "I'm going to be a failure case." (80%)	Shame (100%) Anxiety (100%)	"That's a case of my thinking in 'all or none,' because I CAN organize my thoughts sometimes, including right now. I can do the homework, but it's not easy, and I have a hard time trusting myself to do it right and trusting that others won't think I'm an idiot. I am trying my best to overcome my depression. I am a person, not a failure case."	1st thought (20%) 2nd thought (0%) 3rd thought (50%) Shame 70% Anxiety 80% Began to work on this ATR before leaving my therapy session.

Questions to help compose an alternative response: (1) What is the evidence that the automatic thought is true? Not true? (2) Is there an alternative explanation? (3) What's the worst that could happen? Could I live through it? What's the best that could happen? What's the most realistic outcome? (4) What's the effect of my believing the automatic thought? What could be the effect of changing my thinking? (5) What should I do about it? (6) If _____ (friend's name) was in the situation and had this thought, what would I tell him/her?

Source: J. Beck (1995). Adapted from *Cognitive Therapy: Basics and Beyond*, and used with permission

Would it be better if you decided on your own what you want to do this week?

Would it help if we started doing some of the homework right now, for clarity?

What are some of your constructive criticisms about the homework?

Does it seem like the homework is asking too much, especially given how you feel?

Note that these questions try respectfully and caringly to elicit clients' beliefs pertinent to the issue of helping themselves between sessions during the week. Therapists take great care to minimize the possibility that the clients will perceive a power struggle. For example, therapists can further explore the client's perceptions about therapy homework (while maintaining an atmosphere of collaboration) by doing an exercise of assessing the pros and cons of doing homework and the pros and cons of not doing homework (see Figure 3.3). Aside from explicating some of the perceived advantages and disadvantages of engaging in therapy homework, this method can also elicit some idiosyncratic client beliefs that need modification, perhaps via the use of the ATR. In Figure 3.3 we see that the client lists "I'll feel inept" as a disadvantage of doing therapy homework, a belief that could be subjected to further scrutiny in its own right, such as by doing the homework assignment as a behavioral experiment in its own right, and seeing how much the client really feels inept in the process.

In the spirit of collaboration, therapists should consider the possibility that they themselves can improve the ways in which they assign and manage the client's homework assignments, and that this may improve the client's level of active participation. The following are guidelines to assist cognitive-behavioral therapists in making homework relevant, interesting, clear, and manageable for their clients.

➤ *The homework assignment should be a natural extension of that which was discussed in the therapy session.* This makes the homework timely and relevant. For example, if one of the topics in session was the client's anguish in not being able to speak her

Figure 3.3   Pros and Cons of Doing Homework and Not Doing Homework

	Pro	Con
Doing Therapy Homework	1. My therapist will stop reminding me. 2. I'll get more therapy. 3. I'll get better, quicker. 4. I'll remember the important things from therapy. 5. I'll have a sense of accomplishment.	1. Drudgery, boredom. 2. I'll feel inept. 3. It will be embarrassing showing it to my therapist. 4. Time-consuming. 5. I'll have to think about things that upset me.
Not Doing Therapy Homework	1. I can pretend I know more than my therapist knows. 2. I can procrastinate, which is my area of greatest expertise. 3. I can relax instead.	1. I'll be limiting what I can get out of therapy. 2. Once again, my laziness will mess things up in my life. 3. I'll have nobody to blame but myself if I don't understand the self-help skills. 4. My therapist will lose faith in me.

mind to an important person in her life, a good homework assignment might be for the client to write a mock letter to that person and to practice reading it aloud.

> ➤ *The homework assignment should be well-described*, even to the point of doing a short demonstration in the session (if possible). For example, rather than vaguely saying to a client, "Why don't you do some 'thought trackings' this week?" it is better to say something like, "Each day, use your therapy notebook to jot down some of the thoughts you had at moments when you were feeling particularly sad and lonely, so we can learn more about your state of mind at those important times."

> ➤ *Therapists would do well to elicit as much client participation as possible in the process of brainstorming and designing homework assignments.* Sometimes it is appropriate and useful to say to the client, "Based on what we have discussed in session today, what homework assignment would you be willing to give yourself so as to continue our work during the week?"

> ➤ *Elicit feedback from the client*, rather than simply assuming that the assignment is clear and acceptable to the client. Feel free to ask, "What is your opinion about the homework assignment? What part of it seems potentially helpful? Is there anything in the assignment about which you have some doubts or misgivings?"

> ➤ *Acknowledge that homework is sometimes hard work* and that any efforts on the client's part will be appreciated.

> ➤ In order to *gauge the clients' level of confidence and commitment to the homework*, ask questions such as, "On a scale from 0% to 100%, how likely do you think it is that you will do the homework? On a scale from 0% to 100%, how confident are you that you will be able to get something useful out of doing the homework?" If therapists leave sufficient time at the end of the session for further discussion (e.g., 5 to 10 minutes), it will be possible to discuss and process the clients' answers. For example, if a client gives himself a "0% chance" of doing the homework, it provides a golden opportunity to discuss the client's automatic sense of helplessness and hopelessness, even before he has tried.

> ➤ If clients bristle at the sound of the word *homework* (perhaps due to negative connotations from their academic past), try to find synonyms. Alternative ways to describe homework include, *experiments*, *take-home therapy*, *field tests*, *practical applications*, and *real-world tests*, to name a few.

Although it is certainly possible for depressed clients to make significant gains in CBT even if they rarely or never do therapy homework, the chances of their making improvements as well as the scope and durability of their positive changes are likely to be noticeably enhanced if homework becomes a routine part of treatment. As such, it is a good idea for CBT therapists to set the tone by offering to devise homework assignments at every session and by being ready to review the past week's homework as one of the agenda items of a typical session. As one psychodynamically trained colleague once quipped, "It seems as though homework is a 'permanent object' in CBT!"

Applying Cognitive Behavior Therapy With the Suicidal Client

When treating clinically depressed clients, it is prudent to do regular assessments for suicidal ideation and/or intention. This may be accomplished simply by asking the clients at each session whether (and to what degree) they have been thinking about suicide, and then going into some detail (regarding their intentions, preparation, method, plan, etc.) if the clients' answers are "yes." It is also useful if the clients are asked to complete brief self-report inventories at each appointment, such as the Beck Depression Inventory (Beck, Steer, & Brown, 1996) and the Beck Hopelessness Scale (Beck, Weissman, Lester, & Trexler, 1974), as hopelessness has been shown to be a factor that significantly increases the risk of suicide in depressed clients (Beck, Steer, Beck, & Newman, 1993; Beck, Steer, Kovacs, & Garrison, 1985). A more specific, lengthier method of assessing the client's level of suicidality is to conduct a structured interview, such as the Beck Scale for Suicide Ideation (see Beck, Steer, & Ranieri, 1988), which taps into the client's thoughts, feelings, and intentions toward suicide on the day of the interview, *as well as at the worst time in their lives*. This latter component of the interview is most useful, as one of the best predictors of suicidal risk is the client's maximum level of suicidal thinking and intention in his or her personal history (Wenzel, Brown, & Beck, 2009).

When clients indicate an elevated level of suicidality, it is vitally important to put this topic at the head of the therapeutic agenda and to do everything possible to gain the client's cooperation in refraining from taking any self-harming actions at least until the next session, preferably all the while that therapy is being undertaken, and ideally for all time. At the same time, therapists need to seek to understand the client's subjective reasons for wanting to die, and to provide empathy about the client's emotional pain and suffering. As much as therapists may view suicidal thoughts and intent as being "abnormal," therapists must be able to put themselves in the client's shoes and to communicate this understanding. Doing so will help therapists establish the high degree of credibility necessary to ask clients to refrain from acting on their impulses, and instead to engage in the challenging work of therapy, even if they feel depleted of energy and hope and consumed with negative emotionality.

In order to gauge and assess the clients' episodes of acute suicidality (e.g., from a suicide gesture of low lethality to a frank attempt to kill themselves), it is useful to review the full set of circumstances—both "inside" the client and in the external, situational circumstances—that served as triggers. Therapists can ask the following questions, and more:

When you noticed that you were thinking about hurting or killing yourself . . .

> ➤ Where were you? Who was with you? When did this occur?

> ➤ What was going on around you? What were your situational circumstances?

> ➤ What thoughts were going through your mind? What were you feeling?

> ➤ What action(s) did you take in order to harm yourself?

> ➤ How intent were you on dying? Did you have any second thoughts?

> ➤ What do you think were the main factors that triggered your wish to die?

> ➤ What are your thoughts and feeling *now* as compared to your thoughts and feelings at the time you [harmed yourself] tried to kill yourself?

> ➤ What does this situation teach you about what makes you most vulnerable?

> ➤ What actions can you take the next time in order to safeguard yourself if you should feel similarly again?

The clients' answers to these important questions can be written down for future reference, perhaps in the form of a flow chart that maps out the "suicidal scenario" (see Figure 3.4). Although there is no guarantee that all clients will be willing and/or able to answer the previous questions in a way that will be clinically useful, most suicidal clients will appreciate having the opportunity to explore and explain the reasons and circumstances for their suicidality.

Figure 3.4 "Suicidal Scenario" Flowchart—Sequence of External and Internal Events

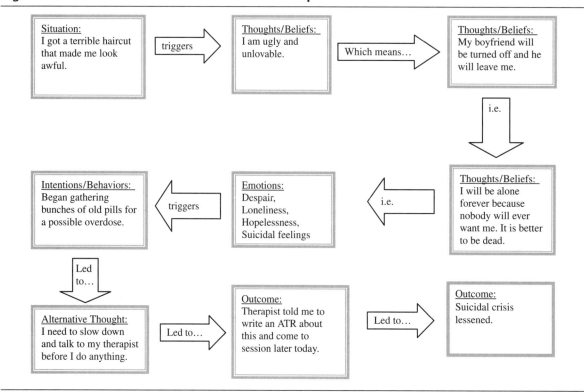

Suicidogenic Beliefs

Another useful heuristic for understanding the client's desire to commit suicide is to look at the "suicidogenic beliefs" they may be harboring (see Newman, 2005). Following is an untested, anecdotal, short list of such beliefs, along with their corresponding therapeutic rejoinders. Clients sometimes openly reveal that they hold one or more of these beliefs, and sometimes therapists need to infer these beliefs and then ask the clients directly to confirm how much they ring true for them. By identifying one or more of these beliefs, therapists will improve their chances of helping clients develop rational responses (via such methods as ATRs between sessions and guided discovery questioning within sessions) that are particularly meaningful in counteracting their purported reason(s) for wanting to kill themselves. For example:

Belief #1: "My problems overwhelm me. The only way to cope is to end all problems at once by killing myself."

Rational response: Death is not a solution. It just passes my problems onto other people, and I don't want to do that. The only way to begin to solve my problems is to start today, one at a time, and to make use of the help I am receiving in therapy and from others who care. With each problem I tackle, I will feel better about myself for having the courage to try.

Belief #2: "I am a burden to others, and they would be immediately better off if I were dead."

Rational response: If my illness truly has become a burden to my family—and this may just be an example of my negative assumptions—then the best way to alleviate this burden is to show them that I am going to devote myself fully to my treatment and commit myself to getting well again. Committing suicide would *really* burden my family, and there would be nothing they or I could do to fix it. At least if I am alive, I can always try my best to improve things and to be more helpful to those I love.

Belief #3: "I hate myself, I can't live with myself, and I deserve to die."

Rational response: If I hate myself, it means I feel ashamed of the way I have lived my life. If I die now I will always leave behind a negative legacy. The best way to overcome my negative feelings about myself is to improve the way I live my life and to "rehabilitate" myself, rather than give myself a "death penalty." It will be very difficult to change my life for the better, and it may even be painful to take stock of myself and take a new path, but this is the best direction to take in order to forgive myself and go on.

Belief #4: "I am in unbearable, intractable pain, and the only way to feel better is to die."

Rational response: I will find a way to take care of my pain without having to die. I will turn my pain and suffering into motivation to help others and to help myself in the process. I will work in therapy to brainstorm healthy ways to feel better at least some of the time, and to appreciate those times more than I ever have before.

Belief #5: "If I kill myself, maybe people will finally understand how I feel, and maybe I will get in the last word that will show everybody that they should have treated me better."

Rational response: The best way to help people understand how I feel is to communicate with words, rather than by acting out violently. I am angry and frustrated, but I will only make things worse if I do something as extreme as trying to kill myself. People will be more understanding if I refrain from doing things that scare them.

The rational responses represent best-case scenario examples of suicidal clients making cognitive changes, but it is possible for them to reach such therapeutic conclusions (and others) through the diligent, patient help of their cognitive therapists. It is best if they write or otherwise record these new, improved ways of thinking, as they can refer back to them at times in the future when they may lapse into feeling particularly depressed or hopeless.

Cognitive Vulnerabilities of the Suicidal Client

Aside from hopelessness and negative beliefs, depressed, suicidal clients demonstrate additional cognitive vulnerabilities that need to receive attention in treatment, such as cognitive rigidity, poor problem solving, deficits in autobiographical recall, and self-punitive perfectionism (Ellis, 2006; Wenzel et al., 2009).

Cognitive Rigidity This problem is most often seen in clients who are prone to look at situations simply in terms of black and white, all or none. Either life is the way I want it to be, or it is worthless. Either I have total confidence in myself, or I have none. Either people love me, or I am rejected and all alone. Either I see a bright future, or I have no future worth anything at all. When therapists spot this sort of dichotomous thinking in their clients, they can craft questions that help the clients to consider gradations or shades of gray. The following are some examples of therapist comments that help clients move away from a purely all-or-none outlook.

➤ I know that you said that nobody cares about you or understands you, but I wonder who in your life *comes the closest* to being able to understand and care about you.

➤ I hear you when you say that all you do is "mess things up, again and again," and I know that this distresses you. However, I wonder if there have been some *exceptions to the rule*, so to speak. I would be interested in hearing about any times when you did something right. Let's not forget the things that are in your favor. Even if "doing things right" is in the minority, let's look at them, because these experiences are important, too.

➤ Can we *rate* what you just said on a scale of 0 to 100? Rather than just say, "I have *no* chance of improving my life," let's look at the *percentage chance*. Even if it's really low, we may be able to learn something about what needs to be done.

➤ I notice that you say the words *always* and *never* a lot, and that you're usually very distraught when you describe your life in those terms. Remember back in school when teachers used to say that in multiple choice tests you can usually rule out the answers that have the word *always* or *never* in them because that is so often not true? Well, the same thing is true in psychology. Most things in life are not *always* or *never*, and so I wonder if we can start examining your life in a way that the "answer to the test question is right."

Problem Solving All too frequently depressed clients underutilize problem-solving skills. They often perceive more problems but generate fewer solutions than nondepressed, nonsuicidal clients, with regard to both individual and interpersonal problems (Weishaar, 1996). Further, suicidal clients are less likely to try to actively deal with their problems than nonsuicidal clients, perhaps out of a sense of hopelessness and helplessness. In general, depressed clients who lack problem-solving skills are at greater risk for suicide than those clients who actively try to practice the principles of "damage control" in everyday life (see Schotte & Clum, 1987). Thus, cognitive therapists would do well to include problem-solving on the list of "things to learn" in the treatment plan (A. Nezu, C. Nezu, & Perri, 1989). This broadly includes learning how to:

➤ Identify and describe a problem in clear, operational terms (e.g., the problem is *not* that *I am a useless nobody*, but that I have become inactive and self-isolative).

➤ Brainstorm possible solutions, and not to censor or otherwise exclude possible solutions right off the bat just because of a sense of hopelessness.

➤ Posit and weigh the pros and cons of each brainstormed solution (perhaps as a homework assignment if there isn't sufficient time in the therapy session to complete this task).

➤ Choose one of the most favorable solutions, plan a method for enacting it, and then attempt to implement it (perhaps for a homework assignment).

➤ Observe the results, make adjustments as needed, give yourself positive feedback for having had the courage and know-how to try to solve the problem and do it again (and/or try to solve an additional problem).

This general stepwise method can be applied to a host of problems, helping depressed, suicidal clients to rebound from setbacks, mend fences with important others, and improve their life situation in ways they may have thought were beyond repair. "It is useful to note . . . that *for every vicious cycle there is an equal and opposite positive feedback loop. One of the goals of cognitive therapy is to find this positive counterpart to the clients' more common downward spiral*" (Newman, 2005, p. 85).

Autobiographical Recall Those who suffer from both unipolar and bipolar depression have been found to have relatively less specific memories about their personal histories (Evans, Williams, O'Laughlin, & Howells, 1992; Scott, Stanton, Garland, & Ferrier, 2000). By extension, these individuals have relatively more difficulty in learning useful lessons from their experiences compared to their nondepressive peers. Similarly, they may fail to give adequate weight to those specific *positive* experiences in their past that otherwise might give them a heightened sense of mastery, confidence, and being cared about by others. Taken together, these cognitive deficiencies make depressed clients relatively more vulnerable to the influence of their generalized, negative beliefs. In response to this problem, cognitive-behavioral therapists encourage depressed clients to discuss and write about significant life experiences in as much specific detail as possible, so as to better appreciate the richness, complexities, and useful lessons from their past. In order to facilitate the encoding of autobiographical information going forward, cognitive-behavioral therapists encourage their clients to keep personal journals and to record their own therapy sessions for future reference, paying special attention to the times they solved problems, had success experiences, and learned important life lessons to help them cope.

Perfectionism Maladaptive perfectionism can be a risk factor for suicide (Blatt, 1995; Hewitt, Flett, & Weber, 1994). Here we are not simply talking about an individual's ambition to perform well and succeed. We are referring to someone's internal demand that things work out "just so," with anything less or different being deemed to be a devastating failure. In this way of thinking, there are no options, and no "second-best solutions." Along with this rigid mind-set comes a punitive tone, such that the individual does not view the less-than-perfect situation as a learning opportunity, but rather as justification for self-castigation and hopelessness. In response, therapists try to encourage these "punitively perfectionistic" depressed clients to appreciate the opportunities for learning and growth inherent in life's difficulties, from the inconveniences and minor mistakes of everyday life to significant personal flaws and setbacks. By making this change in mind-set, clients may be able to appreciate their "good enough" accomplishments, learn valuable life lessons that stem from disappointments, and even occasionally have the pleasure of *exceeding* their expectations (which can never happen when one is constantly expecting perfection).

The effective cognitive-behavioral therapist assists such clients in being more specific, clear, and thorough in their thinking, often by nicely but persistently asking the clients questions that encourage them to consider ways they can help themselves *other* than by giving up, shutting down, and/or engaging in self-harming behaviors. When the client's reply is "I don't know," cognitive therapists should not be deterred. They can reply with the following comments:

➤ It is okay to take an educated guess.

➤ This is a very important topic in your life. It warrants some thought. Let's work together on this. If you can try to answer, I will try to match it with another possible answer, and then we can try the same thing again. Is that okay?

➤ It may be hard to answer for yourself. What would you tell a *friend* in the same situation?

➤ When you say "I don't know," I think what you mean is that you don't know *for sure, right now*. However, it's okay to brainstorm some ideas and to take your time.

➤ Saying "I don't know" is not the end of the story; it is the beginning of our exploration to try to understand. Let's start now.

Pros and Cons

A direct, straightforward way to evaluate and potentially modify a client's reasons for wanting to die is to articulate the pros and cons of suicide, along with the pros and cons of refraining from suicidal behavior (see Ellis & Newman, 1996). This technique does not increase risk, as it simply provides a forum for suicidal clients to articulate the pro-suicide thoughts they have already been harboring, while simultaneously encouraging them to consider alternative, safer viewpoints, all within an accepting and supportive professional environment. A pro-con analysis regarding suicide also allows the therapist to ascertain some of the dysfunctional beliefs the client maintains about suicide. Figure 3.5 shows a sample pro-con analysis in the form of a 2×2 table, revealing (among other things) that the client believes that killing himself will relieve

Figure 3.5   Pros and Cons of Trying Suicide and Not Trying Suicide

	Pro	Con
Trying Suicide	1. People will really understand how much pain I was in. 2. I will no longer be a burden to my family. 3. I won't be overwhelmed by my problems anymore. 4. I will be doing something about my depression, rather than just complaining about it.	1. I might mess it up and wind up in a coma, and become an even bigger burden to my family. 2. I would always be remembered as "that hopeless guy who killed himself." 3. My mother would be scarred for life. 4. My friends would feel guilty for not being able to help me. 5. I would never travel the world like I hoped I would. 6. I would lose any chance of getting better forever.
Not Trying Suicide	1. I won't have to leave a legacy as being a self-destructive person. 2. I might decide to change my life rather than try to end it. 3. Maybe I'll be happier in the future. 4. Maybe it will be a turning point and I can start to get a life. 5. My family won't be stigmatized. 6. I can live and help others who might feel suicidal.	1. I might have to go through more failures in my life. 2. My hopes and dreams still might not come true. 3. People will stop taking me seriously when I tell them I hate my life.

his family of a burden, will spare him from having to deal with his overwhelming problems, will prove something to others, and will somehow represent "doing something" about his depression. These are all "suicidogenic beliefs" that need to be addressed and challenged directly. A similar approach can be taken to reevaluate his cons for living. At the same time, this technique allows the client to consider healthy alternatives in the form of pros for living and cons for suicide.

Therapists may wonder, "What if the client only lists advantages to suicide and fails to consider any advantages to living?" If this occurs, the therapist then acknowledges the client's profound sense of hopelessness and addresses this promptly. Newman (2005) illustrated a therapist response to such a situation, part of which follows:

> By only seeing the pros of dying and the cons of living, you may be setting yourself up for a self-fulfilling prophecy. I am not asking you to have blind optimism. I am inviting you to think about how your future could be better, and how living your life to its natural conclusion in the distant future could present you with advantages you currently do not dare allow yourself to consider. Are you willing to work with me to explore this? (p. 81)

The "Hope Kit"

In order to improve the suicidal client's sense of connectedness to others (and therefore to life itself) and hope for the future, therapists ask their clients to maintain a "hope kit" (Wenzel et al., 2009). This is a compilation of memorabilia and contact information that clients keep in one place (e.g., an old shoebox), which they can access at times when they are in particular need of an emotional lift. Items can include old photos that represent happy events or times, birthday and/or holiday cards that the client has saved over the years, artifacts that represent success experiences (e.g., award or honor certificates), a list of important people along with their phone numbers and e-mail addresses, emotionally significant writings that the clients have done over time that communicate important messages (e.g., old therapy homework assignments that were done well and that helped the client see things in a more hopeful light), and any other items that favorably represent the client's life and times. Sometimes therapists will ask their depressed clients to bring their "hope kit" to session, so that they may discuss its contents, add to them, and otherwise make therapeutic use of this method. The general theme is to give depressed clients concrete evidence of their attachment to their lives and to remind them why their existence is worth preserving and nurturing.

Special Issues

In this section, we review special issues of concern in conducting CBT with depressed adults.

Identify the Client's Strengths

Even the most symptomatic of our depressed clients possess areas of personal strength, and these can be put to good use in therapy. When clients believe that they have experienced a marked decline in their functioning (e.g., typified by thoughts and comments such as, "I am not the person I used to be"), therapists can make use of the clients' memories of how they managed their lives and coped more successfully in the past. As noted earlier, one of the hallmarks of moderate to severe depression is a deficit in autobiographical recall, but therapists can still impress upon their clients the importance of describing incidents in their personal histories when they felt better about themselves. Such memories can be a springboard for generating ideas for better coping in the present, while also giving the clients something they can feel proud to discuss, thus combating demoralization and low self-efficacy. The following, brief therapeutic dialogue illustrates:

Client (C): I'm so overwhelmed. I have a zillion things I have to do for school and work, and I can barely get out of bed in the morning. I'm just going to fall apart. There's no way I can manage all of this. I should just throw in the towel now.

Therapist (T): I know you have a lot on your plate right now. I know it's a lot. I think most people would feel stressed out in your situation. The thing that stands out as being a sign of *depression* is that you are so convinced that you are going to fail completely and miserably that you are ready to quit on yourself before you even see what you're capable of.

C: I think it's pretty clear that I'm not very capable at all right now. I have no idea what I'm going to do.

T: I wonder if we can take a lesson from your own past experience in order to help us with this situation.

C: What do you mean?

T: From what I understand, you've gone through similar situations in the past, working and going to school at the same time, and managing a heavy load. I wonder what personal strengths you brought to bear on those situations in order to help you cope and succeed.

C: I wasn't depressed.

T: Okay, that makes sense, but there are many people who aren't depressed who still aren't able to succeed in work and at school at the same. You did. So, it stands to reason that you have some skills and some experience in enacting those skills that are noteworthy. Maybe we should do an accounting of your methods and see what you could implement now, even though you're depressed.

C: I don't know. My expectations for what I can do are pretty low right now.

T: I do understand that. I don't want to give the impression that I think you can easily overcome all your symptoms, especially the lethargy. On the other hand, I am reluctant to start telling you that you ought to do this or that when you already have a history of knowing how to handle the demands of life quite well. I want to respect your experience and knowledge before I start telling you what to do and essentially re-inventing the wheel.

C: Well, years ago, I believed in myself. I was young and confident. I didn't want to settle for doing a half-baked job at anything. I pushed myself even when I was tired and discouraged.

T: So far starters, you didn't automatically believe that fatigue meant you were helpless. Your goals meant too much to you to get into a defeatist mind-set.

C: Yes, and I'm a far cry from that right now.

T: I wonder if we can work together to revive some of that old mind-set where you believed in yourself. Let's start by talking about what sorts of things you used to say to yourself to get yourself going in the morning and how you structured your time so that you managed to do so much. Maybe we can identify the best of your cognitive and behavioral habits and dust them off again. I'm interested in exploring this with you. How about you?

Even if the client is reluctant to engage in such an exercise, it is likely that he or she will feel respected by the therapist, and this may have some motivational value in itself. In any event, such an intervention has the potential to maximize the client's sense of self-efficacy, which has positive implications for improving maintenance of therapeutic gains.

Another way to utilize clients' strengths to counteract depressive low self-esteem is to demonstrate an active interest in the things they normally do for a sense of accomplishment. If clients have a particular hobby, craft, intellectual interest, or similar pursuit in which they express themselves well or otherwise demonstrate some sort of talent, let this be a part of the therapeutic agenda from time to time. This strategy is consistent with focusing on encouraging the client to be more active by planning and engaging in constructive activities that give them a sense of mastery and/or pleasure, also known as the *Ms* and *Ps*. These Ms and Ps can be rated on a scale of 0 to 10 as part of the client's Daily Activity Schedule (DAS) that they may do for homework.

Beware the "Depressive Identity"

In cases of chronic, early-onset depression, clients sometimes cannot even imagine that being nondepressed could be part of their "natural" state. They may un-fortunately maintain the belief that the only way to feel better is to use drugs or alcohol, or they may mistrust their episodes of good mood, reasoning to themselves that contentment is illusory and short-lived. In fact, some clients report that feeling emotionally good is uncomfortable and unsettling, and they will sometimes admit that they do things that appear to be "self-defeating" just to return to a familiar state again. This is not a "need to suffer," but rather a natural gravitation toward that which is known in favor of that which seems unfamiliar. One of our tasks as therapists is to help the chronically depressed client learn to accept and adapt to the "strange" feeling of a rational improvement in mood and self-image. We must also empathize with our clients who express doubts about recovering from depression, as they equate their identity with their emotional illness, rather than view their depression as an unfortunate encumbrance to their "real" self.

We must consider that some chronically depressed clients actually anticipate feeling a sense of loss if their depression remits, even though they are truly suffering while their depressive symptoms persist. As one client put it, "If I weren't depressed all the time, who would I be?" Although this is a rhetorical question, it begs a literal answer; therefore therapists should be ready to seize the moment to discuss the full range of personal qualities that comprise the client's identity, aside from his or her mood disorder. Similarly, some clients maintain at least partially favorable associations with being pessimistic, cynical, and even suicidal, such as clients who have artistic talents they associate with depression. As one client opined, "All the great writers were depressed." As one might guess, this client aspired to be a serious writer and was loath to give up his membership in such a desired club by becoming more upbeat about himself and his life. Another client openly stated that only people who are simpleminded could possibly be happy to exist in a polluted, violent, fickle, and unjust world such as the one in which we live. For her, feeling emotional relief in the form of a remitted depression would be akin to losing her intelligence. Upon ascertaining this problematic client belief, the therapist would now attempt to discuss the possibility that the client could maintain her personal strength of high intellect while still working to become a happier, more hopeful person. For example, a homework assignment could involve the client's making a list of the persons that he or she knows who seem to possess both good intellect and a generally upbeat demeanor. How does the client account for this? Can the client adapt and emulate this combination of characteristics? These are the sorts of questions that can be entertained in session.

An interesting twist on the above theme occurs when clients point to *you (their therapist)* as being someone who is both smart and optimistic. Sometimes this leads the client to wonder aloud whether you are *really* as positive as you purport to be or whether it is just something you are "supposed to do" when you are a therapist (with the implication that you are not being entirely genuine). Therapists should be prepared to discuss this issue frankly, all toward the goal of helping the client to modify the belief that feeling positively is a sign of not really knowing what's going on. This discussion *really* starts to get interesting if the depressed client believes that you (the therapist) are sincerely happy and therefore doubts your intelligence! Either way, it is all (as they say) "grist for the mill."

When Depressed Clients Are "Phobic" About Hope

Few therapists would argue against the notion that maintaining hopefulness helps people to be more resilient in the face of life stressors. However, some depressed clients seem to be averse to the idea of "getting their hopes up," and are steadfast in their beliefs that nothing can help, and that there is nothing to be done. Rather than getting into an intellectual and philosophical argument with such clients about the merits of feeling hopeful, or risking invalidating their psychological pain and suffering by implying that their feelings of hopelessness are necessarily maladaptive, therapists can *conceptualize* the client's shunning of hope and provide accurate empathy for their apparent "phobia" about hope. By asking the clients about their subjective experiences in "having [their] hopes dashed," we may be able to understand why they recoil from interventions that are designed to help them think more optimistically.

First, in order to be accurately empathic, clinicians need to ask the clients to explain their misgivings about feeling hopeful, and to provide feedback that is understanding of their position. For example, a depressed young woman explained that she planned to return to the college from which she had taken a leave of absence due to her severe depression and hospitalization. She stated to the therapist that she had very low expectations about her ability to readjust to college life and to succeed academically, and that she did not dare to get her hopes up this time around. The following is a summary of the dialogue that ensued:

> Client (C): Everyone is saying that it's great that I'm going back to school and that I should be happy, but I'm just miserable, and I don't see any way that I'm going to be able to cope. Just setting foot on that campus is going to make me feel sick again.
>
> Therapist (T): I guess others are very hopeful for you, but you are having some serious doubts. Help me understand your doubts.
>
> C: I had big hopes when I started school, and it was all just a setup for a disaster. Now I am prepared for the worst. I can't ignore the reality that I may have another breakdown. I'm not going to get my hopes up just to get slammed again.
>
> T: I can understand why you have some concerns about returning to school after what happened last time. [Pause] At the same time, I wonder if you can be prepared for the stressors ahead and still maintain some hope that things will be okay. I don't think that being hopeful is necessarily the same thing as being unprepared to deal with things. What do you think?
>
> C: If I let myself have hope, I'm asking for trouble. If I just expect the worst, then I can't be disappointed.
>
> T: Is it okay if we examine what you just said as a *belief*, rather than as a fact?
>
> C: How so?

T: When you say that you can't be disappointed if you expect the worst, that's a hypothesis. The same thing goes for your belief that if you feel hopeful it will cause trouble. I think we should evaluate these thoughts, because I think you can modify them and still be prepared to handle school again.

C: I just think that the safe thing is to give up my hopes of ever finishing school. [Tearful]

T: Well, it may be "safe" in one sense, but it makes you upset just to think about that possibility. I have had the impression all along that it's really important to you to return to school and get your degree. I want to help you get there, but I think we need to look at your belief that it is foolhardy to have hope. I think that if we combine *hope with a plan*, we can utilize some optimism to *help* to you achieve your goals.

C: It just seems so risky. I don't know if I can cope with another major disappointment.

T: That's assuming that you don't succeed. How disappointed will you be if you never try?

C: I guess I would regret not going back, but I'm just so afraid.

T: That means we have to put together a coping plan, so that you can move forward with hope—not as a setup for a letdown, but as a way to give you the best chance to move forward and achieve your goals. Having *hope plus a plan* means that you're not just wishing upon a star. You are really investing yourself in the best way possible, to maximize your chances of improving your life.

As one can see from this dialogue, it would be easy but misguided for the therapist simply to assume that the client "really doesn't want to go back to school." It is far more instructive to view the client's reactions as reflecting a problematic ambivalence, whereby the client would like to believe that she can pursue an important goal, but she is inhibited by fear, along with the negative belief that striving and hoping can only be trouble for someone so vulnerable. It is also apparent from the dialogue that the client is not going to relinquish her "hope phobia" just because the therapist makes a few comments to the contrary. It is going to require a concerted, collaborative effort to examine her beliefs, to generate alternatives, and to test these alternatives little by little in the form of experiential exposures (e.g., imagery exercises) and/or behavioral experiments (e.g., to "set foot on campus" and to see if she feels "sick," as she predicted).

The Mistake of Micromanaging the Client's Thinking

Identifying and modifying the clients' maladaptive thought processes is central to CBT for depression, and there is strong evidence that clients who learn to implement these skills for themselves make significant progress in treatment (Strunk, Chiu,

DeRubeis, & Alvarez, 2007; Tang, Beberman, DeRubeis, & Pham, 2005). Nevertheless, too much of a good thing can be counterproductive at times, such as when the therapist is hypervigilant to each and every client thought that may need to modified. If the therapist calls the client's attention to too many purportedly maladaptive thoughts in too short a space of time, it may be harmful to the sense of rapport and collaboration that is so important to the process of treatment. Clients often need some time and space in which to vent their concerns, and to believe that their story has been sufficiently heard before they will be optimally responsive to what the therapist has to say in return. If the therapist challenges each and every maladaptive thought in a rapid-fire manner, the client may respond negatively, perceiving that he or she is being psychologically micromanaged. Instead, the therapist would do well to add some reflection and empathy in the process, so as to make the process of questioning the client's thinking a bit more congenial. The following two vignettes illustrate a *problematic* way and a *productive* way to question the functionality of the client's thoughts respectively.

1. Do *not* question the client's thoughts in the following manner:

Client (C): I'm always depressed and anxious because things never work out for me, so it's ridiculous for me to feel calm and confident.

Therapist (T): Is it really true that you are *always* anxious? That sounds rather black and white.

C: Well, I'm anxious a lot of the time, and that's why I'm such a wreck who can't face anything.

T: There you go again, labeling yourself, calling yourself a *wreck*, and then being black and white in your thinking by saying that you can't face *anything*.

C: There are so many things I should be doing, and I can't bring myself to do them because I'm so overwhelmed, and tired, and beaten down, and know I'm just making things worse for myself. I can't just talk my way out of this. I'm messing things up and I don't know how to feel otherwise.

T: The way you condemn yourself in such absolute terms, it's no wonder you feel so depressed and so stuck.

C: But I can't just pretend that things are okay when they're not!

T: Now you're engaging in black-and-white thinking again, and you're negatively filtering what I'm saying as well. I didn't say that you should pretend that everything is fine, because obviously some things are going badly in your life.

C: That's all I'm trying to say in the first place. I don't know. I'm getting confused with this conversation.

2. *Do* question the client's thoughts in the following manner:

Client (C): I'm always anxious because things never work out for me, so it's ridiculous for me to feel calm and confident.

Therapist (T): I think that feeling more calm and confident would be a worthy goal for you, but tell me more about what you mean.

C: No matter how hard I try, I'm just too tired and beaten down to follow through with my plans, and nothing gets done, and I just feel like a complete failure. I can't even do the therapy homework you give me each week. I'm not getting anywhere.

T: I know you're frustrated and upset. I agree that it's hard to be productive when you're depressed, but I'm noticing that your self-criticisms are very punishing. I wonder if we can work together to make your self-criticisms more *constructive*.

C: How can I do that? How would that help?

T: I would be happy to explain. When you angrily call yourself a *complete failure*, it's going to make you feel worse and it won't tell you what you can change, or how to change it. Maybe we can just agree that you are depressed, and far from your best right now, but we can examine what's going on for you to see what sorts of changes would be reasonable and helpful, even now when you're feeling so bad.

C: But I'm not even doing the homework. I'm just letting things fall apart.

T: What are the things that are "falling apart" that we can constructively discuss right now?

C: Aside from not doing my therapy homework? Well, my apartment is a complete wreck, just like I am. I haven't done laundry or dealt with my mail for weeks, I'm behind schedule on some important work assignments, and my friends are giving up on me.

T: For starters, I don't perceive you as being a "wreck," and I am not going to give up on you. I would like to invite you not to give up on yourself either. Instead, let's start working constructively on some of these problems you've just mentioned.

C: I don't think I'm going to be able to make any changes.

T: I know that's what you believe. I hear you, and I take what you're saying seriously. I also know that your comments are a reflection of your depressive thinking, which has become a habit for you. If it's okay with you, I am going to look at your thoughts as being starting points, rather than ending points.

C: What does that mean, exactly?

T: That means that instead of coming to negative *conclusions* before we even start, we are instead going to *test* your beliefs, perhaps by having you try to make gradual, positive changes, and see how it goes. In other words, let's not *prejudge*. Let's actually see what happens when we put together a positive plan and you try to do some of it for homework.

Note that in the first vignette, the therapist is so intent on immediately pointing out the client's myriad dysfunctional thoughts that he or she comes up short in being empathic. The client then feels compelled to justify himself or herself, the discussion moves toward argumentation, and the client simply feels more frustrated and confused. In the second example, the therapist takes the time to learn more about what the client means before giving feedback, and when he or she *does* give feedback it is mixed with empathy and support. Rather than simply contradicting or labeling the client's automatic thoughts, the therapist in the second example questions the level of harshness of the client's thoughts and invites him or her to begin the collaborative process of solving discrete problems. Good CBT is much more than simply swatting away negative thoughts as they emerge. It requires the therapist to be respectful about the ways that clients think, to communicate this understanding with empathy, and to encourage the clients to modify their problematic thoughts and beliefs in a manner that does not seem impatient or otherwise artificially rushed. Cognitive-behavioral therapists in training often believe (erroneously) that they are failing to perform CBT properly if their depressed clients leave a given session without having substantially changed their thinking styles or remitted from their depressive states. In real practice, many clients need additional time to ponder what has been discussed in session and to do their therapy homework assignments—perhaps over the course of numerous weeks—before they begin to modify their longstanding depressive cognitions. However, once the clients begin to master the methods they have learned in session, the positive changes can be quite significant, sweeping, and durable.

Conclusion

Cognitive-behavioral therapy (CBT) offers depressed clients numerous, powerful ways to monitor important aspects of their own functioning (with special emphasis on their thoughts, beliefs, and schemas), and to enact self-help interventions that are advantageous to the quality of their lives. Therapists are most helpful when they impart these skills in a spirit of "collaborative empiricism" (Beck et al., 1979), as they work as a team with the clients to formulate an evolving case conceptualization in the context of a supportive, genuine therapeutic relationship.

It is vitally important that CBT therapists emphasize the psycho-educational aspects of the treatment, so that the clients appreciate the need for them to learn skills that they can use effectively without the presence of the therapist. Success in this area is boosted by the regular use of homework assignments, which plays an important role in the long-term maintenance of gains in treatment.

As depression is a heterogeneous disorder, its treatment does not always follow a smooth, predictable course. This chapter has endeavored to illustrate the sorts of complications that can arise even in delivering an empirically supported treatment such as CBT for depression, including the serious topic of managing clients who are suicidal, as well as less serious difficulties that nonetheless threaten the process of treatment if not identified and addressed adequately (e.g., clients who fear getting their hopes up). The good news is that the practice of CBT for depression is very rewarding, inasmuch as therapists have a good chance of seeing their work come to fruition in the form of client improvement, and clients often emerge from CBT feeling hopeful and empowered.

References

Abramson, L. Y., Alloy, L. B., & Metalsky, G. I. (1995). Hopelessness depression. In G. M. Buchanan & M. E. P. Seligman (Eds.), *Explanatory style* (pp. 113–134). Hillside, NJ: Erlbaum.

American Psychiatric Association (2000). *Diagnostic and statistical manual of mental disorders* (4th ed., text rev.). Arlington, VA: Author.

Beck, A. T., Butler, A. C., Brown, G. K., Dahlsgaard, K. K., Newman, C. F., & Beck, J. S. (2001). Dysfunctional beliefs discriminate personality disorders. *Behaviour Research and Therapy*, *39*(10), 1213–1225.

Beck, A. T., Davis, D. D., & Freeman, A. (2004). *Cognitive therapy of personality disorders* (2nd ed.). New York, NY: Guilford Press.

Beck, A. T., Rush, A. J., Shaw, B. F., & Emery, G. (1979). *Cognitive therapy of depression*. New York, NY: Guilford Press.

Beck, A. T., Steer, R. A., Beck, J. S., & Newman, C. F. (1993). Hopelessness, depression, suicidal ideation, and clinical diagnosis of depression. *Suicide and Life-Threatening Behavior*, *23*, 139–145.

Beck, A. T., Steer, R. A., & Brown G. K. (1996). *Manual for the Beck Depression Inventory II*. San Antonio, TX: Psychological Corporation.

Beck, A. T., Steer, R. A., Kovacs, M., & Garrison, B. (1985). Hopelessness and eventual suicide: A 10-year prospective study of patients hospitalized with suicidal ideation. *American Journal of Psychiatry*, *142*, 559–563.

Beck, A. T., Steer, R. A., & Ranieri, W. F. (1988). Scale for suicide ideation: Psychometric properties of a self-report version. *Journal of Clinical Psychology*, *44*, 499–505.

Beck, A. T., Weissman, A., Lester, D., & Trexler, L. (1974). The measurement of pessimism: The hopelessness scale. *Journal of Consulting and Clinical Psychology*, *42*, 499–505.

Beck, A. T., Wenzel, A., Riskind, J. H., Brown, G., & Steer, R. A. (2006). Specificity of hopelessness about resolving life problems: Another test of the cognitive model of depression. *Cognitive Therapy and Research*, *30*(6), 773–781.

Beck, J. S. (1995). *Cognitive therapy: Basics and beyond*. New York, NY: Guilford Press.

Bennett-Levy, J., Butler, G., Fennell, M., Hackmann, A., Mueller, M., & Westbrook, D. (2004). *The Oxford guide to behavioural experiments in cognitive therapy*. Oxford, UK: Oxford University Press.

Blatt, S. J. (1995). The destructiveness of perfectionism: Implications for the treatment of depression. *American Psychologist*, *50*, 1003–1020.

Burns, D. D., & Spangler, D. L. (2000). Does psychotherapy homework lead to improvement in depression in cognitive behavioural psychotherapy or does improvement lead to increased homework compliance? *Journal of Consulting and Clinical Psychology*, *68*, 46–56.

DeRubeis, R. J., Hollon, D., Amsterdam, J. D., Shelton, R. C., Young, P. R., Salomon, R. N., . . . Gallop, R. (2005). Cognitive therapy vs. medication in the treatment of moderate to severe depression. *Archives of General Psychiatry*, *62*, 409–416.

Ellis, T. E. (Ed.). (2006). *Cognition and suicide: Theory, research, & therapy*. Washington, DC: American Psychological Association.

Ellis, T. E., & Newman, C. F. (1996). *Choosing to live: How to defeat suicide through cognitive therapy.* Oakland, CA: New Harbinger.

Evans, J. M. G., Williams, J., O'Loughlin, S., & Howells, K. (1992). Autobiographical memory and problem-solving strategies of para-suicide clients. *Psychological Medicine, 22,* 399–405.

First, M. B., Spitzer, R. L., Gibbon, M., & Williams, J. W. (1996). *Structured clinical interview for DSM-IV Axis-I disorders, clinician version (SCID-CV).* Washington, DC: American Psychiatric Association.

Giesen-Bloo, J., van Dyck, R., Spinhoven, P., van Tilburg, W., Dirksen, C., van Asselt, T., . . . Arntz, A. (2006). Outpatient psychotherapy for borderline personality disorder: Randomized trial of schema-focused cognitive therapy vs. transference-focused psychotherapy. *Archives of General Psychiatry, 63*(6), 649–658.

Gilbert, P., & Leahy, R. L. (Eds.) (2007). *The therapeutic relationship in the cognitive-behavioral psychotherapies.* London, UK: Routledge-Brunner.

Hewitt, P. L., Flett, G. L., & Weber, C. (1994). Dimensions of perfectionism and suicidal ideation. *Cognitive Therapy and Research, 10,* 439–460.

Hollon, S. D., DeRubeis, R. J., Shelton, R. C., Amsterdam, J. D., Salomon, R. M., O'Reardon, . . . Gallop, R. (2005). Prevention of relapse following cognitive therapy vs. medications in moderate to severe depression. *Archives of General Psychiatry, 62,* 417–422.

Kuyken, W., Padesky, C. A., & Dudley, R. (2009). *Collaborative case conceptualization: Working effectively with clients in cognitive-behavioral therapy.* New York, NY: Guilford Press.

Leahy, R. L., & Holland, S. J. (2000). *Treatment plans and interventions for depression and anxiety disorders: The clinician's toolbox.* New York, NY: Guilford Press.

Newman, C. F. (1991). Cognitive therapy and the facilitation of affect: Two case illustrations. *Journal of Cognitive Psychotherapy: An International Quarterly. 5*(4), 305–316.

Newman, C. F. (2005). Reducing the risk of suicide in clients with bipolar disorder: Interventions and safeguards. *Cognitive and Behavioral Practice, 12,* 76–88.

Newman, C. F., & Beck, A. T. (2009). Cognitive therapy. In R. M. Kaplan & B. J. Saddock (Eds.), *Comprehensive textbook of psychiatry* (9th ed., pp. 2857–2873). Baltimore, MD: Lippincott, Williams, & Wilkins.

Newman, C. F., Leahy, R. L., Beck, A. T., Reilly-Harrington, N., & Gyulai, L. (2001). *Bipolar disorder: A cognitive therapy approach.* Washington, DC: American Psychological Association.

Nezu, A. M., Nezu, C. M., & Perri, M. G. (1989). *Problem-solving therapy for depression: Theory, research, and clinical guidelines.* New York, NY: John Wiley & Sons.

O'Donohue, W. T., & Fischer, J. E. (Eds.) (2009). *General principles and empirically supported techniques of cognitive behavior therapy.* Hoboken, NJ: John Wiley & Sons.

Rees, C. S., McEvoy, P., & Nathan, P. R. (2005). Relationship between homework completion and outcome in cognitive behavior therapy. *Cognitive Behaviour Therapy, 34,* 242–247.

Schotte, D., & Clum, G. (1987). Problem-solving skills in suicidal psychiatric clients. *Journal of Consulting and Clinical Psychology, 55,* 49–54.

Scott, J., Stanton, B., Garland, A., & Ferrier, N. (2000). Cognitive vulnerability to bipolar disorder. *Psychological Medicine, 30,* 467–472.

Strunk, D. R., Chiu, A. W., DeRubeis, R. J., & Alvarez, J. (2007). Patients' competence in and performance of cognitive therapy skills: Relation to the reduction of relapse risk following treatment for depression. *Journal of Consulting and Clinical Psychology, 74*(2), 337–345.

Tang, T. Z., Beberman, R., DeRubeis, R. J., & Pham, T. (2005). Cognitive changes, critical sessions, and sudden gains in cognitive-behavioral therapy for depression. *Journal of Consulting and Clinical Psychology, 67,* 894–904.

Weishaar, M. E. (1996). Cognitive risk factors in suicide. In P. M. Salkovskis (Ed.), *Frontiers of cognitive therapy* (pp. 226–249). New York, NY: Guilford Press.

Wenzel, A., Brown, G. K., & Beck, A. T. (2009). *Cognitive therapy for suicidal clients: Scientific and clinical applications*. Washington, DC: American Psychological Association.

Whisman, M. (Ed.). (2008). *Adapting cognitive therapy for depression: Managing complexity and comorbidity*. New York, NY: Guilford Press.

Wright, J. H. (2004). Integrating cognitive-behavioral therapy and pharmacotherapy. In R. L. Leahy (Ed.), *Contemporary cognitive therapy: Theory, research, and practice* (pp. 341–366). New York, NY: Guilford Press.

Young, J. E., Klosko, J. S., & Weishaar, M. E. (2003). *Schema therapy: A practitioner's guide*. New York, NY: Guilford Press.

CHAPTER 4

Behavioral Activation for Depression

Jonathan W. Kanter, William M. Bowe, David E. Baruch, and Andrew M. Busch

Introduction

Behavioral Activation (BA) has a long history dating back to the late 1960s. During this history variants of BA have appeared, disappeared, and reappeared in new form. Currently two versions of BA are in widespread use (Lejuez, Hopko, & Hopko, 2001; Martell, Addis, & Jacobson, 2001) and these current versions have much in common with, and extend in significant ways, the earlier variants (Hopko, Lejuez, Ruggiero, & Eifert, 2003). Taking a historical perspective, it is clear that a number of techniques fall under the umbrella term BA, or the even larger umbrella term *behavior therapy* for depression (Kanter et al., 2010). A common technique across all variants of BA is the scheduling of specific activities for the client to complete between sessions. Thus, activity scheduling may be seen as the core of BA, and this core is strengthened by a variety of supplemental techniques. The skill of the BA therapist, as discussed later, is in determining what activities to assign, when in the course of therapy to assign them, maximizing the probability of successful completion of assigned activities, and determining when to use supplemental techniques.

Depending on training history, preferred theoretical orientation, and approach to psychotherapy, clinicians may have different reactions when it is suggested that they consider a *behavioral* model of disorder and treatment. Some may think behaviorism is cold, mechanical, superficial, and unable to foster the deep and meaningful psychotherapeutic relationships that many clients and therapists seek and feel are crucial to success (Skinner, 1974). In this chapter we aim to show that BA does not represent that kind of behaviorism, but that it is straightforward, sensible, and approachable, employing a rationale that clinicians and clients easily relate to and understand. The psychotherapeutic relationship in BA can be deep and meaningful, depending on the needs and desires of the client (and therapist). The techniques are easy to learn, are easy to implement, can be integrated without much disruption into ongoing work from other perspectives, and can be used cross-culturally with appropriate modifications and considerations. Most importantly, as Appendix B of this volume describes in detail, research indicates that BA, in terms of outcomes, is equivalent to, if not better than, other empirically supported psychotherapies and as effective as ongoing medication for the treatment of severe depression (Cuijpers, van Straten, & Warmerdam, 2007; Ekers, Richards, & Gilbody, 2008; Mazzucchelli, Kane, & Rees, 2009).

The empirical data in support of BA's effectiveness, in combination with BA's potential ease of dissemination and implementation, places BA at the cutting edge of an extremely important public health issue. Depression—the most burdensome disease in the world according to recent figures (Lopez, Mathers, Essati, Jamison, & Murray, 2006)—requires treatment strategies that are effective, easy to disseminate, and easy to implement for treatment to have maximum reach and impact at the public health level (Glasgow, Vogt, & Boles, 1999). With many individuals reporting reluctance to begin and maintain trials of antidepressant medications, and the majority of individuals reporting a preference for psychotherapy over medication for the treatment of depression, the development of effective psychotherapeutic strategies with BA's qualities becomes important. We believe the data support BA's use as a frontline treatment for a range of depressive presentations (mild to severe) and comorbidities. It also may be an effective adjunct to treatment of primary problems other than depression when depression is a part of the clinical presentation, or in any approach in which homework assignments are given to clients to change their behavior or engage in new behavior.

Theoretical Considerations

Effective psychotherapies, and the theories on which they are based, do not have to be complicated and should not be complicated if the goal is maximum cross-cultural reach. Although the theory of behaviorism on which BA is based is rich and detailed, offering a full account of human behavior in all its complexity (e.g., Skinner, 1953), a BA clinician does not need to be an expert in behavioral theory to understand and implement the techniques effectively. The behavioral theories of depression underlying the variants of BA that have been developed over the years vary from approach to approach but can be distilled into a simple, pragmatic model that is user-friendly for both clinicians and clients (Manos, Kanter, & Busch, 2010). Put nontechnically, the model is this: When people get depressed, they shut down and get stuck. BA, therefore, is about getting people unstuck and active again.

Put more technically, the model is this: Depression results from environments characterized by losses of, reductions in, or chronically low levels of positive, natural reinforcement. It is well known that when natural reinforcers are reduced or lost, behavior is weakened or extinguished (e.g., the person shuts down and gets stuck). BA, therefore, strategically employs behavioral principles to systematically activate the client to maintain and sustain contact with a diverse and stable set of personally meaningful positive reinforcers (see Kanter, Busch, & Rusch, 2009, for a full description of the behavioral model underlying BA).

To behaviorists, reinforcement is the most important piece of the puzzle of human behavior. Here we briefly review the two concepts of positive and negative reinforcement, which play a major role in BA's theory of depression and in provision of BA techniques.

Positive Reinforcement

The primary behavioral concept for clinicians to understand in this model is *positive reinforcement*. When people typically think of reinforcement, *enjoyable rewards* such as candy, tokens, and praise come to mind; when people typically think about scheduling contact with reinforcement in therapy (i.e., activity scheduling), *enjoyable activities* such as watching a movie, getting a massage, dancing, or playing with grandchildren come to mind. In BA, however, reinforcement is not just enjoyment. A positive reinforcer is defined functionally as *any consequence that, when it is introduced following a specific behavior, makes that behavior more likely to occur in the future*. These consequences can be things like candy or praise, but BA primarily is interested in more naturally occurring consequences. On a simple level, examples include the consequence of the car engine starting after the behavior of turning the ignition key, the consequence of a friendly voice on the phone after the behavior of dialing the phone, and the consequence of the warm sun on one's skin after the behavior of going outside for a walk on a nice day. On a more complex level, examples include the consequence of getting a job after months of the behavior of searching for employment, the consequence of increased trust and intimacy after the behavior of a risky self-disclosure to someone you care about, and the consequence of someone giving you what you want after the behavior of an appropriately made assertive request.

Thus, reinforcers in BA are defined not only in terms of what the client enjoys, but also in terms of activities that would bring a sense of mastery or satisfaction: problems to be solved, obstacles to be overcome, and behaviors that are not at all enjoyable but linked to deeply held values (e.g., giving a speech at a funeral, submitting to a necessary medical procedure). The goal is for the client to develop a repertoire of behavior maintained by a *diverse* and *stable* set of positive reinforcers. When this occurs in a person's life, he or she feels that life is rich and meaningful . . . and hopefully, but not necessarily, enjoyable.

Diversity of reinforcers is important such that if one reinforcer is lost, others are still in place. Thus, a recently widowed or retired client may reduce risk for clinical depression by having developed reinforcing pursuits independent of the deceased spouse or previous career; these clients may (and should) feel the appropriate pain of their losses, but the availability of alternate meaningful sources of positive reinforcement will be important in a healthy grieving process and preventing a spiral into clinical depression.

Stability is also important. Heroin, for example, is reinforcing but unstable as a reinforcer (requiring larger and larger doses) and thus is not a good choice as a reinforcer (among many other problems with heroin). Physical attractiveness also is relatively unstable. Thus, a relationship initiated primarily on the grounds of physical attractiveness initially may be reinforcing, but over time other more stable qualities of the partner hopefully become reinforcing if the relationship is to succeed in the long term.

Issues of diversity and stability come into play in BA when working with the client on identifying reinforcing activities to schedule. Ideally, a wide range of activities is identified, some simply that bring a sense of pleasure and enjoyment, others that solve problems, and others that connect the client with long-held values. Activities that lead to stable reinforcement are generally preferred. Thus, an assignment might be for a client, recently relocated in a new city, to travel to the old city to visit old friends. This should improve mood in the short run. A better plan would be to arrange for regular meetings between the client and these friends and to simultaneously help the client establish a new set of friends in the new city that will result in ongoing contact.

The importance of diversity and stability does not imply that it is wrong to be passionate about something in particular at the expense of other reinforcers. The issue is the diversity and stability of reinforcers within one's passion. A baseball player, for example, may be fully committed to a career as a professional; however, age and injury will eventually restrict this behavior. If this pursuit is controlled by being an all-star and breaking records, the risks—from our point of view—outweigh the potential benefits. However, a more complete appreciation for the sport of baseball will allow for reinforcing baseball-related endeavors well past one's athletic prime and could include coaching, broadcasting, writing, teaching one's children and grandchildren, and so on.

Negative Reinforcement

The second behavioral concept for clinicians to understand in this model is *negative reinforcement*. Negative reinforcement also is defined functionally as the process by which successful escape from or avoidance of aversive stimuli makes the escape and avoidance behavior more likely to occur again. For example, when a depressed individual stays in bed all morning, the responsibilities of the day are avoided. When one socially withdraws by not answering the phone, uncomfortable interactions are avoided. To the degree these consequences are salient to the individual, he or she is more likely to stay in bed and socially withdraw in the future. Thus, staying in bed and social withdrawal are seen as avoidance behaviors maintained by negative reinforcement. Avoidance may take the form of active behavior (e.g., giving an excuse for not joining friends to avoid social anxiety, overscheduling to avoid time alone) or general passivity (e.g., watching television all day, not calling a friend). Whether active or passive, the function remains the same—avoidance. Because these behaviors are reinforced, they may become stronger over time, resulting in a spiral into deeper and deeper depression. Instead of actively pursuing valued life goals and utilizing problem-solving skills for life difficulties, a client may become increasingly avoidant over time.

Examples of avoidance behavior in depression are endless and include staying in bed, sleeping too much, calling in sick to work, withdrawing from friends/ family, not doing housework, not looking for employment, drinking and drug use, overusing prescription meds, filling every minute of the day with social activity to avoid facing problems, and attempting suicide. In fact, when presented with the BA rationale, clients readily connect with the fact that avoidance provides a highly effective and immediate emotional coping strategy that, over the long term, strengthens depression.

Rumination is a common avoidance behavior in depressed clients and serves to illustrate how a careful analysis of negative reinforcement can inform treatment. From a behavioral perspective, rumination must provide reinforcement or else it would cease to occur. Often rumination functions as negative reinforcement as it allows a client to be ''lost in thought'' instead of contacting aversive realities or may allow a client to temporarily reduce the pain of past memories or failed interactions. When this occurs, the goal for clients would be to activate more effective, alternative behaviors in situations that evoke rumination. For example, clients may initiate active problem solving that leads to a concrete ''To-Do'' list as opposed to simply stewing about problems. The distinction between a BA approach to rumination versus cognitive restructuring is an important one. Clients are not directed to challenge the content of rumination; rather, clients learn to respond differently to situations that have reinforced ruminating behavior. From a behavioral perspective, this approach helps clients break the reinforcing chain of negative reinforcement and thereby prepares clients to contact diverse and stable sources of reinforcement for healthy, nondepressed behavior.

General Principles of Behavioral Activation

When conducting BA, several general principles are important to keep in mind (Table 4.1). At a basic level, these principles are foundational to any behavioral intervention, not just BA.

Table 4.1 General Principles of Behavioral Activation

Principle	Description
1.	Behavior is best understood functionally, not formally.
2.	BA is best accomplished functionally, not formally.
3.	BA is active, concrete, and focused on the details of client's lives.
4.	BA is focused on the present, not the past.
5.	BA is focused on behavioral, not cognitive, change.

Behavior Is Best Understood Functionally, Not Formally

How do we define any behavior? In BA, it is useful to define behavior in terms of its function rather than its form. Consider a simple activity that would be typical of an activity assignment in BA: gardening. On a formal level (i.e., the *form* of the behavior), gardening involves pulling up weeds, watering the plants, and so forth. But this description tells us little about what is clinically relevant about this behavior. Clinically, rather than exactly *what* the person is doing, we usually want to know *why* the person is gardening (knowing *what* a target behavior is in detail is also important for developing good assignments, which will be discussed later). Is gardening a naturally positive reinforcing activity that the client used to do regularly before becoming depressed? Alternately, perhaps gardening is seen by the client as an unpleasant task, completed to escape continued complaining from one's spouse? Alternately, perhaps the client is lost in thought while gardening, aimlessly pulling weeds but mostly ruminating about a recent fight with his mother? In the first case, gardening is a specific instance of contact with positive reinforcement. In the second case, gardening is a specific instance of negatively reinforced behavior (behavior that stops or avoids something aversive). In the third case, the client is not really gardening at all, and the behavior of interest is ruminating (also negative reinforcement).

Thinking about and describing behavior functionally requires an understanding of positive and negative reinforcement, as discussed earlier. The best way to improve one's skill at thinking about and describing behavior functionally is to always ask about the potential future and achieved past consequences of the behavior. Questions include:

➤ How has the behavior affected others or the environment in the past? And currently?

➤ What is a behavior in the service of?

➤ What has the behavior produced in the past (i.e., positive reinforcement)? And currently?

➤ What has the behavior removed, stopped, or avoided in the past (i.e., negative reinforcement)? And currently?

A full-functional analysis of behavior would also include assessing the contexts in which specific behavior occurs. Later we discuss this more in-depth analysis, but the important point for now is that to understand a behavior's function, the therapist should inquire about the consequences.

BA Is Best Accomplished Functionally, Not Formally

Although BA is a behavioral approach, the therapist does not need to *sound* like a behaviorist in the therapy room. Therapists do not need to describe the rationale with terms such as *reinforcement* or *extinction*. BA therapists use language that is functional, contextual, and pragmatic. We have encountered some behavior therapists who insist on using behavioral terminology with their colleagues and clients; while this may work with like-minded individuals, it may limit effective communication with others (especially those from other cultures). BA allows for the flexible, functional use of language rather than a dogmatic insistence on behavioral terminology.

Therapy also should be conducted functionally. Although this chapter and other manuals on BA provide the therapist specific instructions on what to do in session, these instructions also always should be applied with an eye toward what is working in the therapy room. Thus, we suggest a very specific structure for the therapy session (discussed later), but upholding that structure should not be the priority. The priority in BA always concerns the questions, *Is the client getting active and is the client's mood responding to that activity?* However this happens is fine with BA as long as it happens. No specific form, structure, or technique is mandatory.

Thus, the best BA therapists are those who deeply understand the model and tailor it creatively to the unique presentations of their clients. For example, consider a depressed client who was already very active, spending long hours looking and applying for employment and scheduling lots of activities, such as going to the movies, with friends. The client also reported that she had lost several friends who "could not handle how depressed I am." The therapist, a student trainee who had just learned the BA model, wanted to schedule some activities with the client in the first session (a good idea), and when the client reported what she was already doing, the therapist encouraged the client to keep doing those activities and planned out several of them in detail, including going to the movies with a friend.

Missing from this sequence of events was an attempt by the therapist to understand the behavior functionally. For example, when detailing a plan for going to the movies, the client reported that she used to like going to the movies by herself, but now if she does anything alone she is overwhelmed and is unable to do daily tasks alone (e.g., going to the grocery store). A goal for treatment could actually be spending more time alone. Thus, a better assignment would have been for the therapist to encourage the client to go to the movies by herself. Although in general most people prefer to see movies with friends, in this client's case the avoidance of being alone had become problematic and pervasive.

BA Is Active, Concrete, and Focused on the Details of Clients' Lives

We have heard over and over this common complaint from depressed clients about past therapists: "He was really nice, he listened to me and let me talk, but he rarely said anything and didn't seem to have any ideas about what I should do differently." A recent client compared work with the first author to a past therapist: "I would talk through most of the session, and then at the end she would encourage me to stay busy and fill my weekends with activities, but with you we spend most of our time on *how to do that*—you don't just tell me I should do it and leave it up to me."

Helping clients with how to successfully engage in life again requires being active, concrete, and focused on the details of clients' lives. Consider the following interaction from Kanter and colleagues (2009, p. 105):

> Client (C): Last week was a bad week. I just stayed in bed the whole time and didn't do my homework.
>
> Therapist (T): You do seem really depressed this week. We really need to figure out how to get you out of bed and get you active again.
>
> C: I know I do. It is just so hard—I feel like my whole body is just screaming at me to stay in bed. I'm just so miserable, I feel like I'll never have a life again.
>
> T: Wow. It really is hard to activate when you're feeling that way. But I feel confident that if you get active, you'll start to build the life you want.

This interaction sounds like BA because it is focused on the client's activity level and the clinician is emphasizing activation. Such an interaction would be typical at the beginning of therapy. However, there is much room for improvement in terms of a typical BA interaction. It could be less abstract, more concrete, more focused on the function of the client's behavior, and more focused on exactly what the client can do differently. Consider an alternative to this interaction (modified from Kanter et al., 2009, p. 106):

> C: Last week was a bad week. I pretty much just stayed in bed the whole time and didn't do my homework.
>
> T: You do seem really depressed this week. We really need to figure out how to get you out of bed and get you active again. Can we spend a few minutes on this?
>
> C: Sure.
>
> T: Good. First, you said you were in bed the whole week, but you must have gotten out of bed a few times.
>
> C: Well, I got out of bed earlier on Tuesday.
>
> T: How did you manage that?

C: I just forced myself, I guess.

T: Well, let's figure this out. What time did you get up? How long did you lie in bed after your alarm went off? What did you have to do that day? How late were you up the night before?

In this alternative, the clinician immediately moves from an abstract discussion of the importance of activation to a concrete analysis of a specific instance in the client's life. The clinician wants to understand this instance of behavior in enough detail such that specific, concrete recommendations can be made to help the client activate in that particular situation. We would then expect the client and clinician to continue this discussion, possibly for 5 or 10 minutes, until they have achieved a specific plan for what the client will do to get out of bed on specific days. Developing these plans is the heart of good BA. Without these detailed plans, one may suggest that the clinician is *talking about BA* but not *doing BA*.

BA Is Focused on the Present, Not the Past

It should be clear by now that BA is a present-focused intervention, and the mechanism of action of BA involves changing the client's present behavior. That does not mean, however, that a BA therapist has no interest in the client's past. In fact, understanding the past is important in helping the therapist understand the functions of the client's current behavior, because these functions were determined in the past. It also can be recognized that some important functions may have been determined early in life (e.g., a history of abuse that has led to a pervasive pattern of fear and avoidance of genuine intimate relations with men); thus even discussions of early childhood can be appropriate in BA. In general, clients expect some discussion of their life histories, and therapists may devote some time to this, in the service of such general understanding, providing empathy and developing a good therapeutic relationship.

That said, insight into the past is not the mechanism of BA, and insight into the past *without action in the present* is useless from a BA perspective. Thus, the majority of a BA session should be focused on understanding a client's current environment and current events in the client's life, so action plans for how the client can behave differently can be developed. This is often pitched to the client as "I expect us to discuss the parts of your past that are directly affecting your current behavior."

BA Is Focused on Behavioral, Not Cognitive, Change

In this chapter, we describe BA as a behavioral intervention, but sometimes it is loosely thought of as a cognitive-behavioral intervention as well. The terms *cognitive*, *behavioral*, and *cognitive-behavioral* have been used differently over the years. For example, Dobson and Dozois (2001), in Dobson's (2001) well-used *Handbook of Cognitive-Behavioral Therapies*, suggest that all cognitive-behavioral therapies share three fundamental propositions: (1) cognitive activity affects behavior, (2) cognitive activity may be monitored and altered, and (3) desired behavior change may be affected through cognitive change. By this definition, BA is *not* a cognitive-behavioral therapy!

BA instead focuses on behavior change directly, without assuming that mediating cognitive variables need to change in order to change behavior. There is nothing in BA's theory that states that behavior change cannot be achieved through cognitive change—it is just that cognitive change is not necessarily the only or the best way to achieve behavior change. In fact, several lines of research support the notion that cognitive change is not required for good outcomes in depression treatment (Longmore & Worrell, 2007).

In therapy, however, unless the therapist is in a research trial that *requires* the therapist to avoid implementing cognitive interventions such as restructuring techniques, there is no need for the therapist to dogmatically avoid any discussion of cognition. The primary issue is that cognitive restructuring interventions, in the context of a larger BA rationale that states that the goal is to get active *regardless of negative thoughts and feelings*, can potentially be confusing for clients. Thus, this chapter presents several ways that clinicians can respond to cognitive problems in ways that are consistent with the BA rationale.

Assessment in Behavioral Activation

As a behavior therapy, it is important in BA to assess change in depressive symptoms and behavior change over the course of treatment. Many options for measuring depressive symptoms exist (e.g., Cusin, Yang, Yeung, & Fava, 2010; Hopko, Lejuez, Armento, & Bare, 2004; Nezu, Ronan, Meadows, & McClure, 2000); many BA therapists find the Beck Depression Inventory II (BDI-II; Beck, Steer, & Brown, 1996) or Depression Anxiety Stress Scale (DASS; S. Lovibond & P. Lovibond, 1995) to be useful options as measures of depressive and related symptoms. In BA, a measure such as the BDI-II may be given in the waiting room before the session and quickly scored and checked at the beginning of the session (the BDI-II also affords a useful one-item check on suicidality).

It also is important to assess for behavior change related to BA targets on a regular basis in BA (Manos et al., in press). For this purpose, therapists may use some of the forms discussed later such as activity-monitoring forms, create forms such as simple diary cards to track specific behaviors, or use published measures. Recently, two measures assessing reinforcement and activation have been developed that can be easily inserted into BA practice (given along with the BDI-II before the session). The Behavioral Activation for Depression Scale (BADS; Kanter, Mulick, Busch, Berlin, & Martell, 2007) is a 25-item scale that measures activation and avoidance behaviors relevant to BA. The BADS was designed to be sensitive to weekly changes in activation and avoidance behaviors and therefore provides the BA therapist with a sense of the client's general level of activation to supplement progress made on specific activation assignments. In addition, the Environmental Reward Observation Scale (EROS; Armento & Hopko, 2007) is a 10-item measure that assesses client's subjective experience of reinforcement in his or her daily life. Given that BA posits that depression is caused by the loss of stable and diverse sources of positive reinforcement, the EROS provides a means to track changes in client report of contacted reinforcement. Recently, the Response Probability Index (RPI; Carvalho et al., in press) was developed as an improvement on the EROS and also may be considered as a brief useful measure of this process. While the BADS may be given weekly, the EROS and RPI reference longer periods.

The Therapy Relationship in Behavioral Activation

In BA, as in all therapies, the therapist develops a good therapeutic relationship characterized by warmth, empathy, and genuineness. The therapist is like a coach who has studied the client's depression and current situation and can offer expert guidance, advice, and support to help the client become reengaged in life. In the end, of course, it is the client who must do the work, and it is the client who has direct access to the details of his or her environment and behavior. By working collaboratively, the client and the BA therapist can custom tailor activation assignments. To help make such a collaboration a reality, BA therapists can foster confidence in the basic BA rationale of activating clients via specific, concrete assignments, but do so in a way that they do not dictate or define activation assignments for clients. Instead emphasis can be placed on using assessment information and constant feedback from the client on what the client feels would be a graded improvement, what might be a useful next step, and what the client feels would be challenging, useful, and would produce a sense of accomplishment. Activation assignments may be presented as useful experiments to try, and the outcomes may be discussed collaboratively to bring about a useful next step.

The Structure of Behavioral Activation

In this section, we review the structure of sessions and therapy in behavioral activation.

Session Structure

A BA session typically follows the standard session structure of cognitive-behavioral interventions (Beck, 1995) in which the client's mood and symptoms are reviewed, an agenda is set, previous homework is reviewed, new homework is assigned, and the therapist asks for feedback or summarizes the session at the end (Table 4.2). Homework review and assignment are central to BA and allow the therapist and the client to discuss the details of the client's life in the context of specific activation assignments.

Table 4.2 A Typical BA Session Structure

Element	Description
1.	Brief review of symptoms (e.g., BDI-II)
2.	Set agenda
3.	Review of previous week's homework assignments
	Assess and problem solve failure to complete assignments
4.	Collaborative development of new homework assignments
	Assess and problem solve potential obstacles to completion
5.	Feedback and session summary

As stated earlier, the session structure should not be applied dogmatically. As always, we recommend the clinician think functionally: For which clients will less structure be helpful, and for which clients will more structure be helpful? For example, some clients will resist the structure, and it will be in their interests to help them become more structured. This is particularly the case for clients whose lives outside of therapy are similarly unstructured and chaotic. For such a client, the clinician may provide a rationale for structuring the sessions:

> I think the issue is that having a chaotic life is a risk for depression for you, because it makes it less likely that you'll accomplish your goals for the day or the week. Part of what I have to suggest is a degree of structure that will be new for you. When people say "I don't like structure," it is usually because the structure is imposed by others—things people have to do that others want them to do or that they feel they should do. I want your days to feel less chaotic, more organized, more structured, but it will be a structure that YOU design (with my help), a structure that works for YOU, not one that I SAY you should do or that SOME BOOK says you should do, but one that you really feel captures what is important and meaningful to you. And a good place to start is to make sure that our sessions are structured, to make sure that we accomplish in here what is important and meaningful to you.

Therapy Structure

Variants of BA offer different guidelines on the degree to which therapy follows a structured course. BATD (Lejuez et al., 2001) offers a specific step-by-step protocol in which six units are delivered over 10 to 12 sessions. These units are: (1) introduction, (2) recognizing depression, (3) providing a rationale, (4) preparing for treatment, (5) getting started, and (6) charting progress, with the bulk of the work conducted in the last two units. BA by Martell and colleagues (Martell, Addis, & Jacobson, 2001; Dimidjian, Martell, Addis, & Herman-Dunn, 2008; Martell, Dimidjian, & Herman-Dunn, 2010) highlights the idiographic application of treatment strategies and only offers a general course that treatment may follow. This course is: (1) orienting to treatment, (2) developing treatment goals, (3) individualizing activation and

Figure 4.1 Course of Therapy

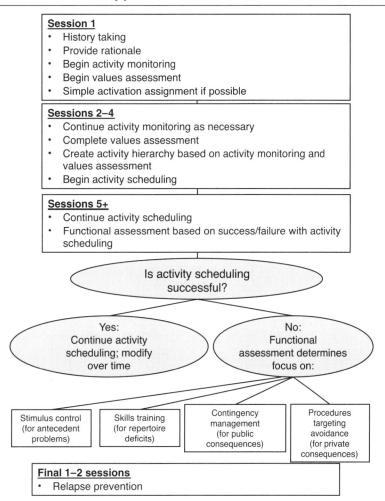

engagement targets, (4) repeatedly applying and troubleshooting activation and engagement strategies, and (5) reviewing and consolidating treatment gains.

The structure obviously should be tailored to the needs of the client and settings of the therapist. In Figure 4.1 we suggest a course of therapy that is initially structured but becomes more flexible over time (Kanter et al., 2009). Specifically, Session 1 includes standard history taking and completing the intake interview, providing the BA rationale, beginning behavioral assessment, and provision of initial activation assignments. Sessions 2 through 4 continue behavioral assessment in order to create an activity hierarchy, which essentially functions like a case conceptualization in BA. During this time, additional activation assignments are given and reviewed. The initial hierarchy can be modified throughout therapy and guides activation assignments in subsequent sessions.

For many clients, these initial activation assignments will be successful and lead to a reduction in depressive symptoms. For these clients, no supplemental interventions will be required. For other clients, however, these initial activation attempts will not be successful and supplemental, more complex interventions will be required. This chapter provides a functional assessment (FA) strategy for the therapist to assess specific obstacles to successful activation. Supplemental interventions are linked to categories of obstacles identified by the FA, providing the BA therapist a simple guide to determine which supplemental strategies to employ for which client problems. This sequence, in which activity scheduling is employed in a fairly structured format, followed by additional techniques tailored to the specific needs of clients only for those for whom activity scheduling alone was not successful, may have several advantages and is an attempt to capitalize on BA's existing strengths of parsimony, ease of implementation, and flexibility.

A particularly cost-effective way to deliver this version of BA is with a combined group and individual approach. In this approach, the therapist initially meets individually with each client to provide the rationale and to develop an initial list of activation targets. This is done in a single session. Then, the client joins a group that meets weekly to review activation assignments and schedule new assignments. This group has a rolling admission where clients may join and leave as appropriate. For clients who are doing well, they may stay in the group and help new clients with their assignments. For clients who are not responding, their group meetings may be supplemented by individual meetings with a therapist who performs the functional assessment and provides more complex interventions to help the client complete activation assignments. Although the current chapter focuses on an individual approach, the strategies may easily be modified for this group approach.

Providing a Rationale in Behavioral Activation

In the first session or two of BA, the clinician will provide two rationales, one for how depression is understood in BA and one for the provision of BA techniques.

Providing a Rationale for the Provision of BA Techniques

The clinician can begin therapy with a simple rationale for the provision of BA techniques:

> When people get depressed, they shut down. This treatment is about getting you active again. Our goal will be to develop action plans and goals for you, and then help you act according to these plans or goals rather than according to your feelings. Our goal will be to first identify how you have shut down, what you have stopped doing, what you are actively avoiding, what gives you a sense of pleasure, what gives you a sense of accomplishment, and what you really, truly care about. Then, our goal will be to activate you to reengage in life, experience more pleasure and accomplishment, start doing what you have stopped, approach the things you are avoiding, solve major life problems, and act consistently with what you really care about.

Some additional phrases to explain the rationale that BA therapists have found helpful include:

Typically we think of acting from the "inside-out" where we wait to feel motivated or inspired before completing tasks. The problem is, we may be waiting a long time for this to happen. Our treatment is about getting you moving now, before you feel better. We are going to try acting from "outside-in," where we behave first and feel later. (This notion of acting from the outside-in was highlighted by Martell et al., 2001, p. 95.)

While typically we may believe that we act according to our moods, your goal will be to learn how to act according to a plan, not a mood, and we will come up with that plan together to best meet your goals. (This notion of following a plan, not a mood, is described as a fundamental principle of BA by Martell et al., 2010, p. 27.)

Have you heard of the phrase, "Plan your work and work your plan"? That is essentially what we will do. In here we will come up with the plan, then during the week you will work it.

I believe that the key to changing how people feel is helping them change what they do. Can you think of times when you were feeling lousy but got up and did something, and that helped you feel better? (This notion of changing what one does in order to change how one feels is described as another fundamental principle of BA by Martell et al., 2010, p. 22.)

Providing a Rationale for Depression

Next, the clinician may describe how depression is understood in BA with the "Two Circles Model" (Figure 4.2). This model depicts the basic relation between environment and behavior that is fundamental in general to behaviorism and specifically to BA. In this model, an arrow depicts how negative life events lead to common responses, which may lead to more negative life events, and this spiral results in clinical depression.

Figure 4.2 The General Two Circles Model

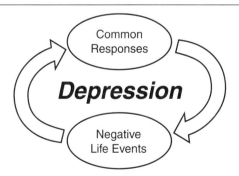

Circle 1: Negative Life Events Clients may present in therapy with a variety of negative life events, problems, daily hassles, stressors, and the like. These negative life events can include:

➤ Divorce, marital stress, and dissatisfaction with or lack of intimate relationships.

➤ Difficulties with obtaining and maintaining employment with a livable wage.

➤ Health problems of all sorts including obesity, physical pain from injuries, and chronic health conditions such as diabetes.

➤ Daily hassles that are increased exponentially when living in poverty or lacking social support, such as use of public transportation, car maintenance, paying the bills, finding quality daycare if employed, and lack of insurance.

➤ Conflicts with friends or family members or lack of friends and family.

➤ Direct and indirect experiences of racism and racial, sexual, gender, or other forms of discrimination.

➤ Isolation from family and friends and loss of extended social support network and community if having recently moved to a new area.

➤ Experiences of trauma and violence.

➤ Disruptive "positive" events including pregnancy and childbirth.

➤ Other major losses, such as widowhood, death of loved ones.

The BA therapist determines collaboratively with the client the specific nature of the problems and stressors causing low mood. Some clients may report just one or two discrete problems or losses, such as death in the family, divorce, or recent unemployment. Others will report on the accrual of multiple smaller hassles and stressors. Others will have been living in chronically stressful and deprived environments for so long that they will at first have no losses to report on, because nothing new has happened or changed in quite some time. Regardless, undoubtedly there will be problems, and it is the job of the BA therapist to emphasize that many of the symptoms of depression make sense given these problems. The therapist should develop a list of these negative life events, write them down, and share them with the client. The therapist may call them "negative life events" and draw a circle around them.

Circle 2: Common Responses It is a natural human response, when bad things happen (either major events, the accrual of smaller events, or the combination), to feel bad and to become passive. We call these *common responses* to emphasize that they are common and that the client is not weak, unusual, or crazy for having them. The important point for the BA therapist to stress is that these responses are common and make sense. Anyone would feel this way given the client's situation. In this model, common responses include cognitive, emotional, and behavioral responses of the client including negative thoughts, lowered self-esteem, depressed mood, anger, irritability, avoidance, passivity, and giving up; in other words, the full psychological response of the client is relevant here. Some common emotional responses include:

- Sadness
- Feeling down
- Feeling blue
- Crying more
- Feeling depressed
- Experiencing less pleasure in things
- Grief reactions
- Fear
- Stress
- Physical symptoms
- Fatigue
- Anger, irritability
- Guilt
- Shame
- Despair
- Hopelessness

The client may also demonstrate a range of behavioral common responses to the negative life events, including the escape and avoidance behaviors discussed earlier:

- Passivity
- Avoidance
- Not wanting to go out any more (e.g., to church)
- Staying in bed
- Sleeping too much
- Calling in sick to work
- Withdrawing from friends/family
- Stopping housework
- Stopping looking for employment or only pretending to look for employment
- Drinking too much, smoking, using drugs, overusing prescription meds
- Filling every minute of the day to avoid facing problems
- Watching television for long periods of time
- Lashing out at others, including family and children
- Eating too much junk food
- Trying to kill oneself
- Acting like life is already over

It is the therapist's task in BA to understand the client's common responses to the negative life events, whatever they are, and to validate and normalize them. As this discussion is occurring, the therapist may develop a list of the client's common responses, write them down, and label them *common responses*. The therapist may circle the list and draw an arrow from the negative life events to the common responses to show that they are an understandable response to the events.

Although emphasizing to the client that these responses are natural and normal and make sense given the negative life events, it is also emphasized that unfortunately these responses, especially the behavioral avoidance responses, tend to produce even more negative life events and create a spiral into depression. This is suggested by drawing an arrow back to the "negative life events" circle from the "common responses" circle. Clients almost always see this point readily and agree that their responses have just made things worse. Thus, the BA therapist compassionately explains to the client that treatment will help the client respond to life events proactively with activation rather than behavioral common responses. This is done by giving the client specific activation assignments based on his or her specific problems, and working closely with the client on designing activation assignments that will succeed.

Strengths of BA's Rationales

We believe these simple rationales are a key strength of BA, because they are simple, easy to understand by clients, and easy to learn and apply by therapists. Research has suggested that these rationales also may be more helpful than traditional explanations of depression that emphasize biological factors in terms of reducing stigma about being depressed and receiving treatment for depression (Rusch, Kanter, & Brondino, 2009; Rusch, Kanter, Brondino, Weeks, & Bowe, 2010). The rationales also are relatively unencumbered by psychological constructs that may complicate adaptation and translation of the rationale for different cultures and languages; instead the BA rationales emphasize negative life events and empowering individuals to persevere in the face of difficult life circumstances, certainly globally accepted experiences and goals (e.g., Santiago-Rivera et al., 2008).

The rationales also do not require psychological sophistication and thus may be useful for clients without well-developed language skills for talking about feelings. For example, when reviewing common responses, some clients may not report any feelings in response to negative life events. For example, in response to the question, "How are you feeling in response to all this?" a recent client said, "I just can't do anything anymore." When the therapist probed again for emotional responses, the client again said, "I just feel like I haven't been able to get anything done." A therapist not practicing BA may see this sort of response as an indication that the client may need to become more aware of his feelings. In BA, however, the therapist may roll with this response and does not have to help the client understand or report on her feelings. In this case, the therapist may just focus on the client's behavior.

Likewise, it is *not* important that the therapist educate the client about depression or the symptoms of depression. In fact, the therapist does not have to use the word *depression* while working with clients. Instead, the therapist should learn the clients' language and descriptors of their problems, and fit the BA model to the clients' language. The therapist should provide a good rationale for treatment that links the treatment techniques to whatever problems the client presents with. For example, a male client presented primarily with complaints of irritability and anger and said he was not depressed (although he met criteria for major depression according to an assessment interview). In such a case, the therapist may state that treatment will target those issues of irritability and anger. According to the "Two Circles" model, irritability and anger would be seen as common emotional responses to negative life events. Thus, treatment would involve activating alternate, more functional behaviors instead of anger expression.

It is possible that a client will emphasize physical rather than emotional symptoms, for example, feeling tired or in pain. This also is not a problem and the client does not need to be convinced to talk in emotional terms. The therapist may use the client's language and terminology for how they are describing their experiences and use the somatic symptoms directly in the model. Usually these somatic symptoms can be seen as "common responses" and the therapist will want to focus on activating the client to maintain healthy lifestyles in the presence of these symptoms.

Dealing With Client Reactions to the Rationale

Some clients may misinterpret the rationale as "I just need to force myself to do things," or "Just do it." They may feel that they have already tried to get more active and have failed. In these cases, it is important for the therapist to emphasize his or her expertise in helping people change their behavior. The therapist may say:

> The difference between what I have to offer you, and what you have already tried, is that I have lots of tips and tricks and ideas that help people make changes. People think it is easy to change their behavior, but if it was so easy you probably wouldn't be here and you would have figured it out on your own. So we can look very closely at what behaviors we should change for you, how these behaviors should be broken down, and where we should start. Also, we can look very closely at how you and others respond when you do activate, and try to make sure that the right consequences are in place. It is not just about doing more things randomly; we are going to be very strategic about what you do and when you do it, and create a plan that over time will get you where you want to be.

Other clients may respond to the rationale by minimizing their own difficulties. A recent client seen by the first author stated, "I always think people are dealing with worse things . . . the death of a parent, abuse of a child . . . I always would just think I'd get over it, I don't have things that tough . . . " In this case, the therapist responded:

> The fact that worse things have not happened in your life is a good thing; I think that if more bad things had happened to you, you would be even more depressed and even more shut down, and it would be even harder to get you moving again. So we can together appreciate that others have things worse than you do, both because you would feel even worse and also because it would make our job harder. I think, given your life, your depression makes sense to me, you have had enough bad things happen, but at the same time certainly it could be worse . . . so I am optimistic that we can get you moving again.

It also may be helpful to emphasize that it is not the severity of the initial life events that matters, but how the client responds to those events—does the client respond with proactive problem solving or does the client respond in a way that perpetuates a spiral into deeper depression? It is important to not pathologize the client's response here but to indicate that it is also a normal and understandable response—it just happens to be ineffective in this case.

A final client reaction to the rationale is to counter the behavioral rationale with a biological rationale: "I understand what you are saying, but my husband [or doctor, friend, etc.] says I have a biochemical imbalance." A similar response to the behavioral model from other professionals such as some psychiatrists is to believe that the behavioral rationale is a good fit for "situational" depression but not real, clinical depression, which requires a pathological biological process rather than a process characterized by a normal response to life events (Horowitz & Wakefield, 2007).

Although certainly the clinician may enjoy a good debate with other professionals, it is important for the BA clinician to roll gently with these responses and not become argumentative with clients. The clinician may want to emphasize that behavior and biology are parallel, not competing, processes:

> You are absolutely right. All behavior has a biological basis, so it is certainly the case that people's brains change when they become depressed. However, there are many ways to change the brain, and therapy is one of them. So I am confident that, if there are any biochemical imbalances in your brain, we can actually work with them in here.

In fact, recent research has demonstrated significant changes in how the brain processes reward over the course of successful BA treatment (Dichter et al., 2009). It may be helpful to show clients this article, as it displays changes in fMRI images, and research has identified that these images are powerful communication tools.

Assessment: Obtaining Information to Guide Activity Scheduling

After presenting the rationales, the primary goal of initial BA sessions is to obtain information useful for scheduling good activation assignments that are tailored to the client's life problems and values. Developing a hierarchical list of specific activation assignments for the client is essentially akin to case conceptualization in BA, so this early stage is about developing a case conceptualization. As stated earlier, the assessment process here is broad and can include:

➤ What has the client stopped doing?

➤ What is the client doing ineffectively?

➤ What is the client actively avoiding doing?

➤ What gives (or used to give) the client a sense of pleasure?

➤ What gives (or used to give) the client a sense of mastery?

➤ What are the client's long-term goals and values?

Here we review four sources of information (summarized in Table 4.3) to be used to assess these areas and build activation assignments. Like everything about BA, any one of these should be seen as optional, and the therapist should always be thinking functionally about obtaining this information in any way possible.

Informal Clinical Interview

Important information can be obtained from the client simply by listening and asking the client informally about his or her life. This informal interviewing, which occurs mostly during the intake assessment, provides information useful to the conceptualization, particularly about things the client used to do and has stopped doing, and problems in the client's life that need solving. Consider this Session 2 interaction with Bill:

Therapist (T): I'd like to find out more about your hobbies and other things that maybe you're not doing now that you used to enjoy, just to get to know you better and figure out things we can do in this treatment. You already told me about photography, that's one. Do you have any other hobbies?

Bill (B): Carnivorous plants.

Table 4.3 Four Sources of Information to Guide Activity Scheduling

Source of Information	Target
1. Informal clinical interview	Activities client used to do and has stopped doing; problems to solve.
2. Activity monitoring	Activities client currently is doing, specific target behaviors; behavioral excesses; moods related to specific behaviors.
3. Values assessment	Behaviors to activate in the service of deeply held values across various life domains.
4. Self-report questionnaires	Pleasant, unpleasant, and interpersonal events.

T: Like a Venus Flytrap?

B: Yeah, I have two or three terrariums of carnivorous plants. I haven't been taking care of them very well lately.

T: Well, maybe that's something we can schedule, too. So, photography, carnivorous plants . . . other hobbies?

B: Computers.

T: Okay, what do you do with computers. Are you just interested in general or do you like certain things?

B: I have an associate's degree, programming and networking stuff. I just play around usually.

T: Do you have a computer of your own?

B: Yes.

T: Any other hobbies?

B: I used to bicycle a lot but not anymore.

T: Do you have a bike?

B: An old one.

T: Now the weather is getting a little colder . . . some people do winter biking.

B: Yeah, last time I rode for 11 miles and that was the only warm day this year.

T: Yeah, I remember that day. Anything else?

B: No.

T: Well, this is a pretty good list: photography, plants, computers, biking. This is a long list as far as hobbies go, sometimes people only have one if they have a hobby at all, so that's good. We can talk about focusing on some of these in here, getting you back to doing some of these things.

As with much of BA, conducting a clinical interview of this sort should be fairly straightforward. The key, in fact, is for the therapist to remain fairly concrete, focused on the details of the activities that the client used to do and has decreased or stopped doing altogether, and what would be required to complete and reengage in the activities (e.g., a bike to go biking), without getting distracted by other possibilities that would complicate the conceptualization. Although the earlier example concerned the client's hobbies, it is expected that the therapist will explore various life domains with the client as they complete their intake assessment. This intake assessment, covering family, social, educational, recreational, occupational, and other areas of functioning, should be a rich source of information for the therapist.

Activity Monitoring

The informal clinical interview described earlier is helpful in identifying what the client is not doing and problems to be solved, but activity monitoring is helpful in identifying what the client already is doing. The traditional tool used in early BA sessions to do this is the activity monitoring form, also called an activity chart. An initial monitoring assignment can occur in Session 1. The therapist may suggest:

> Therapist (T): I want to understand what your week looks like in more detail, so I'd like to ask you to complete this chart for your first homework assignment over the course of this next week. Essentially it simply asks you to describe your activities over the course of the day, hour-by-hour. For example, here [pointing to correct cell in the grid] you would put "therapy," and here [pointing to another cell] you would put "studied for chemistry" as we already discussed. It would be ideal if you could fill this out at the end of every day.

> Client (C): Okay, it seems like a lot of information, though.

> T: It is, and it is not something I will suggest you do every week. But my goal with you at this point is to really get a sense for what your life looks like, hour by hour . . . how you are spending your time, what you are doing, and what you are not doing. I want to be a fly on the wall as you go about your week, and this is the easiest way to do that.

There are several forms of activity charts, and the form chosen depends on the preferences of the client and the therapist. Much like different styles of daily or weekly planners, the client may be given a chart for each day, allowing for more detailed information about each day (Figure 4.3), or a chart for each week, allowing for less detailed information but a better visual summary of the entire week (Figure 4.4). Like

Figure 4.3   Completed Daily Activity Monitoring Sheet

Day of Week:	Activity	Mastery/Pleasure	Mood
Morning (time)			
6–11 AM	Sleep		
11 AM–12 PM	Watched TV, made microwave dinner	0	4 for TV 5 for dinner
Afternoon (time)			
12–5 PM	Watched TV	0	3
Evening (time)			
5–6 PM	Ordered and ate pizza	0	4
6–7 PM	Played video games online	7	8
7–10 PM	Helped son with homework	7	7
10 PM–2 AM	Watched DVDs	3	4

Figure 4.4   Completed Weekly Activity Monitoring Sheet

	Sunday	Monday	Tuesday	Wednesday	Thursday	Friday	Saturday
6–7 AM	Sleeping	Sleeping	Sleeping	Sleeping	Sleeping	Sleeping	Sleeping
7–8 AM	Sleeping	Sleeping	Sleeping	Sleeping	Sleeping	Sleeping	Sleeping
8–9 AM	Sleeping	Sleeping	Sleeping	Sleeping	Sleeping	Sleeping	Sleeping
9–10 AM	Sleeping	Sleeping	Ate breakfast	Sleeping	Sleeping	Sleeping	Sleeping
10–11 AM	Sleeping	Sleeping	Doctor's appointment	Sleeping	Doctor's appointment	Sleeping	Sleeping
11 AM–12 PM	Sleeping	Sleeping	Doctor's appointment	Sleeping	Doctor's appointment	Sleeping	Sleeping
12–1 PM	Sleeping	Sleeping	Doctor's appointment	Sleeping	Doctor's appointment	Sleeping	Sleeping
1–2 PM	Sleeping	Sleeping	Ate lunch/ watched TV	Sleeping	Ate lunch/ watched TV	Sleeping	Sleeping
2–3 PM	Sleeping	Sleeping	Watched TV	Ate lunch	Cleaned kitchen	Sleeping	Sleeping
3–4 PM	Ate lunch/ watched TV	Ate lunch/ watched TV	Watched TV	Watched TV	Surfed the Internet	Ate lunch/ watched TV	Ate lunch/ watched TV
4–5 PM	Watched TV	Grocery shopping	Watched TV	Laundry/watched TV	Surfed the Internet	Watched TV	Went to church
5–6 PM	Watched TV	Paid bills	Went to video store	Laundry/watched TV	Went to store to get newspaper	Watched TV	Went to church
6–7 PM	Surfed the Internet	Surfed the Internet	Watched DVD	Laundry/watched TV	Looked through want ads	Watched TV	Looked online for jobs
7–8 PM	Had dinner/ watched TV	Had dinner and a couple of drinks with friend	Watched DVD	Played video games	Went to movies	Watched TV	Looked online for jobs
8–9 PM	Played video games	Had a couple of drinks with friend	Sleeping	Looked online for jobs	Went to movies	Watched TV	Studied for GED
9–10 PM	Lay in bed	Sleeping	Sleeping	Surfed the Internet	Sleeping	Sleeping	Sleeping
10–11 PM	Lay in bed	Sleeping	Sleeping	Lay in bed	Sleeping	Sleeping	Sleeping

everything about BA, the form of the chart is less important than the function. Thus, some clients may prefer to chart in an existing daily or weekly planner and others may prefer simple lists. Others may develop diary cards to suit their own styles and needs. The important point is that the assessment function is served and the therapist gains useful information about the nature, breadth, and frequency of clinically relevant client behavior over the course of the week.

Activity monitoring assignments may also be elaborated in several ways. First, they can be tailored to track specific behaviors of interest that will be targeted later in therapy, such as job-searching behaviors, studying, or watching television. In addition, the activity chart may include space for the client to rate his or her mood during specific activities. For some clients, we have found the categories mad, sad, scared, angry, and bored work well, but other clients may prefer to supply their own descriptors rather than picking from a predefined list. Similarly, other ratings can be obtained, depending on the particulars of the client, including ratings of pleasure, accomplishment or mastery, pain, and consistency with values. We have found that a 0 to 10 scale for these ratings works well, but there is nothing special about the scale range and it can be modified as necessary.

If a client does not like to complete the monitoring forms, in most cases the therapist should not force the issue and should not lose sight of why monitoring is done.

> Client: Well, I forgot to do the chart again, but as I've said before it really won't tell you much . . . I could summarize my whole week just out loud, I mean most of the time I'm just doing nothing . . . just watching television at home and making food and studying, which has pretty much been my last three days.

Here the therapist has a choice point—to try to get the client to comply with the monitoring or to accept the client's self-report. One solution is to discuss this openly with the client, helping the client understand the purpose of monitoring and working collaboratively with the client to meet that function in different ways:

> Therapist: On the one hand, this therapy is about you and what works for you, so if completing these forms just is not helpful to you, let's not do it. On the other hand, from my perspective I really want to understand this watching TV, making food, studying thing that was your past three days. The thing I'm interested in is the ratio of maybe what we could call good behaviors to bad behaviors. For example, do you feel the amount of time you're spending watching TV is good or are you procrastinating too much? Do you feel good about this balance? So then we can see if we can help you adjust this balance to work better for you, and you can see improvement in the amount of time you're spending on these different things. So we don't *need* the chart for this, but this is the kind of detail I'm after because I really think the devil of depression is in these details. What do you think is the best solution for you?

Values Assessment The third source of information to guide activity scheduling is values assessment.

Values were initially introduced into behavior therapy in Acceptance and Commitment Therapy (ACT; Hayes, Strosahl, & Wilson, 1999), and more recently have been incorporated into the BATD protocol (Lejuez et al., 2001). We have used values in our version of BA as well (Kanter et al., 2009). In BA, the principal role of values is to make activation personally meaningful by having clients develop specific activation goals that are wedded to one's values in various life domains. The linking of client values with specific therapy goals in this context is likely to foster motivation on the part of the client to become more active, and serves as a counterweight to the inertia that is commonly experienced by depressed clients when attempting activation early in treatment.

The connection between values and activation goals is important not only to motivate early attempts at activation, but also to sustain activation over the course of treatment. For instance, consider a depressed client Hal, who became depressed when he lost his job of eight years. During the values assessment, Hal stated that he valued being able to support his wife and children to the best of his ability. This value was tied to a number of specific activation assignments, such as researching different work options, updating his resume and employment references, and applying for various positions. Despite his devotion of many hours to this process, he did not have any luck in procuring job interviews after sending out approximately 15 resumes. Had Hal encountered this kind of repeated failure without having created employment goals in the context of his values, it is likely that he may have become more depressed and given up on persisting in this area. In the face of adversity, however, Hal soldiered on by constantly reminding himself of why his employment goals were important: "It is really a bummer putting in all of this time and not getting anywhere . . . But I have to remember my family. They mean the world to me, and I need to keep trying for them." This description by Hal serves to illustrate that whereas many activation assignments over therapy will be met with failure or perceived as unrewarding, the emphasis on values is likely to provide a longer time horizon for motivation when a client's current life situation is characterized by various short-term setbacks.

The values assessment may be completed early in therapy, and can be given as a homework assignment during the first session. The following script may be useful as an introduction to the values assessment:

> As I mentioned earlier, the point of our work together is to get you active in your life. This does not mean that our goal is to have you become more active simply for the sake of being more active. What it does mean is that I would like you to become active in ways that are personally meaningful to you. Clients have found it particularly helpful to think about areas in their lives that they value and then think about specific activation goals that are in line

with these values. For instance, I already sense that you value being a good father, so we may develop a specific activation goal such as spending more time playing with your children. How would you feel if you were able to consistently do this more? Reminding oneself of why activation assignments are important is often helpful for depressed clients when it seems difficult initially to get going.

We suggest using a Values and Goals Assessment (Figure 4.5). This form is similar to the one used in BATD, which was adapted from the Valued Living Questionnaire (Wilson, Sandoz, Kitchens, & Roberts, 2010). Our form lists 12 valued life domains for the client to consider that represent a diverse range of life domains. When reviewing the form with the client, the therapist may first ask the client to start thinking about relevant valued life domains from this list. From the outset, it is important for the therapist to clarify the distinction between values and goals, emphasizing that values are a direction, and as such, do not have a definable end-point (Hayes et al., 1999). This conception of values is very abstract and may be confusing to some clients. In such instances, it may be helpful for the therapist

Figure 4.5   Blank Values and Goals Assessment Sheet

Think about what you value in the following life areas. For the "I" column, rate how important that valued area is to you from 0 (not important at all) to 10 (extremely important). Then, describe what type of person you would like to be in this area. Then, list some specific, concrete goals you have that are in line with your valued life domains.

Value	I	What type of person would you like to be in this area?	Immediate concrete goals?
Family Relationships (Other than parenting or marriage)			
Marriage/Couples/Intimate Relations			
Parenting			
Friendships/Social Relations			
Employment/Meaningful Work			
Education/Training/Lifelong Learning			
Recreation/Hobbies/Creative and Artistic Expression			
Citizenship/Community/Activism/Altruism			
Physical Well-Being/Health/Nutrition/Self-Care			
Spirituality			
Life Organization/Time Management/ Discipline/Finances			
Other			

to clarify the meaning of "values" with relevant metaphors. Consider the following conversation between a therapist and Kristin:

> Therapist (T): So what exactly do you value about being a parent?
>
> Kristen (K): Well, I feel really bad about missing my son's last five soccer games. I guess I could say I value being there at his games to cheer him on.
>
> T: I really appreciate what you just said. Right now, I'd like to stop for a moment and clarify what I mean by values. When thinking of values, it is helpful to think of a value as a direction in which one lives her life. A value can never be reached.
>
> K: But I can go to all of his games.
>
> T: You are absolutely right. And that is a good example of a goal, or something that can be reached. A value can never be fully reached. For instance, it sounds to me like you value being a supportive mother. How does that sound?
>
> K: Definitely.
>
> T: So attending all of your son's games would certainly be in line with that value, but does completing this goal mean you've exhausted all possibilities for being a supportive mother?
>
> K: Uh, no. There are lots of other areas where I can be supportive.
>
> T: Exactly, so being a supportive mother simply specifies a direction for you to move in. With that direction specified, we can come up with concrete goals like going to the soccer games.
>
> K: I think I get it.

This distinction between values and goals is important, in that properly defined values will be conducive to the generation of multiple concrete goals that can be used to formulate specific activation assignments.

Once the notion of values has been clarified, the therapist can have the client start to explore her valued life domain by asking the client to consider: (a) What type of person would you like to be in this area?; (b) What immediate, concrete goals are relevant to this valued area? The Values and Goals Assessment also includes a column where the client can rate the importance of a value on a scale of 0 (*not important at all*) to 10 (*very important*). A sample of a completed Values and Goals Assessment is provided in Figure 4.6.

The list of values provided on the assessment form is relatively concrete, and clients may often list values that are more abstract in nature. For instance, Mike stated that "he valued being a caring individual." In this situation, it would be helpful for the therapist to question Mike and collaboratively determine how this value is relevant in the more specific valued life domains listed on the sheet. For example, the therapist might ask Mike to elaborate on all of the relevant categories in which he desired to be "caring."

Figure 4.6 Completed Values and Goals Assessment Sheet

Value	I	What type of person would you like to be in this area?	Immediate concrete goals?
Family Relationships (Other than parenting or marriage)	5	Would like to be more tolerant.	Call brother.
Marriage/Couples/Intimate Relations	10	I would like to reconnect with my wife and have that vitality again from when we were first married.	Start doing more activities that we enjoy together. Have more meaningful conversations with wife. Tell my wife I love her more often.
Parenting	10	I would like to be the best father I can be, always being there for my kids.	Play games with them at night. Help with homework.
Friendships/Social Relations	4	Don't have any. Would like some.	Can't think of anything.
Employment/Meaningful Work	7	I would like to have a job that I enjoy and can give 100% effort to.	Start thinking about exactly what I want to do. Start applying to places of interest. Start resume and cover letter.
Education/Training/ Lifelong Learning			
Recreation/Hobbies/ Creative and Artistic Expression	6	I would like hobbies that keep me always learning and try to get in as much time with these as possible.	Start fishing again. Start exercising regularly.
Citizenship/Community/ Activism/Altruism	8	I would like to be able to give back more to the community.	Look for organizations to become involved with.
Physical Well-Being/Health/ Nutrition/Self-Care			
Spirituality	9	I would like to have God back in my life.	Go to church. Read the Bible.
Life Organization/Time Management/Discipline/ Finances			
Other			

Although the values assessment can be relatively straightforward, there are several pitfalls the therapist should try to avoid. First, the therapist should guard against client values or goals of "wanting to feel better." Whereas one of the aims of treatment is the reduction of depression symptoms, it should be recognized that one's feelings and thoughts are largely uncontrollable on a day-to-day basis and will exhibit great variation depending on the context of a specific day. Conceptualizing symptom reduction as a value also is inconsistent with BA's rationale of activating despite one's negative emotions rather than waiting for them to improve. When therapists encounter this problem, the following script may be helpful:

It makes sense to me that you would value feeling less depressed. And hopefully, this treatment will help you start to feel better. The problem with "wanting to feel better" as a value, however, is that everyone, even those who are not depressed, has difficult days when they are not too happy. It's not a matter of not wanting to be happy, it is just sometimes happiness at a given moment is out of our control. We want values to be things you can choose to move toward every day.

Some additional difficulties with the values assessment may stem from individuals trying to conform to societal norms when enumerating values, and individuals who state that they cannot think of any values. If the therapist suspects that the former issue may be a problem, she may remind the client to "list your values and goals as if you are the only person who will ever have access to this form." The second case may be difficult, especially when an individual has been depressed for a long time. Helpful questions from the therapist that may start to generate ideas from the client are "What values did you used to have?" or "What values would you have if you weren't depressed?" Some clients, however, may continue to have trouble generating values, especially at the beginning of treatment. The therapist should not dogmatically persist in this effort with such clients. Instead, the therapist may pursue other avenues for obtaining information to guide activation assignments and consider revisiting the issue of values later in treatment.

Self–Report Questionnaires

Finally, therapists may consider a self-report questionnaire, such as the Pleasant Events Schedule (MacPhillamy & Lewinsohn, 1974; MacPhillamy & Lewinsohn, 1982), as a useful tool to identify activation assignments. The PES contains a list of 320 pleasurable events (e.g., "Hearing jokes," and "Washing my hair") that traditionally are rated by the respondent twice, first rating the frequency of occurrence in the past month of the item and then rating the subjective enjoyability of that event if it occurred. The cross-product of frequency and enjoyability across all items is meant as an indicator of reinforcement received. For clinical purposes, however, the list may be used simply to trigger ideas about behaviors to activate, subsets of items from the list may be used, or additional items may be added to the list. For a complete review of uses of the PES and other self-report measures, see Manos et al. (in press).

Activity Scheduling

Activity scheduling is the hallmark of BA. Most of BA session time is devoted to reviewing previous assignments and scheduling new assignments. Good BA sessions involve very detailed analyses of these assignments, and the assignments are defined very concretely. The therapist and the client will discuss how to do the assignment, when to do it, where to do it, with whom to do it, and what barriers

Table 4.4 Five Tips for Developing Good Activity Scheduling Assignments

Tip	Summary Description
1. Assignments should be guided by the case conceptualization.	Develop an "activity hierarchy" that integrates information obtained during assessment into a list ranked by difficulty level.
2. Assignments should be graded according to task difficulty.	Assigned activities should be slightly challenging but likely to be successful; difficulty can be increased following success.
3. Assignments should be broken down into manageable chunks.	Complex activities should be broken into component activities that can be assigned and achieved individually.
4. Assignments should be specific.	Consider *wwww* (see page 148 for a definition) for good operational definitions of assignments.
5. Assignments should consider barriers and obstacles to completion.	Maximize the chances of success by predicting and problem solving barriers and obstacles to assignment completion.

and obstacles may be encountered while attempting to do it. In Table 4.4, we present five tips for developing good activity scheduling assignments.

Assignments Should Be Guided by the Case Conceptualization

During the first several sessions, the therapist will compile a list of behaviors to activate in therapy; developing this list essentially functions as case conceptualization in BA. As stated earlier, this list is a result of an ongoing multimethod assessment process and should represent stable, meaningful reinforcers, diverse activities, and a range of difficulty levels. It should include pleasant events, problem-solving behaviors, behaviors that the client stopped doing since becoming depressed, and behaviors in the service of deeply held values.

Figure 4.7 presents a blank Activity Hierarchy, which may be used for formally completing this list. The hierarchy form used is adapted from the form used by Lejuez and colleagues (2001), who first introduced such a hierarchy into BA, and we have incorporated it as well. Like an exposure hierarchy in exposure treatments for anxiety disorders, the Activity Hierarchy lists the activities in order of increasing anticipated difficulty. Although the client and therapist need not strictly follow the order of difficulty as per the hierarchy, it can serve as a guide for when various activities are assigned. The Activity Hierarchy includes columns for noting when the activity was assigned, when it was completed, and the actual difficulty of the activity (to be compared with the anticipated difficulty). A sample completed hierarchy (Figure 4.8) illustrates how a hierarchy may be completed and also demonstrates the flexibility of the hierarchy, in that the "assigned" and "completed" columns can be completed with yes/no responses, checkmarks, dates, or hash marks (for activities that repeat regularly) as appropriate.

We recommend use of an Activity Hierarchy over the entire course of treatment, with new assignments added to the bottom of the hierarchy as they are developed and assigned. The hierarchy thus serves as a running record of the client's behavioral activation assignments throughout therapy, as well as a record of if and when each activity was completed and how difficult it was to complete.

Figure 4.7   Blank Activity Hierarchy

Please rate the anticipated and actual difficulty of the task using a 1 – 10 scale (1 = not at all difficult; 10 = extremely difficult) and note date of activity assignment and completion.

Activity	Anticipated Difficulty	Assigned	Completed	Actual Difficulty

Figure 4.8 Completed Activity Hierarchy

Activity	Anticipated Difficulty	Assigned	Completed	Actual Difficulty
Go dancing with wife	6			
Have meaningful conversation with wife every day of week	1	5/10/08	JHT III	1
Tell my wife I love her	1	5/10/08	III	1
Go to Ben's soccer game	4			
Play board games with kids	6			
Check in with kids on homework	5			
Get new job	10			
Start thinking about meaningful work	3	5/17/08	no	3
Start researching companies interested in	4			
Work on resume and cover letter	5			
Apply for jobs	8			
Go fishing with Fred	3	5/17/08	5/19/08	2
Exercise for 30 mins per day	7			
Do community service	7			
Start looking for meaningful volunteer work	4			
Go to church	2	5/10/08	no	5
Read Bible	5			

By the end of therapy, the hierarchy becomes a rich reminder and succinct overview of specific treatment targets, how much the client has accomplished, and what remains to be accomplished.

Like everything in BA, using an Activity Hierarchy is not mandatory. As treatment begins, the therapist may not have obtained from the client enough information, or be sufficiently confident with the information, to commit it to the Activity Hierarchy and share it with the client. Nonetheless, the therapist's attempting to draft a list of potential behaviors to activate over the course of therapy on the Activity Hierarchy on his or her own outside of session may be a useful exercise for the purposes of case conceptualization.

Graded Task Assignment

This tip suggests that easier tasks that are likely to be completed and reinforced should be assigned first, followed by progressively more difficult tasks. This point is intuitive for many therapists and although it is obvious, it is included here because it is important. Technically the issue here is *shaping*, the behavioral term for reinforcing successive approximations to a desired level of behavior. An ideal activation assignment is one that shapes behavior; it is slightly challenging but likely to be successful, and when successful a slightly more challenging behavior is assigned next. If the assignment is too challenging the client will fail, but if it is too easy the client will succeed but not experience it as a success.

For example, a client may have stopped paying bills and opening mail for several months, and in therapy the client may suggest an assignment where "I finally just do all the bills, and then do them every day as they come in." The therapist may work with the client to attain this goal over time but start smaller: "Let's think of something slightly more manageable to start. How long do you think it will take you to do all the bills? How about this week you commit to an hour of doing this? If you spend more than an hour, all the better, but the assignment is to do one hour."

Sometimes the therapist may simply state the issue plainly: "I'd like us to come up with an assignment that is slightly challenging for you, so you have a good chance to succeed but at the same time will feel like it is an accomplishment. Let's not make it too easy, because then you'll feel like you didn't accomplish anything, and not too hard, because then you may not do it. Let's figure this out together so the assignment feels right for you."

Early in therapy, some depressed clients present with the paradox of being unable to accomplish basic tasks because of their depression but at the same time they have expectations of themselves to function at a level consistent with not being depressed. The therapist should encourage the client to think in terms of shaping in this situation: The goal is to determine the client's current level of functioning and develop an assignment that is slightly challenging with respect to current functioning, not to develop assignments that would be considered challenging with respect to previous, higher levels of functioning. This view of task assignment may evoke self-critical responses from the client, such as "I have become such a baby; I never used to have trouble with this," or "I feel so pathetic that I can't even do this basic thing anymore." Although a cognitive therapist may see these statements as opportunities for cognitive change, the BA therapist's task is not to get distracted by them. The therapist should validate that it is common for depressed individuals to think this way at the beginning of treatment, and ask if the thought will get in the way of completing the assignment or if the client can do the assignment while having these self-critical thoughts. The goal is to improve the client's functioning, which—according to the BA model—*will result in an improvement in the self-critical thoughts.* The therapist may say to the client, "It will be difficult for you to have that thought that you are so pathetic if you complete this assignment successfully, won't it?"

Assignments Should Be Broken Down Into Manageable Chunks

Chaining is a behavioral term for linking together a sequence of smaller, simpler units of behaviors to produce a larger, more complex unit of behavior. Essentially the therapeutic task is to think about specific activation assignments and to discuss with the client whether they could and should be broken into smaller parts. Shaping and chaining are similar and easily confused. The important point is that the therapist should consider both task difficulty (shaping) and whether the task can be broken into component parts (chaining) in developing activation assignments. Subsequently, all component tasks should also be considered in terms of difficulty.

For example, consider a client who identified a possible assignment to clean his house over the weekend. Through discussion with the therapist, several component tasks were identified, including buying cleaning supplies and fixing the vacuum cleaner, as well as determining which rooms to clean in what order. The complete chain of behavior determined collaboratively between the client and the therapist was: buy supplies, fix vacuum cleaner, clean bedroom, clean living room, clean kitchen, and clean bathroom. Now thinking about shaping and task difficulty, it was determined that fixing the vacuum cleaner and cleaning the kitchen and bathroom were too difficult for the initial assignment. The client's assignments that week included buying supplies and cleaning the bedroom and living room (sweeping the floors with a broom instead of with the vacuum cleaner).

Assignments Should Be Specific

One of the most common mistakes of therapists new to BA is not being specific and concrete enough with task assignments. Furthermore, many therapists with a less extensive knowledge of BA will say that they are doing BA if they encourage their clients to stay active and engage in pleasant events. For example, a session may be spent discussing the client's feelings about his spouse, and then at the end of the session the therapist may add, "Well, try to stay active this weekend and do something nice for yourself."

As stated earlier, BA focuses not only on providing such instructions to clients but also on working with the client to determine exactly what he or she will do to stay active and how he or she will do it. Typically, between two and five activation assignments are provided in each session (Kanter, Santiago-Rivera, Rusch, Busch, & West, 2010), and one or two of them are discussed in considerable detail. The

Figure 4.9   Blank Homework Activation Sheet

BA Homework Activation Sheet				
Activity	wwww	Obstacles	Solutions to obstacles	Outcome

"Activation Homework Sheet" (Figure 4.9) may be used to structure these detailed discussions. The sheet provides a column to list the assignment, which is taken verbatim from the Activity Hierarchy so there can be consistency between the two forms. The next column, "wwww," stands for *who, what, where,* and *when* and allows the client and the therapist to discuss and agree on the details. A sample of a completed sheet is included in Figure 4.10.

Activity scheduling, from a behavioral point of view, can be seen as a stimulus control intervention. Stimulus control interventions, which have been used successfully by behaviorists for decades (Kanter et al., in press), essentially add prompts into the client's environment to evoke improved behavior, or remove prompts from the cleint's environment to decrease the frequency of problem behavior. Activity scheduling is a stimulus control intervention because the specific homework assignment may be seen as a prompt, which functionally constitutes a rule or instruction to engage in a specific behavior. Thus, the best homework assignments are those that specify the behavior of interest in formal detail, including the what, when, where, and how of the behavior (e.g., go to community center to look for basketball leagues to join at noon on Saturday with son). It is also relevant for the BA therapist to discuss with the client *where* they will place the Activation Homework Sheet, such that it serves as an effective reminder. Other stimulus control interventions, specifically related to when clients forget to do their homework, are discussed in the following sections.

Figure 4.10 Completed Homework Activation Sheet

BA Homework Activation Sheet

Activity	wwww	Obstacles	Solutions to obstacles	Outcome
Complete activity monitoring	Every day; nighttime before bed	May not remember	Place reminder on alarm clock tonight using post-it note. Leave monitoring sheet on my nightstand	Completed 5/7 nights
Do laundry	Sort laundry tonight after dinner into darks and whites. Wash darks Wednesday afternoon. Wash whites Friday morning after breakfast. Fold clothes Friday evening after *American Idol*.	Might not have enough quarters to do wash	Go home today after session and get checkbook; then drive to bank in order to get quarters	Completed all of my darks, but none of my whites
Go fishing with Fred	Call Fred Thursday, 6 pm. Schedule date for fishing. Go to WalMart on Wed after lunch to get new supplies.	May forget to call Fred	Write a note today reminding myself to call Fred; leave note near the phone	Went fishing over the weekend
Go for a jog one time	Tuesday evening before dinner	Workout clothes are dirty	Reschedule to Thursday, after my clothes have been washed	Incomplete: got tied up with a movie

Some clients may resist this level of detail, and it may be helpful for the therapist to provide a rationale to the client for why all the details are helpful:

> Sometimes the details help because it forces you to think through, well, the details, which makes it more likely you'll do the activity. Even if you don't do the activity at the exact time and place we specify, sometimes the process of thinking it through at this level makes it more likely you'll do it at all, because it is more realistic for you versus just some good idea. Also it gives me something specific to latch on to next week, to check in on. If you do it at another time because that made more sense to you, I'm not going to be too concerned, because this therapy is about you after all, not me. But if you didn't do it at all, this gives us an opportunity to say, "Well, what were you doing at 5:00 last Monday?" versus just having some vague conversation about it. The more specific we can be, the more I can help you if you didn't do it, and the more likely you are to do it.

As with everything in BA, the therapist need not insist on the details with a resistant client, and some clients will succeed at assignments without a thorough review of the details. Rather than arguing with a client and forcing a discussion of the details that is tedious and unwanted by the client, the therapist may choose to negotiate with the client: "Well, I have found that thinking through the details is often helpful, but certainly there are some clients for whom it is not. How about we just go with the general assignment this week, but if you end up having trouble getting it done, we can get more detailed next week?"

As clients experience more success from week to week in completing assignments, the focus on the details should be faded out. Ultimately, the goal is for the client to be self-managing his or her activation assignments rather than relying on the structure or intervention of the therapist. This may be explicitly discussed with the client: "I have found that for many depressed clients, at the beginning of treatment they are so depressed that they really benefit from the structure, support, and accountability that therapy provides. As they get more active and engaged in life, however, we really want you to take responsibility from me. We can see how this goes, but I suspect that fairly soon we will be able to move to a relatively quick review of old assignments and a quick collaboration on new assignments, rather than the detailed process that I'm suggesting today."

Assignments Should Consider Barriers and Obstacles to Completion

The Activation Homework Sheet also has columns to list foreseeable obstacles and solutions to obstacles. Although the therapist may not have time in session to review the *wwww* and obstacles related to every activity assigned, we do recommend the therapist spend some time on this for the one or two most important assignments.

In response to the question, "What kinds of obstacles may get in the way of you completing this activity?" clients may initially report that they cannot think of any, but often that response is simply a product of not thinking too deeply about the assignment and the client should be encouraged to do so. Consider this interaction between the first author and Jim:

Therapist (T): So, regarding you going to the museum on Monday, what might get in the way of you doing that?

Jim (J): Nothing that I can think of.

T: Well, take a minute, think about it . . . if you don't complete this assignment, what would be the most likely culprit?

J: I really can't think of anything.

T: Okay, well, can I ask you a few questions about it?

J: Sure.

T: Okay, well, you said you were going to do it after your shift ends on Monday, right?

J: Right.

T: What do you normally do after your shift?

J: Just go home.

T: And now on Monday you will plan to do this instead. Do you think you'll be tired and want to go home?

J: Maybe, but I have been wanting to go to the museum for a while now, so I think I'll be looking forward to it.

T: Well, that's good. Will you be hungry after your shift?

J: No, we eat during the shift.

T: Oh, good. How are you planning to get from work to the museum?

J: I've got my bike, so I guess I will ride it.

T: Is it far?

J: No, it is not exactly on the way home, but it is not really too far out of the way. It should just take 10 minutes.

In this interaction, the therapist had the luxury of enough time in the session to explore this activity in detail. A similar useful strategy here is imaginal rehearsal: Ask the client to imagine completing the assignment in detail, walking through the assignment step-by-step out loud with you. Often this process helps the client consider the difficult details of the activity that he or she otherwise wouldn't consider, and it also provides the therapist sufficient detail to envision potential obstacles as well.

There is nothing special about generating solutions to potential obstacles in BA. The therapist and the client simply should work together to find solutions. It is important for the therapist to remain collaborative here; the client after all knows his or her life better than does the therapist. Sometimes, however, clients are sufficiently depressed that they have lost the skill of persisting in the face of problems, and even solutions obvious to the therapist will not be obvious to the client.

Reviewing Homework

It is as important in BA to spend time reviewing homework as it is assigning homework. Here we organize our discussion of reviewing homework according to (a) when the client is at least partially successful completing the homework and (b) when the client fails to complete the homework. Although no specific criteria are provided for what percentage of homework completion should be considered overall a success versus a failure, in general we have loosely defined success as more than half of the homework completed. The homework review sheet provided by Busch, Uebelacker, Kalibatseva, and Miller (2010) may be useful when conducting a homework review.

Successful Homework Completion

When clients regularly and successfully complete their homework over several sessions, it is expected that over time their depressive symptoms will decrease. If this is not the case, from a BA perspective this is a problem with the case conceptualization. In other words, the wrong assignments (or at least not the right assignments) are being given. The therapist and the client should go back to the Activity Hierarchy and discuss what may be missing from the list. The therapist may state:

> You are feeling a little better, and you are active, but you are still depressed. What are we missing? What feels like it still is missing in your life? It seems like we're not hitting on something crucial to your depression—can we spend a few minutes thinking about what this might be, so we can add it to your list?

As this discussion proceeds, it is important for the therapist to consider the possibility that BA is not a good fit for the client. We do not want to encourage the therapist to persist with a treatment strategy that is not helping the client. At the same time, the therapist should be aware that for some clients, change takes time and both the client and the therapist need to be patient.

When reviewing successful homework completion, it is important for the therapist to highlight the importance of homework completion to the client's improved mood. A primary issue here is shaping, which focuses the therapist on making any successful activation salient to the client, especially early in therapy. For example, consider this therapist response to a client who took several very small steps towards his goals between sessions:

> Listen, I don't want to make too big a deal of it, but I just want to say that from my perspective, what you are doing here is really important, perhaps more

important than anything else I can think of, actually. Depression is not necessarily that complicated, but it is hard, and often what people need to do is simply *stay active*. And when you are active, doing things important to you, not actively avoiding everything, then you feel better. And ultimately, over time, you get better at staying active on a continual basis, and then you are engaged in life and depression gets farther and farther away. So let's spend some time today talking about how you did this and how you can keep it going.

It is also important to focus on partial successes, rather than partial failures. The therapist may say to the client, "Since you are not feeling perfect, I will not expect your homework to be perfect either." Consider a client who did most of his homework assignments but was self-critical because he did not fully complete his activity monitoring chart. The therapist responded: "This is great, this is great, and all the stuff you did is fantastic; and when I look at homework, I look at it altogether. Maybe you didn't keep track the later part of the week but look at all you did." Similarly, consider this interaction between this same client and the therapist later in the session:

> Client (C): I just lay there for two or three hours. I just try and tune things out and just mindlessly wander.
>
> Therapist (T): Do you know if you were avoiding anything at that time?
>
> C: There's always something that I should be doing, but how much I should be doing it is subjective I guess.
>
> T: When I look at all you did this past week, I'm just really impressed. Granted when you're lying in bed and you have things to do, that's the time to get you moving and get you unstuck, but this is really exciting.

Notice in this example, the therapist had a choice to either focus on the improved behavior or focus on the problematic behavior. Following the principle of shaping, the therapist observed that the client's behavior was not perfect but it was an improvement over the previous week's activity; so in this instance, the therapist focused on the improvement and simply ignored the behaviors that were still problematic. Later, the therapist worked with the client directly on the problem behavior, but this occurred only after the client had demonstrated several weeks of continued improvement in other realms. In this way, the tone of therapy stayed positive rather than negative, and problems were addressed according to the case conceptualization and their perceived difficulty, in the context of continued improvement.

When clients regularly and successfully complete their homework and their depressive symptoms are responding, the BA therapist's task is to continue scheduling activities as per the earlier guidelines, fade out weekly sessions (potentially by both shortening the length of individual sessions and increasing the length of time in between sessions) and plan for termination. Termination issues are discussed later in the chapter. Additional BA strategies discussed later simply may not be required for these clients.

Failure to Complete Homework

A key skill of the BA therapist that we feel has been underemphasized in previous writings on BA is the skill of determining why a client failed to successfully complete activation assignments. When a client has not completed his or her homework, the first thing a therapist should do is review the homework assignment in terms of the five principles earlier. Was the assignment related to the client's goals, values, and case conceptualization? Maybe it was just an unimportant assignment that does not have to be revisited? Was the assignment too hard? Was it too complex, with too many components? Was it specific enough? Was the *wwww* specified, and were these details the right details (e.g., maybe the community center is not open at noon on Saturday, when the client said he was going to go)? Reviewing these details essentially is a check for the therapist to determine if the assignment was a good assignment in the first place.

In addition to reviewing these details, there are many additional BA strategies that can be employed when a client does not complete his or her homework. Over the past several years we have cataloged the full array of BA-consistent strategies (Kanter et al., in press) and developed a simple functional assessment (FA) procedure that the BA therapist may employ to assess categories of homework failure that links these categories with BA-consistent strategies. These strategies add a level of complexity to BA as an intervention; thus we suggest that straightforward activity scheduling as per the earlier guidelines be attempted first and that these additional strategies only be employed as necessary for clients who are having trouble getting active.

To understand our FA procedure, one must first understand the traditional behavioral ABC model. According to behaviorists, to fully understand why a behavior occurs, or in this case, does not occur, we must understand the behavior in terms of *antecedents* to the behavior (A), the *behavior* itself (B), and *consequences* to the behavior (C). So far, this chapter has focused primarily on the concept of reinforcement, but notice that in this model, reinforcement falls in the *consequences* category and is only one aspect of the full model. We also briefly have discussed activity scheduling as a stimulus control intervention, which falls under the *antecedents* category of this model. The FA procedure described herein to intervene when a client does not complete an activation assignment captures the full behavioral sequence of the ABC model.

To illustrate this model, consider Angela who, after discussing her values and goals with her therapist, has decided to begin cooking her family's dinner meals as an activation assignment (currently, her mother, who lives with them, has been cooking). First, let us consider whether the appropriate antecedents to this behavior are in place:

➤ Does she have the proper cooking supplies?

➤ Does she have a recipe to follow?

➤ Does she have the proper ingredients?

➤ Does she have time available in the afternoon to follow through on this?

➤ Does she have reminders in place to help her remember to do this new behavior?

Next, let us consider the behavior itself. This is relatively simple:

➤ Does Angela know how to cook?

➤ Can she emit the desired behavior?

Most importantly, let us consider the consequences, which potentially are multifaceted.

➤ How will Angela's mother respond when this task is taken from her? Will she be supportive of Angela, or will she feel slighted? Will she suggest that Angela cannot cook as well as she can?

➤ How will the family respond? Will they express appreciation or pleasure during the meal, or will they be critical and express a preference for Angela's mother's meals? Will the family pitch in to help clean up and do the dishes afterward?

➤ Finally, how will Angela herself respond? When she thinks about starting the task, will she feel a sense of dread and want to avoid the task? Will she get overwhelmed when she tries to read the recipe? When she goes shopping for the food, will she start to ruminate on her past failings and how her mother never believes in her? After the meal, will she feel a sense of pride, relief, accomplishment, or despair?

All of these factors influence the degree to which Angela will successfully complete the task and are of primary concern to the BA therapist. The key is for the therapist to think through the potential antecedents, behaviors, and consequences that are relevant to completing specific activation assignments with specific clients.

The FA questions provided here are designed to quickly assess these domains. Because many of the antecedents to the behavior of interest should already have been discussed with the client when assigning it in the first place, the FA of antecedents focuses on forgetting, a common problem in BA, and links problems with forgetting to stimulus control interventions designed to help the client remember assignments. The FA of the behavior itself focuses on skills deficits and links to skills training procedures. The FA of problems with consequences distinguishes consequences as either public or private because the intervention strategies differ depending on this distinction. Thus, the FA procedure currently consists of four sets of questions, identifying problems related to (1) forgetting, linked to stimulus control strategies, (2) skills deficits, linked to skills training strategies, (3) public consequences, linked to contingency management strategies, and (4) private consequences, linked to strategies targeting avoidance. Although research on this FA procedure is ongoing, an initial pilot study found that the FA was helpful, feasible, and acceptable (Baruch, Kanter, Bowe, & Pfennig, in press).

Conducting the FA simply involves asking the client a series of questions to determine where to intervene. Figure 4.11 provides sample questions for the therapist to consider, but these questions are neither necessary nor exhaustive. The guide does not represent a structured interview; it simply lists sample questions. The therapist should feel free to elaborate or abridge the assessment as necessary—the goal is for the therapist to think about the activation assignment in terms of relevant antecedents, behaviors, and consequences, and to assess these domains to determine where intervention is necessary. Consider this interaction between the first author and Jim, who had been asked to practice a relaxation breathing exercise for five minutes a day every day in between sessions.

Therapist (T): Did you do the relaxation breathing exercise?

Jim (J): Nope, I completely forget.

T: So, after you left the session last week, it was just completely out of your mind until right now?

J: Well . . . until I was sitting in the waiting room just now.

T: Okay, let's talk about that today and decide if it is still something you should try this week, okay?

This interaction completed the FA in this case because the therapist was satisfied that the problem had been correctly diagnosed and there was no need to assess the other categories. In this case, the entire assessment took approximately 20 seconds.

Of course, it is not always so simple. Clients may indicate that obstacles occurred with respect to multiple categories. Our initial research using this procedure suggested that clients most frequently endorsed problems with private consequences, but every category was endorsed occasionally, suggesting the full assessment is useful (Baruch et al., in press). Consider this later interaction with Jim (the FA category the therapist is assessing is indicated after relevant questions):

Therapist (T): Did you make it to the museum on the free Monday, as we discussed last week?

Jim (J): No, I didn't make it.

T: Oh, I'm sorry to hear that. I was optimistic you would make it. Should we talk about what happened?

J: Sure.

T: Okay, well, did you remember to go, or did you just forget? [Forgetting]

J: I remembered, actually I was looking forward to it.

T: So you were planning to go Monday afternoon. Did you remember then? [Forgetting]

Figure 4.11 Functional Assessment Guide

Did you remember to do the assignment?		Did others distract you from starting or completing the assignment? How did others react?	Did you spend a lot of time thinking about the assignment but not doing anything?
	SOCIAL SKILLS Did completing the assignment require you to say no to or ask others for permission? Did you have trouble figuring out how to get these people to listen to you? Did you know what to say and how to say it effectively?		Imagine you are starting the assignment: What do you feel? How does thinking about doing the assignment make you feel?
Did you remember at the right time and place?		Did others do the assignment for you?	
		Is this assignment just really boring and you'd rather not do it?	Did you just avoid doing it?
Did you have it written on your activity monitoring or planner, etc.?	**NONSOCIAL SKILLS** Did you know how to do the assignment effectively? Have you done it before? Do you feel that there are other skills, experiences, etc. that you might need to do this well?	Is this assignment just a chore? Something you don't really care about but just have to do?	Were you just too tired, fatigued, or lacking energy to start the assignment?
		Did you get sidetracked by more enjoyable or easier activities, like watching TV?	Did you feel this assignment was beneath you or childish?

(continued)

Figure 4.11 (Continued)

ANTECEDENT FAILURE: Forgetting	BEHAVIOR FAILURE: Skills Deficit (PROBLEM SOLVING)	CONSEQUENCES FAILURE: Public	CONSEQUENCES FAILURE: Private
Did you try to use any reminders—written or from friends? Do you think this would have helped?	Was the problem fitting this assignment into a packed schedule? Was there just not enough time in the day? Did other unforeseen obstacles interfere? Did you have trouble coming up with solutions to these obstacles?	Did you get anything positive from not doing the assignment?	Did you feel you couldn't do the assignment alone? Were you hopeless about doing the assignment, or hopeless that doing it would help?
⇒	⇒	⇒	⇒
Stimulus Control	Skills Training	Contingency Management	Procedures Targeting Avoidance

J: Yes, but my buddy asked me to stay late at work to cover for him, so I didn't get out of there until 3:30, and the museum closes at 6, so I didn't think I would have enough time to do it.

T: So was it a situation where you had to say "yes" to your buddy [Public consequences], or was it that you didn't know how to say "no"? [Social skills deficits]

J: I pretty much had to. I mean, I guess I could have said "no," but he's done this kind of thing for me before and it would have been pretty rude.

T: Okay, but let me just ask you this for a second. If you had decided that going to the museum was sufficiently important that you were willing to be rude to him, would you have been able to say it? Or would you have been stuck, not knowing how to say "no" to him? [Social skills deficits]

J: I think I would have been able to say it to him—I've turned him down plenty of times before.

T: Okay, that's good. So let me ask you this, then. Could you have gone to the museum for just a briefer period of time, for just a few hours? I mean, why didn't you still go, even for a bit?

J: Well, I think that's a good question. When it was 3:30, I thought, do I really want to go through all that effort to bike down there, find a place to lock it up, wait in line, etcetera etcetera, just for like an hour or so?

T: So when the time got truncated, it just got sort of overwhelming and not worth the effort to you? [Private consequences]

J: Yeah, that's basically what happened.

In this interaction, the therapist has determined that (a) forgetting was not a problem in this instance, (b) social skills deficits do not appear to be a problem (although it may be useful for the therapist to probe a little more into how easy it would be for the client to assertively say "no" to his friend), (c) a public consequence was a problem, but there may not be a viable solution to it in this instance (in that the client made a reasonable decision to respect the friend's request rather than leave work at the scheduled time), and (d) a private consequence was a problem, and there may be room for intervention in this area.

The next section of this chapter presents additional BA strategies as per the FA procedure. Our suggestion is that these strategies are required only when a client does not complete activation assignments as per the activity scheduling guidelines presented earlier, and implementation of the strategies may be based on the FA procedure.

Additional Behavioral Activation Strategies
Stimulus Control Strategies

Stimulus control interventions are used when the client simply forgets to complete specific homework assignments or when the client remembers at inopportune times.

Behaviorally speaking, forgetting is not a matter of laziness, lack of motivation, or lack of caring; it is a function of an environment that is not properly arranged with the necessary prompts to evoke behavior related to homework assignments. The aim of a stimulus control intervention is therefore to have clients strategically place prompts in the environment that will serve as effective reminders to complete assignments.

Some clients may protest that the intervention sounds childish, and that they just need to do a better job of remembering. When responding to these kinds of client reactions, the therapist may find it helpful to provide information normalizing not just the frequent use of reminders by depressed individuals, but also by the gamut of nondepressed individuals in society. The following therapist/client interaction is typical of what therapists may encounter with clients, and may be helpful in responding to such hesitancy on the part of the client.

> Client (C): This idea just seems so silly and kind of infantile to me. I'm not here receiving treatment for Alzheimer's. Really what it boils down to is that I just need to do a better job of remembering.
>
> Therapist (T): Right, it is actually a common concern of clients that using reminders is childish. The truth is, however, many successful nondepressed individuals make use of reminders every day. Think of the busy lawyer who uses reminders from her secretary, BlackBerry, and planner every day to ensure that all of her client appointments and court dates are met. The lawyer does not use all of these reminders because she is stupid or because of some intellectual deficit. She does so because it can be difficult to keep track of multiple life demands. Incorporating some organization into her life makes this task easier.
>
> C: But a lawyer clearly has a lot more going on than I do.
>
> T: That is true. But I want you to take your life as seriously as the lawyer takes hers. Just because you are unemployed and depressed doesn't mean that what you have to accomplish on a day-to-day basis isn't important. Your time is just as valuable as the lawyer's, and what you do every day is just as important. You've lost that sense that what you do matters, and we all need reminders and help getting things done. So just like the busy lawyer, using some reminders is not a reflection of something that you are intrinsically lacking. Reminders are a way to make your life slightly more organized and to increase the chances that you will do the things that are actually important to do.

There are two principal considerations of any stimulus control intervention: (1) the form of the prompt and (2) the location of the prompt. Regarding the form of the prompt, sticky notes are common, but many other mediums can be used. New technologies have resulted in many electronic options such as BlackBerrys, e-mail, cell phones, and other digital organizers that the client can use to send reminder messages to him- or herself at specific times of the day. Whereas these devices can act as stimulus control interventions on their own, they may also be useful as a stimulus control intervention for the stimulus control intervention itself, as in an e-mail message to one's self to remember to put a sticky note on the computer when one gets home. Other less technologically advanced mediums, such as calendars and paper-and-pencil measures, can also be used. The therapist him- or herself may act as a reminder, with phone calls or e-mail, especially early in therapy.

Regarding the location of the prompt, good locations are those that are related to the behavior or assignment in some way. For example, it is likely that a note on the refrigerator to work on a resume may not serve as an effective cue because it is not located in the specific area where the client will work on his resume. Likewise, when a client is having trouble remembering to go jogging, a helpful reminder might be to place the jogging clothes and running shoes in front of the bedroom door before bed so that they are easily seen the next morning. Likewise, if a client is having trouble looking for jobs in the newspaper, it might be helpful for the client to place a newspaper on the alarm clock before going to bed.

The form and location of stimulus control interventions is only limited by the creativity of the client and therapist. Table 4.5 displays several types of stimulus control interventions that can be suggested to clients. Therapists and clients will determine what form of stimulus control works best for individual clients on a case-by-case basis according to the client's level of organizational skill as well as the physical tools (BlackBerry, planner, etc.) that the client may have at his or her disposal.

Skills–Training Strategies

Skills-training interventions should be considered when the functional assessment determines that the client does not possess adequate skills in his or her behavioral

Table 4.5 Common Stimulus Control Interventions

Nature of Prompt	Intervention
Visual	Keep a To-Do List: paper, word processing document, whiteboard. Use a daily planner or calendar: book or online format. Experiment with different paper, color/size for To-Do lists. Write single items to remember on a sticky note. Send an e-mail reminder to yourself or create a computer desktop reminder for self. Ask a friend to send you an e-mail.
Auditory	Leave a voice message for self (can call from session). Record messages on a handheld recorder. Set timers on alarm clocks, cell-phones, ovens, microwaves, etc. Ask a friend to give you a reminder call.
Timing	Set timers on alarm clocks, cell-phones, watches, ovens, microwaves, etc. Use a program to schedule sending a text message/instant message/e-mail. Schedule a time to review To-Do list (e.g., morning/before going to sleep).
Placement	Sticky note on cell phone to remember to call someone. Sticky note on computer monitor to remember to write an e-mail. Place exercise clothes in front of bedroom door to remember morning exercise. Sticky note on TV, computer monitor, game system. Sticky note on pillow to do something before going to bed. Place materials to be read on remote control. Put book to be read on gym bag. Keep To-Do list in pocket/wallet/purse until complete.

repertoire needed to complete a given assignment. Skills deficits may be social or nonsocial in nature, with problem-solving skills further distinguished as a subtype of nonsocial skills; and the purpose of the skills-training intervention is to help the client obtain necessary learning or training experiences outside of therapy and, in some instances, practice skills directly in session.

Social-Skills Social-skills training has been part of BA for decades (Kanter et al., in press). In general, it involves (a) direct instruction on what the client should do differently, (b) modeling of the improved performance with the therapist acting as the client and the client acting as the partner in the interaction, (c) role-playing the performance with the client practicing the performance and the therapist acting as the interaction partner, and (d) assignment of real-world practice as homework after the therapist has decided that the behavior is of sufficient skill to be successful in the natural environment (Segrin, 2003).

We expect most therapists to have some social-skills training repertoire already developed, so here we do not provide detailed instructions but do offer some general comments (for a review of specific techniques, see Becker, Heimberg, & Bellack, 1987; Bellack, Hersen, & Himmelhoch, 1996; Trower, 1995). Consider the following inter- action between a therapist and Amanda about Amanda initiating a conversation with her husband about household chores, which was an activation assignment she failed to complete.

Therapist (T): So it seems like you are having trouble initiating that conversation about household chores with your husband.

Amanda (A): I know. I feel so stupid. It shouldn't be too hard for me to ask him for a little more help around the house.

T: Well, based on what you've told me, it doesn't seem like you have had a lot of practice with asking specific demands of him. At the same time, it seems very important to you to have this conversation.

A: It is really important. I just don't know where to go with it.

T: Okay, let's work on this for a few minutes. Can you practice what you might say to your husband by role-playing with me? I'll pretend to be your husband.

A: I guess we can give it a try.

T: So just go ahead and talk to me as if I am your husband.

A: Okay, I guess I would say something like, "I've really been overwhelmed with all of the housework lately and don't feel like I've been getting very much help." [Amanda fails to make eye contact with her therapist and speaks in a low, almost inaudible tone.]

T: Okay, before we go on, can I point out a couple of things that I noticed while you were talking?

A: Sure.

T: The two things that I noticed were that you didn't make eye contact with me, and that you were speaking in a very low voice, which made it difficult to hear you. Is this how you might be with him?

A: You're right. Let's try this again. [Amanda repeats her question again, this time projecting her voice better and maintaining eye contact.]

T: "Well Amanda, you're making it seem like I sit around doing nothing all day. Maybe we can talk about this later." [Amanda looks down, and does not respond further.]

T: What did you notice about my response, Amanda?

A: Well, you got pretty defensive, and I didn't really know how to respond after you said that. That is actually pretty close to how my husband might respond.

T: Well, can you think of any reasons why your husband might respond defensively to what you have said?

A: I guess my statement did kind of imply that I'm not recognizing how busy he is with other things.

T: Do you think you can rephrase your question to be more sensitive to this point?

A: How about something like this. "Hey honey, I know you are very busy with work and other things, but I was wondering if I could talk to you about maybe getting a little more help with some of the chores around the house." How was that?

T: I think that was much better.

This interaction illustrates that in BA, just like with the assignment of activities, social-skills training is as concrete and specific as possible. The therapist ideally learns about the details and nuances of the social interaction and provides feedback at that level. Therapists need to pay close attention to nonverbal qualities that may detract from the client's message, such as poor eye contact, bad posture, and inappropriate tone, and be able to point out these observations. Sometimes, a good amount of time may need to be spent working on these kinds of nonverbal qualities before the content of the client's message is worked on.

Another issue regards the likelihood that clients will have difficulties generating appropriate material on their own at the beginning of role-play exercises. Therapists may choose to model the interaction first but should be careful that their modeling is consistent with the client's tone, style, and language. The therapist may say, "Here is how I might say it, but we'll need to translate it into something you're comfortable with and that feels right coming from your mouth." After modeling, the therapist may ask the client to role-play, and this sequence may be repeated several times.

Social-skills training interventions need not be limited to work in session. Therapists can work with clients to contact other learning sources outside of session that either supplement or complement ongoing work done directly with the therapist. For example, a client with difficulties initiating and sustaining conversations with people he meets may benefit from keeping up on current events in the world such that he has *small talk* material ready. The therapist and this client may also spend some time thinking up small talk topics of interest to the client in advance, so that he has them ready, as well as practicing small talk in session.

A final recommendation related to the training of social skills in BA sessions comes from Functional Analytic Psychotherapy (Tsai et al., 2009). Specifically, it is suggested that the therapist should always be observing the client's behavior for when the client is engaging in problematic and improved behavior *in session with respect to the therapist*. In other words, although Amanda may benefit from practicing making requests of her husband by role-playing with the therapist, she also may benefit from making requests directly of the therapist. When this happens, the therapist is in a position to reinforce relevant behavior directly, rather than relying on the husband to reinforce the behavior. Procedures for observing and responding to in-session behavior in BA are found in Kanter, Manos, Busch, and Rusch (2008).

When the therapist has determined that the client is ready to try the new behavior in his or her natural environment, as with other assignments in BA, therapists may ask clients to record specific assignments on the Activation Homework Sheet or activity hierarchy. Particular attention should be given to the level of the individual's current behavioral repertoire, and assignments should be developed in a graded fashion. In developing graded assignments related to practicing social skills in the real world, the therapist needs to be cognizant of a client's learning history, given that social-skills deficits are typically conceptualized as a product of the client's environment. Because social-skills deficits likely result from punishment or a lack of reinforcement for targeted behaviors in the past or from a lack of relevant exposure to situations requiring these skills, it is tantamount for the therapist to try to increase the likelihood of success for using skills outside of the session. For instance, if a client's goal is to be more assertive with a difficult family member who is likely to punish a client's attempts, it may be helpful for the therapist to determine whether there are other situations or people with whom the client can practice being assertive. In general, finding other situations should not be difficult, as the social-skills deficits often extend to multiple contexts.

Nonsocial-Skills Deficits There are a potentially large number of nonsocial-skills deficits blocking completion of activation assignments that the therapist may encounter, including issues such as lack of computer experience, difficulties creating a resume, driving a car, learning English, or learning the bus system. In general, therapists will not work on training these specific skills during the session, given time constraints and the likelihood of limited expertise in some of these areas. Rather, the therapist should work collaboratively with the client to facilitate the client receiving pertinent learning experiences outside of session, and should schedule these activities on the Activation Homework Sheet.

In the following exchange, the therapist describes the purpose of a nonsocial-skills intervention to Mike. The functional assessment has highlighted Mike's lack of experience in writing a resume as a reason for why he did not complete a resume for his homework assignment the previous week.

> Therapist (T): Okay. So you mentioned that you didn't really know where to get started with your resume because you haven't had to complete one for a while.
>
> Mike (M): Yeah, it's been about 20 years since I last had to apply for a job.
>
> T: Well, that's quite a while. What do you think about trying to spend some time right now figuring out how you can get some information on resume writing to help you along?
>
> M: Well, I guess I could do a Google search and try to find some information online, or maybe I could go to Barnes and Noble to see if they have any reference books.
>
> T: Both very good ideas. Now I want to make sure we're not putting too much on your plate for the upcoming week, given the other assignments we've already come up with. What do you think? Would you like to add just one of these to your homework sheet for this week and see how far you get?
>
> M: I think that makes sense. Why don't I just start out by working from home and see what I can find online first. Money is kind of tight, so it would be helpful if I didn't have to dole out cash for a new book.

This interaction illustrates that, as with all BA assignments, the therapist should work with the client to make the assignment specific, break it down into component parts, and grade it to fit what the client can do successfully. Although Mike possessed computer skills and a computer at home in this situation, the therapist may want to break down such tasks into smaller component parts to ensure that clients have the necessary skills to complete earlier behavioral links in the chain. For example, with other clients in a similar situation as Mike, the therapist might want to ascertain the client's access to a computer and his or her ability to use it in order to problem solve any potential barriers earlier in the chain.

Problem-Solving Deficits One exception to teaching nonsocial skills in session is teaching clients structured problem solving (D'Zurilla & Goldfried, 1971; Goldfried & Davison, 1994). This intervention can be useful with clients who have difficulties determining the best way to pursue a goal or have problems with effectively managing their time. This intervention will likely be most useful when clients learn the intervention well enough to implement this approach outside of session on their own in the advent of unexpected obstacles that impede completion of assigned homework. Although beyond the scope of this chapter, a simple structured problem-solving protocol can be taught to clients as appropriate as per the guidelines of Goldfried and Davison (1994).

Contingency Management Strategies

The primary goal of BA is for the client to engage in specific behaviors that contact positive reinforcement, broadly defined. Often the problem is not that the client is engaging in no behavior (antecedent problems) or low-quality behavior that does not contact reinforcement (behavior problems), it is that problem behavior is being reinforced instead of the target behavior. Put simply, the client is distracted from the behavior of interest by other more reinforcing activities. Examples range from a client spending his or her evenings watching television to friends unintentionally disrupting clients in various ways (asking to hang out) when the client is planning to complete an assignment.

Behavior isn't right or wrong, good or bad. Instead, it is a description or a commentary on the reinforcement value of one set of behaviors (e.g., employment seeking) relative to other behaviors (i.e., disrupting behaviors). Therefore, if a client is watching television instead of working on activation assignments, instead of suggesting that the client is lazy, we recognize that the reinforcement value of the competing behavior (watching TV) is simply greater. Several variables combine to determine a behavior's reinforcement value (e.g., the reinforcer magnitude, the time it takes to receive reinforcer, and the probability of receiving the reinforcer).

When a functional assessment determines that these sorts of public consequences are a reason for noncompliance, contingency management interventions should be considered. Contingency management interventions often target the public consequences in one's social environment. When a client is depressed, it is common for family members to reinforce depressive behavior. Consider the client whose wife cooks and brings all of his meals to bed so that the client does not have to leave the bedroom all day. Although these actions are usually done in a caring manner meant to help the client, the reinforcement of depressive behavior can act as a major barrier to the client becoming more active. Likewise, a client's attempts at activation can be stymied when family members or others inadvertently punish nondepressed behavior. As an example, consider the client who is asked, "How long are you going to be glued to that computer?" each time the client attempts to search for jobs on the computer. In response to such criticism, the client may likely search for work less frequently.

Individuals are often unaware of the true consequences of their actions and comments on others. Thus, when presenting the rationale for the intervention, it is important to explain how others' reactions are affecting the client's behavior and also to remind the client that others' actions are often unintentional. Here is an example of what this discussion may look like between a therapist and a client named Maria.

Therapist (T): You mentioned how you spent most of your time in bed last week and how your husband Juan brought most of your meals to the bedroom.

Maria (M): Yes, he knew I was having a really down week and was just trying to help.

T: Was there anything else he did for you while you were in bed.

M: Well, he also did the laundry and dishes for me.

T: Well, that was really nice of him. Now even though it seems like your husband had the best of intentions, do you find any of his behaviors problematic in terms of getting you active?

M: Well, maybe. I guess there was really no reason for me to get out of bed when he was taking care of all of my chores for me.

T: Right, so although your husband was lovingly trying to help you, his actions really just made it easier to stay in bed. These types of situations often come up during therapy. When they do arise, we usually ask clients to consider talking with the family member or friend about how his or her behavior is making activation more difficult. We could even ask that person to sign a contract stating that he or she will refrain from specific behaviors that might be interfering with therapy for a specified period of time. How does that sound?

Although the conversation in this example focused on depressed behaviors reinforced by the husband, the same kind of dialogue can easily be modified to address problems relating to the punishment of nondepressed behavior. Once the client agrees to consider trying out the intervention, the therapist and the client can formulate a written behavioral contract, adapted from the version used by Lejuez et al. (2001). Although the filled-out version provided in Figure 4.12 can be used as a template, the therapist and the client have latitude to design their own forms as appropriate.

Figure 4.12 Completed Behavioral Contract

I, **Juan** agree not to engage in the following behaviors that may interfere with **Maria's** goal of becoming more active: Bring Maria breakfast in bed, yell at Maria when she is doing her resume on the computer, take out the trash, do all the shopping.

When I, **Juan** see that **Maria** is making a visible effort to become more active, I agree to reward this active behavior by: taking her out for ice cream at the end of the week; giving her praise; giving her kisses.

Signed:

Juan

_____

Family member/friend

Maria

_____

Client

Regardless of the form used, the filled-out contract should concretely specify which behaviors the family member, friend, or acquaintance is being asked to refrain from, along with the client goals with which these behaviors are interfering. In the example provided in Figure 4.12, Juan's behaviors have been interfering with Maria's ability to search for employment. Notice how the behaviors that Juan is being asked to refrain from are very specific in nature, ranging from not bringing Maria breakfast in bed to not yelling at her while she works on her resume. In addition to proscribing specific behaviors, the contract can also list positive consequences contingent on client engagement in nondepressed behaviors. In this example, Juan has agreed to reward Maria's efforts at activation with praise and going out for ice cream together.

Before the client asks the individual to sign the contract, the therapist may have the client role-play the interaction to ensure that the client's presentation of the contract is sensitive to the feelings of the family member/friend and nonaccusatory. Ideally, the family member can be invited into the session for an explanation of the rationale for the intervention.

Contingency management can also be used when assignments are not particularly pleasurable for clients, as in when a client reports that an assignment must be done, but the assignment simply is boring, a chore, and has no connection with the client's values. In these situations, the client and the therapist can be creative in developing contracts and contingencies that might help the client engage in the behavior. Some examples from previous versions of BA include (Kanter et al., 2010):

➤ Develop with the client a self-reward menu that specifies self-rewards for completion of specific assignments, or points that can be accumulated for larger rewards.

➤ Make the next therapy appointment contingent on completing tasks assigned in the previous session.

➤ Link the number of activities completed to minutes of therapy time.

➤ Develop a "credit" system in which the client's therapy bill is adjusted up or down depending on completion of tasks and compliance with therapy procedures.

➤ Contract with the client that if he or she chooses not to complete an activity, he or she will call the therapist and leave a message stating that he or she is *choosing* not to get active.

➤ Have the client write a check to an organization or charity that he or she dislikes (e.g., a client who is a politically active liberal would write a check to a conservative organization). Hold on to the check, with the agreement that you will send the check to the organization if the client does not complete the assigned activity.

When setting up self-reward systems, two points should be kept in mind. First, the client must agree to not partake in the reward until the activation assignment is completed. For example, if the client agrees that she will only watch television after completing her laundry, she must be willing to change her routine and not watch television at other times. Otherwise, the value of the reward is severely diminished. Second, these arbitrary reward systems should not be seen as long-term solutions. They tend to work best as interim solutions when otherwise the specific target behavior would not occur, but they should be faded out before the end of treatment.

Strategies Targeting Avoidance

Strategies targeting avoidance, primary to BA by Martell and colleagues (2001), flow directly from the negative reinforcement model of depression discussed earlier. These strategies should be used when the FA determines that the private consequences of a specific assignment may be interfering with homework completion. These private consequences may include feeling anxious, sad, stressed, overwhelmed, bored, and so forth. When activation elicits these aversive feelings, it is natural for clients to want to avoid the activation, even if as they are avoiding they are aware that they may be making their problems worse in the long run. Avoidance in this context may take many forms, some active and some passive, and may be relatively tricky to overcome. The power of short-term negative reinforcement in the form of successful escape from or avoidance of painful emotional states is quite strong.

BA's approach to targeting avoidance of private experiences essentially is an acceptance approach, in that the goal is to activate the client *with* the aversive private feelings rather than trying to directly change the feelings. The idea, consistent with how behaviorists have viewed the relations between feelings and behavior for decades, is that aversive feelings make certain behaviors harder to accomplish, but they do not make behavior impossible (Martell & Kanter, in press). Thus, the BA therapist empathically validates the client's experience of aversive private experiences and compassionately persists in helping the client activate, in the presence of those feelings. This approach is similar to that of Acceptance and Commitment Therapy (ACT; Kanter, Baruch, & Gaynor, 2006). However, in ACT, the client is taught explicit strategies, such as mindfulness and defusion, that specifically help with acceptance of aversive experiences, whereas in BA no specific strategies are taught. Instead, BA works on the assumption that compassionately persisting in activation will be sufficient in overcoming avoidance for many clients. In BA, unlike in ACT, the therapist may suggest to the client that over time, aversive private experiences will ameliorate, and that engaging in behavioral activation should be helpful in reducing those experiences over time.

Providing a Rationale for Targeting Avoidance As a first step in targeting avoidance, the therapist may provide a rationale for this work to the client. For this purpose, the Two Circles model presented to clients earlier in treatment can be modified to yield a Three Circles model. The therapist may explain this to the client as follows:

> Do you remember, when we were talking about the cycle of your depression, I presented to you these two circles, "negative life events" and "common responses"? [Draw the two circles as before.] Talking to you now, I would like to add a little bit to that model. Specifically, when we talk about your common responses, I'd like to distinguish two types of responses. One is how you feel in response to the negative life events, and the other is how you act. So the common responses circle from before can become two circles [erase "common responses" circle and replace with two circles as in Figure 4.13], one that we can label "Emotional Responses," like how you feel, and the other that is more what you do. And I'm thinking that perhaps a good label for what you've been doing is "getting stuck" because it seems as if these feelings [point to "emotional responses" circle] have really become a major impediment for you. Or we could call this circle Avoidance. Either way, it represents all the ways you've been reacting to these painful emotions, trying to not feel them, isolating and shutting down, staying in bed all day, like we've been talking about. Does this fit your experience? Does your experience map on to this idea that your life sort of fell apart [pointing to "negative life events"], you started to really feel miserable [pointing to "emotional responses"], and then you sort of shut down and got stuck in avoidance behavior [pointing to "avoidance"]? And all of this sort of cycles and creates more and more depression, because once you're stuck, now you're not doing anything productive at all? So our task is going to be to get you to notice when you are getting stuck (avoiding) and help you specifically get unstuck and keep active specifically in those situations that are hard for you.

Figure 4.13   The Three Circles Model

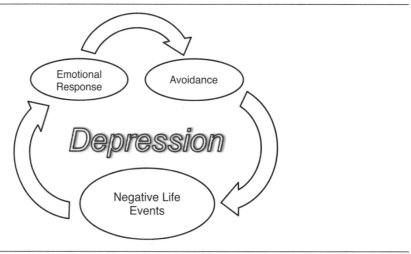

Figure 4.14 A Specific Example of the Three Circles Model

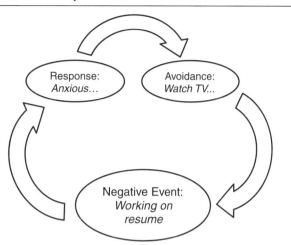

Working With Specific Situations That Evoke Avoidance Although the earlier script may be helpful to therapists in introducing the model broadly, it is also helpful to repeatedly review the model in the context of specific problems surfacing for the client, and to be collaborative with the client when teaching the model. Thus, the model can be used to discuss specific problems as well. Consider this interaction with Shana, who reported that she had not completed her activity of completing her resume and cover letter over the previous week. A sample three-circles model for Shana is shown in Figure 4.14.

Therapist (T): So you had some troubles with your resume.

Shana (S): Yeah, I just couldn't bring myself to do it. It was too hard.

T: Can you tell me a little about what you were feeling and thinking as you sat down to start it?

S: Well, I don't know. I guess I just kind of got anxious, and started thinking about how no matter how much time I put into this resume, it really wouldn't matter a darn bit. There are just so many applicants and so few jobs; I mean I don't have a chance.

T: Okay, that is understandable. Do you remember that "Three Circles" model about depression that we reviewed earlier on?

S: Sure.

T: Well, I'd like to go over the model and see how it relates to this specific situation, and then get your feedback on this. How does this sound?

S: Sure, why not.

T: [Writing on blackboard] So here is our first circle, which before we labeled negative life events, but when we're thinking about applying it to specific situations in your life, we can look at any situation that triggers negative feelings for you. In this instance, we're talking about you trying to get started on your resume. So I am going to write that in here. Next I am going to draw an arrow over to this second circle, which is your emotional response. You said that you were pretty anxious when starting on that resume, so I will put that down. What were some of the other things you were feeling?

S: I just became really stressed out and even cried a little. And then I just kept having all those thoughts about my efforts just not really mattering.

T: All right, I'm going to write in those here, too. So when you started on your resume, you got anxious, stressed, emotional, and couldn't get rid of these negative thoughts that kept coming back to you. So once all of these set in, what was your next move?

S: I'm not really sure of what you're getting at.

T: What did you do once you started feeling this way? Did you keep on writing the resume, getting it partially completed?

S: No, I just left the computer room and watched television for the rest of the day.

T: Okay. Did you come back to the resume later that day or later in the week?

S: No, I just didn't see the point.

T: So I'll put that in this third "Avoidance" circle here. I'll write that you stopped writing the resume, watched television, and did not come back to the resume for the rest of the week. I am also going to add these three arrows here connecting the three circles. Does this make sense to you?

S: Yeah, I guess my getting upset caused me to stop doing my task for the week.

T: Exactly, that's the arrow going from responses to avoidance. And the first arrow going from the event to the responses refers to how trying to write your resume got you anxious and stressed. Now, what about the arrow from watching TV to more negative life events?

S: I know, I know, I'll never get a job if I keep avoiding working on my resume, and then I'll just feel worse. If I could just make myself do it, I know I would feel better.

T: I agree, but I also want to point out that I really believe you are doing the best you can. I mean, if you could just make yourself do it, you wouldn't need me, right? It is really hard to continue working when feeling all the things you are feeling, and it is completely understandable that you would quit. As you know, it is totally unhelpful, but it is understandable. So I want to help you with a really hard task—persisting in working on your resume, knowing that these feelings are going to surface for you and sort of scream at you to quit. I believe you can do this, and we can discuss how.

As in the earlier dialogue, when targeting avoidance, the BA therapist gently and compassionately encourages the client to persist in the task, while feeling the feelings that otherwise would lead them to avoid and quit. Clients, however, will often convey an intellectual understanding of the avoidance model to the therapist, while maintaining that acting in the context of negative private experiences is just too difficult. A common client retort to the presentation of the model is to take the "inside-out" approach to activation; for example, "I could do all of this stuff if I just didn't feel so tired." In response to such concerns, the clinician should remain empathic while shifting the focus to BA's "outside-in" approach. A "fireman" metaphor is sometimes useful in this regard. The therapist may state:

> It's like the "Firemen" approach. Firemen know that going into a burning building is dangerous and scary, but they accept that a part of their job is taking all that fear and anxiety along with them. I remember I once heard a fireman interviewed after he had heroically saved someone from a burning building, and the reporter asked him, "You have so much courage. How can you not feel any fear?" The fireman responded, "Courage is not the absence of fear, it is feeling the fear but doing something anyway. If you didn't feel the fear, it wouldn't be courageous." You are sort of in that situation like the fireman. It's the same here; the goal is to carry that discomfort with you while you are doing the assignment. Your goal is to choose to *keep moving* with the discomfort without getting caught up in the urge to make it go away.

The following dialogue also may be helpful in illustrating this point.

Therapist (T): I understand how it is very hard to get things done when you are having such intense feelings of anxiety. If the feelings would go down just a bit, it would be so much easier to get things done. I totally understand how that feels. With the approach that we are trying, I am asking you to approach the situation from a slightly different angle. Sometimes, it may take a lot of time for these intense emotions and feelings to diminish; if you wait for them to go away, you may be waiting for a while before you can become active. What I am asking you to do is to become active despite the way you are feeling. Try to recognize those feelings of stress, and carry them with you as you try to bang out that resume.

Client (C): But I'm just so stressed, I can't. And doing the resume isn't going to make me less stressed out.

T: And that's a very good point. The stress may not go away. It may even increase because you are coming face-to-face with it. The question is whether getting this resume out and hopefully getting a job sometime soon is important enough to you so that it outweighs the stress you are feeling in the short term. And it is sort of a trap, isn't it? Because while you're waiting for and hoping these feelings go away, in actuality the more you wait, the more stressed you've been feeling! However, if you could just get started on it, that might start to make you feel less stressed. The trick is just to get started; then you've broken that cycle and things start to improve for you. It is kind of like pushing a car from a standstill. It is really hard to get the car moving, but once you've got it moving, then it is much easier to keep it moving.

C: But what if I can't get the car moving?

T: Well, that is what we've got to figure out. Let's rethink the assignment this week—come up with something that is just about getting moving, just a bit. A bite-size piece of work here. Nothing too overwhelming—just enough to get you started? What do you think that would be?

C: Well, how about I just spend 15 minutes on it?

T: If you spend 15 minutes on it, would you feel a sense of accomplishment?

C: Given that I haven't even touched it in the last year, I think so.

T: Okay, good, let's plan that then. And here's the thing: When you sit down to do it, you will feel that anxiety and stress. I suspect it will hit you hard. Your trick will be to not fight it. Let it happen, and tell yourself, "I can keep working, this feeling can't stop me. I don't need to make it go away *before* I can work. And if I work right now, I will feel better afterward." Do you think you can do that?

C: I can try.

Activating clients in the context of avoidance of private experiences is not easy work for the therapist. It is more important than ever to make sure that the five tips for creating good activation assignments are being followed here. Regarding the first tip (assignments should be guided by the case conceptualization), it may be useful to have an explicit discussion of the client's goals and values related to the assignment, to make sure that it fits what he or she truly wants out of therapy. Explicitly linking the assignment to the client's values may offer a bridge over the short-term aversive experiences that working on the assignment will cause. In fact, we have found it helpful to use stimulus control procedures to make the client's values very salient when trying to activate in the context of avoidance. For example, the client earlier may put a picture of her daughter by the computer monitor to remind herself of her desire to be a good role model for her daughter by persisting in trying to find work.

Focusing on values helps clarify that the therapist is not advocating a "grin and bear it" approach. In fact, many clients feel more empowered by focusing on their choice or willingness to choose to pursue their long-term goals while feeling uncomfortable in the short term. Thus, the client is being encouraged to be fully aware of the difficult feeling, notice it, and keep moving. In short, they are encouraged to say to oneself: "Although I am feeling ____, I'm going to keep doing ____ because this task is really important to me."

Graded task assignment (Tip 2) and breaking down tasks into manageable chunks (Tip 3) are extremely important here in order to design assignments that are not overwhelming to clients, and discussing the specific details of the assignment (Tip 4) also will be helpful when reviewing the task the following week because it allows the therapist to ask what the client was doing at the specific time agreed upon for task completion.

Working With Rumination In BA, rumination is treated as avoidance and thus can be submitted to the "Three Circles" model. For example, consider Benton, who reported to his therapist that he spends long periods of time thinking about how self-absorbed he was as a teenager, failing to fully appreciate his mother before she died suddenly. In this case, the negative event can be seen as Benton's mother's death, and the response can be seen as his guilty thoughts. Of primary interest to the BA therapist is not the content of the thoughts or how accurate they are, but how Benton responds to the thoughts. Some questions for the therapist to ask may be:

➤ What was Benton doing while he was having these thoughts?
➤ What was Benton avoiding or missing by having these thoughts?
➤ Was this productive behavior or unproductive?
➤ What does Benton do to avoid having these thoughts?
➤ What can Benton do more productively with respect to his mother's death instead of ruminating about past misdeeds?

In Benton's case, as with grief in general in BA, we would encourage activation assignments as an alternative to rumination that are consistent with the notion of "active grieving," such as scheduling a period each day to journal about his feelings about his mother or more informally simply being open to the experience of grief whenever it surfaces, visiting his mother's grave, talking to family members about the loss, reviewing old photo albums and mementos associated with his mother, and so forth.

When working with rumination, a useful alternate behavior to try to activate, when the client notices that he or she is ruminating, is "attention to immediate experience." This is akin to mindfulness, but there is no need to call it mindfulness or to invoke any Eastern spiritual connotations. Instead, the therapist may simply suggest:

When you notice yourself ruminating, I would like you to instead try to redirect your attention to your immediate experience. Stop and smell the roses, as they say. Although in your case, your immediate experience may not be as pleasant as roses, it is still there to be experienced. What is happening around you? What are the sights, sounds, smells? What is happening in your immediate environment that is there to be experienced?

However, attention to immediate experience is one of many alternatives to rumination. The goal is to keep the client active, however possible. Consider this interaction between the therapist and Bill:

Therapist (T): In here we've been talking about how when you're feeling lousy, the natural reaction is to shut down and not do the things you normally do.

So when you were sitting around daydreaming this week, how were you feeling then?

Bill (B): Trying to tune it all out I guess, daydream more.

T: How did that make you feel when you were trying to tune it all out and make it go away?

B: It got worse.

T: How did it get worse?

B: My problems hadn't got any better so it just . . . got worse over a period of time that I hadn't done anything about them.

T: So how was your mood when you came back to reality?

B: More depressed.

T: So you started to feel depressed and you pulled away and that made you feel worse.

B: Yep.

T: Do you think you could have been doing something else instead of lying on your bed, feeling tired and daydreaming?

B: It would have taken a lot of work . . .

T: Here's what I'd like to ask you to do next time. You are lying there on your bed, right? And you feel exhausted. Next time that happens, just roll right off the bed. Fall on the floor. Now you're not going to want to be just lying there on the floor, will you?

B: That's funny. No, that would be pretty uncomfortable.

T: Okay, good. So now that you're on the floor, what are you going to do?

B: Well, I need to water my plants, and I need to do my dishes. I don't know, there are a million things to do.

T: Well, let's have a specific plan for what you will do if you find yourself on the floor, okay?

Putting It All Together In this final dialogue, the therapist is working with a college student who has become active and has started to feel better. The therapist responds by highlighting the client's values and BA's "outside-in" approach, which involves feeling feelings while staying active.

Client (C): I've been focused on getting reenrolled in school, but it is very complicated. There are only two classes that fulfill the requirement I need to fulfill and they are both at the same time, so I have to take one class at one campus and the other at the other campus . . . . It is so . . . I'm trying not to use the word "frustrating."

Therapist (T): Why are you trying not to use it?

C: Because I'd be, like, everything is frustrating, this is frustrating, that is frustrating . . .

T: Well, that is how you feel.

C: I know, okay, I'm really frustrated.

T: And I want to highlight just one aspect of this . . . It is sort of like you are acting like a real adult here. There are lots of frustrating things we have to do on a daily basis, and we do them, because if we didn't . . .

C: Things would just fall apart.

T: Right, so, I just want to say that I appreciate how you are frustrated, but I think this is really great that you are focused on getting this done and acting like an adult here . . . I mean, the easiest way to make the frustration go away would be to just give up and say, forget it, I don't want to get my degree, it is not worth it.

C: I'm not going to do that.

T: How close are you to giving up?

C: I mean, I have totally thought, "I just want to quit," and in the past, I would have just quit.

T: So this is really terrific. Do you see? Think about it. In a way, your frustration is a good thing, because it is sort of a signal that you are not giving up, that you are acting like an adult. You feel frustrated because you are no longer running from frustration.

C: Yeah, I see what you mean.

Termination

As clients start to improve during BA, there are several things to keep in mind. The primary consideration is making sure that the client's improved activation will continue in the absence of the therapeutic relationship. This can be done by gradually fading the therapy and the accountability the client has to the therapist. The therapist and the client may discuss lengthening the interval between sessions from weekly to bi-monthly to monthly and decreasing the length of sessions from 50 minutes to 30 minutes to brief phone check-ins. Also, after a new behavior has become a routine, the therapist should spend less session time specifically scheduling and reviewing the behavior, to evaluate if the behavior will continue in the absence of direct therapeutic intervention.

For some clients, improvement occurs rapidly, and the therapist may be concerned that the client will terminate therapy as soon as he or she feels better, but before robust changes in behavior and environment have occurred. In these instances, a clear rationale for continuing therapy even when feeling better may be helpful. The therapist may suggest:

It is great that you are feeling better, and it is more important than ever to continue therapy. I want to work with you to build positive changes in your life so the next time you hit rock bottom, you will be prepared. It is like preparing for a hurricane—you know it is coming, you do things to prepare for it, stock up, get food and water, and protect against the storm. That way, when negative life events again happen in your life—and I sure hope they won't, but realistically, some certainly will—you will be prepared and stay active and not fall into the cycle of depression.

Alternatively, it may be helpful to frame therapy as teaching a new skill—the skill of responding with activation when negative life events happen and you feel bad. The therapist may suggest that learning a new skill takes time and that it is important to come to sessions and learn this skill, even if the client starts to feel better immediately.

Finally, when clients start to improve, we have found it helpful to use a "Staying Active Guide" (Figure 4.15). This guide includes simple lists that the client and the therapist may collaboratively define of: (a) ways the client will recognize if she or he is becoming depressed or inactive again (to help the client self-activate as soon as she or he recognizes the spiral), (b) activities that the client enjoys when not depressed, (c) activities that are in line with the client's values that she or he may not feel like doing, (d) obstacles to engaging in #2 and #3 and plans for overcoming those obstacles, and (e) expected future events that may be difficult for the client to handle (holidays, anniversaries, changes of seasons, or specific things the client's partner may do or may not do), and plans for responding to these events. These lists are designed to function as important reminders for the client to take with him or her on the road beyond therapy. The guide may also include the therapist's or clinic's phone number and the invitation to restart therapy if things get rough.

Figure 4.15   Staying Active Guide

Staying Active Guide
Things to remember: What was helpful about therapy? What made me feel the best? What is important to remember?

1. _____
2. _____
3. _____
4. _____

How will I notice if I am becoming depressed again? What specific things do I do that make me depressed?

1. _____
2. _____
3. _____
4. _____
5. _____

Important activities to continue (both activities that I enjoy AND activities that are important to do but I used to avoid):

1. _____

  ◦ Obstacles to doing
    it: _____

  ◦ Plan for overcoming
    obstacles: _____

2. _____

  ◦ Obstacles to doing
    it: _____

  ◦ Plan for overcoming
    obstacles: _____

3. _____

  ◦ Obstacles to doing
    it: _____

  ◦ Plan for overcoming
    obstacles: _____

4. _____

  ◦ Obstacles to doing
    it: _____

  ◦ Plan for overcoming
    obstacles: _____

5. _____

  ◦ Obstacles to doing
    it: _____

  ◦ Plan for overcoming
    obstacles: _____

Think about the next year of your life. What events—holidays, anniversaries, changes of seasons, specific things your partner and/or children may do or may not do—will be difficult for you to handle?

1. _____
2. _____
3. _____
4. _____
5. _____

How will I cope with these events and situations? What specific actions will I take? (This list could include talking to family and friends and calling your therapist for help if you need it.)

1. _____
2. _____
3. _____
4. _____
5. _____

References

Armento, M. E. A., & Hopko, D. R. (2007). The environmental reward observation scale (EROS): Development, validity, and reliability. *Behavior Therapy, 38,* 107–119.

Baruch, D. E., Kanter, J. W., Bowe, W. M., & Pfennig, S. L. (in press) Improving homework compliance in career counseling with a behavioral activation functional assessment procedure. *Cognitive Behavioral Practice.*

Beck, A. T., Steer, R. A., & Brown, G. K. (1996). *Manual for the Beck depression inventory-II.* San Antonio, TX: Psychological Corporation.

Beck, J. S., (1995). *Cognitive Therapy: Basics and Beyond.* New York, NY: Guilford Press.

Becker, R. E., Heimberg, R. G., & Bellack, A. S. (1987). *Social skills training treatment for depression.* New York, NY: Pergamon Press.

Bellack, A. S., Hersen, M., & Himmelhoch, J. M. (1996). Social skills training as a treatment for depression: A treatment manual. In V. B. Van Hasselt & M. Hersen (Eds.), *Sourcebook of psychological treatment manuals for adult disorders* (pp. 179–200). New York, NY: Plenum Press.

Busch, A. M., Uebelacker, L. A., Kalibatseva, Z., & Miller, I. W. (2010). Measuring homework completion in behavioral activation. *Behavior Modification, 34,* 310–329.

Carvalho, J. P., Gawrysiak, M. J., Hellmuth, J. C., McNulty, J. K., Magidson, J. F., Lejuez, C. W., & Hopko, D. R. (in press) The reward probability index (RPI): Design and validation of a scale measuring access to environmental reward. *Behavior Therapy.*

Cuijpers, P., van Straten, A., & Warmerdam, L. (2007). Behavioral activation treatments of depression: A meta-analysis. *Clinical Psychology Review, 27,* 318–326.

Cusin, C., Yang, H., Yeung, A., & Fava, M. (2010). Rating scales for depression. In L. Baer & M.A. Blais (Eds.), *Handbook of clinical rating scales and assessment in psychiatry and mental health* (pp. 7–35). Totowa, NJ: Humana Press.

Dichter, G., Felder, J., Petty, C., Bizzell, J., Ernst, M., & Smoski, M. (2009). The effects of psychotherapy on neural responses to rewards in major depression. *Biological Psychiatry, 66,* 886–897.

Dimidjian, S., Martell, C. R., Addis, M. E., & Herman-Dunn, R. (2008). Behavioral activation in the treatment of major depressive disorder. In D. H. Barlow (Ed.), *Clinical handbook of psychological disorders,* (4th ed., pp. 328–364). New York, NY: Guilford Press.

Dobson, K. (2001). *Handbook of cognitive-behavioral therapies* (2nd ed.). New York, NY: Guilford Press.

Dobson, K., & Dozois, D. (2001). Historical and philosophical bases of the cognitive-behavioral therapies. In K. S. Dobson (Ed.), *Handbook of cognitive-behavioral therapies* (2nd ed., pp. 3–39). New York, NY: Guilford Press.

D'Zurilla, T., & Goldfried, M. (1971). Problem solving and behavior modification. *Journal of Abnormal Psychology, 78,* 107–126.

Ekers, D., Richards, D., & Gilbody, S. (2008). A meta-analysis of randomized trials of behavioural treatments of depression. *Psychological Medicine, 38,* 611–623.

Glasgow, R., Vogt, T., & Boles, S., (1999). *Evaluating the impact of health promotion interventions: The RE-AIM framework. American Journal of Public Health, 89,* 1322–1327.

Goldfried, M., & Davison, G. (1994). *Clinical behavior therapy* (Exp. ed.). Oxford, England: John Wiley & Sons.

Hayes, S. C., Strosahl, K., & Wilson, K. G. (1999). *Acceptance and commitment therapy: An experimental approach to behavior change.* New York, NY: Guilford Press.

Hopko, D. R., Lejuez, C. W., Armento, M. E. A., & Bare, R. L. (2004). Depressive disorders. In M. Hersen (Ed.), *Psychological assessment in clinical practice: A pragmatic guide* (pp. 85–116). New York, NY: Taylor & Francis.

Hopko, D. R., Lejuez, C. W., Ruggiero, K. J., & Eifert, G. H. (2003). Contemporary behavioral activation treatments for depression: Procedures, principles, and progress. *Clinical Psychology Review, 23*, 699–717.

Horowitz, A. V., & Wakefield, J. C. (2007). *The loss of sadness: How psychiatry transformed normal sorrow into depressive disorder*. New York, NY: Oxford University Press.

Kanter, J. W., Baruch, D. E., & Gaynor, S. T. (2006). Acceptance and commitment therapy and behavioral activation for the treatment of depression: Description and comparison. *Behavior Analyst, 9*, 161–185.

Kanter, J. W., Busch, A. M., & Rusch, L. C. (2009). *Behavioral activation: Distinctive features*. London, England: Routledge Press.

Kanter, J. W., Manos, R. C., Bowe, W. M., Baruch, D. E., Busch, A. M., & Rusch, L. C. (2010). What is behavioral activation? A review of the empirical literature. *Clinical Psychology Review, 30*(6), 608–620.

Kanter, J. W., Manos, R. C., Busch, A. M., & Rusch, L. C. (2008). Making behavioral activation more behavioral. *Behavioral Modification, 32*, 780–803.

Kanter, J. W., Mulick, P. S., Busch, A. M., Berlin, K. S., & Martell, C. R. (2007). The behavioral activation for depression scale (BADS): Psychometric properties and factor structure. *Journal of Psychopathology and Behavioral Assessment, 29*, 191–202.

Kanter, J. W., Santiago-Rivera, A., Rusch, L. C., Busch, A. M., & West, P. (2010). Initial outcomes of a culturally adapted behavioral activation for Latinas diagnosed with depression at a community clinic. *Behavior Modification, 34*, 120–144.

Lejuez, C. W., Hopko, D. R., & Hopko, S. D. (2001). A brief behavioral activation treatment for depression: Treatment manual. *Behavior Modification, 25*, 255–286.

Longmore, R. J., & Worrell, M. (2007). Do we need to challenge thoughts in cognitive behavior therapy? *Clinical Psychology Review, 27*, 173–187.

Lopez, A. D., Mathers, C. D., Ezzati, M., Jamison, D. T., & Murray, C. J. (2006). Global and regional burden of disease and risk factors, 2001: Systematic analysis of population health data. *Lancet, 367*, 1747–1757.

Lovibond, S. H., & Lovibond, P. F. (1995). *Manual for the depression anxiety stress scales*. Sydney, Australia: Psychology Foundation.

MacPhillamy, D. J., & Lewinsohn, P. M. (1974). Depression as a function of levels of desired and obtained pleasure. *Journal of Abnormal Psychology, 83*, 651–657.

MacPhillamy, D. J., & Lewinsohn, P. M. (1982). The pleasant events schedule: Studies on reliability, validity, and scale intercorrelation. *Journal of Consulting and Clinical Psychology, 50*, 363–380.

Manos, R. C., Kanter, J. W., & Busch, A. M. (2010). A critical review of assessment strategies to measure the behavioral activation model of depression. *Clinical Psychology Review, 30*, 547–561.

Martell, C., Dimidjian, S., & Herman-Dunn, R. (2010). *Behavioral activation for depression: A clinician's guide*. New York, NY: Guilford Press.

Martell, C. R., Addis, M. E., & Jacobson, N. S. (2001). *Depression in context: Strategies for guided action*. New York, NY: Norton.

Martell, C. R., & Kanter, J. W. (in press). Behavioral activation in the context of "third wave" therapies. In J. D. Herbert & E. Forman (Eds.), *Acceptance and mindfulness in cognitive behavior therapy*. Hoboken, NJ: John Wiley & Sons.

Mazzucchelli, T., Kane, R., & Rees, C. (2009). Behavioral activation treatments for adults: A meta-analysis and review. *Clinical Psychology: Science and Practice, 16*, 383–411.

Nezu, A. M., Ronan, G. F., Meadows, E. A., & McClure, K. S. (Eds.). (2000). *Practitioner's guide to empirically based measures of depression*. New York, NY: Kluwer Academic/Plenum.

Rusch, L. C., Kanter, J. W., Brondino, M. J., Weeks, C. E., & Bowe, W. M. (2010). Biomedical stigma reduction programs produce negative but transient effects on a depressed low-income community sample. *Journal of Social and Clinical Psychology, 29*(9), 1020–1030.

Rusch, L. C., Kanter, J. W., & Brondino, M. J. (2009). A comparison of the contextual and biomedical models of stigma reduction for depression with a non-clinical undergraduate sample. *Journal of Nervous and Mental Disease, 197*, 104–110.

Santiago-Rivera, A., Kanter, J., Benson, G., Derose, T., Illes, R., & Reyes, W. (2008). Behavioral activation as an alternative treatment approach for Latinos with depression. *Psychotherapy Theory, Research, Practice, Training, 45*, 173–185.

Segrin, C. (2003). Social skills training. In W. O'Donohue, J. E. Fisher, & S. C. Hayes (Eds.), *Cognitive behavior therapy: Applying empirically supported techniques in your practice* (pp. 384–390). Hoboken, NJ: John Wiley & Sons.

Skinner, B. F. (1953). *Science and human behavior*. Oxford, England: Macmillan.

Skinner, B. F. (1974). *About behaviorism*. Oxford, England: Knopf.

Trower, P. (1995). Adult social skills: State of the art and future directions. In W. O'Donohue & L. Krasner (Eds.), *Handbook of psychological skills training: Clinical techniques and applications* (pp. 54–80). Boston, MA: Allyn & Bacon.

Tsai, M., Kohlenberg, R. J., Kanter, J. W., Kohlenberg, B., Follette, W. C., & Callaghan, G. M. (Eds.). (2009). *A guide to functional analytic psychotherapy: Using awareness, courage, love, and behaviorism*. New York, NY: Springer.

Wilson, K. G., Sandoz, E. K., Kitchens, J., & Roberts, M. E. (2010). The valued living questionnaire: Defining and measuring valued action within a behavioral framework. *Psychological Record, 60*, 249–274.

5
Cognitive Behavioral Analysis System of Psychotherapy for Chronic Depression

James P. McCullough Jr. and J. Kim Penberthy

Introduction

The format of this chapter is written to illustrate a single case administration of Cognitive Behavioral Analysis System of Psychotherapy (CBASP) to an early-onset, chronically depressed 39-year-old male. Large portions of the text consist of verbatim transcript interactions between the first author, JPM, and the patient. The verbatim exchanges are followed by comment sections to illustrate the underlying rationale guiding the therapist's behavior. Our goal here is to help the reader get "a feel" for the way the CBASP model is administered to a chronically depressed patient. For a more in-depth review of the model, readers should consult the two major CBASP texts (viz. McCullough, 2000, 2006).

Briefly, the essential etiological predicament of the early-onset, chronically depressed patient arises from a developmental history of psychological insults and trauma (McCullough, 2008; Nemeroff et al., 2003; Wiersma et al., 2009) received at the hands of his or her significant others. These preadolescent or adolescent experiences leave early-onset patients sealed off behind a wall of pervasive interpersonal fear. The fear state frequently results in a lifetime pattern of interpersonal avoidance with little or no possibility of spontaneous remission (McCullough et al., 1990a, 1990b; McCullough et al., 1988). One consequence of the fear state is seen in an age-inappropriate level of cognitive-emotive functioning that is best described by Piaget (1926/1923) as *preoperational functioning* (McCullough, 2000, 2006). Early-onset patients are not informed by environmental feedback, so they behave in the intrapersonal and interpersonal-social spheres with patterns of self-contained repetitiveness. They think in a precausal and illogical manner, leaping from premises to negative conclusions with no stops in between. In addition, they evince little emotional control and converse in a monologue fashion. At the outset of treatment, these patients frequently leave psychotherapists feeling helpless, incompetent, and frustrated. When administered medication alone—which is regrettably too often the case among U.S. psychiatrists—approximately 23% will remit (Keller, McCullough, et al., 2000; Kocsis et al., 2009), with relapse and high recurrence rates once medication is withdrawn (Thase, 1992). Approximately 45% to 50% of this patient population will not respond to medication alone. Recent research suggests that optimal treatment strategies should include medication and psychotherapy administered concomitantly (Keller, McCullough, et al., 2000; Schramm & Reynolds, 2010). Summarily, these childlike adult patients do not function adequately in the adult world and without proper treatment they are consigned to a lifetime of misery.

The goals of CBASP psychotherapy address the paramount intrapersonal and interpersonal dilemmas of the early-onset patient. Therapy must neutralize the interpersonal fear and instill felt interpersonal safety. This experience must then be generalized to others while interpersonal approach behaviors such as assertive strategies are taught. McCullough (2000, 2006) has posited that a major outcome goal is the acquisition of *perceived functionality* denoting that the patient is now able to recognize the consequences of his or her behavior. This achievement also implies that the patient is perceptually connected to his or her interpersonal environment and is now informed by the behavior of the therapist as well as others.

Case of Sam Smith

In this section, we provide a case example of an adult male undergoing diagnosis and therapy sessions with Dr. James P. McCullough.

Session 1: Diagnosis of Sam Smith

James P. McCullough (JPM): Hello, Sam.

Sam (S): Hello, Dr. McCullough.

Comment Sam is a large man, 6 feet 2 inches tall, and a heavy but not obese architectural engineer. His handshake, as well as the glancing look in his eyes, is tentative, suggesting extreme interpersonal submission (Kiesler, 1983, 1988, 1996; Kiesler & Schmidt, 1993). Sam looks down quickly while shaking hands and waits for JPM to suggest a place for him to sit in the office. His nonverbal demeanor is reticent. JPM is clearly in charge here. Sam's BDI-II (Beck, 1978) score taken at the first session was 41. Among chronically depressed patients, any score $\geq$ 35 reflects *severe/clinical* *depression*; a score of 24 to 34 denotes *moderate depression* intensity; and a score range of 11 to 23 signals *mild depression* intensity.

JPM: Tell me what brings you my way.

S: I can't get rid of this depression. I'm 39 years old, and I've been depressed for as long as I can remember. It's affected every area of my life, my marriage, my job—everything.

JPM: Have you ever sought professional help before?

S: I've been to three therapists and taken one antidepressant medication. Nothing seems to make any difference.

JPM: Tell me about the therapists. What was your experience with them?

S: The first one was a college counselor. She was very accepting and just listened to what I said. That's all she did, and I finally quit going because I never felt any better. The second person I saw was a clinical psychologist. It was five years ago and he did the same thing. He just listened. I got tired of talking and never feeling better, so I quit. Two years ago I saw another clinical psychologist who had me chanting mantras. I would walk around his office and say repeatedly: "I'm feeling better, I'm feeling better, I'm feeling better." I felt stupid as hell and I never felt any better. He was sort of weird anyway, so I quit going.

JPM: You mentioned taking one medication. Do you remember what it was?

S: Just one. When I saw the clinical psychologist five years ago, he sent me to a psychiatrist who prescribed Zoloft. That helped for awhile and then it no longer worked.

JPM: Do you remember the dosage you took?

S: I ended up taking 150 mg. After I stopped seeing the psychologist, I threw away the pills. The last psychologist didn't ever say anything about my taking the medicine. Do you think I need to take medication for my depression?

JPM: Yes. I'm going to suggest that you do this, but let's wait a moment and let me see what the clinical course of your depression has been like.

S: The what?

JPM: The clinical course, the history of your depression. I want to do several things over the next few minutes. First, I want to find out how severe your depression is right now so I'm going to ask you some diagnostic questions. Then, I'm going to go up to the flip chart and draw a line across the page and let you tell me about the ups and downs of your mood as you think back over your life—as best as you can remember how you felt. We'll work from the present backward in time. But first, let's see where you are right now.

Comment JPM diagnosed Sam using *DSM-IV* criteria (APA, 1994) to determine if, in fact, a chronic depressive disorder was present (Klein, 2008). Then, he used a course timeline procedure that has been described elsewhere (McCullough, 2001; McCullough, Kornstein, et al., 1996) to graphically illustrate the history of Sam's disorder. The patient's clinical course history was illustrated on the flip chart working from the present diagnosis backward in time (from left-to-right on the chart). Each time a shift in mood intensity was reported while working back in time, JPM asked: "Did the intensity of your depression improve, worsen, or return to the normal mood baseline?" The line on the graph should reflect the intensity of changes over time. When the graph was completed, Sam would be looking at an approximation of the clinical course of his depression beginning from the age of onset.

The second question that JPM wanted to answer was whether early-onset dysthymia (DD) was present during adolescence. The presence of DD usually implicates a problematical developmental history. When early-onset "double depression" is diagnosed (i.e., MD with antecedent early-onset DD: Keller & Shapiro, 1982), the goal is not only to rid the patient of the major depression (MD) but also to extinguish the earlier, mild-moderate dysthymic disorder. If dysthymia is not treated successfully, the patient will remain vulnerable to future MD episodes (Keller & Shapiro, 1982; Klein, 2008; Klein, Shankman, & Rose, 2006).

> JPM: I'm going to ask you some questions about your symptoms and I want to know if the symptom has been present continuously for the past two weeks.

Comment JPM administered the *DSM-IV* checklist for major depression (MD). Sam described his dysphoric mood state as (a) being present for the past 2 weeks. He had (b) lost interest and pleasure in all activities and reported (c) weight gain accompanied with bouts of eating even when he was not hungry; (d) he described being restless nightly during the middle of his sleep cycle, which disturbed his sleep, and he stressed that (e) he felt agitated and restless. Sam stated that he (f) felt "worthless" and he'd been having (g) significant difficulty concentrating and making decisions. When asked how long he'd felt just the way he was feeling now, he replied without hesitation: "For the past 2 years." Sam said that he had experienced some relief for a 6-month period prior to the 2-year period, but a serious job crisis had precipitated the present chronic MD episode. As best we could determine, Sam's feeling a "little better" lasted for several months (4 to 5 months) following a work promotion. Before that, Sam said that he'd felt down since graduating from college—the post-graduation period was diagnosed as his first MD episode; however, he said that this MD episode (that lasted about 12 years) had not been as bad as the one now. During college and high school, Sam described a course of DD with an onset age, as best we could determine, around 14 to 15 years. The DD symptoms he endorsed were (a) low energy/fatigue; (b) poor self-esteem; and (c) significant difficulty concentrating and making decisions. He also said that he had always had (d) insomnia problems, even in high school. JPM diagnosed Sam as a *chronically depressed patient* (Klein, 2008; McCullough, Klein, et al. 2003) with *antecedent early-onset DD*—a clinical course described by Keller and Shapiro (1982)

Figure 5.1   Clinical Course of Sam's Early-Onset "Double Depression"

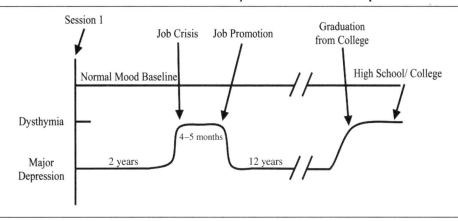

as "double depression." It should be noted that JPM ruled out the presence of bipolar disorder. The clinical course timeline is shown in Figure 5.1.

S: So this is what my clinical history looks like?

JPM: Yes, you've had a rough time with depression ever since you were in middle school. Has anyone ever shown you what you've been dealing with?

S: No. Counselors just had me start talking about how I felt. What good does talking do?

JPM: Not much with this kind of depression. Just talking doesn't help.

S: I just talked about whatever I wanted to when I saw counselors. The only one who was different was that psychologist who had me chant. He got me up and doing things in his office. I felt stupid and it didn't help. You really want me to be honest with you?

JPM: Certainly.

S: I don't think seeing you will do any good. I bet I'm going to stay depressed.

JPM: I'm not surprised you think this. I do hope one thing though.

S: What's that?

JPM: That you will hang around and find out. I think you will be surprised. I also don't think you will have experienced anything quite like what you will experience in working with me. If you stay with me until we're finished, you will not live the way you've been living.

S: Do you really think I can beat this depression—really get over this crap?

JPM: I wouldn't agree to see you if I felt otherwise. Yes, you'll get over this crap! But I'm going to work you hard. I'm going to help you do things over the next several months you've never done before. There's no other way out. Changing the way you live your life is going to be the hardest thing you'll ever do. It will not be easy. We won't chant; however, you will change the way you live. I know this doesn't make much sense to you right now, but stick with me and you'll see what I mean. I'll help you and go with you through the change process.

S: I don't understand why but I feel a little hope right now.

JPM: Good. That's exactly what I want you to feel. You'll just have to count on my hope for awhile. Here's what I want you to do before we meet next time. Think of five or six significant others (SOs) in your life who've influenced you to be the person you are today. These will be the big players. They will not be the many friends and acquaintances we all have over the years. These are the individuals who leave their *marks* or *stamps* on us. They influence us to see the world the way we do, to feel about ourselves the way we do, and to behave the way we do. Their influences can either be positive or negative—helpful or hurtful. Bring your list in and I'll write the list on the flip chart. We'll go through your list together one by one. I'll ask you two questions about each SO. I'll explain this next week.

Comment The patient left the session with a slim ray of hope, which was the best outcome JPM could have hoped to achieve during the initial session. Sam was referred to a psychiatrist who prescribed 50 mg of Zoloft (sertraline), which was titrated to 150 mg over the course of psychotherapy. He will stay on Zoloft after psychotherapy ends and for the foreseeable future.

Preoperational Functioning McCullough (2000, 2006) described the primitive social-interpersonal behavior of chronically depressed adults and suggested that their cognitive-emotional-behavioral style mimics that of preoperational stage children (Piaget, 1926/1923; Vander Molen, 2010). Sam described himself to JPM as a lonely individual and behaved as if he were interpersonally disengaged from others. Since he'd avoided the interpersonal environment for many years, his views about himself and others had never been accessible to hypothesis testing. It is not surprising that he behaved with JPM as a highly egocentric individual and as an adult who was undersocialized. Sam's story at screening had a "sameness" quality about it regardless of whether he talked about the past, the present, or the future. The general theme could be depicted as follows: "This is the way things have always been in my life, this is the way they are today, and tomorrow will just be more of the same." Time for Sam had stopped with the past, present, and future all collapsing into a landscape of rejection and failure. His self-description was analogous to a snapshot picture of reality—that is, it was frozen in time. Not surprisingly, he didn't use logic or causal reasoning when he talked about himself. When he described the way people treated him, he saw no connection between what he did and the reactions of others. Sam talked to JPM in a monologic manner and with a style characterized by an absence of felt or expressed empathy. Treating Sam will be like starting a learning process with a 4- to 6-year-old child—yet, this individual is an adult.

Session 2: Significant Other History (SOH) and Post-Session Impact Message Inventory (IMI)

In this section, we discuss the purpose of the SOH and the IMI; additionally, we provide case examples to illustrate their use in therapeutic settings.

Comment The SOH is designed to provide interpersonal emotional material that will inform the construction of the Transference Hypothesis (TH; McCullough, 2000, 2006). The TH is an emotionally derived interpersonal expectancy predicting how Sam is likely to behave while in therapy with JPM. The SOH evokes memories concerning each SO. As Sam and JPM reviewed each SO on the list, Sam was asked to describe the major influence (i.e., a *stamp* or *mark*) the SO has left on him (see McCullough, 2006) that shaped him to be the kind of person he is today. The Significant Other History procedure is shown below in Table 5.1.

> JPM: Did you bring in a list of your Significant Others (SOs)?
>
> S: Yes.
>
> JPM: Tell me who's on your list, and I'll write each one on the flip chart.
>
> S: My mother, father, wife (Mary), my mother's mother (grandmother) and my mother's father (grandfather). They're all living today and a part of my life.
>
> JPM: Then, let's go through the people in the order you listed them. I'll ask you two questions about each SO: What was it like growing up/being around this

Table 5.1 CBASP Significant Other History Procedure (SOH)

<u>Instructions</u>: Significant Others are the dominant/major players in the patient's life. The list should include no more than four to six Significant Others — individuals who have left their personal "stamp" on the patient and influenced them to be who they are as well as influenced the direction their life has taken. The stamp may either be "positive" or "negative."

Administrative Step One:

Request a list of four to six Significant Others — persons who have shaped the patient to be who he or she is. The stamp may either be a *positive* or a *negative* one.

Administrative Step Two:

Go through the list in the order that the Significant Others are listed.

Administrative Step Three (prompt questions):

Begin with this question: What was it like growing up or being around this person? Let the patient recall several memories, situations, or stories. Then, go to one of the prompts below and say:

Prompt 1: Tell me how this person has influenced you to be the kind of person you are now.

Prompt 2: How has growing up with/around this person influenced the direction your life has taken? What is the direction?

Prompt 3: What kind of person are you as a result of living around this person?

Administrative Step Four:

The goal of this step is to have the patient formulate one Causal Theory Conclusion for each Significant Other. The Conclusion should denote the "stamp" or "legacy" that the patient feels the Significant Other has left on him/her that influenced him/her to be who they are today.

SO, and what is the stamp or mark you bear from this relationship that's influenced you to be the kind of person you are right now? Let's start with your mother, the first person on your list. What was it like growing up and being around your mother?

S: [About his mother] It was not a good relationship, never has been. She's very intellectual in all she does. She was an RN before she retired, and she always worked hard. She worked the 11 PM-to-7 AM shift mostly so I didn't see her much during the day. Her major philosophy can be summed up as, "Get with the program!" She was not an emotional person and everything had to fit into her scheduled program. I never saw her cry or be moody. She held her feelings in check. If I had a problem, she would first find out what was expected of me and then I was told in so many words to "Get with the program." I pretty much did everything she told me to. I was afraid not to. I was compliant and did what I was told—still do. She would call me "a wimp" or "weak person" if I didn't shape up and get with her program.

JPM: What do you take from this relationship that has influenced you to be who you are today—what's the "stamp" that you take from your mother?

Stamp: Do what I'm told and work hard—don't expect much understanding from a woman.

S: [About his father] He was Navy—the physical enforcer around the house. When I was young, he would throw and push me around a lot when he was mad though I don't remember ever being physically hurt. He let me know early that he only respected men who could take care of themselves physically. He and I argued constantly. When he retired from the Navy, he was a telephone employee and I "pushed his buttons" whenever I could. I wouldn't cooperate with what he said. Stayed out past curfew, things like that. I never felt that he knew what he was talking about and thinking back on it now, I don't think that I ever really respected him. Today, things have calmed down between us. We're more like friends but not while I was growing up. It's funny, but I don't think he really knows who I am. I try to keep a stiff upper lip around him—still do. He's a moral man, faithful to his wife and always tells the truth. Guess I'm sorta like that now.

Stamp: I do what's right, I'm faithful to my wife and I always tell the truth.

S: [About Mary, his wife] She's put up with me for 16 years and she married me knowing that I had problems with depression. We go in cycles, good times and bad times, depending on how bad my depression is. She gets things done, is a vice president in a large corporation and she's the one who really keeps the family organized. I think she loves me but she is also critical and judgmental. For example, she's wanted me to ask for a raise for a long time and I just haven't felt like doing it. Frankly, I don't think my work deserves a raise. Mary makes comments to the effect that if they're not going to pay me more, then I need to look for other employment. She wants me to get another job with another company. Her looks from time to time say it all— she thinks I'm a weak man. Why she married me I'll never know.

Stamp: I feel I'm half a man around her. It's like me and my mother all over again, just doing what I'm told and trying to be a "good boy."

S: [About his maternal grandfather] Okay guy and was always in a good mood— still is. He was fun to be around. We hunted together. He was a World War II veteran and was in France for most of the war. He never talked about his experiences. Was wounded in France and was awarded a Purple Heart. He always respected this country. He fought for his country, something I never did, and he's always loved my grandmother. He didn't like weakness in people. I never let him see any in me. Don't think he would like me had he known how weak I feel.

Stamp: I'm moral like him. I try to do my duty.

S: [About his maternal grandmother] She was a very strong person. She divorced her first husband in the early 1940s—can you believe that! People didn't divorce much back then. They just stuck it out. Her ex-husband was an alcoholic and physically abusive. One day, she just took her kids and struck out on her own. She was very religious and ultraconservative—family values and all that. Then, after the war, she married my grandfather. When I was little, she went on hikes with us, took all of us to the beach, she did a lot of baking and was a good cook. I felt she loved "us"— I want to say loved me but I have to say "us." She always had the attitude that she could do anything she put her mind to. I want to feel that way, but I don't.

Stamp: I feel I'm a loser because I can't change my life the way she did.

Comment on the SOH Content Sam's general emotional mood as he described his relationships with his significant others sounded like "the sadness of defeat." He never described instances of feeling equal with his SOs. Ironically, the patient grew up around psychologically strong men and women—strong models to emulate. He married a psychologically strong woman. In addition, he bears no overt physical and psychological scars that frequently accrue from *trauma*—that is, severe physical, sexual, or emotional abuse within the family. Thus, we cannot pinpoint any specific trauma event to explain his refractory mood. So, what do we know based on his SOH? As best JPM could determine, Sam never attached in a positive emotional way to anyone in his family. He learned the social rules of morality and duty but never assimilated the "spirit of the law" that comes from feeling loved and protected by one's caregivers. His SOH matches a pattern seen frequently among chronically depressed patients. The history reveals persons who have been the recipient of repeated and long-standing *psychological insults* (actual instances of emotional rejection, criticism, or negative judgment or repeatedly fearing that one will be rejected, criticized, or negatively judged) (McCullough, 2008). As noted earlier, Sam began psychotherapy interpersonally avoidant (i.e., detached and withdrawn). It was not difficult to hypothesize that what Sam would expect in a relationship with a male such as JPM would be an interpersonal replay of what he learned earlier from his father and grandfather—that being, an ineffectual model in the case of the father and expecting little tolerance for any sign of weakness or vulnerability (father, grandfather). JPM, after carefully reviewing the SOH material, constructed the following Transference Hypothesis (TH): *If I let JPM get to know me (i.e., disclose myself and let him know how inadequate I feel), then JPM will judge me negatively, not like or respect me, because he'll know that I'm a weak person.*

The TH is hypothesized to be an important interpersonal expectancy that Sam will likely transfer to JPM. Thus, JPM begins treatment aware from the patient's interpersonal history that he is unlikely to expect much help from his therapist. The TH will be used in subsequent sessions to make explicit to Sam that JPM is qualitatively different from his significant others.

Using the TH as an Assessment Measure McCullough (2006) operationalized the TH using Shapiro's Personal Questionnaire (PQ) paired comparison technique (Shapiro, 1961, 1964; Shapiro, Litman, Nias, & Hendry, 1973). The PQ was administered at the beginning of each session to reflect the perceptual success (or lack thereof) Sam achieves in emotionally discriminating JPM from his SOs (see McCullough, 2006, pp. 163–167). Four levels of treatment outcome are measurable using the PQ: *illness level* (score = 4: no change); *minimal improvement* (score = 3: some change evident); *significant improvement* (score = 2: partial response); and *recovery level improvement* (score = 1: remission response). Three 3-inch by 5-inch cards are used with the TH stated on Card #1 at an Illness level (*More often than not, when I think about letting JPM get to know me, then I feel he will judge me negatively, not like or respect me because he'll know that I am a weak person*). The Improvement level sentence is written on Card #2 (*Sometimes when I think about letting JPM get to know me, then I feel he won't judge me negatively and that he will like and respect me and conclude that I'm not a weak person*); and the Recovery level sentence written on Card #3 (*More often than not when I think about letting JPM get to know me, then I feel he won't judge me negatively, that he will like and respect me and conclude that I am not a weak person*).

Following Session 2, JPM completed an Impact Message Inventory (IMI: Kiesler & Schmidt, 1993) on Sam. The IMI profile is illustrated in Figure 5.2. The patient obtained peak scores on two octants: the Hostile-Submission (*H-S*) octant (*H-S* items are as follows: Sam appears nervous around JPM; JPM should do something to put him at ease; Sam withdraws from important issues; Sam feels that he cannot do anything; Sam feels that assertion will lead to ridicule; Sam appears to feel inferior to JPM; Sam generally feels uneasy) and a peak score on the Submission (*S*) octant (*S* items are as follows: Sam makes JPM feel in charge; JPM feels dominant around Sam; Sam seems to be unable to disagree with JPM; Sam appears unable to stand up

Figure 5.2 Sam's Impact Message Inventory (IMI) Profile Scores Following Session 2

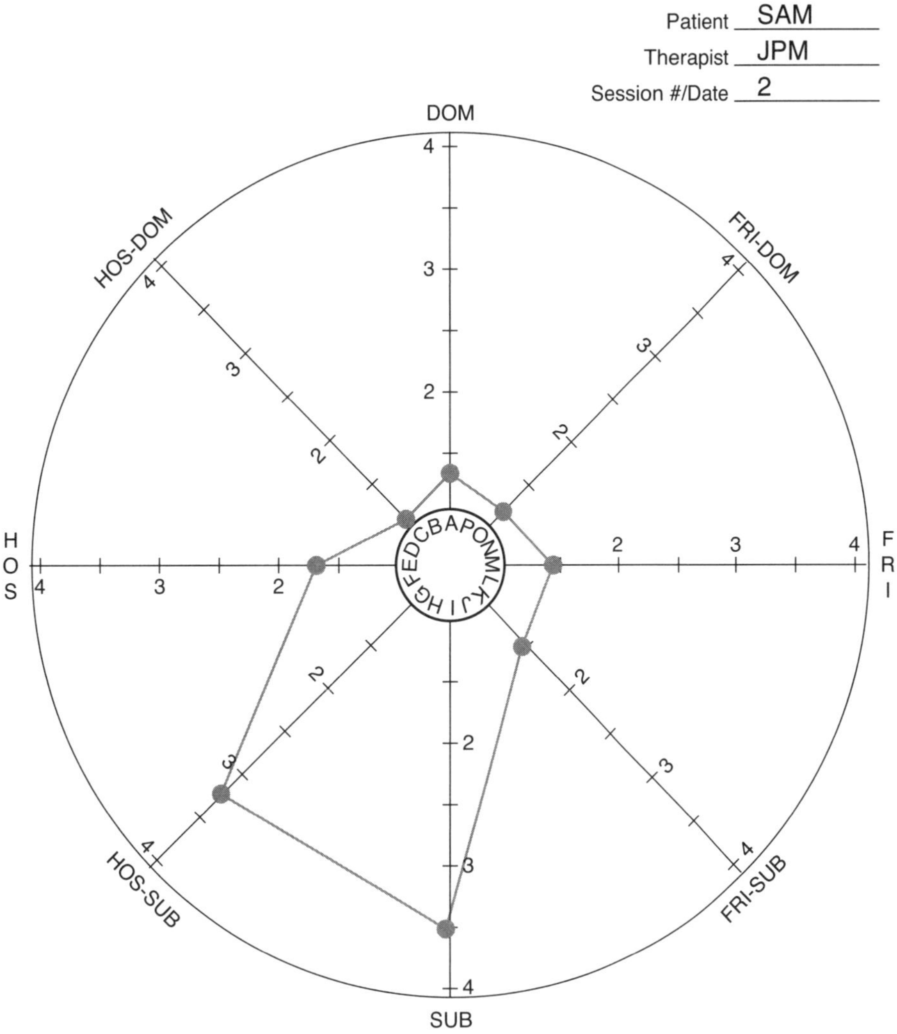

Patient __SAM__

Therapist __JPM__

Session #/Date __2__

for himself; Sam appears to feel that he has few assets; Sam appears to feel that he has no answers; Sam appears to feel inferior to JPM). Kiesler (1988, 1996) defines interpersonal *hostility* as verbal or nonverbal stylistic attempts to avoid interpersonal encounter. Said another way, hostility as well as all the hostile octants on the interpersonal circle (Kiesler, 1983: i.e., H-D: *Hostile-Dominant; H: Hostile; H-S: Hostile-Submissive*) denote an avoidance-of-others interpersonal lifestyle in contrast to an interpersonal approach-of-others lifestyle reflected on the *friendly* side of the interpersonal circle (i.e., F-S: *Friendly-Submissive; F: Friendly; F-D: Friendly-Dominant*).

The potential problems that Sam's interpersonal style presents to JPM are seen in the complementarity pulls (Kiesler, 1983, 1988, 1996) for interpersonal *Hostility* and *Dominance*. Complementarity, as defined by Kiesler (1983, 1988, 1996), means that *H-S* pulls for Hostile-Dominant responses (e.g., "Your efforts are disappointing, I'll have to do it myself.") and *S* pulls for Dominance (e.g., "Do what I say and you'll be okay."). It would be easy for JPM to deliver CBASP therapy and be pulled to react in a frustrated-angry complementary manner (*Hostile-Dominant*) in the face of Sam's detached and withdrawal style; likewise, assuming a "take charge" complimentary role (*Dominance*) given Sam's *Submission* style will also be a strong temptation. Both of these therapist behaviors have been described elsewhere by McCullough (2000, 2006) as "lethal" because they simply reinforce the old damaging interpersonal expectancies. Thus, the interpersonal goals for JPM are to remain on the *Friendly* side of the interpersonal circle and to avoid the complementarity pulls for *Hostility* and *Dominance* (see McCullough, 2000, p. 178).

Kiesler (1983, 1996) describes the interpersonal outcome goals for psychotherapy for these patient types. The goals lie on what Kielser calls the *nadir* octants (see Figure 5.2) that stand directly opposite Sam's original (avoidance) peak octants; nadir octants for Sam lie on the Friendly-Dominant (*F-D*) and the Dominant (*D*) octants, respectively. These octants reflect "approach" behaviors such as taking interpersonal charge of situations (*F-D:* "I'm strong and will impress you with my skills.") and the actualization of more interpersonal control (*D:* "I can take care of my life now").

Sam was also given the *CBASP Patient's Manual* (McCullough, 1993) at the end of Session 2 and asked to read the material prior to the next session. The manual would be discussed at that time. He was also told that he and JPM would begin to do situational analysis (SA), which is discussed at length in the manual.

Session 3: Discussion of the Manual and the First Situational Analysis (SA)

JPM: Did you read the manual?

S: Yes, and I've got a question.

JPM: Let's discuss your question.

S: How will focusing on one problem at a time help me? I've got so many problems.

JPM: It may surprise you how similar your problems are across situations. I'm guessing that what gets you in trouble in one situation may be a problem across a number of situations. Most of us are not that flexible, and I'm talking about myself also. What gets me in trouble in situation A is also present in situation B. This may be hard to believe right now. We'll take one problem at a time and see how much mileage we can get out of it; that is, see how many birds we can kill with one stone, so to speak. We'll take our problem-solving work into all areas of your life before we finish. One lesson I want to teach you in SA is that to solve any problem you must focus on one problem at a time. We can't tackle all your problems at once—can't solve anything that way.

S: So you are going to teach me to solve one problem at a time—is that what you are saying? If you think this will help, I'll do whatever you say.

JPM: That's exactly what I'm saying. There's something else I want to help you learn.

S: What's that?

JPM: You're not as helpless as you think you are. I want to help you see that what happens to you is due in large part to the way you go about reacting to people. You won't believe this until you see this for yourself, but this is the second goal of situational analysis—you'll learn to recognize the effects your behavior has on others. These effects either help you or hurt you. Like the first learning goal of situational analysis, this will take some time to learn. Any more questions?

S: No, that was the main one.

JPM: Let's begin then. I want to show you how situational analysis (SA) works. I'm giving you a Coping Survey Questionnaire (CSQ: McCullough, 2000) to work with while I write on the flip chart [refer to the CSQ in Table 5.1 to follow the SA presented below]. The first step of SA is the situational description. I want you to think of one interaction you've had in the past week that's been stressful. Describe what happened in terms of a "play" that has a beginning, an ending, and some story in between. The rule for Step 1 is that you don't editorialize or try to explain why this or that happened, what you or the other person felt, or what motives you might have had, and so forth. Just tell me *what happened*—this happened, that happened, I said this, he said that, and so

Table 5.2 Coping Survey Questionnaire (CSQ) for Situational Analysis*

Patient: _____

Therapist: _____

Date of Situational Event: _____

Date of Therapy Session: _____

Instructions: Select one stress event that you have confronted during the past week and describe it using the format below. Please try to fill out all parts of the questionnaire. Your therapist will assist you in reviewing this situational analysis during your next therapy session.

Situational Area: Family____   Work/School____   Social___

1. Describe what happened:

2. How did you interpret what happened:

3. Describe what you did during the situation:

4. Describe how the event came out for you (*Actual Outcome*):

5. Describe how you wanted the event to come out for you (*Desired Outcome*):

6. RATE: Did you get what you wanted?   YES____   NO____

*The patient will learn to self-administer the SA over the process of therapy.

on, and then the situation ended, which means that the curtain came down at the end of your play. The endpoint of this *slice of time* or when the curtain comes down is very important. The best endpoint is some behavior on your part that an observer could have seen or heard. You can describe how you felt at the end, but you and I will focus on your behavior.

Step 1 of SA: Elicitation Phase S: Okay. I wanted to talk with my wife about a bill we just got and she was watching TV. I went in the living room and sat next to her on the sofa. I tried to talk to her about the bill and she never looked at me. She kept looking at the screen. I wanted to ask her about our bill from Exxon. I finally got up and walked out of the room. Then, I really got depressed and felt rotten.

JPM: That's a good situation for us to work on. The beginning was your going in the living room and sitting next to your wife. Next, you attempted to talk with her about a bill you got in the mail. She never looked at you and then you got up and walked out of the room. We'll use your walking out of the room as the endpoint of the situation; this is where the curtain comes down on your story.

Step 2 of SA: Elicitation Phase JPM: I've got a good picture of what happened in that slice of time. Sounds like a very difficult event. The second step of SA involves what the situation meant to you. We call it a *situational interpretation*. Interpretations describe the way you or the other person behaves in the situation. It can be a thought, emotion, or behavior on your part or on the other person's part. You do this by answering the question: "What did the situation mean to me?" What I'm looking for are one-sentence interpretations as you look back over the situation. The major rule for Step 2 is that each interpretation must be stated in one sentence and I must understand every word in your sentence. Look back over this slice of time, and tell me what the situation meant to you. Let's take two or three interpretations.

S: My wife is inconsiderate because she didn't talk to me.

JPM: Did it mean anything else to you?

S: She doesn't love me.

JPM: Let's take one more.

S: I'm a complete failure.

JPM: Tell me what you mean by the word *failure*. I want to be sure I understand what you mean.

S: I mean I can't even get my wife to talk to me.

Step 3 of SA: Elicitation Phase JPM: Okay, I got it now. You've carved out a "slice of time" here, and you've told me what sense you made out of the event. Are you with me so far?

S: Yes.

JPM: Now, let's look at the third step of SA. Describe for me what you did in this slice of time; that is, how did you behave? How did you ask your wife to talk to you about the bill? I know what you thought. Now, I need to know what you did and how you went about it.

S: I walked in the living room and sat on the sofa next to my wife. I looked at her and said I wanted to talk about our Exxon bill. She never looked at me. I waited for her to look at me and finally got up and walked out of the room.

JPM: Did you speak her name or just say you wanted to talk about the Exxon bill?

S: I just said I wanted to talk about the bill.

JPM: Was your tone of voice about the way it is right now? You are talking very low, almost so low that I have trouble understanding what you're saying.

S: I think it must have been about the same. I don't ever speak out around her. I just said what I wanted, and she never took her eyes off the screen. It was almost like I wasn't there.

JPM: I'm getting the picture.

Step 4 of SA: Elicitation Phase JPM: Okay. Now we come to the fourth step of SA—the endpoint of the situation, or what I call the *Actual Outcome* (AO). The AO is the point where the curtain comes down on your slice of time, and it's very important. The AO is how the encounter turned out for you. You can think of it as the consequences of your behavior. In this situation, it's how things ended up between you and your wife. The rule for this Step 4 is that the AO must be stated in one sentence and in behavioral terms—a behavior that an observer could have seen or heard. This is why the endpoint of the story in Step 1 is important. The endpoint becomes the AO in SA. Now, look back at your Step 1 and tell me how this situation came out for you—what was the AO?

S: I got up and walked out of the room.

JPM: So, the AO is your walking out of the room?

S: Yes.

Step 5 of SA: Elicitation Phase JPM: The next step of SA, Step 5, is what's called the *Desired Outcome* (DO). You and I have the luxury in SA of looking back at an event and describing how it ended. Then we can formulate a DO or an endpoint that might be more to your liking. If it didn't turn out this way, we can construct a better outcome for you in SA. It's like playing Monday morning quarterback and watching the film of Sunday's game to see how and where we could have improved our performance. The AO for you in this exchange with your wife is what you did when she didn't respond to you. *You* *walked out of the room.* Looking back at the AO now, how would you have liked the endpoint of "walking out of the room" to have come out?

S: I wish it had never happened.

JPM: I bet you do. But, in reality it did. Think about the AO. Can you think of a better ending, something you could have done or said, that would have been a better outcome?

S: I wish she'd responded to me.

JPM: Again Sam, she didn't. That's reality and we can't change it. Focus on what *you* could have done or said that would be better than just walking out of the room.

S: I don't know. I can't think of anything I could have said or done.

JPM: You've given yourself a clue. Think about something you could have said right at that moment.

S: You mean say to her while she's watching TV?

JPM: Yes, and try speaking her name. For example, "Mary, when can . . . ?"

S: Are you suggesting that I could ask for a specific time to talk?

JPM: You're getting the idea. Now, complete my sentence.

S: Mary, can we talk about this Exxon bill when you finish watching TV?

JPM: This is a splendid DO. Instead of walking out of the room, you could have spoken her name and asked her to discuss the bill when she finished watching TV.

S: She probably wouldn't do it.

JPM: We don't know what she would have done. But, does focusing on what you could have said without just walking out of the room sound like a more desirable outcome?

S: Yes. But I don't think it would have done any good.

JPM: Let's don't quit here. I want to show you something about how to get what you want. We're not finished with the SA.

S: I don't understand this. What happened, happened. I can't change my walking out of the room and feeling like crap. Can I?

JPM: You're right. We can't change what actually happened, but we can learn from it. We can "fix it" here with our Monday morning quarterback review, which is the second part of SA. You and I will examine how you played the game and see if adding some plays might have made a difference in the outcome, that is, help you obtain your DO. Our goal here is learning from this event and teaching you how to get what you want so the next time, you don't lose the game. Now, let's turn back to your interpretations to see if the way you are thinking helps or prevents you from achieving what you just said you would have liked to do.

Comment on the Elicitation Phase of SA #1 The autobiographical picture drawn in this SA paints Sam as a weak, inadequate, and ineffectual person around Mary. He reported earlier in the SOH exercise that he's never functioned adequately around significant females. Sam's major coping strategy evident in the SA is interpersonal withdrawal and self-criticism. He was not able to assert himself in the face of the interpersonal challenge. The only viable option he had was to withdraw and leave the room. In this situation, we see the opposite of assertive behavior; instead, we observe interpersonal fear and avoidance. Sam's response to Mary was consistent with the IMI ratings he received from JPM (i.e., Hostile-Submission [*H-S: fear and avoidance*] and Submission [*S: passive behavior*] octants, see Figure 5.2).

JPM drew three conclusions from the Elicitation Phase of SA #1: (1) Sam's depression is appropriate. He is an interpersonal failure and he knows it. What's more, he doesn't know any other way to live; (2) Sam has little or no awareness that his behavior produces the negative interpersonal consequences that characterize Mary's response to him. Said another way, Sam is an operational definition of *helplessness* and *hopelessness* in relationship with Mary.

It is also obvious (3) that Sam doesn't feel safe in the encounter with Mary as evidenced by his avoidance behavior. Bouton (2007) suggests that, "if we want to treat avoidance behavior therapeutically, we will need to extinguish the Pavlovian fear" (p. 386) that he opines motivates the avoidance response (Skinner, 1953, 1968). Bouton's assumption has implications for JPM's treatment of Sam's interpersonal avoidance. JPM will begin to address the avoidance behavior during the Remediation Phase of SA by teaching Sam new approach behaviors. In short, Pavlovian (1927/1960) learning processes are hypothesized to be in operation in this situation (Bouton, 2007), suggesting that as long as Sam remains fearful of Mary, the therapist's and others' motivation to change his behavior remains low. This means that the extinction of his generalized interpersonal fears must first be counter-conditioned in the therapy room with the therapist and replaced with felt safety. Extinction of avoidance begins with JPM who, over time, will become a "safety stimulus" (*S:CS*) for Sam. Once Sam feels safe with his psychotherapist, instituting new approach behaviors with others will be easier.

In the beginning, we described the major intrapersonal problem of the early-onset patient as that of being entrapped behind a wall of refractory interpersonal fear. Consistent with Bouton's (2007) assumption that where there is interpersonal avoidance the motivating factor will be Pavlovian fear, the first goal of CBASP treatment is to address the interpersonal fear and replace it with felt interpersonal safety. The nature of patients' fears is expressed interpersonally in many ways, and sometimes identifying the actual form the fear takes is difficult. Examining the interpersonal path the fear is likely to take in the psychotherapy relationship is the goal of the Significant Other History (SOH) discussed earlier. As noted, the SOH is an emotional history, and the Transference Hypothesis (TH) derived from the SOH operationalizes the hypothesized interpersonal path the fear is likely to take. Modifying the presenting fear state is most easily accomplished within the therapeutic dyad. The therapist will administer the Interpersonal Discrimination Exercise (IDE) repetitively to teach the patient to discriminate between hurtful Significant Others and the salubrious strivings of the clinician. We have found that unless this discrimination is achieved, patients are unlikely to disengage perceptually the therapist from maltreating Significant Others. Until this goal is realized, the achievement of felt safety within the dyad remains an elusive goal.

Summarily, learning to discriminate between JPM (who will not inflict interpersonal ridicule, pronounce negative judgment, or label Sam a weak person) and significant others (who have ridiculed him, pronounced negative judgments, and labeled him weak) is the way CBASP achieves extinction of generalized interpersonal fears in the therapy room. We turn now to the Remediation Phase of Sam's SA #1.

> JPM: The second part of SA is called the *remediation phase*. It's the part where we continue to play Monday morning quarterback and "fix" or talk about the things that prevented you from obtaining your DO. When we finish the remediation phase, you ought to have a better idea of how to obtain the DO.
>
> S: I don't see how anything could be fixed here.
>
> JPM: Let me show you. We'll begin by looking at the way you interpreted the situation. You listed three interpretations (JPM had written the three interpretations earlier on the flip chart):
>
> 1. My wife is inconsiderate.
>
> 2. She doesn't love me.
>
> 3. I'm a complete failure.

Let's look at these reads or interpretations individually and we'll keep your Desired Outcome (DO) in mind as we go through the list. Your DO was: *Mary, can we talk about this Exxon bill when you finish watching TV?* How did your first interpretation contribute to your saying to Mary, *Can we talk about this Exxon bill when you finish watching TV?*

> S: Well, I did think she was rude when she never looked at me.
>
> JPM: She was, but how did it help you say what you wanted to?
>
> S: It didn't, but it surely let me know she wouldn't talk about the bill then.
>
> JPM: So, it didn't take you to the "goal box" or to your DO, but it did signal that the time was not right for any discussion. This is a helpful interpretation. Okay, how did the second interpretation contribute to you saying what you wanted?
>
> S: I don't know. It's just the way I felt. But, it really didn't help me.
>
> JPM: It doesn't keep you focused on what you want does it?
>
> S: No.
>
> JPM: Did you ask Mary if she loved you?
>
> S: No.

JPM: This interpretation is what we call a *mind read*—it's a reaction we have to explain other people's behavior. I'm going to teach you to ask, not to mind-read others. It's a dangerous strategy. So this interpretation didn't help you say what you wanted. Look at your third interpretation. How did it contribute to your asking Mary to talk later?

S: Again, it's how I felt, but it didn't help me get what I wanted.

JPM: You're getting the idea. It's just another global interpretation that you thought, but it didn't contribute to your saying what you wanted. Here's a new step for you. Is there some thought you could have had right at this point that will take you to your DO? Keep the DO in mind. You know Mary doesn't want to talk now and you also know that you want to discuss the bill. What can you think to yourself right here? I call it an *action read*. It would have helped you say what you wanted to say instead of just walking out of the room.

S: I'm not sure what you mean.

JPM: An action read is a short thought or something you could say to yourself in the moment that would take you to the goal box, the DO. Make it short and sweet.

S: Ask her!

JPM: You got it! If you had had that thought in mind, what would have been added to your behavior in that situation? Look at the DO I've written on the flip chart.

S: I would have asked her if we could talk later about the Exxon bill.

JPM: And, had you said that to Mary, would you have gotten what you wanted in this situation?

S: Yes.

JPM: What have you learned in this SA?

S: I'm not sure.

JPM: Look closely at the flip chart, how you first described the situation to me, how you interpreted it, what you did, and what you wanted. Look at what we've changed to help you get to your goal. What do you see?

S: It's hard for me to say what I want or even to know what I want in the moment.

JPM: It surely is. What else can you learn here?

S: To have a goal in mind when I want something.

JPM: Do you realize what you've just said? Learning to have a goal in mind along with the right thoughts and behaviors are the way to win ballgames. Yes, we'll work on helping you keep your goal in mind. Learn anything else?

S: I really get sidetracked with my thoughts. They don't help me here.

JPM: You are right. You want to stop here or do you see something else?

S: This is okay to do here with you, but I could never do this with Mary.

JPM: You don't have to. You and I can work these difficult situations out in the safety of this office and you don't have to go outside and do anything. We'll keep working at it so you'll know what to do in these difficult encounters. However, if sometime you want to try these new skills out, at least you'll know what to do. You've done great here today. I've got one more question to ask you about this SA. You've said you've learned to have a goal in mind and that you get sidetracked by thoughts that don't help you get what you want. Can you think of another situation with someone where you could use what you've learned here today?

S: I had a work situation come up several days ago where I wanted my colleague to check over his work. I'd found several mistakes in his work. I asked him to do it. He never looked up from his desk and, of course, never rechecked the figures. So, I just did it myself. I wanted them to be right before giving them to my boss.

JPM: What have you learned here that you could apply in this work situation?

S: I could have reminded myself several times what I wanted and asked him when we could talk about the errors in his figures. I could have just stood at his desk until he looked up.

JPM: You got it! You've done wonderful work in your first SA.

Comment on Both Phases of SA #1 JPM administered a "mismatching" exercise (Cowan, 1976; Gordon, 1988) to Sam in the SA. The patient functioned at a primitive cognitive-emotional preoperational level during the Elicitation Phase; however, during the Remediation Phase, Sam was required to perform at a higher level of cognitive-emotive functioning in order to resolve the problem. Piagetian therapists (e.g., Cowan, 1976; Gordon, 1988) label this therapeutic strategy "mismatching." It's an essential motif in the SA exercise. Nothing is learned as long as Sam behaves preoperationally and describes his problems from a withdrawal-passive perspective. Learning occurs when he is required to solve the interpersonal problem by behaving at a higher cognitive-emotive level (i.e., at a formal operational level of functioning). Sam, in recognizing how he could obtain his DO, experienced some felt relief during the Remediation Phase. The patient's felt discomfort often increases during the Elicitation Phase when no solution is obvious; the discomfort level is frequently reduced during the Remediation Phase when a solution is recognized and the DO becomes achievable. Reverting to learning theory, Skinner assumes that any behavior that terminates an aversive state is strengthened, and he labels the cessation of discomfort a *negative reinforcer* (Skinner, 1953). Over the process of treatment, Sam will learn how to reduce his felt discomfort by enacting adaptive behavior. Negative reinforcement is the most powerful motivating variable CBASP therapists have (McCullough, 2000) and the reduction of discomfort for approach behavior will be repeatedly demonstrated to the patient during subsequent SAs.

Rating the Quality of SA Performance The SA steps have been operationalized so that the quality of the patient's performance during the exercise can be reliably rated (McCullough, 2000, pp. 202–207) by the therapist or a clinical rater. The goal here is for the patient to learn to self-administer SA without therapeutic assistance. McCullough (2000, pp. 209–210; 2006, pp. 160–175; 2008; in press) describes psychotherapy as a psychological learning experiment and rating Sam's SA performance over sessions provides a measure of acquisition learning. Measuring learning during treatment also provides an opportunity to test the empirical hypothesis that if patients learn the "subject matter" of treatment, the psychopathology will be resolved. Sam will be taught to self-administer the five-step SA procedure and by the end of therapy, he should be performing the self-administration task to criterion. His acquisition learning is assessed by an instrument known as the Patient Performance Rating Form (PPRF: Manber et al., 2003; McCullough, 2000, 2006; 2008, 2010).

Session 4: SA #2 and the First Administration of the IDE

S: You didn't criticize me last session.

JPM: What do you mean?

S: While we were going through my SA last week, you didn't make me feel stupid or judge me in a negative way even though I didn't know what I was doing. I mean, you saw me at my worst.

Comment A hot spot: Sam's comment implicated the Transference Hypothesis because he suggested an interpersonal event where he associates poor performance with rejection and negative judgment. Such in-session occurrences are labeled *hot spots* and signal moments when the IDE can be administered. The historical content (i.e., poor performance during last session's SA) of the situational event is focused on in the IDE. The discrimination exercise concentrates Sam's attention on comparing JPM's behavior and the behavior of maltreating significant others in a situation where he has performed poorly. In the past, poor performance has pulled negative judgments from significant others.

JPM: Let me ask you some about the comments you just made to me concerning how I reacted to your SA performance. Think back about what you and I did in this SA. You remember you were talking about your encounter with Mary and then how you might have asked her to give you a more convenient time to talk. You remember what was going on when the curtain came down at the end—you just walked out of the room.

S: Yes.

JPM: How would your mother have reacted to you had you told her about what you did in the situation with Mary?

S: She would have made it clear that I was not learning my lessons in therapy. I would have felt like a failure. She would have made me feel that I was a weak person.

JPM: How would your father have reacted had you told him?

S: He would have played like he knew all about how to do SA when he really doesn't know anything. He would have said something like: "Just learn it, boy!"

JPM: What about your grandfather? How would he have reacted?

S: He really didn't like weakness. He thought poor performance was weakness personified and he would have been upset and his look would have probably made me feel like crap.

Comment Increase in Felt Discomfort: It was obvious that Sam didn't feel comfortable talking about the reactions he received from his significant others when he performed poorly. The stage was set for the behavioral discrimination to be made between his family members and JPM.

JPM: I want you to think about my reaction to you as we went through your first SA? How did I react?

S: It's like I said, you didn't make me feel bad because I didn't know what to do.

JPM: But, what did I do? How did I behave?

S: You tried to help me through the steps. You seemed interested that I learn what to do.

JPM: You're right. Tell me how I helped you.

S: You went slowly. You tried to get me to see how one step led to the next. You wanted me to understand what we were doing.

JPM: Have you ever had someone try to show you how to solve a problem—a problem you didn't know how to solve?

S: Not that I can recall.

JPM: I'm the first one?

S: I think so. The experience surely felt different.

JPM: And you're sure none of the people we just talked about ever helped you solve a problem?

S: Yes.

JPM: Then, I'll ask one last question. Compare and contrast my behavior and the behavior of your significant others.

S: It's okay if I make a mistake here. It's never been okay before.

JPM: Did you experience any emotional changes as we shifted the focus from the reactions of your significant others to my reactions?

S: Yes.

JPM: What were the changes?

S: For some reason, my shame and embarrassment have gone.

JPM: It looked to me like something changed in the way you felt and that you have ended up feeling a little easier. This shift is important and I don't think it happened by accident. You evidently felt you were safe here compared to the times you spent with your mother, your father, and with your grandfather. If I turn out to be different compared to your significant others, what are the implications for you?

S: I'm not sure, but it surely feels different.

JPM: I think you've pinpointed a key issue here. You may discover that we have a different kind of relationship compared to the relationships you've described with your significant others—especially when it comes to learning how to solve problems. I'm going to keep reminding you of this as we work together.

Comment Some Relief Apparent: The pained expression on Sam's face while we talked about the reactions of his significant others shifted to more a relaxed state when he focused on JPM's behavior. The interpersonal discrimination process has begun. The ultimate goal for Sam is to keep being reminded that the feelings of discomfort and avoidance behaviors associated with his previous caregivers are no longer necessary with JPM—the old consequences of criticism will not occur in the therapy room.

Rating the Quality of IDE Performance Sam will ultimately learn how to self-administer the IDE to criterion without therapeutic assistance. The four-step self-administration performance can be reliably rated by the therapist or a clinical rater using the Form for Scoring the Self-Administered Interpersonal Discrimination Exercise (SAd-IDE: McCullough, January 2009). The four rated IDE steps are shown in Table 5.3.

As noted earlier, the goal of the IDE is to help patients discriminate the clinician from others who have hurt them. If this discrimination is not made explicit, chronically depressed patients are unlikely to do it by themselves. The IDE is designed to heighten and make explicit the felt safety of the patient with his therapist vis-à-vis earlier learning experiences (McCullough, 2008, 2010). As also noted earlier, enhancing motivation to change is difficult to achieve until the chronic Pavlovian fear of an interpersonal encounter with the clinician is extinguished. One interpersonal marker that this change has occurred will be occasions when Sam stops impacting JPM with his *Hostile-Submissive (H-S: avoidance/detachment)* and *Submissive (S: compliant-passive)*

Table 5.3 *CBASP Interpersonal Discrimination Exercise (IDE) Administration and Procedural Guidelines

Note: The CBASP Interpersonal Discrimination Exercise (IDE) four-step procedure is grounded on the Transference Hypothesis and is administered whenever a patient and therapist transverse or enter a *hot spot* area (i.e., talk about material or participate in an in-session event that's implicated by the Transference Hypothesis). The therapist administers the IDE by asking four questions of the patient:

Step One: How would your mother, father, sibling, etc., react to you when you said or did the *content* implicated in the Transference Hypothesis (get close, disclose, make a mistake, or express negative affect)?

Step Two: How have I just reacted to you in this similar Transference area?

Step Three: What are the *differences* between their reactions and mine? What's different about *what* you experienced then and *what* you have just experienced here, with me now?

Step Four: What are the interpersonal implications *for you* if I respond differently to you in this situation than your _____ (significant others) did?

The patient will learn to self-administer the IDE over the process of therapy.

behavior. A decrease in *H-S* behavior will be reflected when Sam addresses his problems more assertively and lets others know what he wants and doesn't want. His submissive (*S*) style will also decrease as he becomes more interpersonally assertive. The proverbial wall of interpersonal fear begins to crumble in the face of stated Desired Outcomes (DOs in the SA exercise). At this point, Sam will obviously begin to take charge of his life and live it the way he wants to.

Comment Therapist Disciplined Personal Involvement: The most unique feature of CBASP is the therapist role, which strives to actualize a Disciplined Personal Relationship (DPR) with patients. McCullough (2006) describes the rationale for the DPR role in the treatment of chronically depressed patient. For more than a century, practitioners have faced the stringent requirements of the personal involvement taboo (Freud, 1963; Hoffer, 2000; Rogers, 1951, p. 494). The consequences of the taboo, more often than not, have limited the therapeutic role to one where practitioners deliver their techniques in a unilateral manner that moves directionally from the therapist to the patient. We have no problems with conducting psychotherapy without engaging in DPR except in those instances where a unilateral technique delivery is not effective. One such instance is where the likelihood of missing the mark involves patients like Sam who confront refractory early-onset fears of interpersonal encounter. Personal involvement in CBASP is an enacted role guided by the well-established operant principles of B. F. Skinner (1953, 1968). Practitioners choreograph personal reaction contingencies (e.g., JPM's behavior toward Sam during the SA exercise), which are then made explicit in the IDE. In these exercises Sam is given repeated opportunities to model and imitate (Bandura, 1976, 1977; Bandura & Walters, 1964; Meichenbaum, 1971) the problem-solving behavior of a comrade who is an interactive participant in the therapeutic process. Disciplined personal involvement doesn't mean that therapists and patients become drinking buddies, business partners, date, sleep together, contact each other when there is nothing else to do, share gossip, meet for coffee after hours, or become chat room pals or that therapists surrender their interpersonal limits in any way.

A disciplined personal relationship is implemented to achieve four specific ends. Adding personal responsivity (emotions, thoughts, and behaviors) to the therapeutic milieu (1) provides the opportunity to "consequate" problematical in-session behavior using the therapist's personal reactions as the consequence; (2) DPR teaches adaptive behavior after illustrating to patients how their negative behavior is interpersonally maladaptive; (3) DPR teaches and models empathic behavior; and lastly, (4) in the Interpersonal Discrimination Exercise, DPR makes explicit the differences that exist between the salubrious behavior of the therapist and the hurtful behavior of maltreating significant others.

From a psychoanalytic point of view, the CBASP contingent response to patients (McCullough, 2006) denotes a personal reaction to the immediate interpersonal impact a patient makes upon the therapist (Kiesler, 1956, 1983); as such, it represents an "objective" (Winnicott, 1949) form of countertransference. This type of reaction stands in stark contrast to a "subjective" form of countertransference (Spotnitz, 1969), whereby therapists react to patients with irrational and defensive behaviors stemming primarily from their own desires or wants. The second countertransference category is *ipso facto* interpersonally destructive because it manipulates patient behavior to meet the needs of the practitioner.

Session 15: SA #11

JPM: Did you bring in a SA today?

S: Yes, another situation happened between me and Mary.

JPM: Let's go through it. Go up to the flip chart and write the steps out and fill the steps in.

Here is what Sam wrote on the flip chart:

Step 1: (The SA was verbally introduced) Two nights ago after the children had gone to bed, Mary and I were discussing how to discipline our oldest son. Bill is eight years old, and he is very sarcastic to his younger sister (three years younger). When we have supper, he rarely misses an opportunity to tease her by not passing food (playing like he doesn't hear her asking him to pass a dish) or teasing her with hurtful comments about the way she looks or dresses or the way she eats. In the past, Mary has pretty much dismissed what I've said and gone on and done what she wanted when it came to discipline. She usually yells at Bill to stop during the meal.

Writing on flip chart: Wednesday, Mary was fussing about Bill's behavior. I told her I had a plan. She kept right on talking. I said: "Mary, I want you to listen to what I'm going to say." She looked surprised but stopped talking. "I want to talk to Bill about his behavior and from now on if he teases or is sarcastic to his sister, I'll give him a warning and tell him that if he repeats this, he will be sent to his room and can finish eating when we are through. Mary agreed to my plan.

Step 2:

1. Mary listened to me.
2. I told her what I wanted to do about Bill's behavior.
3. She agreed with me.
4. To be honest, I was scared to talk to her about this.

Step 3: I said her name and looked right at her. I said what I wanted in a very serious way. I must have looked serious because she listened.

Step 4: She agreed with the plan.

Step 5: I wanted to tell Mary my plan concerning Bill's table behavior.

S: I got what I wanted here because I said what I wanted. I did it just the way we've practiced here.

JPM: Incredible work, Sam! No one could have handled this situation any better. Look over what you've written out and tell me again *why* you got your desired outcome. You've already said it.

S: I knew exactly what I wanted to do and I stayed focused on Mary. I was not going to walk away from this issue. It's been difficult having evening meals in our house lately.

JPM: I thought you said to me a few weeks back that you could never behave this way with Mary. What's going on?!

S: I just did it. I'm tired of running away and being a wimp. I just never knew how to do it before. No one ever taught me how to stand up for myself.

JPM: I've got a feeling that you're not going to repeat what happened to you. You're going to teach your son how to treat his sister in a more appropriate manner and without all the sarcasm. You're also beginning to learn the SA method and have done the steps perfectly today. What you've accomplished here is so important. Let's review what you've learned going through these SAs. Look at the way you've laid this situation out on the flip chart and review what you've learned.

S: I'm thinking more about what I want. I never used to do that. I've also learned to focus on the other person when I talk. I watch them to see what their reactions are. You know what I've discovered? Mary acts like she likes me being more in control. I've just sensed it.

JPM: What does she do that makes you sense this?

S: She smiles more around me. She listens to what I have to say more often. She doesn't interrupt me so much while I'm talking. I just sense she likes me acting like I'm in charge.

JPM: This is a change in her behavior. Who's produced this change?

S: I guess I have. Nothing else has changed.

JPM: You guess?

S: I've done it. It's because I'm more definite about what I want.

JPM: Okay, what else have you learned here?

S: I'm not as afraid around people as I used to be.

JPM: This is a critical breakthrough. Why are you less afraid?

S: I think it's because I'm finding that I'm really not helpless anymore. I can get what I want by going after it. And, I'm also getting good things from other people, even people at work by letting them know what I want and don't want.

JPM: Sam, I want you to keep a daily log and log every time you are with someone during the day—Monday through Sunday. Think specifically about *what you want* and log in the Desired Outcome (i.e., the DO). Then, write in the AO. Briefly describe your behavior in two or three words. Keep the log brief. We'll start reviewing your log at the beginning of each hour before we do anything else. If you can, bring me a copy of your log. My goal here is to help you transfer what we're doing here in the session to your daily life and put it into practice. You should have four columns across the page with *Name, DO, AO,* and *Behavior* at the head of the columns. It should look something like this:

*Day/Date:*_____

Name	*DO*	*AO*	*Behavior*
_____	_____	_____	_____

Comment SA #11: Sam is learning to identify the interpersonal consequences of his behavior. *Perceived functionality* (McCullough, 2000, 2006) or the ability to recognize the consequences he produces in relationship with others, is beginning to modify the refractory feelings of helplessness and hopelessness.

Sam lived for many years behaving as if it didn't matter what he did. His chronic depression was accompanied by a lifestyle in which he lived out a *victim interpersonal role*. At least four things have changed in Sam's life since he began treatment: (1) he has learned that he is interpersonally safe with his psychotherapist; (2) he's acquired the ability to focus on one situation at a time and learned to recognize the interpersonal consequences of his behavior; (3) Sam is acquiring the necessary assertive skills that have enabled him to achieve his desired outcomes in interpersonal encounters; and (4) Sam is talking less globally about himself and other persons he interacts with during the week. Taken together, these acquired novel skills have resulted in greater personal feelings of felt empowerment. It must also be noted that his symptoms of depression have been progressively decreasing over time.

The weekly homework log assignment worked out after SA #11 is designed to help Sam practice his newly learned in-session skills and transfer what he learns to interactions in his daily life. The daily log assignment, an "abbreviated" form of the SA exercise, continues to make explicit that his interpersonal behavior has specific consequences. We will use the log in subsequent sessions to identify what behaviors help Sam achieve his DOs and which ones impede DO attainment.

The Administration of the Interpersonal Discrimination Exercise Following SA 11

JPM: How would your mother have reacted to you had you told her about what happened between you and Mary?

S: I know exactly what she would have said: "It took you long enough to do what Dr. McCullough has been trying to teach you! Why didn't you do this earlier? Mary's been running over you for a long time." (Sam was looking as if the wind had been taken out of his sails.)

JPM: What would your father say?

S: He doesn't like the idea that I'm coming to see you. He would probably react with something like: "I don't see why you just can't take care of yourself without all this therapy stuff."

JPM: What was my reaction to you in this situation? How did I behave?

S: You were happy with me. You looked like you were genuinely proud of me.

JPM: You got it right as far as my reaction to you. Compare what you came out of and what we've got going here. What's different?

S: It's okay if I learn to take care of myself. I never felt it was okay. In fact, I always thought that I should have been born knowing all this stuff. I thought strong men were born—one shouldn't have to learn how to take care of himself. Stupid way to think, isn't it?

JPM: It's absolutely not stupid! In fact, it's just the way you were taught. You learned exactly what you were taught and you learned it well. Of course, it consigned you to one hell of a life, but you learned your lessons well. You are learning some things here that are quite different. You and I have made a great start and we'll keep working on this until you can do all these things in your sleep.

S: Being here with you is really a different experience. It's all so new. Sometimes I feel that maybe I shouldn't change all this stuff about myself. I sorta feel guilty some times.

JPM: I know it's different and I'm not surprised that you feel guilty about all the new changes you're making. Is it like you're becoming another person?

S: Exactly. This isn't really me. I'm becoming someone else. It feels funny and weird.

JPM: I bet it does. Changing one's life after years of living one way and then doing things differently is never easy. You're making some changes now that have to be shaking your foundations on a deep level! I'm not surprised you're feeling guilty and weird. I'm glad you told me about your reactions. We'll keep working at it at your pace, and I'm going with you all the way.

Comment on the Interpersonal Discrimination Exercise Anytime one alters the direction of a chronic and refractory lifestyle, the person discovers that the process itself is often a terrifying experience. Many turn back and refuse to go further because the old ways are at least familiar and less frightening. Coming out of the cellar of chronic depression that's lasted for decades is similar to emerging from darkness into bright sunlight. Patients can easily become overwhelmed. We often report positive therapeutic outcomes (e.g., Keller, McCullough, et al., 2000: $n = 681$ patients who reported being depressed for approximately 20 years) and give little thought to the fight against fears that chronic patients experience in their march from illness to health. Sam is disclosing his fears about being different and about discovering a new interpersonal identity after concluding for years that the way he behaved was the only way he could live. He was wrong, but this discovery was resulting in some startling insights. He found out that not only were his conclusions about himself very limiting, they were also erroneous. Another frequent lament from these patients like Sam concerns the "wasted years" that accompanied one's destructive lifestyle—some patients look back on 30- to 40-plus years! Clinicians who treat chronically depressed patients learn from experience that the health they strive so hard to help patients achieve can be, at least for awhile, as difficult as the illness has been. New learning of this magnitude takes take time to be assimilated and the work of therapy in one sense begins in earnest once Sam achieves his first look at health as he's done in SA #11—now Sam knows that health is an achievable goal.

Readministration of the Impact Message Inventory Post–Session 11

JPM completed an IMI on Sam following the 11th session. The IMI profile is shown in Figure 5.3. Compared to the first rated IMI administration following Session 2, one sees a decreasing amount of space rated on the hostile side of the Interpersonal Circle (Kiesler, 1983). As noted earlier, Kiesler (1996) defines *hostility* as active or passive verbal/nonverbal behavior designed to avoid others by keeping one's distance. Interpersonal hostility may take the form of passive withdrawal or detachment or, in its extreme form, it can become highly aggressive. Rarely do clinicians encounter physical aggression in the therapy room, but many therapists have been the recipients of verbal and nonverbal displays of hostility (e.g., denigrating remarks made about the therapist's competence or overt nonverbal behaviors, such as storming out of the room).

Figure 5.3 Sam's Impact Message Inventory (IMI) Profile Scores Following Sessions 11 and 25

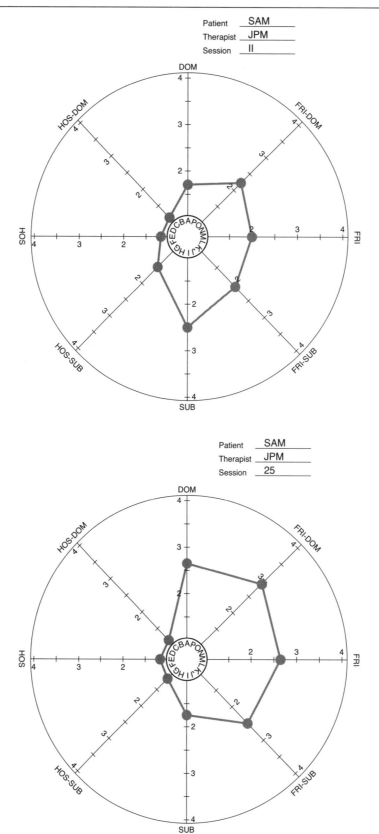

Source: Kiesler, D. J., & Schmidt, J. A. (1993). The Impact Message Inventory: Form IIA Octant Scale Version. Palo Alto, CA: Mind Garden.

Sam's impact on JPM on the *Hostile-Submission* Octant (*H-S:* interpersonally withdrawn, detached) no longer obtained peak status following Session 11. JPM rated the nadir octant opposite the *H-S octant, Friendly-Dominant* (*F-D:* interpersonally more in charge, friendly exhibitionistic) with a higher impact score. The patient's *Submission* Octant (*S:* interpersonal passivity, compliance) decreased somewhat but was still considered a peak octant; however, Sam's *Dominant* nadir octant (*D:* taking charge, being more in assertively in control) increased moderately in impact strength compared to the earlier post-session 2 rating (see Figure 5.2). Interpersonally, Sam's impacts on JPM are moving in the right direction; that is, he's functioning with less interpersonal avoidance and passivity in the session and with more dominance evident in his reported assertive behavior designed to obtain his desired outcomes.

Session 20: Abbreviated SA Work

JPM: Please go up to the flip chart, and pick one day during last week and write out your daily log on the chart. Don't try to write everything—just write enough so we can see *who* you interacted with, *what* you wanted (DO), *how* the event came out for you (AO), and what you did (your behavior). Sam went to the flip chart and wrote the following:

Day/Date: Thursday

Name	DO	AO	Behavior
1. Mary	Decide how to schedule son's homework timetable.	A decision was made.	I stayed focused and urged Mary to help me with our son.
2. Work Colleague	Wanted Bill to do an extra review on the project due next week.	He agreed to do the review.	Invited him for coffee. We talked about the project and I asked him.
3. Next-door neighbor	Wanted my lawn mower back that he borrowed.	Neighbor brought it back.	Asked him nicely but directly—said I needed to mow my grass.
4. Dad fussed at me for letting my car get so dirty.	Told him let's talk about football, don't want to discuss my car.	I turned on the TV and we watched Virginia Tech play.	Sorta chuckled when he fussed and told him directly: "Let's watch the game."

Comment on Sam's Abbreviated SA Work During Session 20 *Perceived functionality*, one of the primary outcome goals of CBASP treatment, is defined as follows: it is the achievement of "a general cognitive set in which the individual perceives that his/her behavior has specific consequences in the environment" (McCullough, 2000, p. 207). In his logged SA work earlier, Sam has provided more evidence that he is now engaging in interpersonal encounters remaining aware of what he wants. Significantly, he provides tangible evidence that he has learned to identify the interpersonal consequences of his behavior. Sam, operating on a perceived functionality basis, has achieved one of the major outcomes goals of treatment. Earlier more primitive forms of preoperational functioning have given way to thinking abstractly or formally when it comes to interpersonal functioning. Sam can now plan ahead, he can learn from his errors, and he is now able to relate empathically with others. Such functioning has been described by other researchers as "means-end" thinking (Platt, Siegel, & Spivack, 1975; Platt & Spivack, 1972, 1974, 1975). It denotes living with others from a goal-oriented perspective.

Post-Treatment Planning The abbreviated SA exercise also provides JPM an opportunity to discuss the importance of continuing to use SA for the remainder of one's life. The rationale here is to awaken Sam to the dangers he will face when treatment ends—researchers frequently describe the post-treatment period in terms of *survival, relapse,* or *recurrence* (Thase et al., 1992), terms that describe the fate of patients when treatment ends. A more appropriate terminology may be to think of the post-treatment period as a dangerous time when Sam will face the threat of the loss of extinction of the older psychopathology. Therapy termination means that Sam will be placed on an extinction schedule when he will no longer have access to the weekly reinforcers in JPM's office. Post-treatment means that Sam will have to create his own reinforcers and keep them in place himself. Bouton (1991, 2002, 2007) writes extensively about the three types of extinction threats that Sam will confront. His list includes *renewal* (a loss of extinction when the dyadic context for Sam is changed after therapy ends; e.g., he no longer attends the weekly sessions in JPM's office and confronts stress in other contexts); *reinstatement* (a loss of extinction when Sam confronts the pre-therapy significant others by himself; e.g., the subtle put-downs of his mother, father, and possibly Mary); and *reacquisition* (a loss of extinction when a pre-therapy state is restored; e.g., Sam encounters the older social milieu in his family on holiday occasions and faces criticism for things he had done wrong).

As suggested earlier, preparing Sam for the post-treatment period means taking into account *what living situations* he'll face following treatment, *who* Sam will encounter on a daily basis and assessing the degree to which he *has learned* to withstand the onslaughts of the older pathological associations. To survive without losing the extinction of the older psychopathology, Sam must engage in daily practice and enact what he wants in all interactions with his mother. Sam will also have to decide how much of himself he wants to share with his father, whom he said "really doesn't know me." Over the past few months Sam has helped his wife Mary become aware of the effects of her negative comments, particularly those that make him feel "less than a man." His grandparents will pose a significant challenge. His grandfather's disdain for weakness and his grandmother's courageous style of living have, in the past, left Sam feeling inadequate. Practicing the maintenance of self-focus, including what he wants / doesn't want, will help Sam stand his ground and avoid behaving inadequately.

In summary, educating Sam about treatment for chronic depression is *basic survival training* and it constitutes the final stage of therapy. Remaining symptom-free will require daily practice. As Sam comes for his final psychotherapy session, his in-session performance suggests that he has learned the lessons of treatment. These gains will be evident below in the SA and the IDE, which Sam self-administers with assistance from JPM.

Session 15: SA 18

JPM: Did you fill out a CSQ today?

S: Yes. Bob called and asked that I come to his office. He wanted to talk about the latest commercial design I'd drawn. Bob and I reviewed the drawings and he didn't have any suggestions or corrections to make. I told him about the hours I'd put in on the drawings. He seemed impressed with my efforts and also with my work. I asked him when would be a good time to talk with him about a yearly raise. He told me to make an appointment with his secretary for Friday of this week. He said that we'd talk about the raise then. I left his office feeling good and set up an appointment to see him on Friday.

Step 2 (Interpretations): The situation meant the following: (1) I went after what I wanted; (2) he liked my work and said so.

Step 3 (Situational Behavior): I made good eye contact during the time I was in his office and when I asked for a time to meet to discuss a raise, I was looking him in the eye.

Step 4 (Actual Outcome): The situation ended with my making an appointment to see Bob on Friday.

Step 5 (Desired Outcome): To start the wheels in motion by asking for a raise.

I got what I wanted here (AO = DO).

I want to do something else. I want to take you through an *Interpersonal Discrimination Exercise* to show you just how different things look to me now compared to several months back.

My mother and father would have probably not been very impressed with my asking for a raise. My mother might have said: "You should have asked months ago. It's about time!" I'm really not sure what my dad would have said. He probably wouldn't have made that much over the fact that I asserted myself. However, my wife was ecstatic! She came up and kissed me when I told her what I'd done. Can you believe that! And you—you've had that big smile on your face ever since I started telling you about this situation. I don't sound like the same person, do I? I've discovered possibilities with you that I've never known before. Seeing that it matters to you and to others has given me the courage to change a lot of things. Now, what I do really matters to me! What I do really matters! This is the big difference.

JPM: You don't sound like the same person compared to the way you behaved when we started. You've made so many changes and your depression has gone. This is the big news. You've taken over your life. You're not a victim anymore. Look out world, here comes Sam!

End of Therapy Assessment

Sam's BDI-II scores are illustrated in Figure 5.4. Two acquisition performance variables are also shown in the figure. Sam's five-step SA performance and his four-step IDE performance across treatment sessions are presented. Beginning in the 11th session, it became obvious to JPM that Sam was accurately identifying the consequences of his behavior as Sam's SA performance scores were nearing a criterion level (i.e., five out of five correct performance steps achieved). Such a perceptual-behavioral achievement frequently suggests two things: (1) an increase in motivation to change one's behavior often accompanies the recognition that one's behavior has interpersonal consequences; and (2) it also becomes apparent that the patient is experiencing decreasing felt helplessness. Helplessness is mitigated because the interpersonal landscape is modified—the emergent issue now becomes the following: *What kind of effects do I want to produce?* Sam reached criterion performance with the SA in the 18th session.

Figure 5.4 shows that the self-administration mastery of the IDE was slower to achieve. Sam reached criterion (i.e., four out of four correct performance steps achieved) in Session 22. His difficulty in performing the exercise was recognizing the "hot spot" points when a discrimination between JPM's behavior versus that of hurtful significant others would be beneficial. This is an important issue. The best

Figure 5.4   Sam's Therapy Assessment Data

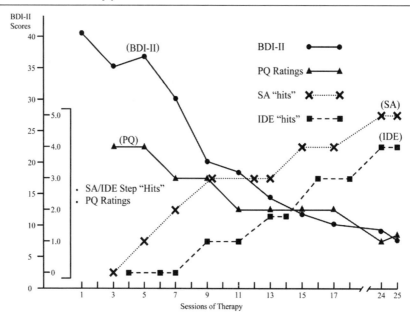

extinction of the older emotional pathology occurs when JPM can be visualized imaginally juxtaposed alongside the maltreating significant others in a previously hurtful situational context (Bouton, personal communication, August 21, 2007). The visual exercise is conducted instructing the patient to view JPM's salubrious in-session behavior discriminated from that of significant others in the hurtful context.

The 25th post-session IMI profile is shown in Figure 5.3. The most important IMI changes were reflected on the *nadir* post-session *XXV* octant ratings compared to post-session 2 (see Figure 5.2). Sam has scored rating gains on the *nadir* Friendly-Dominant (*F-D:* more entertaining, now taking charge, exhibitionistic, and enjoys being with others) and Dominant octants (*D:* taking charge, likes to be the center of attention, standing up for himself, noting his assets, has answers for himself). His Friendly score (*F:* more appreciative and complementary of others, carries his share of the relationship load, welcoming toward others) has notably increased. There is no space taken on the hostile side of the circle suggesting significant decreases in interpersonal avoidance with ample evidence present for assuming interpersonal approach behavior.

Finally, the Personal Question (PQ) paired-comparison scores over the course of treatment are illustrated in Figure 5.4. The Transference Hypothesis (i.e., *If I let JPM get to know me [i.e., disclose myself and let him know how inadequate I feel], then JPM will judge me negatively, not like or respect me because he'll know that I'm a weak person*) was operationalized and the PQ scores reflected four levels of outcome: *illness level* (4.0 rating) at Session 3; *minimal change* (3.0 rating denoting an incremental-to-small change); *significant change* (2.0 signaling a moderate-to-high level of change); *recovery* (1.0: absence of illness). Sam's PQ scores suggested that he experienced "safety" in the sessions with JPM. This shift was slow in coming but it occurred over time. It was assumed that in-session learning would be facilitated to the degree that Sam felt interpersonally safe with JPM. Repetition of the IDE exercise is carried out to draw distinctions between the clinician's behavior and that of hurtful significant others. Enhancing felt safety is important to the counter-conditioning process of CBASP psychotherapy.

Summary

This case was an actual one, though certain alterations have been inserted to protect the real identity of Sam. Interpersonal safety was achieved over the course of treatment and an avoidant lifestyle was apparently overthrown and replaced by a generalized interpersonal approach style. One of the generalized treatment effects (McCullough, 2006) was that Sam's depression intensity levels dropped to negligible levels and he was diagnosed *in remission* two months following the 25th session. At that time, there was no evidence of the vestiges of major depression and Sam did not meet criteria for dysthymic disorder. He had been seen every other week after Session 25 and following the diagnostic follow-up interview, Sam was tapered to one session every three weeks. After several months, the therapy session frequency would be further reduced to once per month.

References

American Psychiatric Association (APA). (1994). *Diagnostic and statistical manual of mental disorders* (4th ed.). Washington, DC: Author.

Bandura, A. (1976). Effecting change through participant modeling. In J. D. Krumboltz & C. E. Thoreson (Eds.), *Counseling methods* (pp. 248–265). New York, NY: Holt, Rinehart & Winston.

Bandura, A. (1977). *Social learning theory*. Englewood Cliffs, NJ: Prentice-Hall.

Bandura, A., & Walters, R. H. (1964). *Social learning and personality development*. New York, NY: Holt, Rinehart & Winston.

Beck, A. T. (1978). Beck depression inventory-II. Philadelphia, PA: Center for Cognitive Therapy.

Bouton, M. E. (1991). Context and retrieval in extinction and in other examples of interference in simple associative learning. In L. W. Dachowski & C. F. Flaherty (Eds.), *Current topics in animal learning: Brain, emotion, and cognition* (pp. 25–53). Hillsdale, NJ: Erlbaum.

Bouton, M. E. (2002). Context, ambiguity, and unlearning: Sources of relapse after behavioral extinction. *Biological Psychiatry, 52,* 976–986.

Bouton, M. E. (2007). *Learning and behavior: A contemporary synthesis* (Chapter 10, pp. 371–419). Sunderland, MA: Sinauer.

Cowan, J. C. (1976). *Piaget with feeling: Cognitive, social, and emotional dimensions*. New York, NY: Holt, Rinehart & Winston.

Freud, S. (1963). *Character and culture* (pp. 234–235). New York, NY: Collier.

Gordon, D. E. (1988). Formal operations and interpersonal and affective disturbances in adolescents. In E. D. Nannis & P. A. Cowan (Eds.), *Developmental psychopathology and its treatment* (pp. 51–73). San Francisco, CA: Jossey-Bass.

Hoffer, A. (2000). Neutrality and the therapeutic alliance: What does the analyst want? In S. R. Levy (Ed.), *The therapeutic alliance* (p. 37). Madison, WI: International Universities Press.

Keller, M. B., McCullough, J. P., Klein, D. N., Arnow, B., Dunner, D. L., & Gelenberg, A. J. (2000). A comparison of nefazodone, a cognitive behavioral analysis system of psychotherapy, and their combination for the treatment of chronic depression. *New England Journal of Medicine, 342,* 1462–1470.

Keller, M. B., & Shapiro, R. W. (1982). "Double depression": Superimposition of acute depressive episodes on chronic depressive disorders. *American Journal of Psychiatry, 139,* 438–442.

Kiesler, D. J. (1983). The 1982 interpersonal circle: A taxonomy for complementarity in human transactions. *Psychological Review, 90,* 185–214.

Kiesler, D. J. (1988). *Therapeutic metacommunication: Therapist impact disclosure as feedback in psychotherapy*. Palo Alto, CA: Consulting Psychologist Press.

Kiesler, D. J. (1996). *Contemporary interpersonal theory and research: Personality, psychopathology, and psychotherapy*. New York, NY: John Wiley & Sons.

Kiesler, D. J., & Schmidt, J. A. (1993). *The impact message inventory: Form IIA octant scale version*. Palo Alto, CA: Mind Garden.

Klein, D. N. (2008). Classification of depressive disorders in *DSM-5*: Proposal for a two dimension system. *Journal of Abnormal Psychology, 117,* 552–560.

Klein, D. N., Shankman, S. A., & Rose, S. (2006). Ten-year prospective follow-up study of the naturalistic course of dysthymic disorder and double depression. *American Journal of Psychiatry, 163,* 872–880.

Kocsis, J. H., Gelenberg, A. J., Rothbaum, B. O., Klein, D. N., Trivedi, M. T., Manber, R., . . . Thase, M. T. (2009). Cognitive behavioral analysis system of psychotherapy and brief supportive psychotherapy for augmentation of antidepressant nonresonse in chronic depression. *Archives of General Psychiatry, 66,* 1178–1188.

Manber, R., Arnow, B. A., Blasey, C., Vivian, D., McCullough, J. P., Blalock, J. A., . . . Keller, M. B. (2003). Patient's therapeutic skill acquisition and response to psychotherapy, alone and in combination with medication. *Journal of Psychological Medicine, 33,* 693–702.

McCullough, Jr., J. P. (2000). *Treatment for Chronic Depression: Cognitive Behavioral Analysis System of Psychotherapy (CBASP).* New York, NY: Guilford Press.

McCullough, Jr., J. P. (2001). *Skills training manual for diagnosing and treating chronic depression: CBASP.* New York, NY: Guilford Press.

McCullough, Jr., J. P. (2003). *CBASP patient's manual.* New York, NY: Guilford Press.

McCullough, Jr., J. P. (2006). *Treating chronic depression with disciplined personal involvement: CBASP.* New York, NY: Springer.

McCullough, Jr., J. P. (2008). Basic assumptions about CBASP emotional mood modification. In J. P McCullough Jr. & R. F. McCullough, *CBASP Intensive Training Workbook.* Richmond, VA: Virginia Commonwealth University.

McCullough, Jr., J. P. (2009, January). *Form for scoring the self-administered interpersonal discrimination exercise (SAd-IDE).* Richmond, VA: Virginia Commonwealth University.

McCullough, Jr., J. P. (2010). Appendix. CBASP, the third wave and the treatment of chronic depression. *Journal of European Psychotherapy, 9*(1), 169–190.

McCullough, J. P., Braith, J. A., Chapman, R. C., Kasnetz, M. D., Carr, K. F., Cones, J. H., . . . Roberts, W. C. (1990a). Comparison of early and late onset dysthymia. *Journal of Nervous and Mental Disease, 178,* 577–581.

McCullough, J. P., Braith, J. A., Chapman, R. C., Kasnetz, M. D., Carr, K. F., Cones, J. H., . . . Roberts, W. C. (1990b). Comparison of dysthymia major and nonmajor depressives. *Journal of Nervous and Mental Disease, 178,* 611–612.

McCullough, J. P., Kasnetz, M. D., Braith, J. A., Carr, K. F., Cones, J. H., & Fielo, J. (1988). Longitudinal study of an untreated sample of predominantly late-onset characterological dysthymia. *Journal of Nervous and Mental Disease, 176,* 658–667.

McCullough, Jr., J. P., Klein, D. N., Borian, F. E., Howland, R. H., Riso, L. P., . . . Keller, M. B. (2003). Group comparisons of DSM-IV subtypes of chronic depression: Validity of the distinctions, Part 2. *Journal of Abnormal Psychology, 112,* 614–622.

McCullough, J. P., Kornstein, S. G., McCullough, J. P., Belyea-Caldwell, S., Kaye, A. L., Roberts, W. C., . . . Kruus, L. (1996). Differential diagnosis of the chronic depressions. *Psychiatric Clinics of North America, 19,* 55–71.

Meichenbaum, D. (1971). Examination of model characteristics in reducing avoidance behavior. *Journal of Personality and Social Psychology, 17,* 298–307.

Nemeroff, C. B., Heim, C. M., Thase, M. E., Klein, D. N., Rush, A. J., Schatzberg, A. F., . . . Keller, M. B. (2003). Differential responses to psychotherapy versus pharmacotherapy in the treatment of patients with chronic forms of major depression and childhood trauma. *Proceedings of the National Academy of Sciences, 100,* 14293–14296.

Pavlov, I. (1927/1960). *Conditioned Reflexes* (Trans. G. V. Anrep). New York, NY: Dover.

Piaget, J. (1926). *The language and thought of the child.* New York, NY: Harcourt, Brace. (Original work published in 1923)

Platt, J. J., Siegel, J. M., & Spivack, G. (1975). Do psychiatric patients and normals see the same solutions as effective in solving interpersonal problems? *Journal of Consulting and clinical Psychology, 39,* 279.

Platt, J. J., & Spivack, G. (1972). Problem-solving thinking of psychiatric patients. *Journal of Consulting and Clinical Psychology, 39,* 148–151.

Platt, J. J., & Spivack, G. (1974). Means of solving real-life problems: I. Psychiatric patients vs. controls and cross-cultural comparisons of normal females. *Journal of Community Psychology, 2,* 45–48.

Platt, J. J., & Spivack, G. (1975). Unidimensionality of the means-ends problem-solving (MEPS) procedure. *Journal of Clinical Psychology, 31,* 15–16.

Rogers, C. (1951). *Client-centered therapy: Its current practice implications, and theory* (p. 494). Boston, MA: Houghton Mifflin.

Schramm, E., & Reynolds, C. (2010, February 9). Letter to the editor: "Where do we go from here?" *Archives of General Psychiatry.* Retrieved from http://archpsyc.ama-assn.org/cgi/eletters/66/11/1178

Shapiro, M. B. (1961, April). A method of measuring psychological changes specific the individual psychiatric patient. *British Journal of Medical Psychology,* 151–155.

Shapiro, M. B. (1964). The measurement of clinically relevant variables. *Journal of Psychosomatic Research, 8,* 245–254.

Shapiro, M. B., Litman, G. K., Nias, D. K. B., & Hendry, E. R. (1973, April). A clinicians's approach to experimental research. *Journal of Clinical Psychology,* 165–169.

Skinner, B. F. (1953). *Science and human behavior.* New York, NY: Free Press.

Skinner, B. F. (1968). *The technology of teaching.* New York, NY: Appleton-Century-Crofts.

Spotnitz, H. (1969). *Modern psychoanalysis of the schizophrenic patient.* New York, NY: Grune & Stratton.

Thase, M. E. (1992). Long-term treatments of recurrent depressive disorders. *Journal of Clinical Psychiatry, 53,* 32–44.

Thase, M. E., Simons, A. D., McGeary, J., Cahalane, J. F., Hughes, C., Harden, T., & Friedman, E. (1992). Relapse following cognitive behavior therapy for depression: Potential implications for longer forms of treatment? *American Journal of Psychiatry, 149,* 1046–1052.

Vander Molen, T. L. (2010). *Preoperational thinking: Is it an essential structural characteristic of early-onset chronic depression?* Santa Barbara, CA: Doctoral Programs of Fielding Graduate University. Unpublished manuscript.

Wiersma, J. E., Hovens, J., van Oppen, P., Giltay, E., van Schaik, A., Aartjan, A., . . . Penninx, B. W. J. H. (2009). Childhood trauma as a risk factor for chronicity of depression. *Journal of Clinical Psychiatry, 7,* 983–989.

Winnicott, D. W. (1949). Hate in the countertransference. *International Journal of Psychoanalysis, 30,* 69–75.

6

One Size Does Not Fit All: Cultural Considerations in Evidence–Based Practice for Depression

Esteban V. Cardemil, Oswaldo Moreno, and Monica Sanchez

The purpose of this book, which is to identify and describe in some detail some of the leading evidence-based approaches to treating and preventing depression, is a laudable one and will prove useful to clinicians interested in providing state-of-the-art mental health services. And yet, the term *evidence-based* should be cautiously applied, given the limited research evaluating the generalizability of that evidence base to populations other than individuals from European-American middle-class backgrounds (Bernal & Scharrón-del-Río, 2001; La Roche & Christopher, 2008; Mak, Law, Alvidrez, & Pérez-Stable, 2007; U.S. Department of Health and Human Services, 2001).

This limitation in the research base is problematic for several reasons. First, within the United States, the demographics of the population have been rapidly changing; estimates suggest that by the year 2050 the number of U.S. residents who self-identify as European American will be below 50% of the total U.S. population (U.S. Census Bureau, 2008). The situation is even more extreme from a global perspective, as almost 85% of the world population lives outside of the United States and Europe (see Arnett, 2008, for a discussion of the limited scope of psychological research in general). Second, there is some research that suggests that important cultural group differences may exist in the prevalence rate of depression. For example, results from both the original National Comorbidity Survey and the more recently completed National Comorbidity Survey—Replication indicated that depression is less prevalent among

Latinos and African Americans than among European Americans (Breslau et al., 2006; Kessler, Chiu, Demler, & Walters, 2005; Kessler et al., 1994). Similarly, some research has documented the existence of culturally specific risk factors for depression, including acculturative stress (Mui & Kang, 2006; Torres, 2010) and racial/ethnic discrimination (Seaton, Caldwell, Sellers, & Jackson, 2008).

And third, considerable research has documented significant mental healthcare disparities affecting individuals from low-income and racial and ethnic minority backgrounds (Snowden & Yamada, 2005; U.S. Department of Health and Human Services, 2001). In addition to being less likely than European Americans to receive formal mental health services (Alegría et al., 2002; Wells, Klap, Koike, & Sherbourne, 2001), low-income and racial/ethnic minorities are more likely to prematurely terminate mental health services once connected (e.g., Organista, Muñoz, & Gonzalez, 1994).

Thus, the changing demographics of the United States, the emerging research showing cultural differences in the prevalence rate and risk factors for depression, and the well-documented mental health care disparities provide a compelling case that clinical psychology needs to more comprehensively consider diversity in the development and evaluation of evidence-based interventions. And, indeed, the past 15 years have seen an increase in efforts to evaluate the efficacy of interventions that have been adapted for particular cultural populations. In this chapter, we briefly review the evidence supporting the efficacy of the various evidence-based interventions described in this book. We then provide more detail regarding the clinical approaches utilized in those interventions that have been rigorously evaluated with different cultural groups.

How Do We Define Diverse Populations?

Before beginning our review of the literature, we first briefly explain our approach to conceptualizing diversity. Diversity in psychology is a broad term that refers to individual, personal, and collective identities, and life experiences across a variety of sociocultural constructs, including race, ethnicity, gender, social class, sexual orientation, religion, and disability. Indeed, scholars have written about all of these constructs as they relate to the application of psychotherapy with different populations. In this chapter, we focus on cultural diversity, a concept that touches on the terms *culture*, *race*, and *ethnicity* (Atkinson, Morten, & Sue, 1998; Helms & Cook, 1999). The term *culture* refers to a shared set of social norms, beliefs, and values that particular groups hold and transmit across generations. These norms, beliefs, and values are thought to be learned and cover a wide range of psychologically relevant topics, including gender and familial roles and relationships, styles of interpersonal communication, and philosophical world views (Betancourt & Lopez, 1993). The term *race* has historically tended to refer to physical or biological characteristics that distinguish particular groups of people from other groups (Atkinson, Morten, & Sue,

1998; Betancourt & Lopez, 1993). Although the existence of biological and genetic underpinnings of different racial categories have not been supported by recent biological and anthropological research (A. Smedley & B. Smedley, 2005), the term *race* nevertheless has social significance and meaning to individuals and is commonly used as a proxy for culture and ethnicity. Finally, the term *ethnicity* is generally used to refer to the historical cultural patterns and collective identities shared by groups from specific geographic regions of the world (Betancourt & Lopez, 1993; Helms & Cook, 1999). Some of these patterns include language, history, customs, and rituals.

Although the terms race, ethnicity, and culture have overlap, there are important distinctions among them (Alvidrez, Azocar, & Miranda, 1996; Betancourt & Lopez, 1993). For example, the racial category *white* includes individuals from different ethnic groups (e.g., individuals of British, French, Russian origin), which have different cultural customs. Further, individuals from the same ethnic group may have different cultural traditions depending on where they were raised (e.g., Asians growing up in Mainland China versus growing up in San Francisco).

In this chapter, we use the term *culture* instead of race or ethnicity when referring to diverse groups of individuals for whom an intervention has been adapted. Using the term *culture* is advantageous because it helps keep salient the fact that culture should be conceptualized as a multidimensional and contextual phenomenon that incorporates a variety of sociopolitical identities, including gender, socioeconomic status, and minority status. The use of the term *culture* can help remind us that it would be problematic to assume homogeneity in cultural worldviews among individuals from the same ethnicity but who vary in their gender, socioeconomic status, and experiences as a minority. This concern is particularly relevant to applying evidence-based practice (EBP) to diverse cultural groups because the overwhelming majority of cultural adaptations have been developed and evaluated with individuals from racial and ethnic minority backgrounds who also come from low-income backgrounds.

Research Evidence for EBP for Depression With Diverse Cultural Groups

There have been three recent reviews of evidence-based psychosocial interventions for racial and ethnic minorities. Each had a slightly different focus, but in general, the reviews found positive effects when examining the efficacy of evidence-based interventions with individuals from different cultural groups (Griner & Smith, 2006; Huey & Polo, 2008; Miranda, Bernal et al., 2005). With regard to depression in particular, several studies that included sufficient numbers of individuals from different cultural backgrounds have found support for the efficacy of cognitive-behavioral therapy (CBT) with Latinos and African Americans (Miranda, Azocar, Organista, Dwyer, Arean, 2003; Miranda, Chung et al., 2003; Miranda, Green et al., 2006; Organista,

Muñoz, & González, 1994; Perez Foster, 2007). In addition, several studies that have focused on specific cultural groups have also found support for the efficacy of CBT with Latino adults and adolescents (Arean & Miranda, 1996; Comas-Diaz, 1981, 1986; Rosselló & Bernal, 1999; Rosselló, Bernal, & Rivera-Medina, 2008), African American women (Kohn, Oden, Muñoz, Robinson, & Leavitt, 2002), and elderly Chinese Americans (Dai et al., 1999). There also exists some support for the efficacy of CBT in the prevention of depressive symptoms among Latino adolescents (Cardemil, Reivich, Beevers, Seligman, & James, 2007; Cardemil, Reivich, & Seligman, 2002) and adults (Cardemil, Kim, Pinedo, & Miller, 2005; Le, Zmuda, Perry, & Muñoz, 2010; Muñoz et al., 1995; Muñoz et al., 2007; Vega, Valle, Kolody, & Hough, 1987).

In addition to CBT, there also exists support for the generalizability of interpersonal therapy (IPT) to Latinos and African Americans in the treatment and prevention of depression, the majority of which have been found with perinatal depression. Some of this work with pregnant women has been conducted with Latina women (Spinelli & Endicott, 2003), low-income and African American women (Crockett, Zlotnick, Davis, Payne, & Washington, 2008; Zlotnick, Miller, Pearlstein, Howard, & Sweeney, 2006), and low-income, Latina and African American adolescents (Miller, Gur, Shanok, & Weissman, 2008). In two studies that did not focus on perinatal depression, Rosselló and Bernal (1999) and Rosselló, Bernal, and Rivera-Medina (2008) also found support for the efficacy of IPT with Puerto Rican adolescents.

Taken together, the research evidence generally supports the efficacy of CBT and IPT with Latinos and African Americans. Unfortunately, the research base for the treatment and prevention of depression is significantly more limited for Asian Americans (one study of CBT for Chinese Americans) and nonexistent for individuals from other cultural groups, including American Indians. This lack of research into the generalizability of EBPs is changing, however, as there is increasing attention to the adaptations of EBPs for different cultural groups (e.g., Hwang, Wood, Lin, & Cheung, 2006; Jackson, Shmutzer, Wenzel, & Tyler, 2006; Renfrey, 1992).

Importantly, the majority of studies investigating the efficacy of CBT with different cultural groups have been variants on a series of manuals developed by Ricardo Muñoz and colleagues (Muñoz & Mendelson, 2005). These manuals were themselves based on the Coping with Depression (CWD) course initially developed by Lewinsohn and colleagues (Lewinsohn, Antonuccio, Breckenridge, & Teri, 1984; see Cuijpers, Muñoz, Clarke, & Lewinsohn, 2009, for an extensive review of the CWD course). Similarly, the studies that have focused on IPT have all based their work in the seminal work of Gerald Klerman, Myrna Weissman, and colleagues (Klerman, Weissman, Rounsaville, & Chevron, 1984; Weissman, Markowitz, & Klerman, 2000).

These studies have generally evaluated adapted versions of a standard intervention that the authors believe better address the needs of the target population. Some of the adaptations have been relatively minor, while others have been more comprehensive. It is also important to note that the majority of the cultural adaptations we reviewed have been developed for low-income populations (e.g., Kohn et al.,

2002; Le et al., 2010; Miller et al., 2008; Miranda et al., 2003; Muñoz et al., 2007). As such, these cultural adaptations have necessarily dealt with issues of poverty and social class. In addition, many of the interventions also specifically targeted women and so attended to issues of gender in the development of their programs. In the following sections, we synthesize the different approaches to adaptation of a standard evaluation and provide concrete recommendations for clinicians interested in adapting and implementing an EBP for depression.

How Should EBP Be Adapted for Diverse Populations?

Although the attention to cultural adaptations of EBP has been increasing, there is no consensus regarding how to adapt EBP to clinical work with individuals from different cultural groups (Cardemil, 2008). For example, there are currently no clear guidelines as to when to adapt an intervention, for which specific populations an intervention should be adapted, the extent to which an intervention should be adapted, or how to evaluate the relative contribution of particular adaptations.

Recently, however, several scholars have offered frameworks for integrating cultural issues into evidence-based practice (Barrera & Castro, 2006; Bernal & Sáez-Santiago, 2006; Hall, 2001; Hwang, 2006; Muñoz & Mendelson, 2005; Whaley & Davis, 2007). One early cultural adaptation framework was developed by Bernal and colleagues (1995, 2006), who focused on ecological validity and rooted their approach in a contextualist perspective. Their framework emphasized eight different dimensions to which attention should be given when adapting, or centering, an intervention for a particular cultural group (for an in-depth discussion of these dimensions, see Bernal & Saéz-Santiago, 2006): (1) the language of the intervention; (2) metaphors to be used in the delivery of the intervention; (3) cultural knowledge about client values, customs, and traditions; (4) recognition and consideration of additional contextual influences in the client's life; (5) the client-therapist relationship; (6) conceptualization and communication of the theoretical approach to treatment; (7) agreement on goals of treatment; and (8) methods for reaching goals of treatment. Attention to these eight dimensions would lead to an adapted intervention that is contextually relevant to the targeted population.

Our approach to adapting evidence-based practice to diverse cultural groups complements this approach, as well as others in the literature (Cardemil et al., 2010). In our depression prevention work with low-income, Latina mothers, we conceptualize culture as a multidimensional, contextual phenomenon that includes aspects of gender, socioeconomic status, and the larger systemic barriers our participants encountered in their daily lives. Thus, our cognitive-behavioral intervention incorporates aspects of four broad sociocultural domains: (1) Latino cultural values and life experiences, (2) gender and gender roles, (3) social class and economic stress, and (4) disempowerment in the form of discrimination and difficulty accessing needed social services. Concretely, our depression prevention program addresses and incorporates different aspects of Latino culture, issues relevant to women and mothers, the life experiences often found in urban, low-income neighborhoods, and the sense of disenfranchisement felt by many cultural minorities. Moreover, as with the other frameworks and approaches to cultural adaptation, our framework is necessarily flexible and does not assume that every participant has relevant life experiences with each of the four domains. Indeed, we have found significant variability in the extent to which individual participants resonate with different aspects of our attempts to incorporate diversity into our work.

Although the various frameworks in the literature have different perspectives and emphases, they share many commonalities, including the recognition that culture is a complex phenomenon that necessitates addressing diversity in many different ways. In our own work, we attended to three issues of diversity throughout the intervention, including (1) when making decisions regarding various structural aspects of the intervention, (2) in the delivery of the program, and (3) in the programmatic content of each of the sessions. Our review of the CBT and IPT literature suggests that these three areas were also the ones to which other research teams attended in their efforts to develop their cultural adaptations. We now describe each of these three domains in more detail.

Diversity Considerations in the Structure of the Intervention

When clinicians and researchers implement an intervention, they need to consider how the intervention should be organized so as to provide the best therapeutic effect. Some general structural considerations include whether the intervention should be delivered individually or in group format, the number and frequency of sessions, the ordering in which content is presented to participants, and the inclusion of extra-session homework.

Attending to diversity should also take place at the structural level, and many of the interventions we reviewed made explicit structural adaptations to standard 16-session CBT. For example, in one study evaluating CBT with low-income, minority women, Miranda and colleagues (2003) added educational information sessions prior to the intervention in order to help some of the women make informed decisions about whether or not to initiate treatment for depression (Miranda et al., 2003). These sessions were developed in recognition of the variability that exists in many cultures' conceptions of health and illness, and they served as a bridge between the authors' conceptions of depression and treatment and the women's own conceptions. In another study that focused on treating depression among low-income primary care patients with CBT, Miranda and colleagues (2003) added supplementary case management to the CBT (Miranda, Azocar, Organista, Dwyer, & Arean, 2003). The purpose of the case management was to help maintain high levels of engagement with the patients in the study. In addition, the case management also focused on helping the patients cope with ongoing life stressors, many of which were related to their low-income status. Some of these stressors included problems in housing, employment, recreation, and relationships with family and friends.

Several of the studies we reviewed made the explicit structural decision to deliver the intervention in group format (e.g., Cardemil, Kim, Pinedo, & Miller, 2005; Comas-Diaz, 1981; Kohn et al., 2002; Miranda et al., 2003; Muñoz et al., 1995; Rosselló, Bernal, & Rivera-Medina, 2008). The use of group approaches appeared to emphasize the development of group cohesion around similar culturally relevant life experiences. Interestingly, some of the approaches limited participation to individuals from a single cultural group (Cardemil et al., 2005; Comas-Diaz, 1981; Kohn et al., 2002), while others included individuals from different cultural groups (Cardemil et al., 2002; Muñoz & Mendelson, 1995; Organista, Muñoz, & Gonzalez, 1994; Satterfield, 1998). There also existed variability in whether the groups were open to ongoing enrollment by participants. For example, Miranda and colleagues (2003) used an open group format in which new participants joined ongoing groups at the beginning of one of three four-week modules. These authors noted that this approach made the intervention more feasible for ongoing medical referrals. Several other research teams also used this open-group approach (e.g., Organista et al., 1994; Satterfield, 1998). In contrast, a few other research teams explicitly used a closed-group approach with the aim of enhancing group cohesion among the participants (e.g., Cardemil, Kim, et al., 2005; Kohn et al., 2002).

Several research groups who focused on Latinos addressed the importance of family within Latino culture through explicit structural adaptations. For example, in their evaluation of CBT and IPT with Puerto Rican adolescents, Rosselló and Bernal (1999) incorporated a parental interview before and after therapy. This interview allowed the therapist to acknowledge the importance of family obligation and support, the traditional hierarchical nature of Puerto Rican families, and the dependence on parents for instrumental and emotional support. Therapists were allowed to discuss treatment issues with the parents, although confidentiality was guaranteed to the adolescents. Similarly, in our work we explicitly incorporated family sessions into our group prevention work with Latina mothers (Cardemil et al., 2005; Cardemil et al., 2010). The purpose of these family sessions was to welcome participants' families into the treatment process, demystify our intervention, and enlist family members into supporting the participant. We used a broad definition of family, which encouraged participants to invite intimate partners if possible, but allowed participants to invite other important adults if preferred. This flexibility allowed us to take advantage of the extended-family structure that is commonly found in Latino families (Falicov, 1998; Gloria, Ruiz, & Castillo, 2004) as well as helping the significant numbers of single mothers feel welcome in our intervention.

In sum, our review of the literature produced many innovative approaches to adapting the structure of the intervention. These efforts are creative in that they extend the traditional conception of psychotherapy beyond the 50-minute therapy hour so as to best reach different cultural groups. Complementing these structural changes is the attention researchers give to the delivery of the intervention, both regarding how therapists interact with the clients and the flexibility in the scheduling of sessions. We now describe these considerations in more detail.

Diversity Considerations in the Delivery of the Intervention

In adapting and applying evidence-based practice to diverse populations, researchers have also focused on the manner in which their intervention has been delivered. A few of the studies we reviewed thought creatively about the location in which the intervention would be delivered and made the decision to hold the intervention in a nonclinical setting. For example, Miller and colleagues (2008), in their prevention and treatment work for postpartum depression among adolescents, held their IPT intervention in school during health classes. Similarly, Cardemil, Reivich, and colleagues (2002, 2007) implemented their CBT depression prevention program during school hours. Holding interventions during school hours has the obvious advantage of making the intervention highly accessible to the participants, normalizing the discussion of mental health topics, and increasing the likelihood that participants feel comfortable.

One innovative approach to this issue was conducted by Vega, Valle, Kolody, and Hough (1987) in their delivery of a cognitive-behavioral depression prevention intervention for Latina women. In their work, rather than use therapists to deliver their intervention in a clinical setting, they used *servidoras*, or indigenous Latina community helpers, and delivered the intervention in community settings. This approach, which has been used in other prevention-oriented health work, is striking in its use of existing community social networks to increase the reach of the intervention.

Researchers have also spent considerable time focusing on therapist behavior when they adapt EBP for diverse populations. Much of this focus has been on having therapists attend to relevant cultural values when interacting with clients. For example, Hwang and colleagues (2006) suggest that clinicians can gain credibility with their Chinese clients by taking into account the importance placed in the Chinese culture on hierarchical relationships, social harmony, and respect for authority figures. Thus, they recommend that therapists present themselves as authority figures with the ability to help their clients solve problems. They also suggest that therapists be proactive in the provision of direction, advice, and teaching skills for symptom relief.

Some of these recommendations are similar to those that have been made when working with individuals from other cultural groups. For example, some researchers have suggested that in American Indian communities, traditional healing practices encourage clients to take on a passive role in deference to the expert healer (Dinges, Trimble, Manson, & Pasquale, 1981). This passive role would encourage a more active, directive approach by the clinician, although as Renfrey (1992) warns, an overly directive style can run the risk of positioning the clinician as a controlling agent of the dominant culture.

With regard to working with Latinos, various scholars have written about the use of certain important Latino values, including *personalismo*, *respeto*, and *familismo* (e.g., Muñoz & Mendelson, 2005; Rosselló & Bernal, 1999). In our own group work with low-income Latinas, we also used these three values in order to gain traction for the delivery of our prevention program. Throughout the intervention, leaders strove to maintain a friendly and relaxed environment so as to sustain an air of *personalismo*, which refers to the emphasis on close interpersonal relationships. This was accomplished in various different ways, namely through self-disclosure, through diffusion of the expert role to include the participants as a source of expertise, and through the provision of food during the sessions. One good example of how self-disclosure can lead to increased rapport with group members can be seen in this exchange following the self-introduction of one of the group leaders:[1]

> Group Leader (GL): Good morning, everyone. My name is Suzette, and I am Venezuelan and I have lived in this country for about 13 years. In that respect, English is my primary language now because I have been using it since I was 12.
>
> Alma (A): I'm sorry; I believed that you were from here.
>
> GL: No, don't worry. Everyone thinks that. I am Venezuelan, I was born there and was raised there up until I was 11 or 12. My family then moved to the United States. So, yes, sometimes I forget my Spanish because that is what happens when you do not use the language all that often. So, at times I'm going to make a mistake, so please have patience with me and help me, please. . . .
>
> A: My children tell me the same thing, because my children came to this country when they were young.
>
> GL: Uh hum.
>
> A: My littlest tells me, he says, "Momma, I am forgetting Spanish" and I tell him not to forget because to speak two languages, one counts for two.

By expressing some vulnerability regarding her Spanish-speaking ability, the group leader reduced some of the distance that commonly exists between therapists and clients. Moreover, the exchange led one of the participants to describe a commonly experienced culturally relevant stressor for Latinos: namely, the desire to have one's children speak Spanish and be connected to one's culture of origin.

This effort to maintain *personalismo* is integrated throughout different facets of our intervention, but it is also tempered by the Latino value of *respeto*—the emphasis on showing respect and differential behavior to others. This is done in several ways, but most obviously through the use of formal language (e.g., using the formal *usted*

---

[1] The names of group members and group leaders have been changed to preserve their confidentiality. In addition, all transcripts have been translated from their original Spanish.

and not the informal *tu* when addressing participants and family members in the second person).

It is important to remember that attention to therapist behavior should not be limited to cultural values. Rosselló and Bernal (2005) describe their attention to issues of poverty among their population. They note that the therapists in their study were sensitized to the economic, racial, and cultural diversity in their clients as well as to the different ways of living that may result from this diversity. They also encouraged therapists to discuss socioeconomic and racial differences with their clients should the need arise. Similarly, we are cognizant of the ways that socioeconomic stress places significant competing demands on many of our participants' schedules (e.g., multiple jobs, various appointments with different social service agencies, transportation difficulties). Thus, we attempt to schedule appointments flexibly, including in the early morning and evening hours as well as on weekends. We also offer bus passes or taxi vouchers to all participants and provide on-site childcare for those participants who need it.

Diversity Considerations in Program Content

In addition to creatively modifying the structure and the delivery of the intervention, efforts to evaluate the generalizability of interventions with different cultural groups invariably also adapt the content of the program. In our review of the literature, we found two main approaches to incorporating diversity issues into program content. Some research teams adapt the intervention manuals to explicitly include modules that address culturally relevant themes. An excellent example of this approach can be seen in the work of Laura Kohn and colleagues (2002), who adapted a cognitive behavioral group treatment for use with depressed low-income African American women. In addition to the standard cognitive-behavioral modules on cognitions, activities, and relationships, these authors added four culturally specific sessions: (1) creating healthy relationships, (2) spirituality, (3) African American family issues, and (4) African American female identity. Of note is that these additions were grounded in the theoretical and clinical research as well as in interviews with therapists who had worked with African American women.

In addition to this approach, many of the adapted interventions modified the material in the manuals that highlighted particular emotion-regulation skills and problem-solving approaches. This standard material often takes the form of stories, didactic exercises like worksheets, and interactive role-play exercises that make the thematic and didactic material more accessible to the clients. This material is usually located in the therapist and participant manuals, with the intention of being used as both in-session work and homework. The cultural adaptations of this material typically consist of highlighting and working through culturally relevant life stressors, including immigration and immigration-related stress, experiences with prejudice and discrimination, and interfamilial stress related to acculturation (e.g., Cardemil et al., 2005, 2010; Muñoz & Mendelson, 2005). Several interventions also emphasized including material that highlighted stressors associated with urban poverty, including exposure to violence, difficulty accessing services, and financial stress (Cardemil et al., 2002, 2007; Miller et al., 2008). Other authors found ways to incorporate spirituality and religion into the intervention (Kohn et al., 2002; Muñoz & Mendelson, 2005). Le, Zmuda, Perry, and Muñoz (2010) describe their use of hand-drawn stories that resembled *telenovelas*, or soap operas, to describe how one's choices can influence one's mood and well-being.

In our depression-prevention program for Latina mothers, for example, we utilize commonly experienced difficult decisions to build rapport and cohesion among the participants. We begin this process early in our first group session by asking our participants to generate a list of difficult experiences related to being a Latina mother. One commonly cited difficulty that participants have mentioned is not being able to communicate with their children's school personnel because of their inability to speak English well. In one group we led, the participants were somewhat quiet, providing relatively short answers to questions from the group leader. However, when one of the participants mentioned not being able to communicate with her child's school teacher, other participants became more engaged in the discussion, sharing their experiences and relating to one another. This conversation unfolded as follows:

> Group Leader (GL): What are some other difficulties related to being a Latina mother?
>
> Julia (J): Not knowing English, so I can't communicate with my child's school.
>
> GL: Has that happened to anybody else?
>
> Erica (E): Yes. It is very difficult when all you know is Spanish and in school the teachers speak English.
>
> Isabel (I): Before, I had this problem. I could not communicate because I only knew a little bit of English. Now, I know more English, so it is not as difficult.
>
> J: A lot of times, [my children] serve as interpreters. They can dominate the language better.
>
> E: That is true; my son is always my interpreter.
>
> GL: So your children help you then?
>
> I: Yes.
>
> J: Yes. He helps me with my writing and I always ask him for help when I need it.
>
> E: I also ask my child for help with English.

As can be seen from this transcript, there was considerable group discussion around this topic. Each of the participants found a way to relate to this issue, including one who no longer experienced it due to the improvement of her English-speaking ability. Further, this discussion led to the spontaneous generation of another commonality—the use of children as interpreters.

Figure 6.1 Worksheet Used in Family Coping Skills Program

Event	Belief/Thought ⟹	Feeling Consequence
	My daughter never seems as happy when she spends time with me. She prefers the babysitter over me.	8—Very Sad
		6—Happy
		3—Anxious

Another example that invariably generates discussion involves having the participants imagine returning from work to find their children playing happily with a babysitter. The babysitter then states that the day went very well, that the children behaved wonderfully, and that there were no problems at all. Invariably, this scenario provokes discussion around motherhood and whether children should be left with nonfamilial caretakers. Many of the participants in our program have told us that they have a strong desire to never leave their children in the care of a nonfamily member (consistent with the cultural value of *familismo*), but that economic circumstances have required them to act against this desire. In addition, this example usually provokes a range of emotional reactions that include pride, regret, disappointment, and surprise. We then transition to cartoon-like worksheets that highlight the relationships among situations, thoughts, and feelings (see Figure 6.1). Thus, because this scenario is meaningful to our participants both through their cultural values and life experiences, it brings to life the cognitive principles of interconnections among situations, thoughts, and feelings.

In addition to the worksheets, we also use interactive role-play exercises that focus on a character's negative thinking around a particular situation. The participants will read aloud the example, identify the negative thinking, and generate several alternative ways of thinking about the situation. One of our role-play situations describes a mother (Susana) whose son resists attending church with the rest of the family, stating that he would prefer to spend Sunday mornings playing with his friends. Some of the mother's negative thoughts include thinking that her son does not care about her family and that she is losing him to the larger U.S. culture. This example has resonated with many of the participants in our program, most likely because it taps into two relevant aspects of Latino culture: family and religion. This can be seen quite well in the following transcript of a different group session with three other participants:

Group Leader (GL): What are the negative thoughts that Susana is having?

Maria (M): Thinking she is a horrible mother.

Juana (J): The thoughts about being a terrible mother.

GL: What more positive things could Susana have told herself so she can feel a little bit better and not feel so bad, like she feels now?

M: She could have talked to her son. Her son could please her and go to church and then she can please him so he can go with his friends.

GL: Then maybe a compromise, right?

J: Exactly.

GL: Come to church with me today and tomorrow you can go with your friends.

Sofía (S): Yeah, let's negotiate. Let's go to church in the morning and after you can go with your friends.

GL: Has something similar ever happened to any of you?

S: Yes

GL: What did you tell yourself when you had to face this situation?

S: In my situation, my son was the Catholic one and was the one that went to church. He wanted to take me to church and invited me; everything changed though. He entered teenage years and his friends would make fun of him saying he looked like a girl at church. He changed his way of thinking and didn't want to go to church because of his friends. Then I started to go and invited him and he said no. I felt uncomfortable because my son learned some good principles and wanted to project them onto me, but when I wanted to project them to him, he didn't want to anymore. I lost that opportunity to be with my son when he needed me.

M: My situation was with my husband. He wanted to take me to church but I would always tell him, give me time. I would join him even when his religion was different, until he stopped going.

GL: Now Susana is telling herself very negative things. "My son does not care about his family." This is an exaggerated thought, right? What could have Susana told herself?

J: Give her son some time and let him go with his friends, but continue to invite him to go.

M: Do not obligate him to go but invite him.

S: Don't push him but remain positive. It might not even be about his family or the values.

GL: She is saying "I am losing him to his friends and to the American culture." This is something that we talked about last week. A change of culture and a change of values are going to be different. What do you think about this? What if your kids don't want to go to church and are losing their cultural values? What could you tell yourself?

S: My son is learning a new culture and value and I will talk to him later so he won't lose ours.

M: I will give him time.

J: Or we invite the friends and we can all go to church, and then we can all go to the movies after.

As can be seen, this role-play led to a good discussion that involved all of the participants. Each of the participants had had personal experiences similar to that described in the role-play, which allowed them to share their own situations, how they thought about them, and how they attempted to resolve their problems.

Other culturally relevant role-plays we use include one in which a mother misses a deadline to register for a free ESL class because she could not find child care, a mother who cannot afford to host a *quinceañera* (sweet 15th birthday) celebration for her daughter, and a mother who worries about communicating in English with her children's teachers. Although not all of the role-plays explicitly address culturally salient issues, they all are designed to allow for the introduction and practice of cognitive-behavioral skills in practice situations that are especially relevant to the participants.

Use of Culturally Relevant Metaphors and Sayings These examples are a few of the exercises we use to infuse our depression prevention program with culturally relevant content. However, as noted earlier, including culturally relevant content is important, but insufficient (Bernal & Sáez-Santiago, 2006; Hwang, 2006). Muñoz and Mendelson (2005) describe how in addition to explicit discussion of relevant content like spirituality and religion, acculturation, and experiences with racism, discrimination, and prejudice, cultural adaptations should include the use of culturally relevant metaphors and stories as a means to convey key therapeutic principles. In their programs, they used culturally relevant images, metaphors, and stories that were used to illustrate key concepts with their Latino clients. For example, the saying, *La gota de agua labra la piedra* (Drops of water can carve a rock) was used to illustrate how pervasive negative thinking can gradually affect one's view of life and produce and maintain depression (Muñoz & Mendelson, 2005). Rosselló and Bernal (2005) note their use of the Puerto Rican expression *Todo se ve a través del cristal con que se mira* (Everything is seen through the crystal with which one looks) to highlight how cognitions can affect one's understanding of situations.

Hwang and colleagues also describe their use of culturally relevant terms and concepts to facilitate the introduction of cognitive-behavioral concepts. In particular, they describe their use of Chinese metaphors and stories embedded in four-word sayings known as *Chengyu*, which are ethical and moral guidelines for individual behavior (Hwang et al., 2006). These principles were used as clinician tools to help clients reframe their maladaptive thinking and engage in healthier activities (Hwang et al., 2006). One example that Hwang cites is a well-known *Chengyu* story about a master artist who practiced using two brushes simultaneously in one hand to create unsurpassed paintings (*shuang guan ji xia*; translated as "two brushes painting together"; Hong, 1987). Hwang and colleagues used this story to highlight for clients the use of employing multiple CBT principles simultaneously (e.g., challenging maladaptive cognitions, developing replacement coping thoughts, and engaging in behavioral strategies to improve mood).

These examples are a few of the many that others in the literature have noted (e.g., Zuñiga, 1991, 1992). And although the use of metaphors, myths, and stories should be undertaken with caution given the within-culture variation that exists in familiarity with individual stories, when judiciously applied, they can nicely integrate some of the active ingredients of the intervention with worldviews and sayings of the particular culture.

Recommendations for Applying EBP With Diverse Populations

The literature we have reviewed highlights the progress that has been made in evaluating the generalizability of EBP for depression, increasing our confidence in applying some EBP with some cultural groups. However, the fact remains that the evidence base is more limited with other EBP, and in general, the evidence base is limited with individuals from some cultural groups. Given the current state of the field, how should clinicians proceed in the delivery of EBP for depression? Our review of the literature yielded a few concrete recommendations that we discuss in turn. Given the limited space in this chapter, we also provide a separate section for additional readings for interested clinicians.

Learn More About the Cultural Groups With Whom You Desire to Work

Despite the obvious nature of this recommendation, its importance warrants explicit mention. Before attempting to adapt an intervention for a particular population, clinicians should familiarize themselves with the extant sociological and psychological literature on that population. The familiarity that the different research teams had with their target populations allowed them to hone their adaptations in ways that were most appropriate and relevant to those particular populations. For example, most of the research teams working with Latino populations touched on topics of immigration and acculturation. These issues would likely be salient when working with other immigrant populations, but would be less so when working with cultural minority groups that were not immigrants (i.e., African Americans, American Indians).

In addition, important subgroup differences may exist that affect the clinical presentation of local populations. For example, while the Latino population in California and the Southwest United States is composed primarily of individuals from Mexico, Latinos in the Northeast United States are predominantly individuals from Puerto Rico, the Dominican Republic, and Central America. Le et al. (2010) provide an excellent description of how they modified some of the Spanish in their intervention to make it more relevant to the Central American women in their study. Similarly, clinicians working with American Indian populations are surely aware of the fact that more than 500 federally recognized American Indian tribes exist and so there exists considerable variation in cultural practices and beliefs (Renfrey, 1992). In addition to differences in cultural beliefs and practices, there are often differences in language and expressions across these groups.

So we recommend that clinicians work to familiarize themselves with the relevant cultural groups in their area. In addition to reviewing the relevant literature, we recommend that clinicians seek out opportunities to gain experiential familiarity with their local populations. This experiential familiarity can be obtained in a variety of ways, including creative outreach efforts to established community leaders like healthcare providers, religious leaders, and school board members (Domenech-Rodriguez & Wieling, 2004; Le et al., 2010). These outreach efforts can even lead to the creation of a community advisory board that can provide regular input on the development and implementation of a novel treatment program. Focus groups with current mental healthcare consumers could also provide valuable information about local stressors and issues (e.g., Nicolas, Arntz, Hirsch, & Schmiedigen, 2009). Through the process of learning about the local community, decisions can be made regarding precisely for whom and how the interventions should be adapted.

Remember to Balance Group and Individual Characteristics

Our next recommendation provides a counterpoint to the first recommendation by highlighting the importance of acknowledging the tremendous heterogeneity that exists within the different cultural groups in adherence to cultural practices, values, and worldviews. Some of this variability may result from individual differences in acculturation, ethnic identity, and life experiences (Chun, Organista, & Marín, 2003; Phinney, 1996). Further, the multidimensionality of culture leads individuals to have multiple sociocultural identities that become more or less salient depending on the context (e.g., gender, sexual orientation, age, religious affiliation). Thus, it is problematic to assume that every individual from a particular cultural group will share characteristics that have been typically ascribed to that cultural group. And yet, to ignore completely the existence of individual connections to a larger cultural group misses a large part of the human identity and experience.

Therefore, incorporating diversity considerations into clinical practice requires balancing an understanding of the values, attitudes, and life experiences at the cultural group level with the values, attitudes, and life experiences that are unique to every individual and that may be related to those of the larger cultural group. Too much attention to the larger cultural group can lead to stereotyping, and too much attention to the individual can lead to misunderstandings related to cultural differences. Achieving this balance between the group and individual-level characteristics is not easy, but it is the same therapeutic skill that is applied regularly by clinicians for noncultural reasons. For example, clinicians who work with recently divorced parents would likely balance their understanding of the stressors commonly associated with divorce and coparenting with recognition that individuals may or may not experience those particular stressors.

Scholars in the area of multicultural counseling have written extensively on this issue and generally emphasize the importance of keeping cultural considerations as hypotheses or questions, rather than as fixed assumptions (e.g., Cardemil & Battle, 2003; Hays, 2009; D. W. Sue & D. Sue, 2008; S. Sue, 1998). Further, building on the first recommendation—increased personal familiarity with different cultural groups—makes it easier to maintain this balance.

Think Broadly About How to Integrate Diversity Considerations

Much of the literature on working with diverse populations focuses on the therapist-client relationship (e.g., La Roche & Maxie, 2003; S. Sue, 1998). However, the literature we reviewed highlights the importance of integrating diversity considerations much more broadly. Studies we reviewed consistently attended to diversity in the structure of the interventions, in the content or material of the interventions, and in the manner in which the intervention was delivered. This comprehensive attention to diversity likely contributed to the success of the adapted interventions, both in terms of efficacy and in terms of retention and engagement of participants.

Thus, clinicians interested in adapting evidence-based practice to diverse populations would do well to think beyond the therapist-client relationship. Although certain logistical and financial factors will likely influence decisions about what particular structural adaptations to make, there is still considerable room for creativity in the implementation of interventions. Some areas where structural considerations could be made to explicitly consider diversity include the modality of treatment (e.g., group versus individual, open versus closed), the frequency and regularity of sessions, and the length of individual sessions. Building on the community work discussed earlier, structural considerations could also include innovative approaches to outreach, psychoeducation, and prevention that are not commonly implemented in formal mental health settings. In general, we encourage clinicians to think flexibly and outside the box regarding how to best implement their EBP and to attend to the feedback they receive from their clients regarding these changes.

Diversify Research, Clinical, and Support Staff

One important fact about the efforts to investigate the generalizability of EBPs to different cultural groups is that the research and clinical have generally themselves been diverse in their make-up. Muñoz and Mendelson (2005) highlight how having individuals from the targeted cultural groups help with intervention development changes the process from one of literal translation into one of true culturally appropriate adaptation. Further, prioritizing diversity in the hiring of clinical and support staff can also play an important role in helping with implementation of EBPs to diverse groups. As we noted in our earlier recommendation, thinking about cultural issues goes well beyond focusing on the therapist-client relationship and so it is important to comprehensively hire diverse staff at all levels of mental health care.

In our own work, we also have a culturally diverse team of researchers and intervention leaders. But just as important, each individual on our team also has considerable experience working with our population of low-income, Latina women. Even though not all of the team members are Latino, each has considerable familiarity and experiencing working with Latinos and low-income clients. More-over, all team members are fluent in both Spanish and English.

Concluding Thoughts

Despite the tremendous advances that have been made in the past 25 years in the evaluation of psychosocial interventions for depression, there remain significant limitations in our ability to make claims about the generalizabilty of these interventions to individuals from different cultural groups. Promising advances have been made documenting the efficacy of CBT and IPT, primarily with Latinos and African Americans, and researchers are beginning to turn their attention to other cultural groups. The extant literature on the cultural adaptation process has led to the formation of a knowledge base for how to proceed with adapting interventions for particular cultural groups, and we are optimistic that this base will allow for increased attention and growth in this area.

In many ways, clinicians are leading the way in the enhancement of this knowledge base, as the increasing diversity of clients precludes waiting for the evidence base to be finalized. And so by carefully reviewing the cultural adaptation literature, following some of the recommendations we provide in this chapter, and maintaining a humble and optimistic approach to the therapy process, clinicians can prepare themselves well for the challenges and rewards of conducting clinical work in the 21st century.

References

Alegría, M., Canino, G., Ríos, R., Vera, M., Calderón, J., Rusch, D., & Ortega, A. N. (2002). Mental health care for Latinos: Inequalities in use of specialty mental health services among Latinos, African Americans, and non-Latino Whites. *Psychiatric Services*, *53*(12), 1547–1555.

Alvidrez, J., Azocar, F., & Miranda, J. (1996). Demystifying the concept of ethnicity for psychotherapy researchers. *Journal of Consulting and Clinical Psychology*, *64*(5), 903–908.

Arean, P. A., & Miranda, J. (1996). The treatment of depression in elderly primary care patients. *Journal of Clinical Geropsychology*, *2*, 241–259.

Arnett, J. J. (2008). The neglected 95%: Why American psychology needs to become less American. *American Psychologist*, *63*, 602–614.

Atkinson, D. R., Morten, G., & Sue, D. W. (1998). *Counseling American minorities* (5th ed.). New York, NY: McGraw-Hill.

Barrera, M., & Castro, F. G. (2006). A heuristic framework for the cultural adaptation of interventions. *Clinical Psychology: Science and Practice*, 311–316.

Bernal, G., & Saéz-Santiago, E. (2006). Culturally centered psychosocial interventions. *Journal of Community Psychology*, *34*, 121–132.

Bernal, G., & Scharrón-del-Río, M. R. (2001). Are empirically supported treatments valid for ethnic minorities? Toward an alternative approach for treatment research. *Cultural Diversity and Ethnic Minority Psychology*, *7*, 328–342.

Betancourt, H., & López, S. R. (1993). The study of culture, ethnicity, and race in American psychology. *American Psychologist*, *48*, 629–637.

Breslau, J., Aguilar-Gaxiola, S., Kendler, K. S., Su, M., Williams, D., & Kessler, R. C. (2006). Specifying race-ethnic differences in risk for psychiatric disorder in a USA national sample. *Psychological Medicine: A Journal of Research in Psychiatry and the Allied Sciences*, *36*, 57–68.

Cardemil, E. V. (2008). Culturally sensitive treatments: Need for an organizing framework. *Culture and Psychology*, *14*, 357–367.

Cardemil, E. V., & Battle, C. (2003). Guess who's coming to therapy? Getting comfortable with conversations about race and ethnicity in psychotherapy. *Professional Psychology: Research & Practice*, *34*, 278–286.

Cardemil, E. V., Kim, S., Davidson, T. M., Sarmiento, I., Ishikawa, R., Sanchez, M., & Torres, S. (2010). Developing a culturally appropriate depression prevention program: Opportunities and challenges. *Cognitive & Behavioral Practice*, *17*, 188–197.

Cardemil, E. V., Kim, S., Pinedo, T. M., & Miller, I. W. (2005). Developing a culturally appropriate depression prevention program: The family coping skills program. *Cultural Diversity and Ethnic Minority Psychology*, *11*, 99–112.

Cardemil, E. V., Reivich, K. J., Beevers, C. G., Seligman, M. E. P., & James, J. (2007). The prevention of depressive symptoms in low-income, minority children: Two-year follow-up. *Behaviour Research and Therapy*, *45*, 313–327.

Cardemil, E. V., Reivich, K. J., & Seligman, M. E. P. (2002). The prevention of depressive symptoms in low-income minority middle school students. *Prevention & Treatment*, *5*(1), Article 8. Retrieved from http://content.apa.org/journals/pre/5/1/8a.html

Chun, K. M., Organista, P., & Marín, G. (2003). *Acculturation: Advances in theory, measurement, and applied research*. Washington, DC: American Psychological Association.

Comas-Díaz, L. (1981). Effects of cognitive and behavioral group treatment on the depressive symptomatology of Puerto Rican women. *Journal of Consulting and Clinical Psychology*, *49*, 627–632.

Comas-Díaz, L. (1986). Cognitive and behavioral group therapy with Puerto Rican women: A comparison of content themes. *Hispanic Journal of Behavioral Sciences*, *7*, 273–283.

Crockett, K., Zlotnick, C., Davis, M., Payne, N., & Washington, R. (2008). A depression preventive intervention for rural low-income African-American pregnant women at risk for postpartum depression. *Archives of Women's Mental Health, 11,* 319–325.

Cuijpers, P., Muñoz, R. F., Clarke, G. N., & Lewinsohn, P. M. (2009). Psychoeducational treatment and prevention of depression: The "coping with depression" course thirty years later. *Clinical Psychology Review, 29,* 449–458.

Dai, Y., Zhang, S., Yamamoto, J., Ao, M., Belin, T. R., Cheung, F., & Hifumi, S. S. (1999). Cognitive behavioral therapy of minor depressive symptoms in elderly Chinese Americans: A pilot study. *Community Mental Health Journal, 35*(6), 537–542.

Dinges, N. G., Trimble, J. E., Manson, S. M., & Pasquale, F. L. (1981). Counseling and psychotherapy with American Indians and Alaska Natives. In A. J. Marsella & P. B. Pederson (Eds.), *Cross-cultural counseling and psychotherapy* (pp. 243–376). New York, NY: Pergamon.

Domenech-Rodríguez, M., & Wieling, E. (2004). Developing culturally appropriate evidence-based treatments for interventions with ethnic minority populations. In M. Rastogi & E. Wieling (Eds.), *Voices of color: First-person accounts of ethnic minority therapists* (pp. 313–333). Thousand Oaks, CA: Sage.

Falicov, C. J. (1998). *Latino families in therapy: A guide to multicultural practice.* New York, NY: Guilford Press.

Gloria, A. M., Ruiz, E. L., & Castillo, E. M. (2004). Counseling and psychotherapy with Latino and Latina clients. In T. B. Smith (Ed.), *Practicing multiculturalism: Affirming diversity in counseling and psychology* (pp. 167–189). Boston, MA: Pearson.

Griner, D., & Smith, T. B. (2006). Culturally adapted mental health interventions: A meta-analytic review. *Psychotherapy: Theory, Research, Practice, Training, 43,* 531–548.

Hall, G. C. N. (2001). Psychotherapy research with ethnic minorities: Empirical, ethical, and conceptual issues. *Journal of Consulting and Clinical Psychology, 69,* 502–510.

Hays, P. A. (2009). Integrative evidence-based practice, cognitive-behavior therapy, and multicultural therapy: Ten steps for culturally competent practice. *Professional Psychology: Research and Practice, 40,* 354–360.

Helms, J. E., & Cook, D. A. (1999). *Using race and culture in counseling and psychotherapy: Theory and process.* Needham Heights, MA: Allyn & Bacon.

Hong, Y. N. (1987). *Chinese saying told in pictures.* Taipei, Taiwan: *Sinora Magazine.*

Huey, S. J., Jr., & Polo, A. J. (2008). Evidence-based psychosocial treatments for ethnic minority youth. *Journal of Clinical Child and Adolescent Psychology, 37,* 262–301.

Hwang, W. (2006). The psychotherapy adaptation and modification framework: Application to Asian Americans. *American Psychologist, 61,* 702–715.

Hwang, W., Wood, J. J., Lin, K., & Cheung, F. (2006). Cognitive-behavioral therapy with Chinese Americans: Research, theory, and clinical practice. *Cognitive and Behavioral Practice, 13,* 293–303.

Jackson, L. C., Schmutzer, P. A., Wenzel, A., & Tyler, J. D. (2006). Applicability of cognitive-behavior therapy with American Indian individuals. *Psychotherapy: Theory, Research, Practice, Training, 43,* 506–517.

Kessler, R. C., Chiu, W. T., Demler, O., & Walters, E. E. (2005). Prevalence, severity, and comorbidity of 12-month DSM-IV disorders in the national comorbidity survey replication. *Archives of General Psychiatry, 62,* 617–627.

Kessler, R. C., McGonagle, K. A., Zhao, S., Nelson, C. B., Hughes, M., Eshelman, S., . . . Kendler, D. S. (1994). Lifetime and 12-month prevalence of DSM-III-R psychiatric disorders in the United States: Results from the national comorbidity survey. *Archives of General Psychiatry, 51,* 8–19.

Klerman, G. L., Weissman, M. M., Rounsaville, B., & Chevron, E. (1984). *Interpersonal Psychotherapy of Depression*. New York, NY: Basic Books.

Kohn, L. P., Oden, T., Muñoz, R. F., Robinson, A., & Leavitt, D. (2002). Adapted cognitive behavioral group therapy for depressed low-income African American women. *Community Mental Health Journal, 38*, 497–504.

La Roche, M. J., & Christopher, M. S. (2008). Culture and empirically supported treatments: On the road to a collision? *Culture & Psychology, 14*, 333–356.

La Roche, M. J., & Maxie, A. (2003). Ten considerations in addressing cultural differences in psychotherapy. *Professional Psychology: Research and Practice, 34*, 180–186.

Le, H., Zmuda, J., Perry, D., & Muñoz, R. F. (2010). Transforming an evidence-based intervention to prevent perinatal depression. *American Journal of Orthopsychiatry, 80*, 34–45.

Lewinsohn, P. M., Antonuccio, D. O., Breckenridge, J. S., & Teri, L. (1984). *The ''Coping with Depression'' course*. Eugene, OR: Castalia.

Mak, W. W. S., Law, R. W., Alvidrez, J., & Pérez-Stable, E. J. (2007). Gender and ethnic diversity in NIMH-funded clinical trials: Review of a decade of published research. *Administration and Policy in Mental Health and Mental Health Services Research, 34*, 497–503.

Miller, L., Gur, M., Shanok, A., & Weissman, M. (2008). Interpersonal psychotherapy with pregnant adolescents: Two pilot studies. *Journal of Child Psychology and Psychiatry, 49*, 733–742.

Miranda, J., Azocar, F., Organista, K. C., Dwyer, E., & Arean, P. (2003). Treatment of depression among impoverished primary care patients from ethnic minority groups. *Psychiatric Services, 54*, 219–225.

Miranda, J., Bernal, G., Lau, A., Kohn, L., Hwang, W., & LaFramboise, T. (2005). State of the science on psychosocial interventions for ethnic minorities. *Annual Review of Clinical Psychology, 1*, 113–142.

Miranda, J., Chung, J. Y., Green, B. L., Krupnick, J., Siddique, J., Revicki, D. A., & Belin, T. (2003). Treating depression in predominantly low-income young minority women: A randomized controlled trial. *JAMA: Journal of the American Medical Association, 290*, 57–65.

Miranda, J., Green, B. L., Krupnick, J. L., Chung, J., Siddique, J., Belin, T., & Revicki, D. (2006). One-year outcomes of a randomized clinical trial treating depression in low-income minority women. *Journal of Consulting and Clinical Psychology, 74*, 99–111.

Mui, A. C., & Kang, S. Y. (2006). Acculturation stress and depression among elderly Asian American immigrants. *Social Work, 51*, 243–255.

Muñoz, R. F., Le, H., Ippen, C. H., Diaz, M. A., Guido, G., Soto, J., . . . Lieberman, A. F. (2007). Prevention of postpartum depression in low-income women: Development of the Mamás y Bebés/ Mothers and Babies course. *Cognitive and Behavioral Practice, 14*, 70–83.

Muñoz, R. F., & Mendelson, T. (2005). Toward evidence-based interventions for diverse populations: The San Francisco General Hospital prevention and treatment manuals. *Journal of Consulting and Clinical Psychology, 73*, 790–799.

Muñoz, R. F., Ying, Y., Bernal, G., Pérez-Stable, E. J., Sorensen, J. L., Hargreaves, W. A., . . . Miranda, J. (1995). Prevention of depression with primary care patients: A randomized control trial. *American Journal of Community Psychology, 23*, 199–222.

Nicolas, G., Arntz, D. L., Hirsch, B., & Schmiedigen, A. (2009). Cultural adaptation of a group treatment for Haitian American adolescents. *Professional Psychology: Research and Practice, 40*, 378–384.

Organista, K. C., Muñoz, R. F., & Gonzalez, G. (1994). Cognitive-behavioral therapy for depression in low-income and minority medical outpatients: Description of a program and exploratory analyses. *Cognitive Therapy and Research, 18*, 241–259.

Perez Foster, R. (2007). Treating depression in vulnerable urban women: A feasibility study of clinical outcomes in community service settings. *American Journal of Orthopsychiatry, 77,* 443–453.

Phinney, J. S. (1996). When we talk about American ethnic groups, what do we mean? *American Psychologist, 51,* 918–927.

Renfrey, G. S. (1992). Cognitive-behavior therapy and the Native American client. *Behavior Therapy, 23,* 321–340.

Rosselló, J., & Bernal, G. (1999). The efficacy of cognitive-behavioral and interpersonal treatments for depression in Puerto Rican adolescents. *Journal of Consulting and Clinical Psychology, 67,* 734–745.

Rosselló, J., & Bernal, G. (2005). New developments in cognitive-behavioral and interpersonal treatments for depressed Puerto Rican adolescents. In E. D. Hibbs & P. S. Jensen (Eds.), *Psychosocial treatments for child and adolescent disorders: Empirically based strategies for clinical practice* (2nd ed., pp. 187–217). Washington, DC: American Psychological Association.

Rosselló, J., Bernal, G., & Rivera-Medina, C. (2008). Individual and group CBT and IPT for Puerto Rican adolescents with depressive symptoms. *Cultural Diversity and Ethnic Minority Psychology, 14,* 234–245.

Satterfield, J. M. (1998). Cognitive behavioral group therapy for depressed, low-income minority clients: Retention and treatment enhancement. *Cognitive and Behavioral Practice, 5,* 65–80.

Seaton, E. K., Caldwell, C. H., Sellers, R. M., & Jackson, J. S. (2008). The prevalence of perceived discrimination among African American and Caribbean Black youth. *Developmental Psychology, 44,* 1288–1297.

Smedley, A., & Smedley, B. D. (2005). Race as biology is fiction, racism as social problem is real: Anthropological and historical perspectives on the social construction of race. *American Psychologist, 60,* 16–26.

Snowden, L., & Yamada, A. M. (2005). Cultural differences in access to care. *Annual Review of Clinical Psychology, 1,* 143–166.

Spinelli, M. G., & Endicott, J. (2003). Controlled clinical trial of interpersonal psychotherapy versus parenting education program for depressed pregnant women. *American Journal of Psychiatry, 160,* 555–562.

Sue, D. W., & Sue, D. (2008). *Counseling the culturally diverse: Theory and practice* (5th ed). Hoboken, NJ: John Wiley & Sons.

Sue, S. (1998). In search of cultural competence in psychotherapy and counseling. *American Psychologist, 53,* 440–448.

Torres, L. (2010). Predicting levels of Latino depression: Acculturation, acculturative stress, and coping. *Cultural Diversity and Ethnic Minority Psychology, 16,* 256–263.

U.S. Census Bureau. (2008). *An older and more diverse nation by midcentury.* Retrieved July 8, 2009, from http://www.census.gov/Press-Release/www/releases/archives/population/012496.html

U.S. Department of Health and Human Services. (2001). *Mental health: Culture, race, and ethnicity—A supplement to mental health: A report of the surgeon general.* Rockville, MD: Author. Retrieved September 26, 2004, from http://media.shs.net/ken/pdf/SMA-01-3613/sma-01-3613

Vega, W. A., Valle, R., Kolody, B., & Hough, R. (1987). The Hispanic network preventive intervention study. In R. F. Muñoz (Ed.), *The prevention of depression: Research foundations* (pp. 217–234). Washington, DC: Hemisphere.

Weissman, M. M., Markowitz, J. C., & Klerman, G. L. (2000). *Comprehensive guide to interpersonal psychotherapy.* New York, NY: Basic Books.

Wells, K., Klap, R., Koike, A., & Sherbourne, C. (2001). Ethnic disparities in unmet need for alcoholism, drug abuse, and mental health care. *American Journal of Psychiatry, 158*(12), 2027–2032.

Whaley, A. L., & Davis, K. E. (2007). Cultural competence and evidence-based practice in mental health services. *American Psychologist, 62*, 563–574.

Zlotnick, C., Miller, I. W., Pearlstein, T., Howard, M., & Sweeney, P. (2006). A preventive intervention for pregnant women on public assistance at risk for postpartum depression. *American Journal of Psychiatry, 163*, 1443–1445.

Zuñiga, M. E. (1991). ''Dichos'' as metaphorical tools for resistant clients. *Psychotherapy, 28*, 480–483.

Zuñiga, M. E. (1992). Using metaphors in therapy: Dichos and Latino clients. *Social Work, 37*, 55–60.

Afterword

Allen Rubin and David W. Springer

If you have just finished reading all the chapters in this book and have not had previous experience with or significant exposure to the interventions they describe, you may be feeling overwhelmed. There is quite a lot to learn if you are considering implementing a new, empirically supported intervention that you've never learned about or provided before—so much to learn, in fact, that even if you have read only one or two of the chapters on just one new intervention approach, you might still be feeling overwhelmed. If you are feeling that way, we urge you not to give up— particularly if the intervention approaches you have been providing to date have not been empirically supported and especially if they have been studied and found to be either ineffective or much less effective than the interventions described in this book.

No matter how overwhelmed you might feel, we hope you will persevere in trying to master one or more of the interventions described in this book. Perhaps the most important reasons for persevering are your professional ethics and compassion for your clients. A cornerstone of professional ethics is a devotion to serving clients in the most effective way possible.

At the same time, we recognize that clinicians often express reasonable rationales for not switching to empirically supported interventions with which they might be unfamiliar and uncomfortable. Perhaps their agency caseload and other require- ments leave them no time to learn to become sufficiently skillful in a new intervention approach and there are no other clinicians in their area who are adept in the empirically supported intervention. Maybe there are such clinicians nearby, but the clients cannot afford the fees of those other clinicians.

Also, the evidence supporting such interventions may be based on studies with clients whose characteristics or problems are unlike those of the clinicians' clients. Clinicians might perceive such interventions as requiring a manualized and mechanistic approach to practice that deemphasizes and devalues therapist flexi- bility, expertise, and relationship skills. In that connection, they might cite studies that have supported the importance of the quality of the therapeutic alliance as having as much or more impact on client outcome than the specific intervention approach chosen.

If clinicians provide a rationale for sticking with interventions that are not evidence-based that is similar to these reasons—or even if their rationale is based on some other reason for thinking that switching would not be in the client's best interest—then even if their reasoning is debatable, they are being professionally ethical in that their reasoning is based on what they think is best for their clients. But one's professional ethics could be questioned if the reason provided for refusing to learn more about a more empirically supported intervention or to refer to a clinician who can skillfully provide that intervention is based merely on what interests the clinician or on the clinician's own unwillingness to invest the work required to try to learn more about something that might be more helpful to their clients.

For example, occasionally we hear from clinical students near completion of their master's degree studies that they just want to provide the interventions that they find most interesting and with which they are most comfortable, regardless of the research evidence about the relative effectiveness of those interventions versus alternative ones. Admittedly, there is some merit to what they say. Clients will not benefit—and perhaps will fare worse—if clinicians provide an empirically supported intervention unenthusiastically and with skepticism about its efficacy or in an incompetent manner because they have not yet mastered the intervention or perhaps feel very awkward and unsure of themselves in providing it.

But there is no excuse for sticking with interventions that lack adequate empirical support merely because one finds those interventions to be more interesting or personally fulfilling than newer interventions that are known to have a greater likelihood of effectiveness. We often respond to students who express such a reason for disliking evidence-based practice with a medical analogy like the one in the box titled "Response to Students: Medical Analogy."

Response to Students: Medical Analogy

Imagine going to a physician for treatment for a medical condition that you recently developed and for which you learned that the most rigorous scientific research studies have agreed that Treatment A is by far the most effective remedy—much more effective than Treatment B. Your physician examines you and agrees that you have the condition you think you have and then tells you she or he will provide Treatment B. You then express your consternation about Treatment B in light of the scientific studies you learned about, and your physician tells you that despite knowing about those studies he or she prefers to provide Treatment B anyway because of lack of skill or discomfort with Treatment A. How would you feel about that physician? Our guess is that you'd view that physician as inadequately compassionate or ethical. You'd probably insist on being referred to a physician who could skillfully and comfortably provide Treatment A.

What if those studies favoring Treatment A existed, and your physician knew about them, but you didn't? What if he or she then merely provided Treatment B without informing you of the evidence supporting the superior effectiveness of Treatment A or offering to refer you to another physician who could skillfully provide it? What if you subsequently—after receiving Treatment B and not benefiting from it—learned about Treatment A's evidence and found out that your physician knew about that evidence but went ahead with Treatment B anyway for the reasons mentioned earlier? You might use more extreme terms to describe the physician than "inadequately compassionate or ethical."

Of course, psychotherapy with depressed clients is not the same as treating a medical condition. Therapist relationship skills and the therapeutic alliance have a much greater impact on treatment outcome than in medical treatment. Even the most evidence-based psychotherapies will not be effective without a strong therapeutic alliance. Moreover, even though they may have the greatest likelihood of success, many clients do not benefit from them. Idiosyncratic client characteristics and preferences can have a profound impact on the choice of intervention, and therapist expertise is critical in determining whether an intervention with the best evidence is really the best fit for a particular client in light of that client's idiosyncrasies.

However, the issue is not an all-or-nothing matter. Being compassionate, professionally ethical, and evidence based does not require that you automatically choose empirically supported interventions in a mechanistic, cookbook fashion and without regard to client preferences. It just means that you will intervene in light of the best evidence and having integrated that evidence with your clinical expertise and knowledge of your client's characteristics and preferences. As is evident in every chapter in this book—and especially in Appendix B—clinical expertise and knowledge of client characteristics and preferences are important elements of evidence based practice and can rightfully imply that an intervention without the best evidence might be the treatment of choice for some clients. Moreover, being evidence based does not mean providing an empirically supported intervention in a rigid manner without room for flexibility based on your clinical expertise. Again, the room for such flexibility is evident in every chapter of this book.

Likewise, your level of comfort and skill in providing a new, evidence-based intervention is not an all-or-nothing, black-and-white issue. All clinicians—no matter what interventions they are providing—have started out being less skillful, less confident, and less comfortable with those interventions than they are now. If you are not yet ready to begin providing an empirically supported intervention due to skill or comfort concerns, that's understandable. But those are not compelling reasons to avoid trying to become more skillful and comfortable with those interventions. And the chapters in this book have identified various additional resources and ways for trying to become more comfortable and skillful with them.

Additionally, it may be helpful to lean on the five steps of the evidence-based process when feeling overwhelmed by all of this. If you are interested in digging in and unpacking the evidence-based process in more detail, we refer you to Rubin's (2008) text on the topic, *Practitioner's Guide to Using Research for Evidence-Based Practice*, as well as Appendix B in this volume, in which Rubin describes the evidence-based practice process in detail.

Of course, we all encounter shifting pieces as we navigate the evidence-based practice (EBP) process. Despite the reasonable concerns and the real-world pragmatic obstacles that we encounter, many clinicians embrace evidence-based practice. We hope that you, reader, have been spurred by this book to learn more about evidence-based practice and about the interventions described herein. We also hope that this book may have given you enough expertise to begin gaining experience in providing one or more of these interventions.

Reference

Rubin, A. (2008). *Practitioner's guide to using research for evidence-based practice*. Hoboken, NJ: John Wiley & Sons.

A

Research Providing the Evidence Base for the Interventions in This Volume

Christopher G. Beevers

The interventions included in this volume have a great deal of research support indicating they are effective for the treatment of depression among adolescents and adults. Indeed, a number of organizations have identified these interventions as having the best empirical evidence for the treatment of depression. The Society of Clinical Child and Adolescent Psychology (SCCAP; http://www.abct.org/sccap) identifies cognitive behavioral therapy (CBT) as one of only two "well-established" psychological treatments for adolescent depression (interpersonal psychotherapy is the other well-established treatment). SCCAP suggests that well-established treatments have the strongest research support to date. This means that there are at least two large-scale clinical trials that have demonstrated superiority of CBT to a comparison group (e.g., another treatment or placebo). This research has to be conducted by at least two independent teams of investigators, in part to minimize researcher allegiance to a particular form of treatment (for more information, see David-Ferdon & Kaslow, 2008).

Similarly, the Society of Clinical Psychology (Division 12 of the American Psychological Association) has summarized research support for a variety of psychological interventions across many psychiatric disorders in adults. For the treatment of depression, CBT, Behavioral Activation (BA), and Cognitive Behavioral Analysis System of Psychotherapy (CBASP) were each identified as having "strong research support," the highest level of empirical support possible in this rating system (information accessed, July 19, 2010, from http://www.psychologicaltreatments.org). To achieve this designation, several well-designed studies from independent investigators must provide consistent evidence supporting a treatment's efficacy. Each of the treatments included in this volume meet or exceed this standard. What follows is an overview of the evidence base for each of the interventions included in this volume.

Cognitive Behavioral Treatment for Adolescent Depression

Although evidence is accumulating, a relatively small number of studies have examined the efficacy of CBT versus other treatments for adolescent depression. One meta-analysis examined six studies involving 217 participants and found that CBT was superior to wait list, relaxation therapy, and supportive treatment (Reinecke, Ryan, & DuBois, 1998). These effects were maintained during follow-up 1 to 24 months later. The Treatment for Adolescent Depression Study (TADS) suggests that CBT alone may not be significantly more effective than pill placebo in the first 12 weeks of treatment (Treatment for Adolescents With Depression Study Team, 2004). However, CBT paired with fluoxetine (Prozac) produced the best depression response rate after 12 weeks of treatment. Longer-term follow-up also indicated that combined treatment (fluoxetine plus CBT), CBT alone, and fluoxetine alone were similarly effective after 36 weeks of treatment. The average response rate was approximately 80% (Treatment for Adolescents With Depression Study Team, 2007). Thus, when delivered alone, CBT may take longer to reach its therapeutic effect than medication among adolescents. Nevertheless, CBT appears to be an effective treatment for adolescent depression, particularly when paired with antidepressant treatment.

There is also growing evidence that psychological treatments may be effective for preventing depression onset among adolescents. In a meta-analysis of 32 prevention programs with a variety of theoretical orientations evaluated in 60 trials, 13 (41%) produced significant reductions in depressive symptoms compared to controls (Stice, Shaw, Bohon, Marti, & Rohde, 2009). Although the number of trials that lead to symptom reduction may seem modest, this is higher than rates observed for prevention programs for eating disorders (29%), obesity (21%), and HIV (22%). Stice and colleagues (2009) reported that larger prevention effects were observed for programs that targeted high-risk individuals, had samples with more females and older adolescents, utilized homework assignments, and were delivered by professional interventionists.

Most relevant to this review, four prevention programs have been shown to significantly reduce future onset of manic depressive disorder (MDD) among adolescents. Three of these prevention interventions were CBT-based prevention programs (Clarke, Hawkins, Murphy, & Sheeber, 1995; Clarke, Hornbrook, et al., 2001; Garber et al., 2009; Stice, Rohde, Seeley, & Gau, 2008). The fourth program that also reduced future MDD onset was interpersonal psychotherapy (Young, Mufson, & Davies, 2006). Thus, CBT may be effective for the treatment of current depression and may also help prevent the onset of MDD among adolescents at high risk for the disorder.

Cognitive Behavioral Treatment for Adult Depression

A conservative estimate is that more than 85 clinical trials of CBT for depression in adults have been conducted since 1977 (Gloaguen, Cottraux, Cucherat, & Ivy-Marie, 1998). A number of meta-analyses of these trials have been conducted (for a review, see Butler, Chapman, Forman, & Beck, 2006), most concluding that CBT is an efficacious treatment for adult depression. For instance, Dobson (1989) first reported that cognitive therapy for depression is superior to untreated controls, wait list, medication, and behavior therapy. The Dobson meta-analysis was critiqued for not controlling for sample size or research allegiance; however, even after these factors were accounted for, CBT was more effective for adult depression than wait list, attention control, and other psychotherapies (Gaffan, Tsaousis, & Kemp-Wheeler, 1995).

Demonstrating greater effectiveness than wait list or attentional control is encouraging, but how does CBT compare to other established treatments? Antidepressant treatment is a treatment with established efficacy that is most frequently compared to CBT. A comprehensive meta-analysis found that CBT was superior to medication (Gloaguen et al., 1998); however, there were some important caveats. The comparison may have been overly favorable for CBT because one study started to taper medication prior to the end of treatment and another study had an unusually low response to medication.

More recent direct comparisons suggest that CBT is equally efficacious as antidepressant treatment following the acute treatment phase. A study of CBT versus paroxetine (Paxil) for the treatment of severe depression reported that response rates for medication (50%) and CBT (43%) 8 weeks after initiating treatment were significantly better than pill placebo (25%). At 16 weeks, CBT and medication showed a similar response rate (both were 58%); however, analyses also indicated that CBT was even more effective when delivered by more experienced CBT therapists but less effective when delivered by inexperienced clinicians (DeRubeis et al., 2005). Nevertheless, CBT appears to be equally effective as medication, particularly when delivered by individuals with strong CBT expertise.

A large ($35 million) multisite study involving 2,876 participants conducted over 6 years attempted to identify optimal treatments for people who fail to respond to an initial course of pharmacotherapy (Rush et al., 2004). After initial treatment, 1,439 participants who did not improve after receiving citalopram (Celexa) were given the option of switching to a new treatment or continuing to take citalopram while adding another treatment. Treatment was not randomly assigned, as this study was trying to emulate conditions in real-world practice. The new treatments included cognitive therapy and one of three other medications. Of this group, 147 either switched to CBT or added it to citalopram. Results indicated that depression improved in 25% of patients who received CBT alone and 23% of patients who added CBT to citalopram (Thase et al., 2007). This was comparable to those who received medication only, suggesting that CBT is just as effective as switching to a new antidepressant medication among people who initially fail to respond to antidepressant treatment.

Although treatment response to CBT and antidepressant medication appears to be similar, the beneficial effects of CBT may be much more enduring (Hollon, Thase, & Markowitz, 2002). A meta-analysis of eight studies examined relapse rates in the year following treatment discontinuation (Gloaguen et al., 1998). Prior CBT was associated with a significant preventative effect in five of the eight studies. Overall, the rate of depression relapse was 30% for patients withdrawn from CBT and 60% for patients withdrawn from antidepressant medication treatment.

A large multisite trial of CBT versus medication treatment for severe depression found that relapse rates during a 12-month follow-up period were significantly lower among people withdrawn from CBT (31%) compared to medication (76%). Relapse rates for people withdrawn from CBT were similar to patients who continued to take medication (31% versus 47%) during the 12-month follow-up (Hollon et al., 2005). Consistent with this evidence, CBT has been shown to reduce relapse among patients who do not fully remit from MDD during acute phase pharmacological or psychological treatment (Vittengl, Clark, Dunn, & Jarrett, 2007). Thus, the main benefit of CBT may not lie in its initial effectiveness (which could also be achieved with medication), but in its ability to prevent the recurrence of future depression once acute treatment is complete.

Behavioral Activation

Behavioral Activation (BA) has been implemented in a number of formats that emphasize different aspects of BA (e.g., Kanter, Busch, & Rusch, 2009; Lejuez, Hopko, & Hopko, 2001; Martell, Addis, & Jacobson, 2001). These treatments have more in common with each other than other forms of treatment, and most reviews treat these BA variants as a single treatment, so we will do the same in our review.

A recent meta-analysis of 10 studies comparing Behavioral Activation to control conditions, either a wait list or a psychological placebo condition (e.g., supportive listening), found that BA was significantly more effective than the control treatment (Cuijpers, van Straten, & Warmerdam, 2007). The advantage of BA over control treatments was quite large and comparable to effects observed for other psychological and antidepressant medication interventions (Gloaguen et al., 1998). Further, this effect appears to be lasting, as the BA treatment effects remained intact during follow-up.

Fourteen studies have compared behavioral activation to other psychological treatments. A meta-analysis of this comparison documented a slight advantage for BA, although the effect did not reach statistical significance (Cuijpers et al., 2007). Further, in 10 studies that directly compared BA to cognitive therapy, there was virtually no difference in outcome for BA versus CBT. Thus, BA appears to be an effective treatment for depression, with an effectiveness rate that is similar to CBT.

There have been two large, influential studies of BA, so we briefly summarize findings from these important studies as well. One of the first tests of modern BA was completed by Jacobson and colleagues, who examined whether individual components of CBT were as effective as the full CBT treatment (Jacobson et al., 1996). They randomized 150 outpatients to receive BA, BA plus treatment to modify automatic thoughts, or the full CBT treatment. Results indicated that each of the treatments was approximately equally effective, as rates of improvement ranged from 61% for BA to 68% for CBT. Relapse rates did not significantly differ between the treatment conditions 6 months and 2 years later (Gortner, Gollan, Dobson, & Jacobson, 1998). This preliminary evidence suggested that BA was as effective as CBT.

A second recent study sought to replicate this initial finding and compare the effectiveness of BA to CBT and antidepressant treatment (Dimidjian et al., 2006). This trial randomized 241 outpatients to behavioral activation, cognitive therapy, antidepressant medication, or pill-placebo control. Overall the treatments were equally effective and superior to placebo. There was also evidence that BA was more effective than CBT among individuals with higher levels of depression, as response rates were 75% versus 48%, respectively. Among treatment responders, patients previously exposed to CBT experienced significantly less relapse than patients withdrawn from medication during a 2-year follow-up period (24% versus 52%). Similar results were observed for the comparison between BA and medication (26% versus 52%); however, this difference fell just short of statistical significance (Dobson et al., 2008). Thus, BA appears to be an effective treatment with comparable efficacy to CBT that continues to prevent depression relapse after BA treatment has been withdrawn.

Cognitive Behavioral Analysis System of Psychotherapy for Depression

CBASP is a relatively new treatment for chronic depression, so there have only been a handful of clinical trials testing its efficacy. However, these trials have been large, high-quality studies, using established treatments (typically pharmacotherapy) as comparison treatments. The first clinical trial randomly assigned 681 adults with chronic depression to 12 weeks of outpatient treatment with nefazodone (also known as Serzone, which incidentally is no longer available in the United States due to rare instances of increased liver damage in patients taking the medication), CBASP (16 to 20 sessions), or both treatments (Keller et al., 2000). The overall response rate at the end of treatment was 48% for both nefazodone and CBASP and 73% for combined treatment. Response rates were even higher for patients who completed a full course of treatment ($n = 519$): 55% for nefazodone, 52% for CBASP, and 85% for combined treatment. A follow-up study using data from this trial reported that CBASP was twice as effective as nefazodone for adults who were chronically depressed and experienced early life trauma (Nemeroff et al., 2003).

A subset of patients who did not respond to CBASP or nefazodone ($n = 156$) in the original trial received 12 weeks of additional treatment. Patients who previously received CBASP were switched to nefazodone, and patients who previously received nefazodone were switched to CBASP. Overall response rates were higher for patients who switched to CBASP from nefazodone (57%) than for patients who were switched to nefazodone from CBASP (42%). In a parallel study, patients who responded to CBASP treatment ($n = 82$) in the original trial were then randomly assigned to receive maintenance CBASP on a monthly basis for 1 year or to receive assessment only (Klein et al., 2004). Significantly fewer patients (3% versus 21%) had a recurrence of MDD in the CBASP condition compared to assessment only.

Finally, a recent study examined whether augmenting antidepressant treatment with CBASP enhanced remission rates compared to antidepressant treatment alone (Kocsis et al., 2009). In this trial, 808 patients first received 12 weeks of flexible medication treatment (i.e., the same antidepressant was not administered to all participants but instead a flexible treatment algorithm was implemented based on prior response to antidepressant treatment). Patients whose depression did not remit after medication treatment ($n = 491$) were then randomly assigned to receive continued medication treatment plus 12 weeks of CBASP, continued medication treatment plus 12 weeks of supportive psychotherapy, or continued medication treatment alone. Although 38% of the sample responded to treatment, the augmentation of antidepressant treatment with CBASP or supportive psychotherapy did not significantly enhance rates of remission. The authors speculated that the broad inclusion criteria (used in an effort to recruit patients that would typically present for treatment), brief course of treatment, and high psychiatric comorbidity might have made it difficult to detect differences between treatment conditions.

Taken together, these data suggest that CBASP (particularly when combined with antidepressant treatment) is an effective depression treatment. Further, if a patient does not respond to antidepressant medication, switching to CBASP may be beneficial. Indeed, a 57% response rate is quite high when you consider that chronic depression is difficult to treat and that patients who switched to CBASP failed to respond to antidepressant treatment. These data also suggest that providing CBASP as a maintenance treatment (e.g., monthly sessions rather than weekly or biweekly) after symptoms have remitted may help to minimize depression recurrence. Finally, in an effort to identify which treatments work for whom, CBASP might be optimally suited for adults with chronic depression who have also experienced significant childhood adversity.

References

Butler, A. C., Chapman, J. E., Forman, E. M., & Beck, A. T. (2006). The empirical status of cognitive-behavioral therapy: A review of meta-analyses. *Clinical Psychology Review, 26,* 17–31.

Clarke, G. N., Hawkins, W., Murphy, M., & Sheeber, L. B. (1995). Targeted prevention of unipolar depressive disorder in an at-risk sample of high school adolescents: A randomized trial of group cognitive intervention. *Journal of the American Academy of Child and Adolescent Psychiatry, 34,* 312–321.

Clarke, G. N., Hornbrook, M., Lynch, F., Polen, M., Gale, J., . . . Beardslee, W. (2001). A randomized trial of a group cognitive intervention for preventing depression in adolescent offspring of depressed parents. *Archives of General Psychiatry*, *58*, 1127–1134.

Cuijpers, P., van Straten, A., & Warmerdam, L. (2007). Behavioral activation treatments of depression: A meta-analysis. *Clinical Psychology Review, 27*, 318–326.

David-Ferdon, C., & Kaslow, N. J. (2008). Evidence-based psychosocial treatments for child and adolescent depression. *Journal of Clinical Child and Adolescent Psychology, 37*, 62–104.

DeRubeis, R. J., Hollon, S. D., Amsterdam, J. D., Shelton, R. C., Young, P. R., O'Reardon, J. P., . . . Salomon, R. M. (2005). Cognitive therapy vs medications in the treatment of moderate to severe depression. *Archives of General Psychiatry, 62*, 409–416.

Dimidjian, S., Hollon, S. D., Dobson, K. S., Schmaling, K. B., Kohlenberg, R. J., Gallop, R., . . . Addis, M. E. (2006). Randomized trial of behavioral activation, cognitive therapy, and antidepressant medication in the acute treatment of adults with major depression. *Journal of Consulting and Clinical Psychology, 74*, 658–670.

Dobson, K. S. (1989). A meta-analysis of the efficacy of cognitive therapy for depression. *Journal of Consulting and Clinical Psychology, 57*, 414–419.

Dobson, K. S., Hollon, S. D., Dimidjian, S., Schmaling, K. B., Kohlenberg, R. J., Rivzi, S.L., . . . Gallop, R. J. (2008). Randomized trial of behavioral activation, cognitive therapy, and antidepressant medication in the prevention of relapse and recurrence in major depression. *Journal of Consulting and Clinical Psychology, 76*, 468–477.

Gaffan, E. A., Tsaousis, I., & Kemp-Wheeler, S. M. (1995). Researcher allegiance and meta-analysis: The case of cognitive therapy for depression. *Journal of Consulting and Clinical Psychology, 63*, 966–980.

Garber, J., Clarke, G. N., Weersing, V. R., Beardslee, W. R., Brent, D. A., Gladstone, T. R. G., . . . DeBar, L. L. (2009). Prevention of depression in at-risk adolescents: A randomized controlled trial. *JAMA: Journal of the American Medical Association, 301*, 2215–2224.

Gloaguen, V., Cottraux, J., Cucherat, M., & Ivy-Marie, B. (1998). A meta-analysis of the effects of cognitive therapy in depressed patients. *Journal of Affective Disorders, 49*, 59–72.

Gortner, E. T., Gollan, J. K., Dobson, K. S., & Jacobson, N. S. (1998). Cognitive-behavioral treatment for depression: Relapse prevention. *Journal of Consulting and Clinical Psychology, 66*, 377–384.

Hollon, S. D., DeRubeis, R. J., Shelton, R. C., Amsterdam, J. D., Salomon, R. M., O'Reardon, J. P., . . . Lovett, M. L. (2005). Prevention of relapse following cognitive therapy vs medications in moderate to severe depression. *Archives of General Psychiatry, 62*, 417.

Hollon, S. D., Thase, M. E., & Markowitz, J. C. (2002). Treatment and prevention of depression. *Psychological Science, 3*, 39–77.

Jacobson, N. S., Dobson, K. S., Truax, P. A., Addis, M. E., Koerner, K., Gollan, J. K., . . . Gortner, E. (1996). A component analysis of cognitive-behavioral treatment for depression. *Journal of Consulting and Clinical Psychology, 64*, 295–304.

Kanter, J. W., Busch, A. M., & Rusch, L. C. (2009). *Behavioral activation: Distinctive features*. New York, NY: Routledge/Taylor & Francis.

Keller, M. B., McCullough, J. P., Klein, D. N., Arnow, B., Dunner, D. L., Gelenberg, A. J., . . . Markowitx, J. C. (2000). A comparison of nefazodone, the cognitive behavioral-analysis system of psychotherapy, and their combination for the treatment of chronic depression. *New England Journal of Medicine, 342*, 1462–1470.

Klein, D. N., Santiago, N. J., Vivian, D., Blalock, J. A., Kocsis, J. H., Markowitz, J. C., . . . McCullough, J. J. P. (2004). Cognitive-behavioral analysis system of psychotherapy as a maintenance treatment for chronic depression. *Journal of Clinical Psychology, 72*, 681–688.

Kocsis, J. H., Gelenberg, A. J., Rothbaum, B. O., Klein, D. N., Trivedi, M. H., Manber, R., . . . Keller, M. B. (2009). Cognitive behavioral analysis system of psychotherapy and brief supportive psychotherapy for augmentation of antidepressant nonresponse in chronic depression: The REVAMP Trial. *Archives of General Psychiatry, 66,* 1178–1188.

Lejuez, C. W., Hopko, D. R., & Hopko, S. D. (2001). A brief behavioral activation treatment for depression: Treatment manual. *Behavior Modification, 25,* 255–286.

Martell, C. R., Addis, M. E., & Jacobson, N. S. (2001). *Depression in context: Strategies for guided action.* New York, NY: Norton.

Nemeroff, C. B., Heim, C. M., Thase, M. E., Klein, D. N., Rush, A. J., Schatzberg, A. F., . . . Ninan, P. T. (2003). Differential responses to psychotherapy versus pharmacotherapy in patients with chronic forms of major depression and childhood trauma. *Proceedings of the National Academy of Sciences USA, 100,* 14293–14296.

Reinecke, M. A., Ryan, N. E., & DuBois, D. L. (1998). Cognitive-behavioral therapy of depression and depressive symptoms during adolescence: A review and meta-analysis. *Journal of the American Academy of Child and Adolescent Psychiatry, 37,* 26–34.

Rush, A. J., Fava, M., Wisniewski, S. R., Lavori, P. W., Trivedi, M. H., Sackeim, H. A., . . . Thase, M. E. (2004). Sequenced treatment alternatives to relieve depression (STAR∗D): Rationale and design. *Controlled Clinical Trials, 25,* 119–142.

Stice, E., Rohde, P., Seeley, J. R., & Gau, J. M. (2008). Brief cognitive-behavioral depression prevention program for high-risk adolescents outperforms two alternative interventions: A randomized efficacy trial. *Journal of Consulting and Clinical Psychology, 76,* 595–606.

Stice, E., Shaw, H., Bohon, C., Marti, C. N., & Rohde, P. (2009). A meta-analytic review of depression prevention programs for children and adolescents: Factors that predict magnitude of intervention effects. *Journal of Consulting and Clinical Psychology, 77,* 486–503.

Thase, M. E., Friedman, E. S., Biggs, M. M., Wisniewski, S. R., Trivedi, M. H., Luther, J. F., . . . Fava, M. (2007). Cognitive therapy versus medication in augmentation and switch strategies as second-step treatments: A STAR∗D report. *American Journal of Psychiatry, 164,* 739–752.

Treatment for Adolescents With Depression Study Team. (2004). Fluoxetine, cognitive-behavioral therapy, and their combination for adolescents with depression: Treatment for adolescents with depression study (TADS) randomized controlled trial. *Journal of the American Medical Association, 292,* 807–820.

Treatment for Adolescents With Depression Study Team. (2007). The treatment for adolescents with depression study (TADS): Long-term effectiveness and safety outcomes. *Archives of General Psychiatry, 64,* 1132–1143.

Vittengl, J. R., Clark, L. A., Dunn, T. W., & Jarrett, R. B. (2007). Reducing relapse and recurrence in unipolar depression: A comparative meta-analysis of cognitive-behavioral therapy's effects. *Journal of Consulting and Clinical Psychology, 75,* 475–488.

Young, J. F., Mufson, L., & Davies, M. (2006). Efficacy of interpersonal psychotherapy-adolescent skills training: An indicated preventive intervention for depression. *Journal of Child Psychology and Psychiatry, 47,* 1254–1262.

APPENDIX B

The Evidence-Based Practice Process

Allen Rubin

As mentioned in this volume's introduction, in its original and most prominent definition, evidence-based practice is a five-step process for making practice decisions. The term *evidence-based practice* (EBP) sprang from the term *evidence-based medicine* (EBM), which was coined in the 1980s and was ultimately defined as "the integration of best research evidence with clinical expertise and patient values" (Sackett, Straus, Richardson, Rosenberg, & Haynes, 2000, p. 1). By including clinical expertise and patient values in the definition, EBM was distinguished from the notion that it was an unchanging list of approved interventions that physicians should implement even if they seemed to be contraindicated in light of the physician's knowledge about the patient. Nevertheless, as the concept of EBM spread to the non-medical helping professions with the label EBP, some critics disregarded its integration component and misconstrued it as recommending that practitioners mechanistically implement scientifically approved interventions regardless of their clinical expertise and knowledge about client attributes, values, and preferences.

Pointing out the integration component of the EBP process is not meant to diminish the importance of the role of empirically supported interventions in EBP. The best research evidence is a key component of the EBP process. Indeed, this entire volume has aimed to facilitate your ability to find and implement interventions that have the best research evidence regarding their effectiveness with substance-abusing clients. In fact, the ultimate priority of the EBP process is to maximize the chances that practice decisions will yield desired outcomes in light of the best scientific evidence. Thus, the integration component of EBP is not meant to give practitioners so much wiggle room that they can disregard or diminish the importance of the best scientific evidence in making practice decisions. It just recognizes the need to blend that evidence with clinical expertise and client attributes.

There are various practical obstacles to the feasibility of the EBP process often encountered by clinicians. Key among those obstacles are the time, expertise, and other resources required to find relevant research evidence, to critically appraise various studies and sort through their bewildering array of inconsistent findings to ascertain which interventions are supported by the *best* evidence, and ultimately to learn how to implement one or more of those interventions. This volume has been geared to practitioners for whom those daunting obstacles make implementing the entire EBP process infeasible. However, if you would like to try to implement that process, the remainder of this appendix can guide you in a step-by-step fashion.

Step 1. Formulate a Question

The first step in the EBP process involves formulating a question based on a practice decision that you need to make. The question could pertain to any level of practice, including questions bearing on administrative or policy decisions. Here are four common types of EBP questions (Rubin, 2008):

1. What intervention, program, or policy is most effective?
2. What factors best predict desirable or undesirable outcomes?
3. What's it like to have had my client's experiences?
4. What assessment tool should be used?

At the clinical level, you are most likely to formulate the first type of question above—one geared to choosing the intervention that has the best chance to be effective for your client. This volume has been geared to that type of question.

To make the next step in the EBP process both expedient and productive, you'll need to add as much specificity to your question as possible—without making it so specific that you'll find no evidence bearing on it. To illustrate questions that are too broadly worded, while writing this appendix I went online to the *PsycINFO* literature database and requested that it show each published work that included all of the following three search terms somewhere in its text: *effective, treatment, trauma.* My implicit question was, "What intervention is most effective for treating trauma?" More than 1,000 published works came up. Too many!

My question was too broad. After all, there are many different types of trauma. So I redid my search, substituting *PTSD* for *trauma*. My implicit question was, "What intervention is most effective for treating PTSD?" That reduced the listed results to 677 publications. Still a lot. Assuming that my client was a victim of sexual abuse, I added the term *sexual abuse* to the search, with the implicit EBP question, "What intervention is most effective for treating PTSD among victims of sexual abuse?" That reduced the list to 51 published works—much more manageable and relevant to my hypothetical client.

To illustrate adding more specificity, I repeated my search by adding the term *African American* to the search, with the implicit EBP question, "What intervention is most effective for treating PTSD among African-American victims of sexual abuse?'' However, no works were found when I added that search term. The same happened when I substituted *Hispanic* for *African American.*

In formulating your EBP questions, it's usually best to go in the opposite direction, formulating a very specific question, and then broadening it in your search if necessary. That way, you can skip the search term tries that give you too many publications that are irrelevant or tangential to your specific practice decision or client, and add (broadening) terms only as needed.

Not all EBP questions about effectiveness are open-ended, without specifying one or more specific interventions in advance. For example, perhaps you know that both EMDR and exposure therapy are accepted as the most effective treatments for PTSD and are wondering which has the best evidence. Your EBP question therefore might be, ''Is EMDR or exposure therapy more effective in treating PTSD?'' When I asked PsycINFO to find all publications that contained all of the following search terms–*EMDR, exposure therapy,* and *PTSD*—it listed 23 results.

Step 2. Search for Evidence

As a busy practitioner, the least time-consuming way to search for evidence is to use Internet search engines and electronic literature databases. *PsycINFO*, as discussed previously, is one useful option. Using it requires a subscription, but there are ways to get around that cost if your work setting does not have such a subscription. One way is to see if you can get free access through any university faculty members or internship students with whom you are affiliated (especially if you serve as an adjunct faculty member or a field internship instructor). Another way is through your local library. Many local libraries provide free access to databases like *PsycINFO* for residents with a library card. You probably will not have to go to the library to use its computers; you should be able to do it all online from your own computer. There are many alternative electronic literature databases, including Google Scholar and MedLine. The nice thing about MedLine is that the National Library of Medicine offers free access to it at www.nlm.nih.gov.

Although various professional literature databases typically require the entering of search terms to retrieve studies, they differ in their search rules and procedures. You'll need to scan their search guidelines before proceeding so that you can expedite your search. For some databases, you can connect the various parts of your search term with words like ''AND,'' ''OR,'' and ''NOT.'' Using ''AND'' limits the number of studies that come up to only those that contain all of the keywords in your search term. For example, if you want to find studies that compare EMDR with exposure therapy, you could enter ''EMDR AND exposure therapy.'' Using ''OR'' will expand the number of studies that come up. Thus, if you enter ''EMDR OR exposure therapy,'' studies that come up will include those that look only at EMDR, only at exposure therapy, and at both (whereas using ''AND'' would include only those studies that look at both). If you enter "EMDR AND exposure therapy NOT pilot study," the list of references that come up will include those that address *both* EMDR *and* exposure therapy, but will exclude pilot studies. For some databases, such as *PsycINFO*, you will not have to enter the connecting words like AND, OR, and NOT. Instead, you can enter the keywords in different boxes that are prefaced with the connecting words.

So far I've been discussing the search for evidence in terms of looking for individual studies. Implicit in this approach is the need to critically appraise (in the next step of the EBP process) the quality of the evidence in each of the relevant studies that you find. A more expedient alternative would be to look first for systematic reviews of the studies already completed by others. This would also include meta-analyses, which are systematic reviews that pool the statistical results of the reviewed studies. Systematic reviews are expedient in several ways. First, they save you the time of searching for and reading individual studies. Second, they spare you the difficulty of critically appraising the research methodology of each study, which can be a daunting task for clinicians with limited expertise in research design, methods, and statistics. Third, even those studies that are methodologically rigorous and that supply the best evidence often report findings that are inconsistent from one study to another, and for some EBP questions, that inconsistency can be bewildering. A good systematic review will synthesize the various findings and provide you with a bottom line as to which interventions have the best evidence, for what types of clients and problems, and under what conditions.

Of course, an even more expedient way for busy practitioners to engage in EBP is to rely on volumes like the one you are reading. If you read Appendix A, you saw a synopsis of the ample empirical support—including systematic reviews and meta-analyses—for the interventions selected for this volume. However, if your EBP question is one for which no systematic reviews or books like this have been published, you may have no alternative to searching for and appraising individual studies. When you start your search, you won't know in advance what you'll find. Assuming that time and other practical constraints make searching for individual studies an undesirable option from the standpoint of feasibility, I recommend that you begin looking for systematic reviews and volumes like this and then look for individual studies only as a last resort. That said, however, you need to be careful that the authors of systematic reviews or books like this do not have a vested interest in the interventions that they depict as having the best evidence. If my co-editor and I, for example, had developed or run workshops on the interventions described in this volume, then the credibility of our previous appendix on the supportive research would be highly suspect, and the value of this book's chapters therefore would suffer. In case you are wondering, we have no vested interests in any of the interventions described in this book.

You should also bear in mind that for some problem areas, different systematic reviews might produce different conclusions regarding which interventions have the best evidence supporting their effectiveness with that problem. For example, some authors with well-established reputations in EMDR have conducted reviews that concluded that EMDR is more effective than exposure therapy, while other authors have conducted reviews that reached the opposite conclusion, while still others conducted reviews that concluded that both interventions appear to be equally effective. Systematic reviews should be transparent about the presence or lack of vested interests by the authors of the review. Reviews that lack that transparency should be viewed with suspicion, as should reviews that admit to a vested interest, while reviews in which the authors have no vested interests probably should have the most credibility (all other criteria being equal, as will be discussed below).

Two highly regarded sources for unbiased and methodologically sophisticated systematic reviews are the Cochrane Collaboration and the Campbell Collaboration. Both are international non-profit organizations that recruit into review teams researchers, practitioners, and consumers without vested interests in the subjects of their reviews. Each of their sites can be accessed online. If you can find a review bearing on your EBP question in the onsite library at either of those sites, you can probably rely on it to answer your question and thus save you the trouble of searching for and appraising other sources of evidence. Moreover, their libraries also contain comments and criticisms of their own reviews as well as abstracts of other reviews, bibliographies of studies, reviews regarding methodology, and links that can help you conduct your own review. The Cochrane Collaboration focuses on reviews in the areas of health and mental health and can be accessed at www.cochrane.org. Its sibling organization, the Campbell Collaboration, focuses on reviews in social welfare, education, and criminal justice. You can access its website at www.campbellcollaboration.org.

Step 3. Critically Appraise the Evidence

The next step of the EBP process involves critically appraising the evidence found in the previous step. Being published is no guarantee that a study's evidence is sound. Some studies are better than others, and some have fatal flaws that severely undermine their utility for guiding practice decisions. All studies have at least one or two minor flaws. Your prime task is not looking for the holy grail of a perfectly flawless study, but rather looking for one or more studies (or systematic reviews) whose strengths and relevance to your practice decision far outweigh their minor flaws.

The criteria to use in critically appraising any study depend on the nature of your EBP question. For questions such as, "What's it like to have had my client's experiences?" studies that employ qualitative research methods are likely to provide better evidence than quantitative studies such as experiments or surveys. For questions like, "What factors best predict desirable or undesirable outcomes?" studies that employ multivariate correlation analyses along with survey designs, case–control designs, or longitudinal designs may be your best bet. For questions like,

Table B.1 Evidentiary Hierarchy for Questions about Effectiveness (Best Evidence at the Top)

Level 1	Systematic reviews and meta-analyses
Level 2	Multisite replications of randomized experiments
Level 3	Randomized experiments
Level 4	Quasi-experiments
Level 5	Single-case experiments
Level 6	Correlational studies
Level 7	Other:
	➤ Anecdotal case reports
	➤ Pre-test–post-test studies without control groups
	➤ Qualitative descriptions of client experiences during or after treatment
	➤ Surveys of clients as to what they think helped them
	➤ Surveys of practitioners as to what they think is effective

Note: This hierarchy assumes that each type of study is well designed. If not well designed, then a particular study would merit a lower level on the hierarchy. For example, a randomized experiment with egregiously biased measurement would not deserve to be at Level 3, and perhaps would be so fatally flawed as to merit dropping to the lowest level. The same applies to a quasi-experiment with a severe vulnerability to a selectivity bias.

"What assessment tool should be used?" you'll need to examine studies that administer assessment tools to large samples of people and calculate the tools' reliability, validity, and sensitivity.

As mentioned earlier, however, the most commonly asked EBP question asks something like, "What intervention, program, or policy is most effective?" For questions about effectiveness, the evidentiary hierarchy in Table B.1 should guide your appraisal of the evidence.

It is beyond the scope of this appendix to explain everything in Table B.1. If you have had one or more good courses on research methods, perhaps you already have sufficient familiarity with the terminology and standards of research rigor to guide your appraisal. To brush up on that material, you might want to examine my book, *Practitioner's Guide to Using Research for Evidence-Based Practice* (Rubin, 2008). In the meantime, five key criteria to keep in mind when appraising individual studies are as follows:

1. Was a control group used?
2. Was random assignment used to avoid a selectivity bias that would make one group more likely to have a successful outcome than the other?
3. If random assignment was not used (i.e., in a quasi-experiment), do the authors provide solid evidence and a persuasive case for considering a selectivity bias to be unlikely?
4. Was the outcome (or outcomes) measured in an unbiased manner?
5. Were the attrition rates in both groups roughly equivalent?

Although the above list does not exhaust all the criteria to consider, if the answers to questions 1, 4, and 5 are all *yes*, coupled with an affirmative answer to *either* question 2 or 3, then chances are the study is supplying some relatively strong evidence regarding whether a policy, program, or intervention is effective.

When appraising systematic reviews (including meta-analyses), you should ask whether the reviewed studies were appraised in connection to the preceding types of evidentiary standards. Reviews can do so in two ways. One way is for the authors of the review to take the strengths and weaknesses of the reviewed studies into account when deriving their conclusions and guidelines for practice. The other way is to exclude from the review any studies that fail to meet certain evidentiary standards, such as the ones listed previously.

As mentioned earlier, another important consideration when appraising a systematic review is whether the authors have vested interests in any of the policies, programs, or interventions addressed in the review and whether they are transparent about such vested interests. They also should identify the inclusion and exclusion criteria that they used in selecting studies for their review and describe how comprehensively they searched for studies. For example, if they excluded studies of clients with substance abuse comorbidity from their review of treatment for PTSD, and your client has such comorbidity, then their review might have less value to you than one that included such studies. As to comprehensiveness, a key issue is whether the authors searched well for unpublished studies to include in their review, based on the notion that if only published studies are included, the deck might be stacked toward studies with findings supporting the effectiveness of interventions, since studies with null findings often are not submitted for publication.

Step 4. Integration, Selection, and Implementation

As mentioned earlier, the EBP process is not merely a mechanistic, cookbook approach in which practice decisions are made and implemented based solely on the best evidence regardless of clinician expertise and knowledge of client attributes and preferences. Consequently, after appraising the evidence, the next step of the EBP process involves selecting an intervention and implementing it only after integrating the critical appraisal of the evidence with your clinical expertise and knowledge of client circumstances and preferences. You might, for example, opt to implement an intervention that has the second- or third-best evidence because the studies done on that intervention involved clients like yours, whereas the studies done on the interventions with the best evidence involved only clients very unlike yours in ways that you deem to be very important. Likewise, your client might refuse to participate in an intervention supported by the best evidence, such as when some parents cannot be persuaded (through psychoeducation) to permit their child to undergo EMDR or exposure therapy because they fear that such treatment would re-traumatize their child.

Feasibility issues also must be considered. What if you lack training in the intervention supported by the best evidence? Is it possible to get the needed training? Can you afford the time and money that will be required? Can you get it soon enough? If you cannot get it, can you refer the client to another service provider who has the expertise to provide the desired intervention? If the answers to these questions are negative, the client might be better off if you provide an intervention that has the second- or third-best evidence, but is one that you have the expertise to provide competently. If the preferred intervention is one covered in this volume, perhaps reading the pertinent chapter will suffice to get you started.

Step 5. Monitor/Evaluate Outcome

In the final step of the EBP process, you monitor or evaluate the outcome of the intervention (or other practice decision that is implemented in Step 4). You might wonder why this final step is needed. After all, haven't you implemented the option that has already been evaluated and found to have the best evidence supporting its effectiveness? There are several answers to these questions. One reason is that even in studies providing the best evidence, some of the participants do not benefit from the empirically supported interventions. A related reason is that those studies might not have included participants with some of your client's key attributes. A third reason is that in Step 4 you may have opted for an intervention that does not have the best evidence.

Moreover, you might complete all four preceding steps and find no empirically supported intervention that fits your client. You may therefore have to proceed according to theory or clinical judgment alone, thus implementing an intervention that lacks empirical support. Keep in mind that doing so does not mean you have violated the EBP process. The fact that you completed the preceding steps means you have implemented the EBP process even if your search is fruitless. But if that is so, then it is all the more important to complete the final step of the process, that is, to evaluate whether the intervention you have chosen attains the desired outcome.

A final reason for the final step of the EBP process is the possibility that you might not implement the selected intervention in a sufficiently competent manner. Remember, even the best evidence is only probabilistic. Rather than ensure treatment success, it merely means that the chosen intervention has the best *likelihood* of success.

Now that you see the rationale for this final step, you might wonder how to do it. Your options are many, and some might be a lot more feasible for you than you think. The most feasible options pertain to situations where you have implemented an intervention that has already been supported by strong studies. In such situations, you should not feel the need to employ a sophisticated evaluation design aimed at producing causal inferences about whether the chosen intervention is really the cause of any client outcomes. Instead, all you need to do is monitor client outcomes. That is, you just need to see if the client achieves his or her desired outcome, regardless of the cause. That's because previous studies have already produced probabilistic causal evidence about the intervention, and your task as a practitioner (and not as a researcher), therefore, is merely to see if your client gets where he or she wants

Figure B.1 An Individualized Daily Rating Scale for Depressed Mood*

Instructions At the end of each day, enter the day's date and then circle a number to approximate how depressed you felt on average for that day.

	Average Level of Depression for the Day						
Date	**Not at all** →			**Moderate** →			**Severe**
___	0	1	2	3	4	5	6	7
___	0	1	2	3	4	5	6	7
___	0	1	2	3	4	5	6	7
___	0	1	2	3	4	5	6	7
___	0	1	2	3	4	5	6	7
___	0	1	2	3	4	5	6	7
___	0	1	2	3	4	5	6	7

*The development of this scale was inspired by ideas in *Evaluating practice: Guidelines for the accountable professional* (5th ed.), by M. Bloom, J. Fischer, and J. G. Orme, 2006, Boston: Allyn & Bacon. This scale can be adapted for other target problems or goals by substituting those problems (anxiety, anger, etc.) or goals (self-confidence, assertiveness, etc.) for "depressed" or "depression."

to go after receiving that intervention and whether (assuming a desired outcome is not attained) a different intervention may need to be introduced.

For a comprehensive guide to monitoring client progress, you can examine Chapter 12 of the book I mentioned earlier (Rubin, 2008). For example, if you are monitoring a client's PTSD symptoms, the client could self-monitor one or more symptoms (including perhaps just one overall rating of the day's symptoms) by completing an individualized self-rating scale each day, such as the one shown in Figure B.1 from Rubin (2008, p. 259).

You could graph the daily ratings chronologically, as appears below to see if the desired level of progress is being achieved. The graph in Figure B.2 would indicate a successful outcome was being achieved in reducing an undesirable symptom (or overall rating of PTSD symptoms in general).

Figure B.2 Illustration of a Successful Outcome in Reducing an Undesirable Symptom

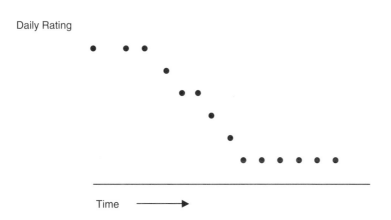

Source: From *Practitioner's guide to using research for evidence-based practice* (p. 257), by A. Rubin, 2008, Hoboken, NJ: John Wiley & Sons.

Figure B.3 Illustration of an Unsuccessful Outcome for Intervention A Followed by a Successful Outcome for Intervention B

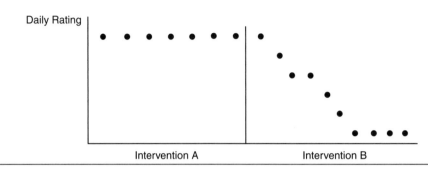

Source: From *Practitioner's guide to using research for evidence-based practice* (p. 257), by A. Rubin, 2008, Hoboken, NJ: John Wiley & Sons.

In contrast, the graph in Figure B.3 illustrates an outcome in which progress was not being made with the selected intervention (Intervention A), but then after an alternative intervention (Intervention B) was introduced the desired progress was being achieved in reducing an undesirable symptom (or overall rating of PTSD symptoms in general).

If you have implemented an intervention that lacks adequate prior empirical support, you might want to employ a more sophisticated evaluation design that aims to produce causal inferences (assuming, of course, that such a design is feasible for you). Such designs include experiments, quasi-experiments, time-series designs, and single-case experiments.

The above examples were discussed in the context of clinical practice with a specific client. However, they can be adapted to a macro level of practice in which you want to monitor or evaluate outcomes with a large number of clients or with an entire community. For example, if you want to see whether a new crisis intervention modality is more effective than previous efforts to prevent PTSD among victims of natural disasters, you could compare the incidence of PTSD among its recipients to the incidence among victims who received alternative or no crisis intervention modalities. To learn more about such macro evaluations, see Rubin and Babbie (2011).

The main thing to keep in mind about this phase of the EBP process, however, is to implement it in whatever way that is feasible for you. As a practitioner, you should not feel immobilized just because a rigorous research evaluation design is beyond your reach. Remember, all practitioners routinely have to make judgments as to whether what they are doing is working and whether they need to try something different. The same applies regardless of what you find and implement in the previous steps of the EBP process. The ideas presented here and in the suggested reference volumes can help you make your monitoring or evaluation efforts more systematic and doable. Just do the best you can, and good luck!

References

Bloom, M., Fischer, J., & Orme, J. G. (2006). *Evaluating practice: Guidelines for the accountable professional* (5th ed.). Boston: Allyn & Bacon.

Rubin, A. (2008). *Practitioner's guide to using research for evidence-based practice.* Hoboken, NJ: John Wiley & Sons.

Rubin, A., & Babbie, E. (2011). *Research methods for social work* (7th ed.). Belmont, CA: Thomson Brooks/Cole.

Sackett, D. L., Straus, S. E., Richardson, W. S., Rosenberg, W. M. C., & Haynes, R. B. (2000). *Evidence-based medicine: How to practice and teach EBM* (2nd ed.). New York: Churchill Livingstone.

Professional Resources and Recommended Reading

THEORETICAL FRAMEWORKS AND GUIDELINES FOR ADAPTING EBP

Barrera, M., & Castro, F. G. (2006). A heuristic framework for the cultural adaptation of interventions. *Clinical Psychology: Science and Practice, 13*, 311–316.

Bernal, G., & Saéz-Santiago, E. (2006). Culturally centered psychosocial interventions. *Journal of Community Psychology, 34*, 121–132.

Le, H., Zmuda, J., Perry, D., & Muñoz, R. F. (2010). Transforming an evidence-based intervention to prevent perinatal depression. *American Journal of Orthopsychiatry, 80*, 34–45.

Muñoz, R. F., & Mendelson, T. (2005). Toward evidence-based interventions for diverse populations: The San Francisco General Hospital prevention and treatment manuals. *Journal of Consulting and Clinical Psychology, 73*, 790–799.

GENERAL INFORMATION FOR WORKING WITH DIFFERENT CULTURAL GROUPS

American Psychological Association. (1993). Guidelines for providers of psychological services to ethnic, linquistic, and culturally diverse populations. *American Psychologist, 48*, 45–48.

Chun, K. M., Organista, P. B., & Marín, G. (2003). *Acculturation: Advances in theory, measurement, and applied research*. Washington, DC: American Psychological Association.

Helms, J. E., & Cook, D. A. (1999). *Using race and culture in counseling and psychotherapy: Theory and process*. Needham Heights, MA: Allyn & Bacon.

Sue, D. W., & Sue, D. (2008). *Counseling the culturally different: Theory and practice* (5th ed.). New York, NY: John Wiley & Sons.

U.S. Department of Health and Human Services. (2001). *Mental health: Culture, race, and ethnicity—A supplement to mental health: A report of the surgeon general*. Rockville, MD: U.S. Department of Health and Human Services, Substance Abuse and Mental Health Services Administration, Center for Mental Health Services.

ONLINE MANUALS AND RESOURCES

CBT manuals for the prevention of depression in low-income, Latina mothers

http://www.clarku.edu/faculty/ecardemil/

CBT Manuals for the treatment of depression in Puerto Rican adolescents

http://ipsi.uprrp.edu/recursos.html

CBT Manuals from the Latino Mental Health Research Program (LMHRP)

http://www.medschool.ucsf.edu/latino/manuals.aspx

Author Index

Subject Index

Page numbers in *italic* type indicate figures and tables.

STUDY PACKAGE
CONTINUING EDUCATION
CREDIT INFORMATION
Clinician's Guide to Evidence-Based Practice:
Treatment of Depression in Adolescents & Adults

Our goal is to provide you with current, accurate and practical information from the most experienced and knowledgeable speakers and authors.

Listed below are the continuing education credit(s) currently available for this self-study package. *Please note: Your state licensing board dictates whether self study is an acceptable form of continuing education. Please refer to your state rules and regulations.*

COUNSELORS: PESI, LLC is recognized by the National Board for Certified Counselors to offer continuing education for National Certified Counselors. Provider #: 5896. We adhere to NBCC Continuing Education Guidelines. This self-study package qualifies for **4.0** contact hours.

SOCIAL WORKERS: PESI, LLC, 1030, is approved as a provider for continuing education by the Association of Social Work Boards, 400 South Ridge Parkway, Suite B, Culpeper, VA 22701. www.aswb.org. Social workers should contact their regulatory board to determine course approval. Course Level: All Levels. Social Workers will receive **4.0** (Clinical) continuing education clock hours for completing this self-study package.

PSYCHOLOGISTS: PESI, LLC is approved by the American Psychological Association to sponsor continuing education for psychologists. PESI, LLC maintains responsibility for these materials and their content. PESI is offering these self- study materials for **4.0** hours of continuing education credit.

ADDICTION COUNSELORS: PESI, LLC is a Provider approved by NAADAC Approved Education Provider Program. Provider #: 366. This self-study package qualifies for **4.5** contact hours.

Procedures:

1. Review the material and read the book.

2. If seeking credit, complete the posttest/evaluation form:

-Complete posttest/evaluation in entirety; including your email address to receive your certificate much faster versus by mail.

-Upon completion, mail to the address listed on the form along with the CE fee stated on the test. Tests will not be processed without the CE fee included.

-Completed posttests must be received 6 months from the date printed on the packing slip.

Your completed posttest/evaluation will be graded. If you receive a passing score (70% and above), you will be emailed/faxed/mailed a certificate of successful completion with earned continuing education credits. (Please write your email address on the posttest/evaluation form for fastest response) If you do not pass the posttest, you will be sent a letter indicating areas of deficiency, and another posttest to complete. The posttest must be resubmitted and receive a passing grade before credit can be awarded. We will allow you to re-take as many times as necessary to receive a certificate.

If you have any questions, please feel free to contact our customer service department at 1.800.844.8260.

PESI LLC
PO BOX 1000
Eau Claire, WI 54702-1000

 **PESI**

Clinician's Guide to Evidence-Based Practice: Treatment of Depression in Adolescents & Adults

PO BOX 1000
Eau Claire, WI 54702
800-844-8260

For office use only
Rcvd. _____
Graded _____
Cert. sent _____

Any persons interested in receiving credit may photocopy this form, complete and return with a payment of $20.00 per person CE fee. A certificate of successful completion will be sent to you. To receive your certificate sooner than two weeks, rush processing is available for a fee of $10. Please attach check or include credit card information below.

Mail to: PESI, PO Box 1000, Eau Claire, WI 54702 or fax to PESI (800) 554-9775 (both sides)

CE Fee: $20: (Rush processing fee: $10)   **Total to be charged** _____

Credit Card #: _____ **Exp Date:** _____ **V-Code*:** _____
(*MC/VISA/Discover: last 3-digit # on signature panel on back of card.) (*American Express: 4-digit # above account # on face of card.)

LAST   FIRST   M.I.

Name (please print): _____   _____   _____

Address: _____ Daytime Phone: _____

City: _____ State: _____ Zip Code: _____

Signature: _____ Email: _____

Date Completed: _____ Actual time (# of hours) taken to complete this offering: _____hours

Program Objectives After completing this publication, I have been able to achieve these objectives:

1. Identify and apply evidence-based psychological treatments for adults and adolescents with major depressive disorder across a range of clinical settings.	1.	Yes No
2. Weigh the pros and cons of using specific psychological evidence-based practices in the treatment of unipolar depression, based upon factors such as the course of the depressive episode, the characteristics of the client, and the corresponding research evidence.	2.	Yes No
3. Assess for the presence and severity of major depressive disorder in adults and adolescents.	3.	Yes No
4. Differentiate the application of cognitive behavioral therapy (CBT) with adolescents and adults with major depressive disorder.	4.	Yes No
5. Identify and refute commonly held myths associated with the use of CBT to treat major depressive disorder in adolescents and adults.	5.	Yes No
6. Delineate and apply the core techniques of CBT.	6.	Yes No
7. Describe an appropriate course of psychological treatment for a suicidal client.	7.	Yes No
8. Apply activity scheduling, a hallmark technique of Behavioral Activation, in the treatment of clients with major depressive disorder.	8.	Yes No
9. Describe the leading psychological treatment for chronic depression.	9.	Yes No
10. Design a treatment plan for a diverse range of clients, including people of different racial and ethnic backgrounds.	10.	Yes No

PESI LLC
PO BOX 1000
Eau Claire, WI 54702-1000

CE Release Date: 1/13/2011

Participant Profile:
1. Job Title: _____ Employment setting: _____

1. Which of the following is NOT a symptom of Major Depressive Disorder (MDD):
a. Depressed mood.
b. Insomnia.
c. Feelings of worthlessness.
d. Hypervigilance for threats.

2. In cognitive-behavioral therapy (CBT), which of the following would most likely be considered a cognitive distortion?
a. a therapists' interpretation of something a client stated in therapy.
b. monitoring a client's mood during therapy.
c. a therapist's emotional response to a client.
d. overlooking the positive aspects of a situation.

3. In cognitive-behavioral therapy (CBT), which of the following behaviors would be considered behavioral activation?
a. engaging in more fun activities.
b. talking more often during a therapy session.
c. challenging distorting thinking outside of the therapy session.
d. sleeping on a regular schedule.

4. In cognitive-behavioral therapy (CBT), what is a behavioral experiment?
a. An opportunity for the client and the therapist to hypothesize about the client's presenting problem.
b. The use of unproven therapeutic intervention.
c. An opportunity for a client to act in a way that the therapist believes will lead to a healthy and positive change in the client.
d. An over-reliance on behavioral techniques during CBT treatment.

5. In cognitive-behavioral therapy (CBT), what is an automatic thought?
a. client's spontaneous, depressive thoughts.
b. an attempt to correct a negative thought.
c. an idea that the therapist shares with the client.
d. a type of identity that a depressed person often adopts.

6. Which of the following is NOT a principle of Behavioral Activation (BA):
a. Behavior is best understood functionally, not formally.
b. BA is active, concrete, and focused on the details of the client's life.
c. BA is focused on past behavior, not present behavior.
d. BA is focused on behavioral not cognitive change.

7. In Behavioral Activation (BA), why is it important to assess a client's values?
a. In order to predict whether the patient will respond to BA.
b. To help clients develop BA goals that are consistent with their life goals.
c. To challenge unwanted, negative thoughts.
d. To determine whether medication treatment might be a better option for the client.

8. A unique feature of Cognitive Behavioral Analysis System of Psychotherapy (CBASP) for Chronic Depression is the therapist role, which strives to have a disciplined personal relationship (DPR) with clients. Which of the following is NOT a benefit of a DPR?
a. it allows a therapist to use his/her own reactions to the client in session.
b. it can be used to teach clients how their behavior is interpersonally maladaptive.
c. it teaches and models empathic behavior.
d. it facilitates friendships between therapists and clients once therapy has been terminated.

9. One of the important goals of Cognitive Behavioral Analysis System of Psychotherapy (CBASP) for Chronic Depression is for the client to develop perceived functionality. This is defined as:
a. Improved ability to function in vocational settings.
b. An awareness that a client's behavior has specific consequences in the environment.
c. Improvements in social functioning that can be perceived by other people.
d. Increasing the number of friendships a person is able to maintain at any given time.

10. When treating individuals from diverse backgrounds with evidence-based treatments, which of the following should be considered?
a. the structure of the intervention.
b. the content of the intervention.
c. how to deliver the intervention.
d. all of the above.

PESI LLC
PO BOX 1000
Eau Claire, WI 54702-1000